CHILD

DEVELOPMENT & PEDAGOGY

Paper 1 & 2 of CTET & all STET's

Thoroughly revised & edited

- **Exhaustive Theory as per CBSE syllabus**
- **Previous Year CTET & STET questions**
- **Practice MCQ Exercise**

Useful for :

- UPTET
- RTET
- HTET
- BTET
- PTET
- MPTET
- TNTET
- APTET

- **Corporate Office :** 45, 2nd Floor, Maharishi Dayanand Marg, Corner Market, Malviya Nagar,
  New Delhi-110017
  Tel. : 011-49842349/49842350

Typeset by Disha DTP Team

Edited by : Nimisha Aggarwal (UGC-NET Qualified)

For further information about books from DISHA,

Log on to **www.dishapublication.com** or email to **info@dishapublication.com**

Contents

MOCK TESTS 1-4

Child Development (Primary & Elementary Stage)   (15 Questions)

- Concept of development and its relationship with learning
- Principles of the development of children
- Influence of Heredity & Environment
- **Socialization processes:** Social world & children (Teacher, Parents, Peers)
- **Piaget, Kohlberg and Vygotsky:** Constructs and critical perspectives
- Concepts of child-centered and progressive education
- Critical perspective of the construct of Intelligence
- Multi Dimensional Intelligence
- Language & Thought
- Gender as a social construct, Gender roles, gender-bias and educational practice
- Individual differences among learners, understanding differences based on diversity of language, caste, gender, community, religion etc.
- Distinction between Assessment for learning and assessment of learning
- School-Based Assessment, Continuous & Comprehensive Evaluation(CCE) : Perspective and practice
- Formulating appropriate questions for assessing readiness levels of learners; For enhancing learning and critical thinking in the classroom and for assessing learner achievement.

Concept of Inclusive education and understanding children with special needs

(5 Questions)

- Addressing learners from diverse backgrounds including disadvantaged and deprived
- Addressing the needs of children with learning difficulties, 'impairment' etc
- Addressing the Talented, Creative, Specially abled Learners.

Learning and Pedagogy   (10 Questions)

- How children think and learn; how and why children 'fail' to achieve success in school performance
- Basic processes of teaching and learning; Children's strategies of learning; Learning as a social activity; Social context of learning
- Child as a problem solver and a 'scientific investigator'
- Alternative conceptions of learning in children
- Understanding children's 'errors' as significant steps in the learning process.
- Cognition & Emotions
- Motivation and learning
- Factors contributing to learning-personal & environmental.

Child Growth and Development Concepts, Principles and Influences

INTRODUCTION

Humans are not static beings. During their lives, they change in size, appearance and psychological makeup. However, the way they change differs from individual to individual. But the fundamental patterns of growth and development remain more or less the same and take place in an orderly way. Each individual, with his unique heredity and environment determines the way he traverses the broad path of his life at his rate of progress. The knowledge of the pattern of human development helps teachers know what to expect of children. It also helps them to know approximately at what age behavioural changes take place, and when these patterns are generally replaced by more mature patterns. This is significant since, if too much is expected of children, they develop a feeling of inadequacy. On the other hand if too little is expected of them, they do not have an incentive to realize their potential.

Before understanding child development, it is imperative to understand the term 'growth'. The terms growth and development are often used interchangeably. But they are conceptually different and complement each other. Human growth deals with just the physical aspects of development whereas human development includes not only human growth but also takes into consideration the psycho-social aspects of development.

GROWTH

Growth is an increase in the size of the body as a whole or the size attained by different parts of the body by multiplication of cells during the period starting from fertilization to physical maturity. It is a fundamental characteristic of all living organisms. The physical size is measured in terms of centimeters and kilograms or metabolic balance that is retention of hydrogen and calcium in the body.

Stages of Growth

The stages or phases of growth have been classified differently by different researchers.

1. **Prenatal Period :** The prenatal period comprises, on the average, about 9 calendar months or 40 weeks. A fertilized egg of a multi-cellular animal is transformed into an embryo by cell division, growth and differentiation. This formation into the embryo is called prenatal growth. In the prenatal period (before birth) the embryo is formed with rudiments of all organs and systems.

Prenatal growth has three distinct stages:

- the fertilized ovum (egg) (first 2 weeks)
- the embryo (from 2 to 8 weeks) and the
- the foetus (from 2 to 10 lunar months)

The human ovum during the first part of this period it is like a homogeneous mass. During the embryonic stage, though the rate of growth is slow, yet the differentiation process to form various regions which later on give rise to different parts like head, arm, leg, etc. begins. By the eighth week the embryo becomes child-like in appearance. During foetus stage the rate of growth in length as well as weight is quite high.

2. **Postnatal Period**

Postnatal growth is commonly divided into the following age periods.

(a) *Infancy :* Infancy comprises the first year of life. This is a period of rapid growth in most bodily systems and dimensions and rapid development of the neuromuscular system. The growth is mostly by addition of more cells or increase in the protoplasm. The rate of growth increases after birth and there is an increase in size, shape and weight. In case of weight, the peak is reached at two months after birth. The cells become larger in size. The cervical and lumber curvatures of the spine show up as the baby starts to straighten the head and tries to sit up and stand.

(b) *Childhood :* Childhood spans from the end of infancy (the first birthday) to the start of adolescence. This period is often divided into early childhood, middle childhood and late childhood. The early childhood is the period of eruption of milk teeth. The middle childhood (7 to 10 years) is the period of eruption of permanent teeth, though not all erupt. The late childhood starts from the pre-pubertal period and continues up to the time of puberty. Childhood is a period of relatively steady progress in growth and maturation and rapid progress in neuromuscular or development.

(c) *Adolescence :* Adolescence follows childhood. In this period the hormonal influences play a leading role in order to attain sexual maturity. During this period there is a marked acceleration of the adolescence growth spurt. The adolescence spurt is a constant phenomenon and occurs in all children, though it varies in intensity and duration from one child to another. In boys it takes place, on an average from age 12 to 15. In girls the spurt begins about two years earlier than in boys. Differentiation in primary and secondary sexual characteristics marks the adolescence period. There are changes in the reproductive organs, in body size and shape, in the relative proportions of muscle, fat and bone and in a variety of physiological functions.

(d) *Maturity or Adulthood :* The endocrine glands under the direction of pituitary hormones prepare the body for adulthood. An important sign of maturity is reproductive maturity. During adolescence, reproductive maturity begins but not completed. The active reproductive period extends up to 40 or 45 years of age in the human beings. The end of growth of height is also regarded as a sign of maturity.

Development

The term development refers to certain changes that occur in human beings between birth and death. The term is not applied to all changes but rather to those that remain for a reasonably long period of time. A temporary change caused by a brief illness, for example, is not considered a part of development. Some developmental psychologists prefer to restrict the notion of development only to changes which lead to qualitative changes in the structure of behaviour, skill or ability. For example, Heinz Werner, a developmental psychologist believed that development consisted of two processes: **integration** and **differentiation**. According to him, development "proceeds from a state of relative lack of differentiation to a state of increasing differentiation and hierarchic integration" at all levels of the person.

Integration refers to the idea that development consists of the integration of more basic, previously acquired behaviours into new, higher level structures. For example, according to Piaget, the baby who learns to successfully reach for objects has learned to coordinate a variety of skills such as keeping an upright posture, moving the arm, visually coordinating the position of the hand and the object, and grasping the object under an integrated structure called a scheme. New developments build on and incorporate what has come before.

Differentiation is the idea that development also involves the progressive ability to make more distinctions among things, for example, learning to adjust one's grasp to pick up small objects (which requires the use of the fingers) versus larger objects (which only require closing the hand around the object and less motor control). Werner defined development as a combination of these two processes of integration and differentiation.

Human development can be divided into a number of different domains:

1. **Physical Domain :** Physical domain consists of development of body structure including muscles, bones and organ systems. It includes:

    (a) Gross motor development using large muscles for example legs and arms.

    (b) Fine motor development or precise use of muscles, for example hands and fingers.

    (c) Sensory development which is development of vision, hearing, taste, smell and touch.

    Physical domain also includes

    (a) Cephalo-caudal development which means that a child starts with development from head to toe. According to this principle, the child first gains control of the head, then the arms, then the legs. Infants gain control of head and face movements within the first two months after birth.

    (b) Proximo-distal starts in the centre (like our chests) then moves to periphery. Accordingly, the spinal cord develops before other parts of the body. The child's arms develop before the hands, and the hands and feet develop before the fingers and toes. Fingers and toes are the last to develop.

2. **Cognitive Domain :** Referred to as intellectual or mental development, includes thinking, perception, memory, reasoning, concept development, problem-solving and abstract thinking. Language is one of the most important and complicated cognitive activities. Understanding and formulating language is a complex cognitive activity. Speaking, however, is a motor activity. Language and speech are controlled by different parts of the brain. **Jean Piaget** was a significant influence in this domain because of his **'theory of cognitive development'.**

3. **Moral Domain :** Moral domain consists of development of character, right attitudes and behaviour towards other people in society, based on social and cultural norms, rules and laws. Understanding the difference between right and wrong is the essence of moral development. Piaget believed in two basic principles relating to moral education:

   - Children develop moral ideas in stages and
   - Children create their conceptions of the world.

   According to Piaget, "the child is someone who constructs his own moral world view and forms ideas about right and wrong. Piaget believed that children made moral judgments based on their own observations of the world.

   Kohlberg proposed a detailed sequence of stages of moral reasoning or judgments about right or wrong. He divided moral development into three levels:

   - Pre conventional
   - Conventional
   - Post conventional

4. **Social and Emotional Domain : Social development** includes the child's interactions with other people and the child's involvement in social groups. It includes

   - relationships with adults and peers,
   - social roles,
   - adoption of group values and norms,
   - adoption of a moral system, and
   - productive role in society

   Learning to live with others in both our family and society is one of the most important tasks, the one in which family and friends play an important role. Socialization is all about learning to cope in the family and society we live in. The socialization process varies in different societies and from family to family.

   - Primary socialization takes place within the family, in the first years of a child's life. It helps children to learn how to interact with others, sense of right and wrong, what is acceptable and what is not.
   - Secondary socialization starts when children come into regular contact with people and settings outside their home. This includes playgroup, school and neighborhood and continues throughout life. Secondary socialization teaches children how to interact with adults, friends and others who are not family.

Emotional Development Includes

- the development of personal traits and characteristics, including a personal identity, self-esteem,

- ability to enter into reciprocal emotional relationships,

- feelings and emotions that are appropriate for one's age and situation.

Important Aspects of Emotional Development are:

(a)   **Attachment and bonding :** The development of the deep bonds of attachment between parents or care givers and their children comes about through day to day interaction. This attachment is helped in the early months by a number of things including: skin contact, talks, parents' voices, feeding, bathing, play, eye-to-eye contact, etc. Children who develop close bonds with several important people will be far more secure than children who have not done so. If a child has a strong sense of security, he is less likely to face emotional traumas and turmoil in life.

(b)   **Self-concept and personal identity :** A child's self-concept and personal identity are closely linked to the quality of parenting in early years. Quite often, adults who harm others or carry out serious crimes have had very negative experiences as children and have a very poor self-concept.

GENERAL PRINCIPLES OF DEVELOPMENT

1.   **Development is an Ongoing Process :** Development begins before birth, since the genetic basis for any individual's development is present in the reproductive cells of that individual's parents, and development continues until death. Earlier theories suggested that all important developmental milestones were achieved before adulthood. But it is known know, that development is an ongoing process with important milestones and stages occurring throughout life.

2.   **People develop at different rates :** While the rate of growth may vary at different times in the life cycle and among individuals, it is always a continuous process. In your own classroom, you will have a whole range of examples of different developmental rates.

3.   **Development is directional :** Development typically proceeds from simple to complex. For example, we all began as a single cell and developed into a complex organism with millions of cells that are highly differentiated by both structure and function. These cells are organized into more and more complex, interacting structures as development proceeds. The same basic pattern is repeated in the progression of motor development. The rudimentary and uncoordinated motor movements of a newborn infant become increasingly complicated and efficient as the child grows.

4. **Development is relatively orderly and may involve stages :** At certain predictable times in the developmental process, particular tasks or activities emerge often referred to as "stages." Stages represent a qualitative change in development, which results in the emergence of an ability or trait. After the emergence of a new skill or behaviour, there is usually a period of "leveling off," when the new skills or abilities are practiced, mastered, and integrated into the child's behaviour. For example, after an infant has learned to walk, he may spend several months perfecting balance, coordination, and stability. Stages represent the emergence of more complex behaviour patterns that often replace earlier, less effective ones. A four-year old with well developed language and good social skill is less likely to respond to frustration by having a tantrum than a two-year old in the same situation.

5. **Development is Cumulative :** Early developmental tasks form the foundation for the development of later, more complicated tasks. For example, the ability to engage in reciprocal interpersonal relationships is based on trust, a developmental milestone of the first year of life. A child who fails to master early tasks will have more difficulty mastering the demands of later stages, and without remedial intervention, the child's development becomes more delayed, or shows increasingly abnormal patterns, over time. The negative effects of early developmental deficits increase as the child grows and as demands become more complex. A deficit such as the inability to recognize letters of the alphabet does not critically affect the life of a 6-year-old. However, an adult who cannot read faces serious difficulties in social and economic functioning.

6. **Development is gradual :** Very rarely do changes appear overnight. A student who cannot manipulate a pencil or answer a hypothetical question may well develop this ability, but the change is likely to take time.

FACTORS INFLUENCING GROWTH AND DEVELOPMENT

1. **Hereditary Factors :** Human beings have a common genetic structure that determines the course of their development. This means there are basic similarities in the structure and functions of their bodies and differences between humans and other species. Many traits are inherited, including eye color, hair color, body type, height, and skin color. These are genetically determined.

    The pattern of physical development during the first year of life is largely genetically determined. A child will not be able to walk until his physical structure, bones, and muscles, have developed sufficiently to support upright body posture and to bear weight.

    Infants in all cultures are biologically ready to walk somewhere between age 9- 15 months, however, environment can influence when a child actually begins to walk. A child carried on his mother's back for the first three years of life will not walk at a year. However, if that same child is allowed to roam freely on the ground, he would likely have walked around age one. Abilities that result from maturation do not have to be taught in the same way we teach a child to hold a paintbrush or to ride a bicycle. The child will have to practice a maturational skill to be proficient; however, the emergence of the skill is not dependent upon environmental factors.

2.　**Environmental Factors :** While children are born with different potentials, the capacity for each child to develop healthily is dependent on a nurturing and supportive environment provided to that child. Multiple environments can positively influence the potential for healthy development.

- Prenatal environment: It includes the chemical balance of mother's body, and the presence of substances or conditions that can enhance or hinder developmental processes (for example, a nutritious diet and vitamins, or conversely, the mother's use of alcohol or drugs during pregnancy.)

- Physical environment: It includes the quality of air the child breathes, the food the child eats, and exposure to conditions that can cause disease or injury including child abuse and neglect.

- Learning environment: It includes the degree and type of stimulation available to the child.

- Social and cultural environment: This comprises the norms, belief system, values, and standards of behaviour that positively regulate a child's life. These codes of conduct regulate more or less all aspects of social life including parenting, family life, interacting with outsiders and authority figures and expectations regarding children's' development and conduct.

- Emotional Environment: The emotional environment comprises of the child's interpersonal relationships and the extent of nurturance provided to them. Human relationships are the building blocks of healthy development. Children grow and thrive in close and dependable relationships that provide love and nurturance, developmentally appropriate discipline, security, and encouragement for exploration. The emotional environment shapes personality and affects self-esteem, trust, social responsibility, and resilience.

MATURATION VERSUS EXPERIENCE IN DEVELOPMENT: THE NATURE–NURTURE DEBATE

In developmental psychology's past, extreme positions have been taken on the nature-nurture debate. Arnold Gesell (1928) was a strong advocate of the position that the course of our development was largely dictated by genetic factors. Our genetic heritage specifies the set of biological processes which determine the patterns of growth that we observe, which Gesell referred to as **maturation**. Simply put, maturation is the sequence of growth which is specified and controlled by our genes. Gesell used studies of identical twins to study how experience and maturation lead to development

In contrast to Gesell's maturationist position, John B. Watson (1928) argued for the dominance of the environment on children's development. Watson believed that genetic factors placed no limits on how environments could shape the course of children's development.

The positions and arguments held by Gesell and Watson regarding the relative roles of maturation and environment on development are essentially extremist positions which are no longer supported in light of current research on child development. Today, most developmental psychologists recognise that nature and nurture both play an important role in development. Rather than discussing nature versus nurture, we commonly talk about the interaction between nature and nurture. Given the widespread recognition that both nature and nurture play crucial roles in shaping development, the challenge which lies before us now is to examine the interplay between biological and environmental factory, figuring out how they interact to produce developmental change. The interaction between nature and nurture, referred to as *epigenesis,* has been characterised as being less of an answer to the nature-nurture debate than as a starting point for the study of development. Elman et al. (1996) point out that the interactionist position is certainly the correct position to take on the nature-nurture debate.

One way we can approach the interaction between nature and nurture is through an examination of the extent to which our biological programming can be altered by environmental influences. The biologist C.H. Waddington (1975) used the term *canalization* to refer to this phenomenon. In other words, is the genetic influence on a particular development robust across varied environments or does it show susceptibility to change? Highly canalized behaviours are relatively unaltered by changes in the environment. For example, the tendency to acquire a language is a highly canalized development in that it occurs across a wide degree of environmental variation. In contrast, some behaviours are easily modified by environmental factors and are less canalized. Intelligence is a trait which is dramatically altered by environmental variations.

Exercise 1 : Previous Year Questions of CTET & STET

1. In which of the following stages do children become active members of their peer group?
   [CTET-2011-I]
   (a) Adolescence
   (b) Adulthood
   (c) Early childhood
   (d) Childhood

2. "Development is a never ending process." This idea is associated with *[CTET-2011-I]*
   (a) Principle of inter-relation
   (b) Principle of continuity
   (c) Principle of integration
   (d) Principle of interaction

3. 'Toy age' refers to *[RTET-2011-I]*
   (a) Early childhood
   (b) Late childhood
   (c) Babyhood
   (d) All of these

4. Which of the following is not a characteristic of early childhood? *[RTET-2011-I]*
   (a) Pre-gang age
   (b) Imitative age
   (c) Questioning age
   (d) Play age

5. In late childhood period children understand the conversion of which physical entity(ies)?
   [RTET-2011-I]
   (a) Mass
   (b) Mass and number
   (c) Number
   (d) Mass, number and area

6. Which of the following development tasks is not appropriate to the late childhood ?
   [RTET-2011-I]
   (a) Learning physical skills necessary for ordinary games
   (b) Achieving a masculine or feminine social role
   (c) Achieving personal independence
   (d) Learning to get along with age-mates.

7. The current view of childhood assumes that
   [UPTET-2011-I]
   (a) children are similar to adults in many ways
   (b) children are best treated as young adults
   (c) childhood is basically a 'waiting period'
   (d) childhood is a unique period of growth and change.

8. The best method to study growth and development of the child is: *[PTET-2011-I]*
   (a) Psychoanalytic Method
   (b) Comparative Method
   (c) Developmental Method
   (d) Statistical Method

9. Term PSRN in development implies:
   [PTET-2011-I]
   (a) Problem solving, reasoning & numeracy
   (b) Problem solving relationship & numeracy
   (c) Perceptual skill, reasoning & numeracy
   (d) Perceptual skill, relationship & numbers

10. The concept of developmental task was first used by *[TNTET-2011-I]*
    (a) Herbart   (b) Bruner
    (c) Hull   (d) Havighurst

11. Development of concepts is primarily a part of
    [CTET-2011-II]
    (a) emotional development
    (b) intellectual development
    (c) physical development
    (d) social development

12. Heredity is considered as a social structure.
    [CTET-2011-II]
    (a) primary   (b) secondary
    (c) dynamic   (d) static

13. Human development is based on certain principles. Which of the following is not a principle of human development?
    [CTET-2011-II]
    (a) Continuity
    (b) Sequentiality
    (c) General to Specific
    (d) Reversible

14. Human development is the product of joint contribution of both *[RTET-2011-II]*
    (a) parents and teachers
    (b) sociological and cultural factors
    (c) heredity and environment
    (d) none of these

15. Character is developed by *[UPTET-2011-II]*
    (a) will power
    (b) conduct and behaviour
    (c) morality
    (d) all of these

16. Child development is defined as a field of study that *[UPTET-2011-II]*
(a) examines change in human abilities
(b) seeks to explain behaviour across lifespan
(c) compares children to adults to senior citizens
(d) accounts for the gradual evolution of a child's cognitive, social and other capacities

17. The part of the brain which is induced by Emotional stimuli is *[TNTET-2011-II]*
(a) Hypthalamus
(b) Pons
(c) Medulla oblongata
(d) Cerebellum

18. Human personality is the result of *[CTET-2012-II]*
(a) interaction between heredity and environment
(b) only environment
(c) only heredity
(d) upbringing and education

19. Which of the following is a principle of development? *[CTET-2012-II]*
(a) Development is always linear
(b) It is a discontinuous process
(c) All processes of development are not inter-connected
(d) It does not proceed at the same pace for all

20. Which of the following is predominantly heredity related factor? *[CTET-2012-II]*
(a) Participation in social activities
(b) Attitude towards peer group
(c) Thinking pattern
(d) Colour of the eyes

21. Environmental factors that shape development include all of the following except *[CTET-2012-II]*
(a) culture
(b) quality of education
(c) physique
(d) quality of nutrition

22. Physical growth and development is called *[UPTET-2014-I]*
(a) Readiness   (b) Maturation
(c) Mobility   (d) Heredity

23. The central focus of Child Psychology is *[UPTET-2014-I]*
(a) Good teacher
(b) Child
(c) Teaching process
(d) School

24. In Child Development- *[UPTET-2014-I]*
(a) Emphasis is on process
(b) Emphasis is on the role of environment and experience
(c) It is study from conception to adolescence
(d) All of the above

25. Scope of study of Child Development is *[UPTET-2014-I]*
(a) Study of different stages of Child development
(b) Study of effects of environment on Child development
(c) Study of individual differences
(d) All of the above

26. Survival of the fittest is the principle of *[UPTET-2014-I]*
(a) Lamarck   (b) Harrison
(c) Darwin   (d) McDougall

27. Factors influencing the emotional development are *[UPTET-2014-I]*
(a) Physical health
(b) Mental abilities
(c) Fatigue
(d) All of the above

28. The type of personality of a person expressing his Libido outward is *[UPTET-2014-I]*
(a) Cognitive Personality
(b) Aesthetic Personality
(c) Extrovert Personality
(d) Religious Personality

29. Who has central place in Education according to Child Psychology ? *[UPTET-2014-II]*
(a) The Child
(b) The Teacher
(c) The Guardian
(d) The Administrator

30. "Child is a book which the teacher has to learn from page to page." Who has stated the abvoe ? *[UPTET-2014-II]*
(a) Plato   (b) Aristotle
(c) Rousseau   (d) Ross

31. Emotion is originated through _________. *[UPTET-2014-II]*
(a) habits
(b) instincts
(c) physical development
(d) formation of concepts

32. Which of the following statements is not true ?
    [UPTET-2014-II]
    (a) "Heredity is the transmission of traits from parents to offspring".
    (b) "Development is the product of the interaction fo the organism and its environment."
    (c) "Heredity is the sublimation of inborn individual traits."
    (d) "Heredity is the transmission from parents to offsprings of physical and mental characteristics".

33. The best method to growth and development of the child is: *[PTET-2014-I]*
    (a) Psychoanalytic Method
    (b) Comparative Method
    (c) Developmental Method
    (d) Statistical Method

34. Which one of the following is the true statement corresponding to Cephalocaudal Principle of Child's Development: *[PTET-2014-I]*
    (a) Development is from head to foot
    (b) Development is from foot to head
    (c) Development is from middle to periphery
    (d) None of these

35. The transmission of traits from parents to off-springs is called: *[PTET-2014-II]*
    (a) environment   (b) genes
    (c) heredity   (d) homeostasis

36. A process by which a parent assumes that his child's traits are all positive because one trait is positive is termed as: *[PTET-2014-II]*
    (a) halo effect
    (b) hawthorne effect
    (c) law of effect
    (d) reverse hallo effect

37. In which stage is the Physical growth is rapid
    [TNTET-2014-I]
    (a) Early childhood   (b) Infancy
    (c) Adolescence   (d) School age

38. Excessive secretion of Growth Hormone by the Pituitary Gland leads to _________
    [TNTET-2014-I]
    (a) Dwarfism   (b) Cretinism
    (c) Gigantism   (d) Goitre

39. The book titled 'Dream Analysis' was published by *[TNTET-2014-II]*
    (a) John Dewey
    (b) William James
    (c) Edward Tichenes
    (d) Sigmund Freud

40. During fertilization the chromosome received from the male partner is *[TNTET-2014-II]*
    (a) Y   (b) X
    (c) XY   (d) XX

41. Adolescence is a period of storm and stress – said by *[TNTET-2014-II]*
    (a) Brickson
    (b) Cole
    (c) Stanley Hall
    (d) William Mcdougall

42. The main ductless gland that regulates the physiological and psychological functioning of a person is _____________ *[TNTET-2014-II]*
    (a) The pituitary gland
    (b) Thyroid gland
    (c) Para thyroid gland
    (d) Adrenal gland

43. The transfer of physiological and genetic characters from parents to off springs through generations is called *[TNTET-2014-II]*
    (a) Evolution
    (b) Transfer to next generation
    (c) Biological heridity
    (d) None of the above

44. Personality traits such as introvertism and extrovertism personality was explained by
    [TNTET-2014-II]
    (a) Cattell   (b) Eysenck
    (c) Kemp   (d) Yung

45. Understanding Human Growth and Development enables a teacher to *[CTET-July-2013-I]*
    (a) gain control of learners' emotions while teaching.
    (b) be clear about teaching diverse learners.
    (c) tell students how they can improve their lives.
    (d) practice her teaching in an unbiased way.

46. Which one of the following is true about the role of heredity and environment in the development of a child? *[CTET-July-2013-I]*
    (a) The relative contributions of peers and genes are not additive.
    (b) Heredity and environment do not operate together.
    (c) Propensity is related to environment while actual development requires heredity.
    (d) Both heredity and environment contribute 50% each in the development of a child.

47. A child coming to pre-school for the first time cries profusely. After two years when the same child goes to the primary school for the first time, he does not express his tension by crying rather his shoulder and neck muscles become tense. This change in his behaviour can be explained on the basis of which of the following principles?

[CTET-Feb.-2014-I]

(a) Development proceeds in a sequential manner

(b) Development is gradual

(c) Development is different in different people

(d) Development is characterized by differential and integration

48. A teacher found that a student is facing difficulty in drawing a square. He/She assumes that this student would also find it difficult to draw a diamond. He/She applies which of the following principles to arrive at his/her assumption?

[CTET-Feb.-2014-II]

(a) Development tends to follow an orderly sequence

(b) Development is saltatory

(c) Development is gradual

(d) Development is different for different people

49. Which one of the following statements is true regarding the role of heredity and environment in human development? *[CTET-Feb.-2014-II]*

(a) The role of environment is almost fixed, whereas the impact of heredity can be altered

(b) The theories based on the 'behaviourism' are largely based on the role of 'nature' in human development

(c) The relative effects of heredity and environment vary in different areas of development

(d) The policy of compensatory discrimination of the Government of India is based on the role of 'nature' in human development

50. The nature-nurture debate refers to

[CTET-Sept.-2014-I]

(a) genetics and environment

(b) behaviour and environment

(c) environment and biology

(d) environment and upbringing

51. Which of the following facts has been least discussed in the psychology of emotion ?

[CTET-Sept.-2014-II]

(a) Emotion is a subjective feeling and varies from person to person

(b) Emotions may not occur within individual students, but also also within the entire class

(c) Emotions are a complex pattern of arousal and cognitive interpretation

(d) Emotional process involves physiological as well as psychological reactions

52. 'Which one of the following is best suited for emotional development of children ?

[CTET-Feb.-2015-I]

(a) Democratic classroom environment

(b) No involvement of the teachers as it is the task of the parents

(c) Controlled classroom environment

(d) Authoritarian classroom environment

53. "Anyone can become angry - that is easy, but to be angry with the right person, to the right degree, at the right time, for the right purpose, and in the right way - that is not easy." This is related to

[CTET-Feb.-2015-I]

(a) Emotional development

(b) Social development

(c) Cognitive development

(d) Physical development

54. In the context of 'nature - nurture' debate, which one of the following statements seems appropriate to you ? *[CTET-Feb.-2015-II]*

(a) Children are genetically predisposed to what they would be like irrespective of whatever environment they grow up in.

(b) A child is like a blank slate whose character can be moulded by the environment into any shape.

(c) Environmental influences only have a little value in shaping up a child's behaviour which is primarily genetically determined.

(d) Heredity and environment are inseparably interwoven and both influence development.

55. Which one of these is a principle of child development ? *[CTET-Feb.-2015-II]*

(a) Development can accurately predict the pace of each individual child.

(b) Development occurs due to interaction between maturation and experience.

(c) Experience is the sole determinant of development.

(d) Development is determined by reinforcement and punishment.

56. The pace of development varies from one individual to another, but it follows ...... pattern. *[CTET-Feb.-2016-I]*

(a) a toe-to-head

(b) a haphazard

(c) an unpredictable

(d) a sequential and orderly

57. Which one of the following is correct about development?   *[CTET-Feb.-2016-I]*

(a) Development begins and ends at birth.

(b) 'Sociocultural context' plays an important role in development.

(c) Development is unidimensional.

(d) Development is discrete.

58. Early childhood is .... period for language development.   *[CTET-Feb.-2016-I]*

(a) a not-so-significant

(b) an unimportant

(c) a sensitive

(d) a neutral

59. Which of the following statements about children are **correct**?   *[CTET-Sept.-2016-I]*

A.   Children are passive recipients of knowledge.

B.   Children are problem solvers.

C.   Children are scientific investigators.

D.   Children are active explorers of the environment.

(a) A, B and D

(b) B, C and D

(c) A, B, C and D

(d) A, B and C

60. Which of the following is the most effective method to encourage conceptual development in students?   *[CTET-Sept.-2016-I*

(a) New concepts need to be understood on their own without any reference to the old ones.

(b) Replace the students' incorrect ideas with correct ones by asking them to memorize.

(c) Give students multiple examples and encourage them to use reasoning.

(d) Use punishment till students have made the required conceptual changes.

61. The cephalocaudal principle of development explains how development proceeds from :   *[CTET-Sept.-2016-I]*

(a) general to specific functions

(a) differentiated to integrated functions

(c) head to toe

(d) rural to urban areas

62. A 6-year-old girl shows exceptional sporting ability. Both of her parents are sportspersons, send her for coaching everyday and train her on weekends. Her capabilities are most likely to be the result of an interaction between :   *[CTET-Sept.-2016-I]*

(a) heredity and environment

(b) growth and development

(c) health and training

(d) discipline and nutrition

63. Which one of the following statements about development is correct?   *[CTET-Feb.-2016-II]*

(a) Developmental changes go forward in a straight line.

(b) Development proceeds from birth to adolescence in a forward manner and then it goes backwards.

(c) Development occurs at a different rate among different Individuals.

(d) Development occurs at a very fast pace from birth till adolescence and then it stops.

64. "Environmental factors do not play any role in shaping an individual, since growth of each individual is determined by his genetic makeup." This statement is   *[CTET-Feb.-2016-II]*

(a) correct, since genetic makeup of an individual is very strong.

(b) incorrect, since there have been several researches to prove that environment can have a major influence on development.

(c) correct, since there have been several researches to prove that genetic material alone predicts an individual's development.

(d) incorrect, since environmental factors contribute little in an individual's growth and development.

65. Which of the following statements about principles of development is incorrect?   *[CTET-Sept.-2016-II]*

(a) Development is a quantitative process which can be measured precisely.

(b) Development depends   on maturation and learning.

(c) Development takes place due to a constant interaction between heredity and environment.

(d) Every child goes through stages of development, yet there are wide individual differences among children.

66. The unique interaction of ___ and ___ can result in different paths and outcomes of development.

[CTET-Sept.-2016-II]

(a) exploration; nutrition

(b) challenges; limitations

(c) heredity; environment

(d) stability; change

67. Match the following principles of development with their correct descriptions:

[CTET-Sept.-2016-II]

Principle		**Description**
(A) Proximodistal trend	(i)	Different children develop at different rates
(B) Cephalocaudal trend	(ii)	Head to toe sequence
(C) Interindividual differences	(iii)	In a single child, the rate of development can vary from one domain of development to the other
(D) Intraindividual differences	(iv)	From the centre of body to outwards
	(v)	Progression from simple to complex

	A	B	C	D
(a)	(v)	(ii)	(i)	(iii)
(b)	(v)	(ii)	(i)	(iii)

(c) (ii) (iv) (i) (iii)

(d) (ii) (iv) (iii) (i)

68. In a normal zygote, the number of chromosomes in pair is *[UPTET-2017-I]*

(a) 22   (b) 23

(c) 24   (d) none of the above

69. Whose name is associated with 'Father of the Eugenics?' *[UPTET-2017-I]*

(a) Crow and Crow   (b) Galton

(c) Ross   (d) Woodworth

70. One of the following statements is true *[APTET-May.-2018-I]*

(a) Development is a short term process

(b) There are no individual differences in development

(c) Development is not uniform in all the developmental stages

(d) Development is not predictable

71. The study that supports the influence of Heredity on development of an individual *[APTET-May.-2018-I]*

(a) Pearson – Darwin's family

(b) Freeman – Miltred Rooth

(c) Skodak – Foster children

(d) Gordon – Gipsy children

72. A child without have proper mental development lags behind in his social development also. The development principle here is *[APTET-May.-2018-II]*

(a) Development is the process of interaction

(b) Developments proceed with interrelation

(c) Development proceeds from general to specific

(d) Development is cumulative

73. Physical factor that affects learners learning is *[APTET-May.-2018-II]*

(a) Interest   (b) Attitude

(c) Intelligence   (d) Maturity

Answer Key

1.	(a)	11.	(b)	21.	(c)	31.	(b)	41.	(c)	51.	(b)	61.	(c)	71.	(a)
2.	(b)	12.	(d)	22.	(b)	32.	(c)	42.	(a)	52.	(a)	62.	(a)	72.	(b)
3.	(a)	13.	(d)	23.	(b)	33.	(c)	43.	(c)	53.	(a)	63.	(c)	73.	(d)
4.	(d)	14.	(c)	24.	(d)	34.	(a)	44.	(d)	54.	(d)	64.	(b)		
5.	(d)	15.	(d)	25.	(d)	35.	(c)	45.	(b)	55.	(b)	65.	(a)		
6.	(b)	16.	(d)	26.	(c)	36.	(d)	46.	(a)	56.	(d)	66.	(c)		
7.	(d)	17.	(a)	27.	(d)	37.	(b)	47.	(d)	57.	(b)	67.	(b)		
8.	(c)	18.	(b)	28.	(c)	38.	(c)	48.	(a)	58.	(c)	68.	(b)		
9.	(a)	19.	(a)	29	(a)	39.	(b)	49.	(c)	59.	(b)	69.	(b)		
10.	(d)	20.	(d)	30.	(c)	40.	(c)	50.	(a)	60.	(c)	70.	(c)		

45. (b) When a teacher know about the growth and development of children enables him to be clear about teaching diverse learners.

47. (d) Human development involves changes. Development is a product of maturity and learning. A child reacts differently the same situation due to maturity and learning and integrates himself.

48. (a) The process of development takes place in an orderly manner. Development proceeds from general to specific. In all areas of development general activity always preceds specific activity.

49. (c) All that we inherit from our parents and forefathers is called heredity and the environment is every thing that affects the individual except the gens. Both have a very important role in development. In physical development, heredity is more important than environment, while in social development environment is more important.

56. (d) The speed of development is different from one person to another but it follows a chronological and systematic pattern. As you see the growth in the first year of a child follows cephalocaudal and proximodistal pattern i.e the patter it follows in terms of height and weight in childhood and other stages.

57. (b) Development is a constant process like learning". The development of a person is related to one's environment, social life. etc. Hence, 'socio-cultural context' plays an important role in development.

58. (c) Early childhood stage of a child is accompanied with language acquisition. As a child reaches the age 5, he becomes familiar with sounds and grammar of he mother tongue. Subsequently he acquires the vocabulary of that language.

62. (a) Heredity and environment both are the enhancing features to make the child develop his personality. Thus a child learns from home and society both.

68. (b) In humans, each cell normally contains 23 pairs of chromosomes, for a total of 46. Twenty-two of these pairs, called autosomes, look the same in both males and females. The 23rd pair, the sex chromosomes, differ between males and females.

70. (c) Development is not same in all developmental stages according to the stages given by Piaget and other psychologists. Therefore it is a true statement saying that Development is not uniform in all development stages.

71. (a) Darwin's family, is the theory given by Pearson the study that supports the influence of Heredity on development of an individual

Exercise 2 : Test Yourself

1. One of the three stages during the prenatal growth is
   (a) Embryo
   (b) Infancy
   (c) Puberty
   (d) Multi-cellular growth

2. Early childhood is a period of
   (a) Eruption of milk teeth
   (b) Straightening of head
   (c) Progress in neuromuscular development
   (d) Rapid growth of bodily systems

3. Heinz Werner explained the concept of
   (a) Simulation and Organization
   (b) Assimilation & Accommodation
   (c) Integration and Differentiation
   (d) Perception and Judgment

4. The detailed sequence of stages of moral reasoning or judgments about right or wrong was proposed by
   (a) Kohlberg   (b) Erikson
   (c) Piaget   (d) Vygotsky

5. The pattern of physical development which is genetically determined is
   (a) Habitual
   (b) Environmental
   (c) Situational
   (d) Hereditary

6. Development is directional means
   (a) There is an emergence of a new skill or behaviour
   (b) Development typically proceeds from simple to complex
   (c) All important developmental milestones were achieved before adulthood
   (d) Development continues until death

7. Physical growth and development is called
   (a) Readiness   (b) Maturation
   (c) Mobility   (d) Heredity

8. Development is not
   (a) A change in desirable direction
   (b) A multi-sphere change
   (c) A spontaneous change
   (d) A planned change

9. Development is a never ending process." This idea is associated with
   (a) Principle of integration
   (b) Principle of interaction
   (c) Principle of interrelation
   (d) Principle of continuity

10. The development that proceeds in the direction of the longitudinal axis i.e., head to foot is termed as ………. .
    (a) Cephalo-caudal development
    (b) Proximo distal
    (c) Interrelation
    (d) Integrative

11. The development that proceeds from the centre to the periphery is termed as:
    (a) Spiral development
    (b) Linear development
    (c) Proximo-distal
    (d) None of the above

12. Environmental factors that shape development include all of the following except
    (a) Quality of learning
    (b) Intelligence
    (c) Nutrition
    (d) Culture

13. Another name for a newborn baby is
    (a) Embryo   (b) Neonate
    (c) Zygote   (d) Fetus

14. A normal child of 12 years of age is most likely to
    (a) Have difficulty with gross motor coordination
    (b) Have feelings of anxiety about pleasing adults
    (c) Confine his/her interests to here and now
    (d) Be eager for peer approval

15. The current view of childhood assumes that
    (a) Children are similar to adults in most ways
    (b) Children are best treated as young adults.
    (c) Childhood is basically a "waiting period."
    (d) Childhood is a unique period of growth and change.

16. The key difference between evolutionary and cultural change is that evolutionary change alters __________ whereas cultural change alters __________ .
    (a) Reproduction; environment
    (b) Heredity; environment
    (c) Environment; behaviour
    (d) Development; learning

17. Development of concepts is primarily a part of
    (a) Emotional development
    (b) Intellectual development
    (c) Physical development
    (d) Social development
18. Lower classes, play-way method of teaching is based on
    (a) theory of physical education programs
    (b) principles of methods of teaching
    (c) psychological principles of development and growth
    (d) sociological principles of teaching
19. Human development is based on certain principles. Which of the following is not a principle of human development?
    (a) Continuity
    (b) Sequentiality
    (c) General to specific
    (d) Reversible
20. Developmental psychology postulates one regulative principle of development; which is
    (a) an orthogenetic principle
    (b) a psycho-social principle
    (c) A Cognitive principle
    (d) A differentiation principle
21. In comparative physical growth curves, female
    (a) Develop more slowly than males
    (b) Develop more rapidly than males
    (c) Develop at the same rate as males
    (d) Develop more rapidly than males during the first six years and more slowly thereafter
22. Physical growth & development is called
    (a) readiness   (b) maturation
    (c) mobility   (d) heredity
23. Adoloscence is a period of 'storm and stress', was said by
    (a) G. Stanely hall
    (b) B.F. Skinner
    (c) Jean Piaget
    (d) None of these
24. The meaning of development is
    (a) progressive series of changes
    (b) progressive series of changes as a result of motivation
    (c) progressive series of changes as a result of motivation and experience
    (d) series of changes as a result of maturation and experience.

25. Which of the following statements is not correct about development ?
    (a) Each phase of the development has hazards
    (b) Development is not aided by stimulation
    (c) Development is affected by cultural changes
    (d) Each phase of the development has characteristic behaviour.
26. Which one of the following is the true statement corresponding to Cephalocaudal   Principle of Child's Development:
    (a) Development is from head to foot
    (b) Development is from foot to head
    (c) Development is from middle to periphery
    (d) None of these
27. Development of human values which are universal in nature means
    (a) indoctrination   (b) adoption
    (c) imitation   (d) manifestation
28. Which one of the following is not an internal factor on the growth and development of children
    (a) Bilogical factor
    (b) Intelligence
    (c) Emotional factor
    (d) Environment in the womb of the mother
29. The literal meaning of Emotion is
    (a) aggression and fear
    (b) affection and love
    (c) excitement or disturbance in feelings
    (d) None of these
30. First stage to learn skill is
    (a) Reality   (b) Imagination
    (c) Co-ordination   (d) Imitation
31. What is the principal psychological characteristic of childhood?
    (a) Dependence on others
    (b) Feeling of gregariousness
    (c) Religious feeling
    (d) Lack of tendency of imitation
32. Cognitive Development means :
    (a) Development of intelligence
    (b) Development of child
    (c) Development of Physical Skills
    (d) Development of individual
33. A development perspective involves concern with changes occurring over time in:
    (a) form   (b) rate
    (c) sequence   (d) all of these

34. In the above figure the line 'A' is perceived to be shorter than the line 'B'. This is due to ___________
(a) Poyendoffs illusion
(b) Horizontal – Vertical line illusion
(c) Zollener's illusion
(d) Muller-Lyer illusion

35. The most apt method of evaluating a person's personality is through
(a) Autobiography   (b) Self rating
(c) Questionnaire   (d) Attitude scale

36. Super ego stage occurs at the age of
(a) 1-3   (b) 3-6
(c) 6-9   (d) 9-12

37. Which one of the following is correctly matched?
(a) Physical Development–Environment
(b) Cognitive Development– Maturation
(c) Social Development– Environment
(d) Emotional Development–Maturation

38. All the following facts indicate that a child is emotionally and socially fit in a class except
(a) develop good relationships with peers
(b) concentrate on and persist with challenging tasks
(c) manage both anger and joy effectively
(d) concentrate persistently on competition with peers

39. Which of the following statements support role of environment in the development of a child ?
(a) Some students quickly process information while others in the same class do not.
(b) There has been a steady increase in students' average performance on IQ tests in last few decades.
(c) Correlation between IQs of identical twins raised in different homes is as high as 0.75.
(d) Physically fit children are often found to be morally good.

40. Which of the following statements is true?
(a) Genetic makeup impacts responsiveness of an individual to qualities of the environment
(b) Adoptive children possess same IQs as their adoptive siblings
(c) Experience does not influence brain development
(d) Intelligence remains unaffected by the schooling

41. Cognitive development is supported by
(a) conducting relevant and well-designed tests as frequently as possible
(b) presenting activities that reinforce traditional methods
(c) providing a rich and varied environment
(d) focusing more on individual activities in comparison to collaboration

42. Human development is
(a) quantitative
(b) qualitative
(c) unmeasurable to a certain extent
(d) both quantitative and qualitative

Answer Key

1.	(a)	**10.**	(a)	**19.**	(d)	**28.**	(a)	**37.**	(c)
2.	(a)	**11.**	(c)	**20.**	(a)	**29.**	(c)	**38.**	(d)
3.	(c)	**12.**	(b)	**21.**	(b)	**30.**	(d)	**39.**	(b)
4.	(a)	**13.**	(b)	**22.**	(b)	**31.**	(b)	**40.**	(a)
5.	(d)	**14.**	(d)	**23.**	(a)	**32.**	(a)	**41.**	(c)
6.	(b)	**15.**	(d)	**24.**	(c)	**33.**	(d)	**42.**	(d)
7.	(b)	**16.**	(b)	**25.**	(b)	**34.**	(d)		
8.	(c)	**17.**	(b)	**26.**	(a)	**35.**	(c)		
9.	(d)	**18.**	(c)	**27.**	(b)	**36.**	(b)		

Constructs and Critical Perspectives on Development

Swiss psychologist Jean Piaget showed that intelligence is the result of a natural sequence of stages and it develops as a result of the changing interaction of a child and its environment. He devised a model describing how humans go about making sense of their world by gathering and organizing information.

According to Piaget development is a spontaneous process tied to embryogenesis whereas learning is provoked by external situations. Embryogenesis concerns the development of the body, as well as the development of the nervous system and the development of mental functions. Learning presents the opposite case. *In general, learning is provoked by situations-provoked by a psychological experimenter, or by a teacher, with respect to a didactic point,* or by an external situation. It is provoked in general, as opposed to spontaneous.

Cognitive development is much more than the addition of new facts and ideas to an existing store of information. According to Piaget, our thinking processes change radically, though slowly from birth to maturity because we constantly strive to make sense of the world. Piaget identifies four factors namely biological maturation, activity, social experiences, and equilibration that interact to influence thinking.

- **Maturation:** Maturation is the unfolding of the biological changes that are genetically programmed. Parents and teachers have little influence on this aspect of cognitive development except to be certain that children get the nourishment and care they need to be healthy.

- **Activity:** With maturation comes the increasing ability to act on the environment and learn from it. For example, when a young child's coordination is reasonably developed, the child may discover principles about balance by experimenting with a sea saw. Thus, the child acts on the environment as it explores, tests, observes, and eventually organizes information.

- **Social transmission:** The process of development also involves interacting with the people around us. According to Piaget, our cognitive development is influenced by social transmission, or learning from others. The amount people can learn from social transmission varies according to their stage of cognitive development.

- **Equilibration:** The actual changes in thinking take place through the process of equilibration- the act of searching for a balance. Briefly the process of equilibration works like this:

If we apply a particular scheme to an event or situation and the scheme works, then equilibrium exists. If the scheme does not produce a satisfying result, then disequilibrium exists and we become uncomfortable. This motivates us to keep searching for a solution through assimilation and accommodation, and thus our thinking changes and moves ahead. The concepts assimilation and accommodation are explained below.

Invariant Functions of Thinking

According to Piaget, all species inherit two invariant functions.

- Organization

- Adaptation

Organization: We are born with a propensity to organize our thinking processes into psychological structures. These structures are our systems for understanding the world. These are called schemes. Simple structures are continually combined and coordinated to become more sophisticated and thus more effective. For example, very young infants can either look at an object or grasp it when it comes in their hands. They cannot coordinate looking and grasping at the same time. As they develop, however, infants organize these two separate behavioural structures into a coordinated higher-level structure of looking at, reaching for, and grasping the object.

In Piaget's theory, schemes are the basic building blocks of thinking. Schemes may be very small or specific, for example, the sucking-through-a-straw scheme or the recognizing-a- flower scheme. Or they may be larger or more general- the drinking scheme or the categorizing-plants scheme. As a person's thinking processes become more organized and new schemes develop, behaviour also becomes more sophisticated and better suited to the environment.

Adaptation: People also inherit the tendency to adapt to their environment through two basic complementary processes.

(a) Assimilation

(b) Accommodation

Assimilation : takes place when people use their existing schemes to make sense of events in their world. Assimilation involves trying to understand something new by fitting it into what we already know. At times, we may have to distort the new information to make it fit.

- For example, the first time many children see a skunk, they call it a "kitty". They try to match the new experience with an existing scheme for identifying animals.

- Assimilation is like adding air into a balloon. You just keep blowing it up and it gets bigger and bigger. For example, a two year old child's schema of a tree is "green and has a bark"and over time the child adds more information that is some trees lose their leaves, some trees have names, there is a maple or Christmas tree etc.

Accommodation: occurs when a person must change existing schemes to respond to a new situation. If data cannot be made to fit any existing schemes, then more appropriate structures must be developed. We adjust our thinking to fit the new information, instead of adjusting the information to fit our thinking.

- For example, children demonstrate accommodation when they add the scheme for recognizing skunks to their other systems for identifying animals.

- For example, all dogs are thought to be black and if a child's pet dog is black, seeing a white dog needs the schema to be changed.

Piaget's Four Stages of Cognitive Development

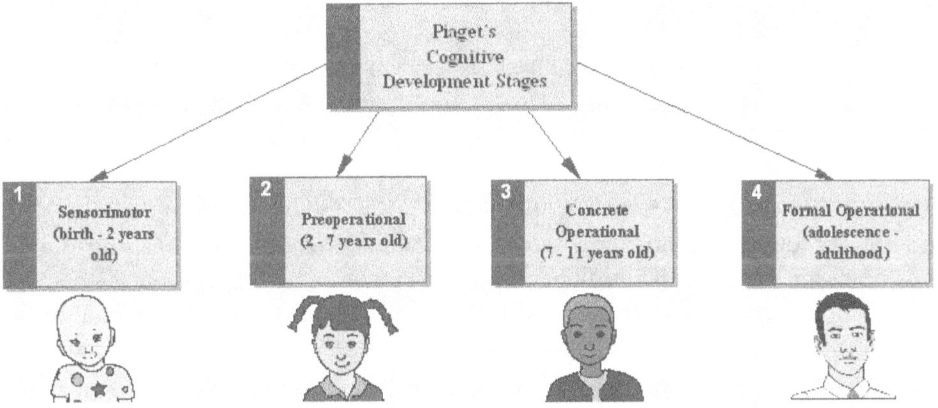

Infancy : The Sensory Motor Stage (0-2 years)

This period is called the sensory motor stage because the child's thinking involves seeing, hearing, moving, touching, tasting and so on. Piaget called each specific "way of knowing" a scheme. During this period, the infant develops object permanence, the understanding that objects exist in the environment whether the baby perceives them or not. As most parents discover, before infants develop object permanence, it is relatively easy to take something away from them. The trick is to distract them and remove the object while they are not looking-"out of sight out of mind". The older infant who searches for a ball that has rolled out of sight is indicating an understanding that objects still exist even when they are not in view.

This period also marks the beginning of goal-directed actions. For example, the container toy for babies is usually plastic with a lid and contains several colorful items that can be taken out and replaced. A six-month old baby is likely to become frustrated trying to get to the toys inside. An older child who has mastered the basics of the sensory motor stage will probably be able to deal with the toy in an orderly fashion by building a "container toy" scheme:

1.   Take the lid off

2.   Turn the container upside down

3.   Shake if the items jam

4.   See the items fall.

Separate lower level schemes have been organized into a higher-level scheme to achieve a goal.

The child is soon able to reverse this action by refilling the container. Learning to reverse actions is a basic accomplishment of the sensory-motor stage. But learning to imagine the reverse of a sequence of actions takes much longer.

Early Childhood to the Early Elementary Years: The Preoperational Stage (2-7 years)

The ability to form and use symbols- words, gestures, signs, images, and so on- is a major accomplishment of the preoperational period and moves children closer to mastering the mental operations of the next stage. This ability to work with symbols, such as using the word "fish" or a picture of a fish to represent a real fish that is not actually present, is called the semiotic function.

The child's earliest use of symbols is in pretending or miming. Children who are not yet able to talk will often use action symbols- pretending to drink from an empty cup or touching a comb to their hair, showing that they know what each object is for. This behaviour also shows that their schemes are becoming more general and less tied to specific actions. The eating scheme, for example, may be used in playing house. During the preoperational stage, we also see the rapid development of that very important symbol, language. Between the ages of 2 and 4, most children enlarge their vocabulary from about 200 to 2000 words.

As the child moves through the preoperational stage, the developing ability to think about objects in symbolic form remains somewhat thinking in one direction only, or using one-way logic. It is very difficult for the child to "think backward" or imagine how to reverse the steps in a task. Reversible thinking is involved in many tasks that are difficult for the preoperational child, such as the conservation of matter.

Conservation is the principle that the amount of something remains the same even if the arrangement or appearance is changes, as long as nothing is added and nothing is taken away. You know that if you tear a piece of paper into several pieces, you will still have the same amount of paper. To prove this, you know that you can reverse the process by taping the pieces back together.

A classic example of difficulty with conversation is found in the preoperational child's response to the following Piagetian task. A 5-year-old, is shown two identical glasses, both short and wide in shape. Both have exactly the same amount of colored water in them.

Interviewer : Does one glass have more water, or are they the same?

Child : Same

The experimenter then pours the water from one of the glasses into a taller, narrower glass.

Interviewer : Now, does one glass have more water, or are they the same?

Child : The tall one has more

Interviewer : How do you know?

Child : It goes up more here (points to higher level on taller glass)

The child shows a basic understanding of identity (it's the same water) but not an understanding that the amounts are identical. Piaget's explanation for the child's answer is that he is focusing, or centering, attention on the dimension of height. He has difficulty considering more than one aspect of the situation at a time, or decentering. The preoperational child cannot understand that increased diameter compensates for decreased height, because this would require taking into account two dimensions at once.

Later Elementary to the Middle School Years: The Concrete-Operational Stage (7-11 years)

Piaget called the concrete operations, the stage of "hands-on" thinking. The basic characteristics of this stage are the recognition of the logical stability of the physical world, the realization that elements can be changed or transformed and still conserve many of their original characteristics, and the understanding that these changes can be reversed.

According to Piaget, a student's ability to solve conservation problems depends on an understanding of three basic aspects of reasoning:

- Identity
- Compensation
- Reversibility

Identity: The child understands identity that is he knows that if nothing is added or taken away, the material remains the same.

Compensation: With an understanding of compensation, the child knows that an apparent change in one direction can be compensated for by a change in another direction. That is, if a liquid rise higher in the glass, the glass must be narrower.

Reversibility: And with an understanding of reversibility, the child can mentally cancel out the change that has been made.

Another important operation mastered at this stage is classification. Classification depends on a student's abilities to focus on a single characteristic of objects in a set and group the objects according to that characteristic. Given 12 objects of assorted colors and shapes, the concrete operational student can invariably pick out the ones that are square.

Classification is also related to reversibility. The ability to reverse a process mentally now allows the concrete operational student to see that there is more than one way to classify a group of objects. The student understands, for example, that buttons can be classified by color, reclassified by size or by the number of holes.

With the abilities to handle operations such as conservation and classification, the student at the concrete operational stage has finally developed a complete and very logical system of thinking.

Junior and Senior High: Formal Operations: (11-adult)

Formal thinking is reversible, internal and organized in a system of interdependent elements. The focus of thinking shifts, however, from what is to what might be. Ask a young child how life would be different if people did not sleep, and the child might say, "People do sleep!"In contrast, the adolescent who has mastered formal operations can consider contrary-to-fact questions. In answering, the adolescent demonstrates the hall-mark of formal operations-hypothetico-deductive reasoning meaning deductive logic becomes important during the formal operational stage. The formal thinker can consider a hypothetical situation (people do not sleep) and reason deductively (from the general assumption to specific implications, such as longer workdays, more money spent on energy and lighting, or new entertainment industries). Formal-operational thinkers can form hypotheses, set up mental experiments to test them, and isolate or control variables in order to complete a valid test of the hypotheses. The ability to solve a problem in a logical and methodical way develops and children are often able to quickly plan an organized approach to solving a problem.

Another characteristic of this stage is adolescent egocentrism. Unlike egocentric young children, adolescents do not deny that other people may have different perceptions and beliefs; the adolescents just become very focused on their own ideas. They analyze their own beliefs and attitudes. There is a feeling that everyone is watching. Thus, adolescents believe that others are analyzing them: "Everyone noticed that I wore this shirt twice this week." "The whole class thought my answer was dumb!" The feeling of being "on stage" seems to peak in early adolescence by age 14 or 15.

Implications of Piaget's Theory for Teachers

According to Piaget, students must be neither bored by work that is too simple nor left behind by teaching they cannot understand. Disequilibrium must be kept "just right" to encourage growth.

Setting up situations that lead to errors can help create an appropriate level of disequilibrium. When students experience some conflict between what they think should happen (a piece of wood should sink because it is big) and what actually happens (it floats), they may rethink the situation, and new knowledge may develop.

Construction of Knowledge

Piaget's fundamental insight was that individuals construct their own understanding and that learning is a constructive process. At every level of cognitive development, you will also want to see that students are actively engaged in the learning process.

Active experience should include not only physical manipulation of objects but also mental manipulation of ideas that arise out of class projects or experiments. For example, after a social studies lesson on different jobs, a primary-grade teacher might show the students a picture of a woman and ask, "What could this person be?" After answers such as "teacher", "doctor", "secretary", "lawyer", "saleswoman", and so on, the teacher could suggest, "How about a daughter?" Answers such as "sister", "mother", "aunt" and "granddaughter" may follow. This should help the children switch dimensions in their classification and center on another aspect of the situation.

VYGOTSKY'S SOCIO-CULTURAL PERSPECTIVE

It is a well-known fact today that the child's culture shapes cognitive development by determining what and how the child will learn about the world. For example, young children in some countries learn complicated ways of weaving cloth through informal teachings of adults in their communities and in some places, without going to school, children who sell sweets or candy on the streets learn sophisticated mathematics in order to buy from wholesalers, sell, barter, and make profit. Cultures that treasure cooperation and sharing teach these abilities early, whereas cultures that encourage competition nurture competitive skills in their children.

A major spokesperson for this socio-cultural theory was Lev Semenovich Vygotsky, a Russian psychologist. His ideas about language, culture and cognitive development have become major influences in psychology and education and have provided alternatives to many of Piaget's theories.

Vygotsky's theory offers an insight into the fact that development is inseparable from human social and cultural activities. Vygotsky was of the view that human activities take place in cultural settings and cannot be seen apart from these settings. One of his key ideas was that our specific mental structures and processes can be traced to our interactions with others. These social interactions create our cognitive structures and thinking processes. In fact, "Vygotsky conceptualized development as the transformation of socially shared activities into internalized processes".

The Social Sources of Individual Thinking

Vygotsky assumed that every function in a child's cultural development appears twice, first on the social level and later on the personal level;

- first between people (inter-psychological) and then

- inside the child (intra-psychological)".

In other words, higher mental processes appear first between people as they are co-constructed during shared activities. Then the processes are internalized by the child and become part of the child's cognitive development. For Vygotsky, social interaction was more than influence. It was the origin of higher mental processes such as problem solving.

Consider this example:

A six-year old has lost a toy and asks her father for help. The father asks her where she last saw the toy: the child says "I can't remember". He asks a series of questions-did you have it in your room? Outside?, Next door? To each question, the child answers "no". When he says "in the car?" she says" I think so" and goes to retrieve the toy. (Tharp and Gallimore, 1988)

It was remembered by the father or the daughter? No, neither the father nor the daughter, but the two together. The remembering and problem-solving was co-constructed between people, that is, both of them in the process of their interaction. But the child may have internalized strategies to use next time something is lost. At some point, the child will be able to function independently to solve his kind of problem.

Both Piaget and Vygotsky emphasized the importance of social interactions in cognitive development, but Piaget saw a different role for interaction.

- Piaget believed that interaction encouraged development by creating disequilibrium-cognitive conflict that motivated change. Thus, Piaget believed that the most helpful interactions were those between peers because peers are on an equal basis and can challenge each other's thinking.

- Vygotsky, on the other hand, suggested that children's cognitive development is fostered by interactions with people who are more capable and advanced in their thinking-people such as parents and teachers.

CULTURAL TOOLS AND COGNITIVE DEVELOPMENT

Vygotsky believed that cultural tools and symbolic tools play very important roles in cognitive development.

Cultural tools:

- Printing presses
- Abacus
- Internet
- Rulers
- Computers

Symbolic tools:

- Numbers
- Braille
- Maps
- Signs and codes

- Mathematical systems
- Sign language
- Works of art
- Language

For example, as long as the culture provides only Roman numerals for representing quantity, certain ways of thinking mathematically-from long division to calculus – are difficult or impossible. But if a number system has a zero, fractions positive and negative values, and an infinite number of numbers, then much more is possible. The number system is a cultural tool that supports thinking, learning, and cognitive development. This symbol system is passed from adult to child through formal and informal interactions and teachings.

The Role of Language

Language is critical for cognitive development. It provides a means for expressing ideas and asking questions, the categories and concepts for thinking, and the links between the past and the future,. When we consider a problem, we generally think in words and partial sentences.

The specifically human capacity for language enables children to provide for auxiliary tools in the solution of difficult tasks, to overcome impulsive action, to plan a solution to a problem prior to its execution, and to master their own behaviour.(Vygotsky, 1978)

LANGUAGE AND CULTURAL DIVERSITY

If we study language across cultures, we see that different cultures need and develop different language tools.. Vygotsky placed more emphasis than Piaget on the role of learning and language in cognitive development. In fact, he believed that language in the form of private speech (talking to yourself) guides cognitive development.

Vygotsky on Private Speech

- Vygotsky suggested that the mutterings which children indulge in play an important role in cognitive development by moving children towards self-regulation, the ability to plan, monitor and guide one's own thinking and problem-solving.

- Vygotsky believed that self-regulation developed in a series of stages:

    (a) First, the child's behaviour is regulated by others, usually parents, using language and other signs such as gestures. For example, the parent says, "No!" when the child reaches towards a candle flame.

    (b) Next the child learns to regulate the behaviour of others using the same language tools. The child says, "No!" to another child who is trying to take away a toy, often even imitating the parent's voice tone. Along with learning to use external speech to regulate others, the child begins to use private speech to regulate its own behaviour, saying "no" quietly to itself as it is tempted to touch the flame. Finally, the child learns to regulate her own behaviour by using silent inner speech. This series of steps is another example of how higher mental functions appear first between people as they communicate and regulate each others' behaviour, and then emerge again within the individual as cognitive processes.

Cognitive Self-instruction

Because private speech helps students to regulate their thinking, it makes sense to allow, and even encourage, students to use private speech in school. Insisting on total silence when young students are working on difficult problems may make the work even harder for them. You may notice when muttering increases- this could be a sign that students need help. One approach called cognitive self instruction, teaches students to use self talk to guide learning. For example, students learn to give themselves reminders to go slowly and carefully.

Vygotsky believed that learning was an active process that does not have to wait for readiness. In fact, properly organized learning results in mental development and sets in motion a variety of developmental processes that would be impossible apart from learning. He saw learning as a tool in development up to higher levels and social interaction is a key in learning.

The Role of Adults and Peers

Vygotsky believed that cognitive development occurs through children's conversations and interactions with more capable members of the culture- adults or more able peers. These people serve as guides and teachers, providing the information and support necessary for children to grow intellectually. Thus the child is not alone in the world "discovering" the cognitive operations of conservation or classification. This discovery is assisted or mediated by family members, teachers and peers. Jerome Bruner called this adult assistance scaffolding. The term aptly suggests that children use this help for support while they build a firm understanding that will eventually allow them to solve the problems on their own.

Implication of Vygotsky's Theory of Teachers

Vygotsky was most concerned with instructed learning through direct teaching or through structuring experiences that support another's learning, but his theory supports the other forms of cultural learning as well. He advocated Assisted Learning which suggests that teachers need to do more than just arrange the environment so that students can discover on their own. Children cannot and should not be expected to reinvent or rediscover knowledge already available in their cultures. Rather, they should be guided and assisted in their learning. So Vygotsky saw teachers, parents, and other adults as central to the child's learning and development.

Assisted learning or guided participation in the classroom requires scaffolding-giving information, prompts, reminders, and encouragement at the right time and in the right amounts, and then gradually allowing the students to do more and more on their own. Teachers' can assist learning by

- adapting materials or problems to students' current levels

- demonstrating skills or thought processes

- walking students through the steps of a complicated problem

- doing part of the problem (for example, in algebra, the students set up the equation and the teacher does the calculations or vice versa)

- giving detailed feedback

- allowing revisions

- asking questions that refocus students' attention

  Cognitive self-instruction is an example of assisted learning.

THE ZONE OF PROXIMAL DEVELOPMENT

According to Vygotsky, at any given point in development there are certain problems that a child is on the verge of being able to solve. The child just needs some structure, clues, reminders, help and remembering details or steps, encouragement to keep trying and so on. Some problems, of course, are beyond the child's capabilities, even if every step is explained clearly. The zone of proximal development is the area where the child cannot solve a problem alone, but can be successful under adult guidance or in collaboration with a more advanced peer. This is the area where instruction can succeed, because real learning is possible.

- **Private Speech and the Zone:** Often, an adult helps the child to solve a problem or accomplish a task using verbal prompts and structuring. This scaffolding may be gradually reduced as the child takes over the guidance, perhaps first by giving the prompts as private speech and finally as inner speech.

- **Teaching :** Students have to be put in situations where they have to reach to understand, but where support from other students or from the teacher is also available. Sometimes the best teacher is another student who has just figured out the problem because this student is probably operating in the learner's zone of proximal development. Students should be guided by explanations, demonstrations, and work with other students-opportunities for cooperative learning. Having a student work with someone who is just a bit better at the activity would also be a good idea. In addition, students should be encouraged to use language to organize their thinking about what they are trying to accomplish. Dialogue and discussion are important avenues to learning.

The Psycho-social Theory of Erikson

Erikson was of the view that human personality develops in a series of stages, each with its particular goals, concerns, accomplishments, and dangers. The stages are interdependent: Accomplishments at later stages depend on how conflicts are resolved in the earlier years. Each stage in Erikson's theory is concerned with becoming competent in an area of life. If the stage is handled well, the person will feel a sense of adequacy and if the stage is handled poorly, the person will develop a sense of inadequacy. At each stage, Erikson suggests that the individual faces a developmental crisis- a conflict between a positive alternative and a potentially unhealthy alternative. The way in which the individual resolves each crisis will have a lasting effect on that person's self image and view of society.

The following are the 8 stages in Erikson's theory which he also called the eight ages of man.

	Stages	Approximate Age	Important Event	Description
1.	Basic trust versus basic mistrust	Birth to 12-18 months	Feeding	The infant must form a first loving, trusting relationship with the caregiver or develop a sense of mistrust. Trust depends on quality of parenting or the caregiver. If trust is build successfully, the child feels secure or else insecure.
2.	Autonomy versus shame/doubt	18 months to 3 years	Toilet training	The child's energies are directed towards the development of physical skills, including walking, grasping, controlling the sphincter. The child learns control but may develop shame and doubt if not handled well. Controlling one's body functions gives a sense of independence. Also important is control over food choices, toy preferences and choosing clothing.
3.	Initiative versus guilt	3 to 6 years	Independence	The child continues to become more assertive and to take more initiative but may be too forceful, which can lead to guilt feelings. If successful in social interaction, children feel capable and able to lead. Those who fail develop doubt, guilt and lack of initiative.
4.	Industry versus inferiority	6 to 12 years	School	The child must deal with demands to learn new skills or risk a sense of inferiority, failure and incompetence. Those who are encouraged by parents and teachers develop a feeling of competence and belief in oneself.
5.	Identity versus role confusion	Adolescence	Peer relationships	The teenager must achieve identity in occupation, gender roles, politics, and religion. With proper encouragement and reinforcement, children become more secure and have the ability to maintain their individuality.

6.	Intimacy versus isolation	Young adulthood	Love relationships	At this stage, people are normally exploring personal relationships. The young adult must develop intimate relationships or suffer feelings of isolation. Those with a poor sense of self tend to have less committed relationships and are likely to suffer isolation and loneliness.
7.	Generativity versus stagnation	Middle adulthood	Parenting/ Mentoring	The focus is on career and family. Each adult must find some way to satisfy and support the next generation. Those who are successful at this stage will feel they are contributing to the society by being active and productive members.
8.	Ego integrity versus despair	Late adulthood	Reflection on and acceptance of one's life	The culmination is a sense of acceptance of oneself and a sense of fulfillment. The phase focuses on reflecting back on life. Unsuccessful people feel they have many regrets in life and that they have wasted this life. Those who are proud of their accomplishments will feel a sense of integrity and satisfaction with few regrets

Kohlberg's Stages of Moral Development

Lawrence Kohlberg proposed that moral development is a continual process that occurs throughout the lifespan of an individual. Kohlberg proposed a detailed sequence of stages of moral reasoning or judgments about right and wrong. He divided moral developments into three levels:

1. Pre-conventional- where judgment is based solely on a person's own needs and perceptions.

2. Conventional- where the expectations of society and law are taken into account; and

3. Post-conventional-where judgments are based on abstract, more personal principles that are not necessarily defined by society's laws.

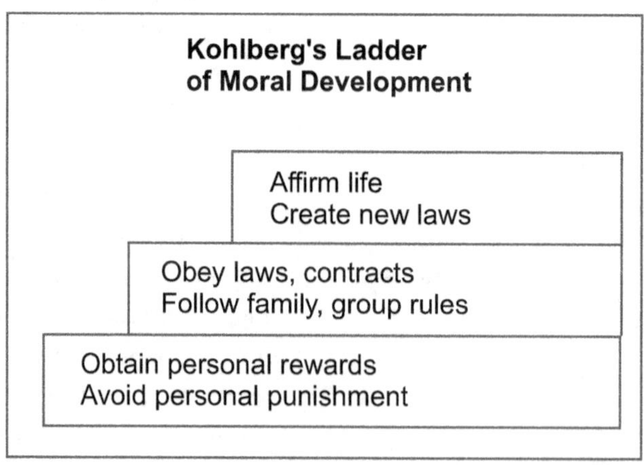

Kohlberg has evaluated moral reasoning of both children and adults by presenting them with moral dilemmas, or hypothetical situations in which people must make difficult decisions and give their reasons.

"The Heinz Dilemma"

Heinz Steals the Drug

"In Europe, a woman was near death from cancer. There was one drug that the doctors thought might save her. It was a form of radium that a druggist in the same town had recently discovered. The drug was expensive to make, but the druggist was charging ten times what the drug cost him to make. He paid only $200 for the radium and charged $2,000 for a small dose of the drug.

The sick lady's husband, Heinz, went to whosoever he knew to borrow money, but he could only collect $ 1,000 which is half of what it cost. He told the druggist that his wife was dying and asked him to sell it cheaper or let him pay later. But the druggist told him that he discovered the drug and he is going to make money from it." So Heinz got desperate and broke into the man's store to steal the drug-for his wife. Should Heinz have done that?"

Kohlberg was not interested so much in the answer to the question of whether Heinz was wrong or right, but in the reasoning for each participant's decision. The responses were then classified into various stages of reasoning in his theory of moral development.

Level 1 Preconventional Morality

At level-1, the child's answer to the drug dilemma above might be "Its wrong to steal because you might get caught". This answer reflects the child's basic egocentrism. The reasoning might be: "What would happen to me if I stole something? I might get caught and punished".

- Stage 1 - Obedience and Punishment- The earliest stage of moral development and reasoning is common both in young children and adults. At this stage, the rules are seen as fixed and absolute. Obeying the rules is important because it is a means to avoid punishment.

- Stage 2 - Individualism and Exchange- At this stage of moral development, children judge actions based on how they serve individual needs. In the Heinz dilemma, children argued that the best course of action was the choice that best served Heinz's needs. Reciprocity is possible at this point in moral development, but only if it serves one's own interests.

Level 2 Conventional Morality

At level 2 (the conventional level), the subject is able to look beyond the immediate personal consequences and consider the views, and especially the approval, of others. Laws, religious or civil, are very important and are regarded as absolute and unalterable. One answer stressing adherence to rules is, "It is wrong to steal because it is against the law". Another answer, placing high value on loyalty to family and loved ones but still respecting the law, is, "Its right to steal because the man means well- he's trying to help his wife. But he will still have to pay the druggist when he can or accept the penalty for breaking the law".

- Stage 3 - Interpersonal Relationships -This stage is often referred to as the "good boy-good girl" orientation, this stage of moral development and is focused on living up to social expectations and roles. There is an emphasis on conformity and being nice.

- Stage 4 - Maintaining Social Order- This stage of moral development is concerned with considering the society as a whole when making judgments. The focus is on maintaining law and order by following the rules, doing one's duty and respecting authority.

Level 3 Postconventional Morality

At level 3 (the post-conventional level), an answer might be "It is not wrong to steal because human life must be preserved. The worth of a human life is greater than the worth of property." This response considers the underlying values that might be involved in the decision. A person reasoning on this level understands that what is considered right by the majority may not be considered right by an individual in a particular situation. Rational, personal choice is stressed.

- Stage 5 - Social Contract and Individual Rights- Rules of law are important for maintaining a society, but members of the society should agree upon these standards.

- Stage 6 - Universal Principles- This final level of moral reasoning is based upon universal ethical principles and abstract reasoning. At this stage, people follow these internalized principles of justice, even if they conflict with laws and rules.

Exercise 1 : Previous Year Questions of CTET & STET

1. "Children actively construct their understanding of the world" is a statement attributed to
   [CTET-2011-I]
   (a) Piaget   (b) Pavlov
   (c) Kohlberg   (d) Skinner

2. The stage in which a child begins to think logically about objects and events is known as
   [CTET-2011-I]
   (a) Sensori-motor stage
   (b) Formal operational stage
   (c) Pre-operational stage
   (d) Concrete operational stage

3. Which is the place where the child's 'cognitive' development is defined in the best way?
   [CTET-2011-I]
   (a) Playground
   (b) School and classroom environment
   (c) Auditorium
   (d) Home

4. During 6 to 10 years children start taking interest in
   [RTET-2011-I]
   (a) Religion   (b) Human body
   (c) Sex   (d) School

5. Which theory believes that human mind is like an iceberg mostly hidden and has three levels of consciousness?
   [RTET-2011-I]
   (a) Trait theory
   (b) Type theory
   (c) Psychoanalytical theory
   (d) Behaviourist theory

6. Which of the following behaviours is not a manifestation of emotional disturbance?
   [RTET-2011-I]
   (a) Delinquency   (b) Bullying nature
   (c) Truancy   (d) Autism

7. For primarily school children, which of the following is better?
   [RTET-2011-I]
   (a) Video simulation
   (b) Demonstrations
   (c) Hands-on-experiences
   (d) All of these

8. Four distinct stages of children's intellectual development were identified by
   [UPET-2011-I]
   (a) Kohlberg   (b) Erikson
   (c) Skinner   (d) Piaget

9. Which is the place where the child's cognitive development is defined in the best way?
   [UPET-2011-I]
   (a) Playground   (b) School and classroom
   (c) Auditorium   (d) Home

10. Emotional adjustment of students is effective in
    [UPTET-2011-I]
    (a) personality formation
    (b) class teaching
    (c) discipline
    (d) all of these

11. Vygotsky proposed that Child Development is:
    [PTET-2011-I]
    (a) Due to genetic components of a culture
    (b) A product of social interaction
    (c) A product of formal education
    (d) A product of assimilation & accommodation

12. Cognitive Development means: *[PTET-2011-I]*
    (a) Development of intelligence
    (b) Development of child
    (c) Development of Physical Skills
    (d) Development of individual

13. 'Gang age period' is *[TNTET-2011-I]*
    (a) Infancy   (b) Childhood
    (c) Adolescence   (d) Middle age

14. Children are capable of forming concepts
    [TNTET-2011-I]
    (a) before verbalisation
    (b) soon after verbalisation
    (c) during childhood
    (d) after childhood

15. According to Piaget, during the first stage of development (birth to about 2 years age), a child learns best *[CTET-2011-II]*
    (a) by using the senses
    (b) by comprehending neutral words
    (c) by thinking in an abstract fashion
    (d) by applying newly acquired knowledge of language

16. Children's thinking is grounded in concrete experiences and concepts rather than abstractions. it is the stage from *[RTET-2011-II]*
    (a) 7 to 12 years   (b) 12 to adulthood
    (c) 2 to 7 years   (d) birth to 2 years

17. Which of the following is not among the four determinants of intellectual growth stated by Piaget? *[RTET-2011-II]*
    (a) Social transmission (b) Experience
    (c) Equilibration   (d) None of these.
18. Though number of psychologists like freud, Piaget explain personality development in terms of stages but only piaget talked of *[RTET-2011-II]*
    (a) developmental stages which are determined by the environment
    (b) restricted effects of stages to early infant experience only
    (c) cognitive transformation to explain stages
    (d) none of these
19. Which statement is not true about interest? *[RTET-2011-II]*
    (a) Interests are innate and acquired
    (b) Interests change with time
    (c) Interests change with time
    (d) Interests are not reflection of attraction and aversion in behaviour.
20. Which of the following is NOT an example of a concrete concept? *[PTET-2011-II]*
    (a) ability   (b) chair
    (c) force   (d) motion
21. Feeling and reflecting of others emotions like happiness and anger is *[TNTET-2011-II]*
    (a) passive sympathy (b) sensitive
    (c) imitation   (d) active sympathy
22. The concept of __________ was introduced by Alfred Adler *[TNTET-2011-II]*
    (a) Oedipus complex (b) Inferiority complex
    (c) Mental health (d) Boorish and coarse
23. Scapegoatism is an example of *[TNTET-2011-II]*
    (a) Rationalisation (b) Introversion
    (c) Compensation (d) Displacement
24. Loitering and pointing others for his faults are the characteristics of *[TNTET-2011-II]*
    (a) Introvert   (b) Short temper
    (c) Extrovert   (d) Ambivert
25. Cathartic theory of play activities has close relation with__________school of psychology *[TNTET-2011-II]*
    (a) Naturalism   (b) Behaviourism
    (c) Psycho–analysis (d) Purposivism
26. In moral development the preconventional stage occurs during the age limit of *[TNTET-2011-II]*
    (a) 2 – 7 years   (b) 3 – 7 years
    (c) 5 – 10 years   (d) 4 – 10 years

27. Vygotsky emphasized the significance of the role played by which of the following factors in the learning of children? *[CTET-2012-I]*
    (a) Moral   (b) Physical
    (c) Social   (d) Hereditary
28. According to Kohlberg, a teacher can instill moral values in children by *[CTET-2012-I]*
    (a) laying clear rules of behaviour
    (b) involving them in discussions on moral issues
    (c) giving strict instructions on 'how to behave'
    (d) giving importance to religious teachings
29. According to Piaget's stages of Cognitive Development, the sensori-motor stage is associated with *[CTET-2012-I]*
    (a) ability to solve problems in logical fashion
    (b) ability to interpret and analyse options
    (c) concerns about social issues
    (d) imitation, memory and mental representation
30. According to Piaget's cognitive theory of learning, the process by which the cognitive structure is modified is called *[CTET-2012-II]*
    (a) Accommodation (b) Assimilation
    (c) Schema   (d) Perception
31. Thinking is essentially *[CTET-2012-II]*
    (a) a psychomotor process
    (b) a psychological phenomenon
    (c) an affective behaviour
    (d) a cognitive activity
32. A good teaching method for infancy stage is *[UPTET-2014-I]*
    (a) Montessory method
    (b) Playway method
    (c) Kindergarten method
    (d) All of them
33. Best method of giving value-education at primary level is *[UPTET-2014-I]*
    (a) telling importance of values
    (b) giving punishment on not obeying the values
    (c) to set values in behaviour of teachers
    (d) All of the above
34. It is not included in classification of values : *[UPTET-2014-I]*
    (a) Spiritual values
    (b) Earning money by any means
    (c) Moral values
    (d) Cultural values

35. Nature of personality organisation is
    [UPTET-2014-I]
    (a) Social-Economical
    (b) Psychological-Physical
    (c) Social-Political
    (d) Psychological-Spiritual

36. It is not the theory of language development:
    [UPTET-2014-I]
    (a) Conditioning Theory
    (b) Theory of limitation
    (c) Surplus Energy Theory
    (d) Theory of Maturation

37. How is intensity of emotions expressed during adolescence period ?   *[UPTET-2014-II]*
    (a) Adverse family relations
    (b) Problem of occupation
    (c) Adjustment with new situation
    (d) All above

38. For the development or formation of concept in the student, the teacher should *[UPTET-2014-II]*
    (a) follow simple to complex method of teaching
    (b) provide opportunity to the student for ample experience.
    (c) provide opportunity to the student for transfer of formed concepts.
    (d) follow all the above activities

39. Laws of Association are *[UPTET-2014-II]*
    (a) Law of Similarity   (b) Law of Contrast
    (c) Law of Contiguity   (d) All the above

40. What is called he tendency of self love ?
    [UPTET-2014-II]
    (a) Self centred tendency
    (b) Egoistic tendency
    (c) Tendency of Narcissism
    (d) Tendency of Hypnotism

41. "A child can think logically about objects & events" This is the characteristic given by Piaget of stage: *[PTET-2014-I]*
    (a) Sensory Motor
    (b) Pre Operational
    (c) Concrete Operational
    (d) Formal Operation

42. The term Identical Elements is closely associated with: *[PTET-2014-I]*
    (a) Similar test questions
    (b) Jealousy between peers
    (c) Transfer of learning
    (d) Group Instructions

43. Which of the following theories identifies four stages of child's intellectual development (sensory-motor, pre-operational, concrete operational & formal operational)?   *[PTET-2014-I]*
    (a) Erickson's theory of psycho-social development
    (b) Freud's theory of psycho-sexual development
    (c) Jean Piaget's theory of cognitive development
    (d) Kohlberg's theory of moral development

44. Which of the following is NOT an example of discrete variable?   *[PTET-2014-II]*
    (a) age   (b) gender
    (c) marital status   (d) place of residence

45. The Stage in which the "Self Initiative Skill" of a child develops when it is let free *[TNTET-2014-I]*
    (a) 2-3 years   (b) First year
    (c) 6th year onwards (d) 4-6 years

46. The term used by Piaget to refer "one's cognitive structure"   *[TNTET-2014-I]*
    (a) Iconic   (b) Schema
    (c) Action Schema   (d) Egocentric

47. How many stages are there in psycho-social growth of man according to Erickson?
    [TNTET-2014-I]
    (a) 6 Stages   (b) 4 Stages
    (c) 10 Stages   (d) 8 Stages

48. The psychologist who defined moral development
    [TNTET-2014-I]
    (a) McDougall   (b) Thorndike
    (c) Pavlov   (d) Piaget

49. Which of the following approach is not related to cognitive learning   *[TNTET-2014-I]*
    (a) Problem solving   (b) Learning by doing
    (c) Project Method   (d) Rote Memory

50. Piaget's principle is related to child's____________
    [TNTET-2014-I]
    (a) Psychological Development
    (b) Emotional feelings
    (c) Cognitive Development
    (d) Physical Development

51. Types of Mental Conflicts are ___________
    [TNTET-2014-I]
    (a) 4   (b) 2
    (c) 3   (d) 8

52. Which of the following cognitive verbs are used to analyse the information given ?*[CTET-July-2013-I]*
    (a) Identify   (b) Differentiate
    (c) Classify   (d) Describe

53. Which one of the following is true ?
[CTET-July-2013-I]
  (a) Development and learning are unaffected by socio-cultural contexts.
  (b) Students learn only in a certain way.
  (c) Play is significant for cognition and social competence.
  (d) Questioning by teacher constrains cognitive development.

54. A teacher wishes to help her students to appreciate multiple views of a situation. She provides her students multiple opportunities to debate on this situation in different groups According to Vygotsky's perspective, her students will __________ various views and develop multiple perspectives of the situation on their own.
[CTET-July-2013-I]
  (a) internalize   (b) construct
  (c) operationalize   (d) rationalize

55. Sita has learned to eat rice and dal with her hand. When she is given dal and rice, she mixes rice and dal and starts eating. She has ________ eating rice and dal into her schema for doing things.
[CTET-July-2013-I]
  (a) Accommodated   (b) Assimilated
  (c) Appropriated   (d) Initiated

56. A teacher shows two identical glasses filled with an equal amount of juice in them. She empties them in two different glasses one of which is taller and the other one is wider. She asks her class to identify which glass would have more juice in it. Students reply that the taller glass has more juice. Her students have difficulty in dealing with
[CTET-July-2013-II]
  (a) Accommodation   (b) Egocentrism
  (c) Decentring   (d) Reversibility

57. Karnail Singh does not pay income tax despite legal procedures and expenses. He thinks that he cannot support a corrupt government which spends millions of rupees in building unnecessary dams. He is probably in which state of Kohlberg's stages of moral development *[CTET-July-2013-II]*
  (a) Conventional   (b) Post Conventional
  (c) Pre Conventional   (d) Para Conventional

58. Which of the following is based on Vygotsky's sociocultural theory?   *[CTET-Feb.-2014-I]*
  (a) Operant conditioning
  (b) Reciprocal teaching
  (c) Culture-neutral cognitive development
  (d) Insight learning

59. A teacher says to her class, "As individual assignments are designed to help individual students learn more effectively, all students should complete assignments prescribed without any assistance, she is referring to which of the following stages of Kohlberg's moral development?   *[CTET-Feb.-2014-I]*
  (a) Conventional stage 4 – law and order
  (b) Post-conventional stage 5 – social contract
  (c) Pre-conventional stage 1 – punishment avoidance
  (d) Pre-conventional stage 2 – individualism and exchange

60. Which of the following theorists would be of the option that students study hard for their personal growth and development?   *[CTET-Feb.-2014-I]*
  (a) Bandura   (b) Maslow
  (c) Skinner   (d) Piaget

61. Which of the following figures correctly represents the development according to Piaget's developmental theory?   *[CTET-Feb.-2014-II]*

(a) 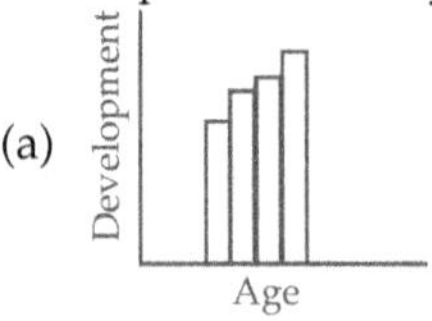

(b) 

(c) 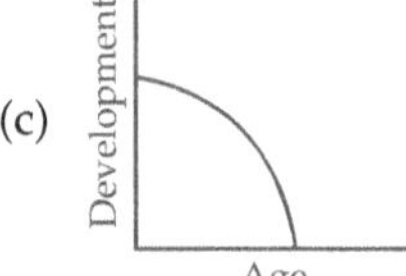

(d) 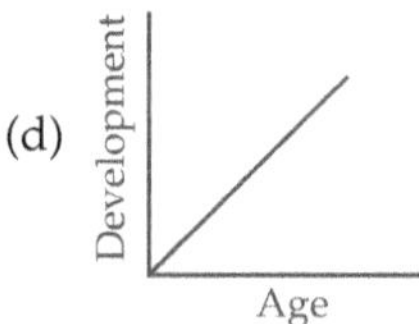

62. Which of the following implications cannot be derived from Piaget's theory of cognitive development?   *[CTET-Feb.-2014-II]*
  (a) Sensitivity of children's readiness to learn
  (b) Acceptance of individual differences
  (c) Discovery learning
  (d) Need of verbal teaching

63. Which of the following is a characteristic of Kohlberg's stages of moral development?
[CTET-Feb.-2014-II]
   (a) Variable sequence of stages
   (b) Stages are isolated responses and not general pattern
   (c) Universal sequences of stages across all cultures
   (d) Stages proceed in a non-hierarchic manner

64. In the context of language development, which of the following areas was underestimated by Piaget? *[CTET-Feb.-2014-II]*
   (a) Heredity
   (b) Social interaction
   (c) Egocentric speech
   (d) Active construction by the child

65. Cognitive apprenticeships and instructional conversations *[CTET-Feb.-2014-II]*
   (a) conceive learning as a social activity
   (b) are based on application of inductive reasoning
   (c) emphasize on systematic organization of textual material
   (d) highlight the need of practical training to achieve efficiency

66. In Vygotsky's theory, which aspect of development gets neglected ? *[CTET-Sept.-2014-I]*
   (a) Social   (b) Cultural
   (c) Biological   (d) Linguistic

67. Which of the following stages are involved when infants "THINK" with their eyes, ears and hands? *[CTET-Sept.-2014-I]*
   (a) Concrete operational stage
   (b) Pre-operational stage
   (c) Sensory motor stage
   (d) Formal operational stage

68. Concept maps are most likely to increase understanding of new concepts by *[CTET-Sept.-2014-I]*
   (a) transferring knowledge between content areas
   (b) focusing attention on specific detail
   (c) prioritizing academic content for study
   (d) increasingly ability to organize information logically

69. The fact that children require culturally relevant knowledge and skills is attributed to *[CTET-Sept.-2014-II]*
   (a) Charles Darwin
   (b) B.F. Skinner
   (c) Urie Bronfenbrenner
   (d) Lev Vygotsky

70. As a teacher you firmly believe in 'saying no to ragging and bullying' and put up posters and form committees in schools. The young adolescents who join you with strong beliefs, are at which of the following stages ? *[CTET-Sept.-2014-II]*
   (a) The conventional level
   (b) The pre-conventional level
   (c) The post-conventional level
   (d) Social order maintaining level

71. Retrieving hidden objects is an evidence that infants have begun to master which of the following cognitive functions ? *[CTET-Sept.-2014-II]*
   (a) Intentional behaviour
   (b) Object-permanence
   (c) Problem-Solving
   (d) Experimentation

72. Which one out of the following provides information about the roles and behaviours which are acceptable in a group, during early childhood period ? *[CTET-Feb.-2015-I]*
   (a) Siblings and Teachers
   (b) Teachers and Peers
   (c) Peers and Parents
   (d) Parents and Siblings

73. Which of the following age groups falls under later childhood category ? *[CTET-Feb.-2015-I]*
   (a) 11 to 18 years   (b) 18 to 24 years
   (c) Birth to 6 years   (d) 6 to 11 years

74. The teacher noticed that Pushpa cannot solve a problem on her own. However, she does so in the presence of adult or peer guidance. This guidance is called *[CTET-Feb.-2015-I]*
   (a) Lateralization
   (b) Pre-operational thinking
   (c) Zone of proximal development
   (d) Scaffolding

75. In Lawrence Kohlberg's theory, which level signifies the absence of morality in the true sense ? *[CTET-Feb.-2015-I]*
   (a) Level III   (b) Level IV
   (c) Level I   (d) Level II

76. Which one of the following statements best summarizes the relationship between development and learning as proposed by Vygotsky ?

[CTET-Feb.-2015-II]

(a) Learning and development are parallel processes.

(b) Development is independent of learning.

(c) Development process lags behind the learning process.

(d) Development is synonymous with learning

77. A major difference between the perspectives of Vygotsky and Piaget pertains to

[CTET-Feb.-2015-II]

(a) their conception of children as active constructors of knowledge.

(b) their critique of behaviourlstic principles.

(c) the role of providing a nurturing environment to children.

(d) their views about language and thought.

78. According to Vygotsky, zone of proximal development is *[CTET-Feb.-2015-II]*

(a) what the child can do on her own which cannot be assessed.

(b) zone demarking the support offered by the teacher.

(c) the gap between what the child can do independently and with assistance.

(d) the amount and nature of support provided to the child to achieve her potential.

79. Piaget proposes that pre-operational children are unable to conserve. He attributes this inability to which one of the following factors ?

[CTET-Feb.-2015-II]

(a) Lack of high-level abstract reasoning

(b) Inability of hypothetico-deductive reasoning

(c) Personal fable

(d) Irreversibility of thought

80. According to Piaget's theory, children learn by

[CTET-Feb.-2015-II]

(a) changing their behaviour when offered appropriate rewards.

(b) memorizing information by paying clue attention.

(c) scaffolding provided by more able members of the society.

(d) processes of adaptation.

81. .... views children as active builders of knowledge and little scientists who construct their own theories of the world. *[CTET-Feb.-2016-I]*

(a) Skinner   (b) Pavlov

(c) Jung   (d) Piaget

82. Which one of the following is a correctly matched pair? *[CTET-Feb.-2016-I]*

(a) Concrete operational child—Is able to conserve and classify

(b) Formal operational child—Imitation begins, imaginary play

(c) Infancy—Applies logic and is able to infer

(d) Pre-operational child—Deductive thought

83. According to Piaget, children's thinking differs in .... from adults than in ....

[CTET-Feb.-2016-I]

(a) amount, kind   (b) size, correctness

(c) kind, amount   (d) size, type

84. According to Vygotsky, children learn

[CTET-Feb.-2016-I]

(a) when reinforcement is offered.

(b) by maturation.

(c) by imitation.

(d) by interacting with adults and peers.

85. Kohlberg has given *[CTET-Feb.-2016-I]*

(a) the stages of cognitive development.

(b) the stages of physical development.

(c) the stages of emotional development.

(d) the stages of moral development.

86. According to Piaget, which one of the following factors plays an important role in influencing development? *[CTET-Feb.-2016-II]*

(a) Language

(b) Reinforcement

(c) Experience with the physical world

(d) Imitation

87. The cognitive ability that comes in pre-operational period is *[CTET-Feb.-2016-II]*

(a) ability for abstract thinking.

(b) hypothetico-deductive thinking.

(c) ability of goal-directed behaviour.

(d) ability to take other's perspective.

88. Which one of the following is a correctly matched pair?   *[CTET-Feb.-2016-II]*
   (a) Punishment and obedience orientation-Laws are not fixed, but can be changed for the good of society.
   (b) Social contract orientation-Physical consequences of an action determine whether it is good or bad.
   (c) Good boy and good girl orientation-One earns approval by being nice.
   (d) Law and order orientation-Ethical principles are self-chosen on the basis of the value of human rights.

89. The concept of 'private speech' of children as proposed by Vygotsky   *[CTET-Feb.-2016-II]*
   (a) illustrates that children are egocentric.
   (b) shows that children are stupid and thus need guidance of adults.
   (c) shows that children love themselves.
   (d) illustrates that children use speech to guide their own actions.

90. According to Vygotsky, learning **cannot** be separated from   *[CTET-Feb.-2016-II]*
   (a) its social context.
   (b) perception and attentional processes.
   (c) reinforcement.
   (d) a measurable change in behaviour.

91. In a constructivist classroom as envisioned by Piaget and Vygotsky, learning*[CTET-Feb.-2016-II]*
   (a) is constructed by the students themselves who play an active role.
   (b) is offering of reinforcement by the teacher.
   (c) is dictated by the teacher and the students are passive recipients of the same.
   (d) happens by pairing of a stimulus and a response.

92. Nowadays, there is a tendency to refer to 'wrong concepts' of children as 'alternative conceptions'. This could be attributed to   *[CTET-Feb.-2016-II]*
   (a) recognition that children are capable of thinking and their thinking is different from that of adults.
   (b) children's understanding being nuanced and their being passive in their own learning.
   (c) using fancy terms to describe children's errors.
   (d) children being thought of as adult-like in their thinking.

93. Middle childhood is the period from   *[CTET-Feb.-2016-II]*
   (a) birth to 2 years   (b) 10 years onwards
   (c) 2 years to 6 years   (d) 6 years to 11 years

94. As a teacher, who firmly believes in social constructivist theory of Lev Vygotsky, which of the following methods would you prefer for assessing your students?   *[CTET-Sept.-2016-I]*
   (a) Collaborative projects
   (b) Standardized tests
   (c) Fact-based recall questions
   (d) Objective multiple-choice type questions

95. Primary school children will learn most effectively in an atmosphere :   *[CTET-Sept.-2016-I]*
   (a) where their emotional needs are met and they feel that they are valued
   (b) where the teacher is authoritative and clearly dictates what should be done
   (c) where the focus and stress are only on mastering primarily cognitive skills of reading, writing and mathematics
   (d) where the teacher leads all the learning and expects students to play a passive role

96. Which of the following is a sensitive period pertaining to language development?   *[CTET-Sept.-2016-I]*
   (a) Prenatal period
   (b) Middle childhood period
   (c) Adulthood
   (d) Early childhood period

97. According to Lev Vygotsky, the primary cause of cognitive development is :   *[CTET-Sept.-2016-I]*
   (a) equilibration
   (b) social interaction
   (c) adjustment of mental schemas
   (d) stimulus-response pairing

98. In the context of Kohlberg's stages of moral reasoning, under which stage would the given typical response of a child fall?
   "Your parents will be proud of you if you are honest. So you should be honest."   *[CTET-Sept.-2016-I]*
   (a) Punishment-obedience orientation
   (b) Social contract orientation
   (c) Good girl-good boy orientation
   (d) Law and order orientation

99. According to Jean Piaget, which of the following is necessary for learning?   *[CTET-Sept.-2016-I]*
   (a) Active exploration of the environment by the learner
   (b) Observing the behaviour of adults
   (c) Belief in immanent justice
   (d) Reinforcement by teachers and parents

100. A 5-year-old girl talks to herself while trying to fold a T-shirt. Which of the following statements is **correct** in the context of the behaviour displayed by the girl? *[CTET-Sept.-2016-I]*

(a) Jean Piaget and Lev Vygotsky would explain this as egocentric nature of the child's thoughts.

(b) Jean Piaget would explain this as egocentric speech, while Lev Vygotsky would explain this as the child's attempt to regulate her actions through private speech.

(c) Jean Piaget would explain this as social interaction, while Lev Vygotsky would explain this as an exploration.

(d) Jean Piaget and Lev Vygotsky would explain this as the child's attempt to imitate her mother,

101. Which of the following statements about students' failure in schools are correct? *[CTET-Sept.-2016-II]*

A. Students belonging to certain castes and communities fail since they do not have ability.

B. Students fail in schools because appropriate rewards are not offered for their learning.

C. Students fail because teaching is not done in a manner in which it is meaningful to them.

D. Students fail because school system does not cater to individual child's needs and interests.

(a) B and D   (b) C and D

(c) A and B   (d) B and C

102. Which of the following statements is **correct** about Jean Piaget's theory of cognitive development? *[CTET-Sept.-2016-II]*

(a) The sequence of the stages can vary according to the cultural context of children.

(b) Piaget argues that instead of progressing through stages, cognitive development is continuous.

(c) Piaget has proposed five distinct stages of cognitive development.

(d) The stages are invariant which means that no stage can be skipped.**17.** The concept of 'conservation' as proposed by Jean Piaget means that : *[CTET-Sept.-2016-II]*

(a) taking the perspective of others into consideration is an important cognitive ability

(b) it is important to protect wildlife and forests

(c) certain physical properties remain the same even when outward appearances change

(d) one can arrive at the correct conclusion by systematically testing hypothesis

103. The concept of 'conservation' as proposed by Jean Piaget means that : *[CTET-Sept.-2016-II]*

(a) taking the perspective of others into consideration is an important cognitive ability

(b) it is important to protect wildlife and forests

(c) certain physical properties remain the same even when outward appearances change

(d) one can arrive at the correct conclusion by systematically testing hypothesis

104. According to Lev Vygotsky : *[CTET-Sept.-2016-II]*

(a) children learn language through a language acquisition device

(b) interaction with adults and peers does not influence language development

(c) language development changes the nature of human thought

(d) culture plays a very small role in language development

105. Lawrence Kohlberg's theory of moral reasoning has been criticized on several counts. Which of the following statements is **correct** in the context of this criticism? *[CTET-Sept.-2016-II]*

(a) Kohlberg has based his study primarily on a male sample.

(b) Kohlberg has not given typical responses to each stage of moral reasoning.

(c) Kohlberg has duplicated Piaget's methods of arriving at his theoretical framework.

(d) Kohlberg's theory does not focus on children's responses.

106. Which of the following statements describes Piaget and Vygotsky's views on language and thought correctly? *[CTET-Sept.-2016-II]*

(a) Both view language as emerging from the child's thought.

(b) According to Vygotsky, thought emerges first and according to Piaget, language has a profound effect on thought.

(c) According to Piaget, thought emerges first and according to Vygotsky, language has a profound effect on thought.

(d) Both view thought as emerging from the child's language.

107. Which of the following is a primary law of physical development? *[UPTET-2017-I]*

(a) Law of difference from mental development

(b) Law of irregular development

(c) Law of rapid growth

(d) Law of relation from imagination and emotional development

108. Which of the following is *not* the theory of development? *[UPTET-2017-I]*
(a) Theory of conditioned reflex
(b) Theory of continuous growth
(c) Theory of interrelation
(d) Theory of uniform pattern

109. "Development results in new characteristics and new abilities." This statement is given by *[UPTET-2017-I]*
(a) Gesell
(b) Hurlock
(c) Meredith
(d) Douglas and Holland

110. The tendency of 'Feeling of Revolt' is concerned with which of the following ages? *[UPTET-2017-I]*
(a) Childhood
(b) Infancy
(c) Early adolescence
(d) Middle adolescence

111. The third stage in the order of language development is *[APTET-May.-2018-I]*
(a) Bobbling stage
(b) Prelingual stage
(c) Language comprehension stage
(d) Sound imitation stage

112. Lack of concept of irreversibility is related to this stage of Piaget's Cognitive development *[APTET-May.-2018-I]*
(a) Sensory motor stage
(b) Pre-operational stage
(c) Concrete operational stage
(d) Formal operational stage

113. The stage of 'obedience for avoiding punishment' is in this level of Kohlberg's moral development *[APTET-May.-2018-I]*
(a) Pre-moral or Pre-conventional
(b) Conventional moral level
(c) Self accepted moral or Late conventional level
(d) Natural moral level

114. Irrespective of his intention to participate in the essay competition the child doesn't participate in it because of his fear of poor performance and not being able to get a reward. *[APTET-May.-2018-I]* The defense mechanism related to this is
(a) Regression
(b) Identification
(c) Projection
(d) Withdrawal

115. This developmental stage is called as "Stage of Identity" *[APTET-May.-2018-II]*
(a) Adulthood
(b) Late Childhood
(c) Early Childhood
(d) Adolescence

116. Construction of knowledge is done through experiences –
This was stated by *[APTET-May.-2018-II]*
(a) Pavlov
(b) Bandura
(c) Piaget
(d) Skinner

117. Process of transformation of a person born who as a living organism into human being is *[APTET-May.-2018-II]*
(a) Mental Development
(b) Moral Development
(c) Social Development
(d) Emotional Development

118. Lowest level and foremost objective in Psychomotor Domain is *[APTET-May.-2018-II]*
(a) Imitation
(b) Precision
(c) Naturalization
(d) Manipulation

119. The approach proposed by Carl Rogers to understand human relations and personality is *[APTET-May.-2018-II]*
(a) Subject centered approach
(b) Nature centered approach
(c) Person centered approach
(d) Relation centered approach

120. According to Erickson, virtue called 'Hope' is developed in this psychosocial critical situation *[APTET-May.-2018-II]*
(a) Trust Vs Mistrust
(b) Autonomy Vs Shame and Doubt
(c) Initiative Vs Guilt
(d) Intimacy Vs Isolation

Answer Key

1.	(a)	11.	(b)	21.	(b)	31.	(d)	41.	(c)	51.	(c)	61.	(a)	71.	(b)	81	(d)	91	(a)	101	(b)	111	(d)
2.	(d)	12.	(a)	22.	(d)	32.	(d)	42.	(c)	52.	(b)	62.	(d)	72.	(d)	82	(a)	92	(a)	102	(d)	112	(b)
3.	(b)	13.	(b)	23.	(d)	33.	(c)	43.	(c)	53.	(c)	63.	(c)	73.	(d)	83	(c)	93	(d)	103	(c)	113	(a)
4.	(d)	14.	(d)	24.	(b)	34.	(b)	44.	(a)	54.	(a)	64.	(b)	74.	(d)	84	(d)	94	(a)	104	(c)	114	(d)
5.	(c)	15.	(a)	25.	(b)	35.	(b)	45.	(a)	55.	(b)	65.	(a)	75.	(c)	85	(d)	95	(a)	105	(a)	115	(b)
6.	(d)	16.	(a)	26.	(c)	36.	(c)	46.	(b)	56.	(c)	66.	(c)	76.	(c)	86	(c)	96	(d)	106	(c)	116	(a)
7.	(c)	17.	(a)	27.	(c)	37.	(d)	47.	(d)	57.	(b)	67.	(c)	77.	(d)	87	(d)	97	(b)	107	(c)	117	(d)
8.	(d)	18.	(c)	28.	(b)	38.	(d)	48.	(d)	58.	(b)	68.	(d)	78.	(c)	88	(c)	98	(a)	108	(a)	118	(b)
9.	(b)	19.	(d)	29.	(d)	39.	(d)	49.	(d)	59.	(a)	69.	(d)	79.	(d)	89	(d)	99	(d)	109	(b)	119	(a)
10.	(c)	20.	(a)	30.	(b)	40.	(c)	50.	(c)	60.	(b)	70.	(c)	80.	(d)	90	(a)	100	(c)	110	(c)	120	(b)

52. (b) According to Bloom's Taxonomy of Cognitive Domain:
Differentiate is used as cognitive verbs to analyse the given information.

56. (c) Decentering - Where the child takes into account multiple aspects of a problem to solve it. For example, the child will no longer perceive an exceptionally wide but short cup to contain less than a normally-wide, taller cup.

57. (b) At post conventional stage of moral development, people begin to account for the differing values, opinions and beliefs of other people. Rules of law are important for maintaining a society, but members of the society should agree upon these standards.

58. (b) Reciprocal Teaching is a contemporary application of Vygotspy's theories. It is used in improve student's ability to learn from text. In this method teacher and students collaborate in learning and practicing four key skills : summarizing, questioning, clarifying and predicting.

59. (a) Lawrence Kohlberg investigated how children reason about rules that govern their behavior in certain situations. In this question, Kohlberg's conventional level, stage tour has been defined.
Conventional level -Stage 4 - Law and order orientation: This means to perform one's own duty properly and show respect for authority.

60. (b) Students study hard for their personal growth and development, means, they need "Self-determination from the humanistic perspective, Abraham Maslow defined the concept of self and personal potential.

61. (a) Jean Piaget, a pioneer in the study of child intelligence regarded knowledge growth as something that happens continually in a sequential process consisting of logically embedded process consisting of logically embedded structures succeeding one another throughout an individual life time. This is devided into stages of development.

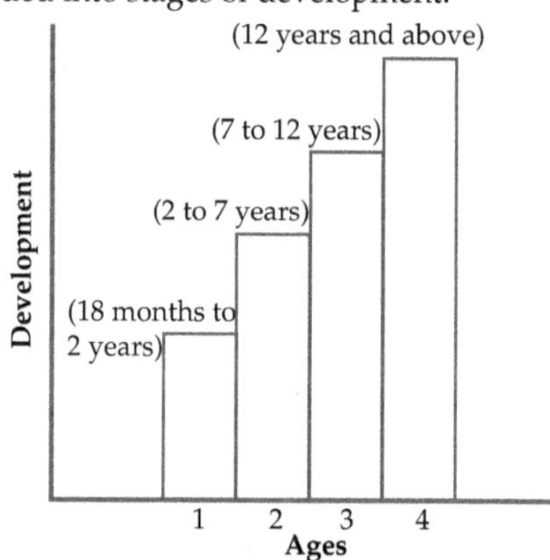

1. The sensorimotor stage (18 months to 2 years)
2. The preoperational stage (2 to 7 years)
3. The concrete operational stage (7 to 12 years)
4. The formal operational stage (12 years and above)

62. (d) First and second options are related to Piaget's concepts of accommodation and assimilation. Discovery learning is related to problem solving. The need of verbal teaching is not related to Piaget's theory.

63. (c) Lawrence Kohlberg described theory of normal development outlined six stages within three different levels. His theory is based upon universal sequences of stages and principles across all cultures.

64. (b) Jean Piaget has underestimated the concept of social interaction while very young children are much more competent and can also be very social rathan than egocentric in their speech. He put too much emphasis on the individual's internal search for knowledge and not enough on external motivation.

81. (d) The cognitive development theory given by Jean Piaget states that children are the dynamic builders of knowledge and little scientists who create their own theories.

82. (a) The concrete operational stage starts from 7 years of age and lasts till 11 years. At this stage, an individual develops becomes more logical, organized and rational in thinking and working out problems to reach the effective solutions.

83. (c) According to the theory of Piaget, children think in diverse ways as compared to adults. They realize the world around them by altering their ideas and experience difference between what they know and what they find out.

84. (d) Vygotsky did an extensive research into cognitive development and propounded a theory of sociocultural development He was of the thought that children thinking is based on social knowledge. It is developed through social interaction with respect to their culture. They learn customs and languages of their respective culture automatically.

85. (d) Kohlcberg is a psychologist who gave a thought on Piaget's theory by briefing the development of moral reasoning in children. He pointed more o the process of analyzing how children and adults govern their behavior in a given situation which needs thoughtful progression.

86. (c) According to Piaget, experiencing with physical world is the best way to learn as child develops learning by age and experience which he observed in his children.

87. (d) Pre-operational stage is a stage where a child depends on other's reactions and thus works with other's perspective because he cannot perform what he or she is thinking due to under developed mind.

89. (d) The concept of "private speech "given by Vygotsky states that speech spoken to oneself for message, self-guidance, and self regulation of a behavior. It is a sign of cognitive childishness where as Vygotsky supported it.

90. (a) Vygostksy emphasized on socialization as it is the best source to learn therefore child should be encourage to socialize.

94. (a) Collaborative projects is an ideal method where a teacher can check the constructive ability of a student.

97. (b) Social interaction is a must to develop child's learning, it was a theory given by Lev Vygotsky who emphasized the importance of socialization in the life of a child or else he will become a bookworm.

108. (a) Conditioned reflexes. A reflex response to a new stimulus can be learned. A Russian scientist called Pavlov trained dogs to expect food whenever he rang a bell.

110. (c) The adolescent and teenage years are a time when youths are trying to understand their place in society. Besides trying to establish self-identity, peer pressure becomes stronger throughout the middle and high school years, putting a young person under more stress.

111. (d) Sound imitation is the third stage of language development when child imitates the sounds of the people around him.

112. (b) According to Piaget's Cognitive development theory In the Pre-operational stage a child has lack of concept of irreversibility.

113. (a) According to Kohlberg's moral development theory Pre-moral or Pre-conventional is the stage of 'obedience to avoid punishment and self – interest orientation.

Exercise 2 : Test Yourself

1. Which is the correct sequence of Piaget's stages of cognitive development?
   (a) Sensori-motor, concrete operational, formal operational, post-operational
   (b) Pre-operational, concrete operational, formal operational, sensori-motor
   (c) Sensori-motor, pre-operational, concrete operational, formal operational
   (d) Pre-operational, informal operational, formal operational, post-operational

2. During the formal operations stage, children begin to
   (a) Accurately use concepts of time, space and number
   (b) Think primarily about concrete objects or situations
   (c) Develop the concept of object permanency
   (d) Think in terms of abstract principles and hypothetical situations

3. A child is largely nonverbal, is learning to coordinate purposeful movements with sense information, and is developing the concept of object permanence. The child is in Piaget's .... stage.
   (a) Sensori-motor
   (b) Preoperational
   (c) Concrete-operational
   (d) Formal operations

4. According to Piaget, adaptation is the process of adjusting schemes in response to the environment by means of Assimilation and ....
   (a) Schemes
   (b) Disequilibrium
   (c) Constructivism
   (d) Accommodation

5. According to Vygotsky, young children use what mechanism to turn shared knowledge into their personal knowledge?
   (a) Conservation of energy
   (b) Private speech
   (c) Autonomous morality
   (d) Sensori-motor behaviour

6. When John was 5 months old, he looked at a toy bear, but when his view of the bear was blocked, he did not search for it. Now that he is 9 months old he does look for it, reflecting the presence of
   (a) Object permanence
   (b) Self-differentiation
   (c) Assimilation
   (d) Schemata

7. Kohlberg's contribution to moral reasoning as advanced from Piaget's theory was that his work with children involved
   (a) Posing moral dilemmas
   (b) Observing children in action
   (c) Asking parents
   (d) Creating game-like situations

8. The Piagetian stage during which understanding of the world comes about through sensory experiences and motor actions is the
   (a) Sensori-motor stage
   (b) Pre-operational stage
   (c) Concrete operational stage
   (d) Formal operational stage

9. Piaget's most famous conservation study involved
   (a) Identical beakers of liquid
   (b) Rows of coins
   (c) Balls of clay
   (d) Shapes and numbers

10. In Piaget's theory, operations refer to
    (a) Physical behaviours
    (b) Words and visual images
    (c) Abstract levels of thinking
    (d) Internalized mental actions

11. A mechanism that Piaget proposed to explain how children shift from one stage of thought to the next is called
    (a) Equilibration
    (b) Conservation
    (c) Transitivity
    (d) Knowledge transfer

12. Reversible mental actions are called
    (a) Focal points
    (b) Symbolic thought
    (c) Abstractions
    (d) Operations

13. In Piagetian terms, the cognitive ability to solve problems that develop in adolescence is called
    (a) Trial and error reasoning
    (b) Hypothetico-deductive reasoning
    (c) Concrete thinking
    (d) Transitivity

14. According to Lev Vygotsky's concept of the zone of proximal development (ZPD), learning is
    (a) Achieved by discovering which answers will lead to rewards.
    (b) Achieved by assimilating new understandings to accommodate the demands of the world.
    (c) Affected by how the environment and genetically programmed learning ability interact during a critical period.
    (d) A social activity between a less knowledgeable child and another adult or child who is more knowledgeable.

15. A toddler is likely to learn something in the zone of proximal development if
    (a) The toddler has mastered all the skills necessary
    (b) Parents or teachers do not interfere.
    (c) The task is more difficult than the child can do alone.
    (d) The toddler needs little or no help from a parent or teacher.

16. Which of the following reflects Lev Vygotsky's beliefs about language and thought?
    (a) Children who use a lot of private speech are usually less socially competent.
    (b) Children use internal speech earlier than they use external speech.
    (c) Language and thought initially develop together and then become independent.
    (d) All mental functions have social origins.

17. Vygotsky's theory of cognitive development best reflects an
    (a) Behaviourist approach
    (b) Information-processing approach.
    (c) Structuralist approach
    (d) Social constructivist approach

18. Which of the following educational practices is supported by Piaget's theory of cognitive development?
    (a) Teachers should treat children as passive receptacles
    (b) Assessment should focus on the use of standardized tests
    (c) Teachers should require rote learning that is tested frequently
    (d) Classrooms should be less structured, allowing for discovery learning

19. Vygotsky's theory of cognitive development is similar to Piaget's theory in that it
    (a) Emphasizes that children actively construct their knowledge and understanding.
    (b) Describes how children develop by interacting with the physical world
    (c) Proposes four stages of development that are age-related.
    (d) Emphasizes how children develop through social interaction.

20. ----------- occurs when a teacher adjusts his or her level of support and guidance to the level of skill of the student.
    (a) Modeling
    (b) Assimilation
    (c) Scaffolding
    (d) Transference

21. According to Erikson, which of these is the most important aspect of the ego?
    (a) Self-conscious ego
    (b) Perceived ego
    (c) Ego identity
    (d) Realistic ego

22. In contrast to Freud, Erikson
    (a) Placed more emphasis on unconscious motivation
    (b) Placed more emphasis on the ego
    (c) De-emphasized social and historical influences on personality
    (d) All of the above

23. The psychosocial crisis of early childhood is
    (a) Basic trust versus basic mistrust
    (b) Intimacy versus Isolation
    (c) Industry versus Inferiority
    (d) Autonomy versus Shame and doubt

24. The psychosocial crisis of the school age is
    (a) Autonomy versus Shame and doubt
    (b) Trust versus Mistrust
    (c) Identity versus Identity confusion
    (d) Industry versus Inferiority

25. Self-regulation of learners refers to
    (a) their ability to monitor their own learning
    (b) creating regulations for student behaviour
    (c) rules and regulations made by the student body
    (d) Self-discipline and control

26. Who is the father of genetic epistemology?
    (a) Piaget
    (b) Bruner
    (c) Vygotsky
    (d) Dewey

27. These two were concerned with language as a vehicle for understanding how thought patterns develop in the child
    (a) Jean Piaget and L. S. Vygotsky
    (b) Carl Lewis and Derreck Rogers
    (c) Harlambos and Hoblorn
    (d) Dorothy Macarthy and JM Baldwin

28. Who linked egocentricism to the child's tendency to personalize thought:
    (a) Bruner   (b) Piaget
    (c) Hull   (d) Dewey

29. Who determined that the incidence of egocentric speech decreased sharply when children were placed in the company of others who could not possibly understand them — deaf and dumb children or children speaking a foreign language
    (a) Vygotsky   (b) Karl Rogers
    (c) Piaget   (d) Kohlberg

30. The ZPD is necessarily a concept where the teacher and learner roles are
    (a) interdependent and asymmetric
    (b) dependent and symmetric
    (c) directional and integrative
    (d) methodical and cyclic

31. The dynamic structuralism of -------- was aimed at capturing both the developmental process and the continuous maintenance of existing organizational forms
    (a) Piaget   (b) Bergson
    (c) Bruner   (d) Erickson

32. Arrange the following in chronological order.
    1. Pre-operational stage
    2. Formal operational stage
    3. Concrete operational stage
    4. Sensorimotor stage
    (a) 1, 2, 4, 3   (b) 2, 3, 4, 1
    (c) 4, 1, 3, 2   (d) 2, 1, 3, 4

33. Kohlberg's moral development stages are closely related to
    (a) Freud's psychosexual stages
    (b) Piaget's cognitive development stages
    (c) Erikson's psychosocial stages
    (d) Sollivan's interpersonal stages

34. In Piaget's theory, the sensorimotor stage marks the period from
    (a) 1 year to 3 years
    (b) 2 years to 4 years
    (c) Birth to 2 years
    (d) Birth to 4 years

35. Piaget's theory, the pre-operational stage marks the period from
    (a) 7 to 11 years
    (b) Birth to 2 years
    (c) 10 to 12 years
    (d) 2 to 6 years

36. Which stage of Piaget's theory of cognitive development, language development starts?
    (a) Sensorimotor
    (b) Pre-operational
    (c) Concrete operational
    (d) Formal operational

37. How many stages of cognitive development are associated with Piaget?
    (a) Seven stages   (b) Four stages
    (c) Two stages   (d) Six stages

38. Which represents the correct order of Piaget's stages of intellectual development?
    (a) Sensorimotor, concrete operational, formal operational, postoperational
    (b) Preoperational, concrete operational, formal operational, sensorimotor
    (c) Sensorimotor, preoperational, concrete operational, formal operational
    (d) Preoperational, informal operational, formal operational, postoperational

39. Regarding Kohlberg's theory of moral reasoning, which of the following statements is false ?
    (a) Kohlberg later added a transition level between levels II & III in which people placed their moral decision on personal feelings
    (b) Very few people reach level III of moral reasoning
    (c) Research has supported most aspect of Kohlberg's theory
    (d) In this theory it is the reasoning underlying a person's response to a moral dilemma

40. According to Piaget, at which of the following stages does a child begin, to think logically about abstract propositions?
    (a) Concrete operational stage (07 - 11 years)
    (b) Formal operational stage (11 years and up)
    (c) Sensori-motor stage (Birth - 02 years)
    (d) Pre-operational stage (02 - 07 years)

41. Frobel's most important contribution to education was his development of the
    (a) Vocational school
    (b) Kindergarten
    (c) Public School
    (d) Latin school

42. According to Piaget, Egocentrism occurs in
    (a) sensori motor stage
    (b) pre-operational stage
    (c) concrete operational stage
    (d) formal operational stage
43. 'Praising or criticising affects the success of the child' is said by
    (a) Hurlock   (b) Galton
    (c) Pearson   (d) Woods
44. The attitude is
    (a) an emotionalized tendency organised through experience to react positively or negatively towards a psychological object
    (b) a characteristic that is symptomatic to the individual's ability to acquire with some specified training, some knowledge or skill in a given field
    (c) a potential ability of an individual of a specialized kind
    (d) none of these
45. The stage of cognitive development according to Piaget, in which a child displays 'object permanence' is
    (a) Formal operational stage
    (b) Sensorimotor stage
    (c) Pre-operational stage
    (d) Concrete operational stage
46. According to Kohlberg, the thinking process involved in judgments about questions of right and wrong is called
    (a) Moral reasoning   (b) Moral realism
    (c) Moral dilemma   (d) Morality co-operation
47. Which of the following is NOT an example of a concrete concept?
    (a) ability   (b) chair
    (c) force   (d) motion
48. According to piaget _________ is the 3rd stage in the cognitive growth of an individual
    (a) Pre-operational stage
    (b) Concrete operational stage
    (c) Sensory Motor stage
    (d) Formal operational stage
49. Which one of the following pair is least likely to be a correct match ?
    (a) Children enter in the   – Chomsky
        world with certain
        knowledge about
        language

    (b) Language and   – Vygotsky
        thought are initially
        two different activities
    (c) Language is   – Piaget
        contingent on thought
    (d) Language is a   – B.F. Skinner
        stimuli in environment
50. Ria does not agree with Rishabh about setting up a class picnic. She thinks that the rules can be revised to suit the majority. This kind of peer disagreement, according to Piaget, refers to
    (a) Heteronomous morality
    (b) Cognitive immaturity
    (c) Reaction
    (d) Morality of cooperation
51. Phonological awareness refers to the ability to
    (a) reflect and manipulate the sound structure
    (b) speak fluently and accurately
    (c) know, understand and write
    (d) master the rules of grammar
52. According to Socio-cultural theory of Vygotsky
    (a) culture and language play a crucial role in development
    (b) the child thinks in different domains and does not a complete perspective
    (c) children think in abstract terms if presented abstract material at a lower age
    (d) self-directed speech is the lowest stage of the scaffold
53. Fitting new information into existing schemes is known as
    (a) Accommodation   (b) Equilibration
    (c) Assimilation   (d) Organisation
54. According to Piaget theory, which one out of the following will not influence one's cognitive development ?
    (a) Language   (b) Social experiences
    (c) Maturation   (d) Activity
55. What is a major criticism of Koh1berg's theory ?
    (a) Kohlberg did not give clear cut stages of moral development.
    (b) Kohlberg proposed a theory without any empirical basis.
    (c) Kohlberg proposed that moral reasoning is developmental.
    (d) Kohlberg did not account for cultural differences in moral reasoning of men and women.

Answer Key

1.	(c)	**11.**	(a)	**21.**	(c)	**31.**	(a)	**41.**	(b)	**51.**	(a)
2.	(d)	**12.**	(d)	**22.**	(b)	**32.**	(c)	**42.**	(b)	**52.**	(a)
3.	(a)	**13.**	(b)	**23.**	(d)	**33.**	(b)	**43.**	(a)	**53.**	(c)
4.	(d)	**14.**	(d)	**24.**	(d)	**34.**	(c)	**44.**	(a)	**54.**	(b)
5.	(b)	**15.**	(c)	**25.**	(a)	**35.**	(d)	**45.**	(c)	**55.**	(d)
6.	(a)	**16.**	(d)	**26.**	(a)	**36.**	(b)	**46.**	(a)		
7.	(a)	**17.**	(d)	**27.**	(a)	**37.**	(b)	**47.**	(b)		
8.	(a)	**18.**	(d)	**28.**	(b)	**38.**	(c)	**48.**	(b)		
9.	(a)	**19.**	(a)	**29.**	(a)	**39.**	(c)	**49.**	(d)		
10.	(d)	**20.**	(c)	**30.**	(a)	**40.**	(b)	**50.**	(d)		

Socialization Process

- Socialization is the process by which one learns the ways of a society or social group so that one can function within it. Socialization includes both the learning and internalizing of appropriate patterns, values, and feelings. The child ideally not only knows what is expected of him and behaves accordingly; he also feels that this is the proper way for him to think and behave. It also means learning the ways of a group such as an immigrant becomes socialized into the life of his new country; a recruit into the life of the Army; a new sales executive into the patterns of his company and his job.

- The entry of a new member into a family, or into any unit, changes the group. It is not just the old group with one added person; it is a new group with new relationships and a new organization.

- From the point of view of socialization, the child is not viewed primarily as a possessor of drives and needs which require satisfaction, but rather as someone who is capable of learning the patterns, symbols, expectations, and feelings of the world surrounding him.

Perspectives of Society

From the perspective of society, the function of socialization is to transmit the culture and motivation to participate in established social relationships in society.

There is the perspective of *norms and values*. Norms are rules specifying what behaviours are acceptable in society. For example, there are norms about how to speak. How you address your grandfather is probably different from how you talk with your spouse, and this is also different to how you speak to your boss, or your children. Your choice of words, your tone, and your body language are all norm-based. Social norms express preferences and value judgments. They govern the specifications of a role and the standards by which behaviour is judged. Therefore, social norms are primarily evaluative, not descriptive. Values concentrate on different areas: some may be general life values, but there are family values, cultural values, and work values too. And as people have values, so do organizations. Today, nearly everybody who has worked for a company is acquainted with the concept of company values.

A second perspective is that of *status and role*. A status is a position in the social structure, and a role is the expected behaviour of someone who holds a given status. We can cooperate with others because we know the rights and obligations associated with each status. The taxi driver has the right to ask for your fare and the obligation to drive you to your destination; the doctor has the right to ask about your symptoms and an obligation to try to cure you. Similarly, role behaviour is expected of the teacher, student, mother, father, daughter, grocery clerk, taxi passenger, and doctor's patient. Each person has many statuses which define his expected behaviour in given situations.

A third perspective is that of *institutions*, each of which focuses about a segment of life and consists of many norms and statuses. One such institution is the school, whose primary function is to transmit, in a more or less formal way, a large share of the intellectual traditions of a society. Within the school there are norms relating to attendance, assignments, behaviour, sports, events, courses, and holiday celebrations; and patterned status relationships among the teachers, students, principal, and other educators.

A fourth perspective focuses on *social class*. Individuals in our society vary in the amount of wealth, prestige, and power they possess, and associated with these are differences in values and ways of life. At one end may be the upper-class individual who is wealthy, has an important position, lives in a luxury, sends his children to elite schools, and is into globetrotting. At the other extreme may be the lower-class individual who works as an unskilled laborer, school dropout, lives in a slum area, and has "crude" table manners. Between these extremes there are other rankings too. It is evident that no single characteristic clearly differentiates class groups and the lines between them are blurred but a stratification system of a kind does exist.

AGENCIES OF SOCIALIZATION

- Socialization occurs in many settings and in interaction with many people. For purposes of analysis, it is helpful to distinguish between organized groups, such as the family, school, and peer group, and settings, such as the media of mass communication, that have significant characteristics in common. We speak of both groups and settings as agencies of socialization.

- Each agency socializes the child into its own patterns and its own values. The family has certain rituals, the school its rules of order, the child peer group its codes and games, and the media of mass communication their traditional forms and story plots. Moreover, each agency --and this is more significant for our purposes--helps to socialize the child into the larger world. Parents, teachers, peers, and mass media are surrogates of wider social and cultural orders, and their impact extends beyond their own organizational limits.

1. The Family and Parental Influences

Families are different, and the role of the family is changing. Each family is unique in the expectations of the people in various roles, in its patterns of interaction, its history of development, and its relationship with other systems". However, family categories usually fall into three groups:

1. The nuclear family consists of a mother, father, and offspring living together.

2. When two or more families live together, this is known as an extended family. Within this group are grandparents, uncles, aunts, or other relatives.

3. The third family group is that of single parent households.

Dimensions of Parental Behaviour

Researchers believe that acceptance-rejection and control-autonomy are contributing factors that determine a family's attitude toward child rearing. The structure of the family and the personality characteristics of individual parents make a difference in socialization as will be demonstrated in the following examples.

Tom, a father of two young children, believes that spending time each day with his children is vital to developing strong family ties. During this time, the children talk about their day, engage in some type of physical activity, such as going for a walk, playing with their pet, or enjoying simple games. Hugging his children, telling them how important they are in Tom's life is a part of each day. In return, his children feel accepted in this warm environment. His friends often comment, "Your children show such responsibility and self-control. What are you doing to make them so responsible?" When children feel this level of acceptance, they want to please and parents become their best role model.

Next, let's look at Aastha, a mother of a six-year-old. At the end of a long workday, Aastha is tired. Instead of giving her daughter a few minutes of quality time when she is back home, she quickly starts working on the domestic chores. "Every time I want to talk to my mother, she is too busy, too tired, or says 'wait we will chat later," remarks her daughter. Later never seems to come. Parents who use rejection in their behaviour may have children who develop hostility and aggressive attitude toward others.

4. Then there is a home of six youngsters where the children were extremely well behaved. One of the sons remarked, "On occasion, my father had to watch us while our mother ran to the grocery store. He made each one of us sit on the couch and dared us to move. A large paddle stood nearby. We were scared to death of him." Restrictive parents who use strict control usually have children who are well behaved. However, these children may be highly dependent on the parents.

5. On the other hand, parents and teachers that are highly permissive allow children to make the rules. In these settings, the child is clearly the "boss." Take for example, Samy and her three year-old son. "Whenever my friends visit, my son interrupts constantly, jumps on the furniture, and is loud and noisy," says Samy. "Often I have to count to three several times. Nothing seems to help." Children who see freedom and autonomy as a form of parental behaviour may be sociable and assertive youngsters who are aggressive.

6. Achieving a balance between these dimensions of parental behaviour seems to be the ideal, yet it is difficult to accomplish.

The Effects of Punishment and Discipline

- The approach to punishment and discipline is another developmental task of learning. When children misbehave, teachers or parents may use some form of discipline. This approach may be in the form of spanking, scolding, shouting, embarrassing, or making the child feel inferior or unloved. Often a combination of these is involved. These negative approaches may produce undesirable results.

- Parents and teachers that rely on a positive approach to discipline teach the child the appropriate behaviour and reinforce that behaviour, which makes it less likely to recur in the future. For example, if a child turns over their milk at the table, have them clean up the spill instead of punishing.

- Consistency is vital in guiding children to a higher level of socialization. Often parents or teachers scold or punish a child for a behaviour one day, and the next day, they appear to ignore the same behaviour because of their mood swings. Consistency in discipline allows the child to know what is acceptable and what is not. Parents and teachers can assist children in socialization by building a sense of trust and a feeling they can have some control over their life.

- Children who are disruptive and seek attention may draw attention to self through silly behaviours, immature or regressive actions, loud talking, and making inappropriate noises or gestures. Educators suggest that parents terminate disruptive attention-seeking behaviours and increase cooperative, pro-social interactions.

Empathy

Parents' sensitive responding to child distress can facilitate children's empathic capacity. Empathy and sympathy are other-oriented emotional responses to the distress or need state of another and are important motivators of pro-social action. Parents who respond with sensitivity to their children's distress model empathy and compassion, which children are likely to emulate later when interacting with others. Responsive reactions to children's negative emotions also facilitate their ability to accurately read others' emotions which can promote empathy.

Deficits in empathic capacity may make anti-social behaviour more likely. Individuals who cannot reflect on and identify with other persons' feelings and mental states will not experience guilt or discomfort as a consequence of hurting others. Indeed, Bowlby's first empirical paper, which focused on the etiology of juvenile delinquency, drew linkages between early experiences of lack of a consistent, supportive caregiver and the development of an "affectionless" personality and delinquent behaviour.

Trust in the Parent

Children whose parents are typically available and supportive in times of need should be more likely to perceive parental prescriptions and prohibitions as manifestations of caring and goodwill than as malevolent and coercive. As a result they would be more likely to comply and cooperate with their parents (and subsequently with others with whom they establish a secure relationship), and to accept parental values as appropriate and just. For adolescents, the impact of parental responsiveness to distress might be particularly great with respect to health-threatening activities such as alcohol and drug use. Protection is also important for the ability to openly seek help when in need and is thus likely linked to the ability to accept and cooperate with such help once it is offered.

Sibling Relationships as Contexts for Socialization

Three characteristics of sibling relationships in childhood and adolescence stand out from systematic research—

1. The first is the emotional quality of the relationship; between siblings, both intense positive and negative feelings are frequently and uninhibitedly expressed from infancy through adolescence. For many young siblings, the relationship is one in which mixed feelings are evident—both positive and negative feelings freely expressed.

2. The second feature of sibling relationships that heightens their potential for influence on socialization is the familiarity and intimacy of the relationship. From the preschool years through middle childhood siblings spend more time together and in interaction with each other than they do with parents or peers They know each other very well, and this intimacy means that they can provide effective support or that they can tease and undermine each other.

3. The great range of individual differences between siblings that research has documented in observational, interview, and experimental studies.

Influence of family culture on child development

Increasingly, students today have only one or no sibling or live with single parents or homes where both parents work. In such situations, students are likely to be alone or unsupervised much of the time outside school. In addition, separation and divorce are stressful events for all participants, even under the best circumstances. The actual separation of parents may have been preceded by years of conflict at home. During the divorce itself, conflict may increase as property and custody rights are being decided.

After the divorce, more changes may disrupt the children's lives. The parent who has custody may have to move to a less expensive home, find new sources of income, go to work for the first time, or work longer hours. For the child, this can mean leaving behind important friendships in the old neighborhood or school, just when support is needed the most. It may mean having just one parent, who has less time than ever to be with the children. In some divorces, there are few conflicts, ample resources, and the continuing support of friends and extended family. But divorce is never easy for anyone.

Effects of divorce: The first two years after the divorce seem to be the most difficult period for both boys and girls. During this time, children may have problems in school or just skip school, lose or gain an unusual amount of weight, develop difficulties sleeping, and so on. They may blame themselves for the breakup of their family or hold unrealistic hopes for reconciliation. Long-term adjustment is also affected. Boys tend to show a higher rate of behavioural and interpersonal problems at home and in school than either girls in general or boys from intact families. Girls may have trouble in their dealings with males. However, living with one fairly content, if harried, parent may be better than living in a conflict-filled situation with two unhappy parents. And adjustment to divorce is an individual matter; some children respond with increased responsibility, maturity and coping skills.

Access to Resources

For socialization to proceed in positive directions, the basic needs of infants and children must be met. These include sufficient nutrition, adequate shelter, protection from dangers, and access to opportunities for socialization. In most parts of the Western world, basic needs such as food and shelter are generally purchased using a family's economic resources.

In as much as family financial resources play a central role in providing for the needs of infants, children, and adolescents, wealth and poverty are central issues for research on socialization. When families are impoverished, the difficulties in socialization of infants and children are multiple. Infants and children from low-income families are less likely than those from more affluent families to receive adequate nutrition and appropriate health care. Low birth-weights, poor childhood health, stunted growth, and poor nutrition are all more common in impoverished than in affluent families. Similarly, low-income families are less likely than others to have adequate housing. They have greater exposure to toxins like lead-based paint and to environmental harms such as exposure to air pollution, experience of community or family violence, and direct victimization by physical abuse or neglect. Research has consistently shown that parents with low incomes and less access to resources show poorer socialization practices and less authoritative parenting styles, compared to more financially well off parents. Parents with fewer economic resources have been found to be less confident in their parenting, less warm and engaged with their children, and more verbally and physically punitive than parents with greater financial resources. Children from impoverished families are less likely than those from more affluent homes to have access to enriching opportunities. They are less likely to live in homes that contain many books, less likely to have access to music or to works of art, and less likely to visit libraries and museums. Overall, family economic circumstances are a major determinant of socialization outcomes for infants and children.

2.   Social Networks

Positive social relationships outside the family are another element of supportive environments for children. The other family members, adult friends, and community members with whom parents have regular contact may support parental socialization efforts. Support can be emotional, bolstering a parent's confidence and providing an outlet for stress, informational, giving useful advice about child rearing, or instrumental, offering practical assistance. Other adults can also act as additional socialization agents for children, through their involvement in child care, provision of social or material resources to children, or status as models of healthy adult social functioning. Supportive social networks benefit both parents and children. Parents with greater social support are less stressed, are more authoritative, and have warmer interactions with their children. Children of parents who maintain more frequent and satisfying contacts with their social networks themselves have more friends and are more socially competent. Access to supportive adults through parents' social networks has also been found to protect children from the adverse effects of risk factors as economic hardship.

3.   Peer Relationship

Peer relationships play a significant role in healthy personal and social development. There is strong evidence that adults who had close friends as children have higher self esteem and are more capable of maintaining intimate relationship than adults who had lonely childhoods. The characteristics of friends and the quality of the friendships matter too. Having stable, supportive, relationships with friends who are socially competent and mature enhances social development, especially during difficult times such as parents' divorce or transition to new schools. Adults who were rejected as children tend to have more problems, such as dropping out of school or committing crimes.

Problems with Peers

Students who are aggressive, withdrawn, and inattentive-hyperactive are more likely to be rejected. But classroom context matters too, especially for aggressive or withdrawn students. In classrooms where the general level of aggression is high, being aggressive is less likely to lead to the rejection by peers. And in classrooms where solitary play and work are more common, being withdrawn is not as likely to lead to rejection. Thus, part of rejection is being too different from the norm. Also, pro-social behaviours such as sharing, cooperating, empathy, and friendly interactions are associated with peer acceptance, no matter what the classroom context. Many aggressive and withdrawn students, lack these social skills; inattentive-hyperactive students often misread social cues or have trouble controlling impulses, or their social skills suffer. A teacher should be aware of how each student gets along with the group. Are there outcasts? Do some students play the bully role? Careful adult intervention can often correct such problems, especially at the middle-elementary-school level.

Peer culture also plays a powerful role in children's development. Peer cultures are groups of students who have a set of "rules"- how to dress, talk, style their hair. The group determines which activities, music or other students are in or out of favour. It encourages conformity to the group rules.

Peer relationships in particular contribute a great deal to both social and cognitive development and to the effectiveness with which we function as adults. He states that "the single best childhood predictor of adult adaptation is not school grades, and not classroom behaviour, but rather, the adequacy with which the child gets along with other children. Children who are generally disliked, who are aggressive and disruptive, who are unable to sustain close relationships with other children, and who cannot establish a place for themselves in the peer culture are seriously at risk". The risks are many: poor mental health, dropping out of school, low achievement and other school difficulties, and poor employment history.

Because social development begins at birth and progresses rapidly during the preschool years, it is clear that early childhood programs should include regular opportunities for spontaneous child-initiated social play. It is through symbolic pretend play that young children are most likely to develop both socially and intellectually. Thus, periodic assessment of children's progress in the acquisition of social competence is appropriate.

The set of items presented below is based on research on elements of social competence in young children and on studies in which the behaviour of well-liked children has been compared with that of less-liked children.

The Role of Parents in the Development of Peer Group Competence

As the child leaves infancy and approaches toddlerhood, one of the tasks parents face is introducing the child to the peer group. To be sure, parents are interested in their child's earliest interactions with peers, but in time, parents become more seriously invested in their children's ability to get along with playmates. Getting along has different meanings for different parents, but in general, parents want their child to enjoy the company of other children, be liked by them, be well-behaved in their presence (for example, share and cooperate with them), and resist the influence of companions who are overly boisterous, aggressive or defiant of adult authority.

How do parents help their child become a socially competent, well-liked playmate who is not too easily influenced by ill-behaved peers? The three parenting styles differ particularly on two parenting dimensions: the amount of nurturance in child-rearing interactions and the amount of parental control over the child's activities and behaviour.

Authoritarian parents tend to be low in nurturance and high in parental control compared with other parents. They set absolute standards of behaviour for their children that are not to be questioned or negotiated. They favour forceful discipline and demand prompt obedience. Authoritarian parents also are less likely than others to use more gentle methods of persuasion, such as affection, praise and rewards, with their children. Consequently, authoritarian parents are prone to model the more aggressive modes of conflict resolution and are lax in modeling affectionate, nurturant behaviours in their interactions with their children.

In sharp contrast, *permissive parents* tend to be moderate-to-high in nurturance, but low in parental control. These parents place relatively few demands on their children and are likely to be inconsistent disciplinarians. They are accepting of the child's impulses, desires, and actions and are less likely than other parents to monitor their children's behaviour. Although their children tend to be friendly, sociable youngsters, compared with others their age they lack knowledge of appropriate behaviours for ordinary social situations and take too little responsibility for their own misbehaviour.

Authoritative parents, in contrast to both authoritarian and permissive parents, tend to be high in nurturance and moderate in parental control when it comes to dealing with child behaviour.

It is this combination of parenting strategies that researchers find the most facilitative in the development of social competence during early childhood and beyond. The following discussion describes specific behaviours used by authoritative parents and the role these behaviours play in fostering social development.

4.　Processes of socialization within school settings

Structural features of schools, such as school and class size, teacher-student ratios, and funding, can influence the amount and quality of resources and opportunities available to students. Social interactions and relationships with teachers and peers describe the more proximal contexts that can influence student adjustment.

Social Interactions with Teachers

In the classroom, teachers play a very important pedagogical function of transmitting knowledge and training students in academic subjects. However, during the course of instruction, teachers also promote the development of behavioural competencies by way of classroom management practices and by structuring learning environments in ways that make social goals more salient to students. For example, cooperative learning activities can be devised to promote the pursuit of social goals for cooperation and helping each other, to be responsible to the group, and to achieve common objectives. Students report stronger levels of satisfaction when given the opportunity to learn within cooperative learning settings.

Researchers have documented that many teachers hold negative stereotypes of minority and low-achieving students, expecting less competent behaviour and lower levels of academic performance from them than from other students. Of particular importance is that teachers' false expectations can become self-fulfilling prophecies, with student performance changing to conform to teacher expectations. Although the effects of these expectations tend to be fairly weak, self-fulfilling prophecies tend to have stronger effects on students from low socioeconomic backgrounds and low achievers. Moreover, teachers who communicate high expectations can bring about positive changes in performance: Teachers' overestimations of ability seem to have a somewhat stronger effect in raising levels of achievement than teachers' underestimations have on lowering achievement, especially for low-performing students.

Social Interactions with Peers

Interactions with peers also can lead directly to resources and information that help students to be socially competent. Even in preschool settings, peers can create beneficial as well as risky contexts for the development of self-regulatory skills. At older ages, peers provide information and advice, modeled behaviour, or specific experiences that facilitate learning social expectations for behaviour. Students frequently clarify and interpret their teacher's instructions concerning what they should be doing and how they should do it and provide mutual assistance in the form of volunteering substantive information and answering questions. Classmates also provide each other with important information about themselves; information concerning social self-efficacy and skills can be gleaned by observing social competencies and skills demonstrated by peers.

Other evidence suggests that peer expectations have the potential to provide the most proximal input concerning whether doing something might be important or fun. For instance, middle school students who perceive relatively high expectations for pro-social behaviour from their peers also pursue goals to behave pro-socially for internalized reasons, or because they think it is important; in contrast, perceived expectations from teachers are associated with pro-social goal pursuit in order to stay out of trouble or to gain social approval. Therefore, peers who communicate a sense of importance or enjoyment with regard to specific types of behaviour are likely to lead others to form similar attitudes. This is especially true if students are friends; strong emotional bonds associated with friendships tend to increase the likelihood that friends will imitate each other's behaviour. This latter point highlights the quality of students' interpersonal relationships as an additional, potential influence on their social and academic functioning. This aspect of socialization in school settings is discussed next.

Teacher's role : Teachers today have to deal with issues that once stayed outside the walls of schools. The first and most important task of a teacher is to educate, but student learning suffers when there are problems with personal and social development. Teachers are sometimes the best source of help for students facing emotional or interpersonal problems. When students have chaotic and unpredictable home lives, they need a caring and firm structure in schools. They need teacher who set clear limits, are consistent, enforce riles firmly but not punitively, respect students, and show genuine concern. As a teacher, you can be available to talk about personal problems without requiring that your students do so.

5. Mass media

In the last 50 years the media influence has grown exponentially with the advance of technology. We live in a society that hinges on information, communication and technology to keep moving and do our daily activities like work, entertainment, health care, education, personal relationships, traveling etc. The mass media introduced worldwide cultures and norms that the child would otherwise not become aware of. The other agents of socialization, family, peer groups, and school are most commonly a part of one society and one culture, but the mass media enlarges one's exposure to the social world.

The amount of time that youth now-a-days devote to media consumption, the lack of parental awareness and control over that media exposure, and the reduction in time that some children might spend on other socializing activities, one has to be concerned with the role of the mass media in socializing children. The very act of engaging with the mass media either alone or with peers provides learning opportunities that socialize children, and what children observe through the mass media alters their beliefs, attitudes, and behaviours. Since the introduction of television in the 1950s, the mass media steadily gained influence in socializing children while more traditional socializing organizations like schools, family etc. steadily lost influence. Because much of the content of the mass media to which children are exposed contains stereotyped, unrealistic and anti-social models of social behaviour, it is only natural that social scientists have focused more on understanding the negative influences of the mass media in socializing children. Yet, the mass media also provides opportunities for positive socialization. Whether the mass media teaches pro-social or antisocial behaviour more easily certainly depends on how the behaviour is presented, but the same learning processes are involved in both cases.

Short-Term Effects of mass media : Most short-term effects of exposure to television, films, video games, or Internet web pages are a consequence of three processes: (1) priming of already existing cognitions or scripts for behaviour; (2) immediate mimicking (imitation) of observed behaviours; or (3) changes in emotional arousal and the misattribution of that arousal (excitation transfer)

Priming : Priming is an increased sensitivity to certain stimuli because of prior experience. It can occur following perceptual, semantic, or conceptual stimulus repetition. For example, if a person reads a list of words including the word tamarind, and is later asked to complete a word starting with tam, the probability that he or she will answer tamarind is greater than if not so primed. Another example is if people see an incomplete sketch that they are unable to identify and they are shown more of the sketch until they recognize the picture, later they will identify the sketch at an earlier stage than was possible for them the first time.

Neuroscientists and cognitive psychologists posit that the human mind acts as an association network in which ideas are partially activated, or primed, by stimuli with which they are associated. Thus an encounter with an event or object can prime related concepts, ideas and emotions in a person's memory, even without the person being aware of it. For example, the mere presence of a weapon in a person's visual field can increase aggressive thoughts or behaviour. Alternatively, exposure to a scene of helping behaviour can stimulate related pro-social thoughts and supportive feelings.

Repeated exposure to specific media content, therefore, has the potential to bias individuals towards thinking, feeling or behaving in ways relevant to that content.

Imitation : Immediate mimicry of specific behaviours can be viewed as a special case of the more general long-term process of observational learning. Humans have an innate tendency to imitate whomever they observe. Observation of specific facial expressions or social behaviours increases the likelihood of children immediately displaying those expressions or behaviours. In fact, many studies have shown that most young children frequently mimic the behaviours of those characters they observe in the media.

Arousal and excitation transfer : Media portrayals are often high-action sequences that can be very arousing for youth, as measured by increased heart rate, and other physiological indices of arousal. When a child has been generally aroused by a media stimulus, the specific emotion, for example, anger generated by a subsequent real world event for example an insult may be felt as more severe.

Exercise 1 : Previous Year Questions of CTET & STET

1. Which of the following is not related to the socio-psychological needs of the child? *[CTET-2011-I]*
   (a) Need for appreciation or social approval
   (b) Need for emotional security
   (c) Regular elimination of waste products from the body
   (d) Need for company

2. Adjustment means accommodating oneself to various circumstances in order to satisfy *[RTET-2011-I]*
   (a) others   (b) motives
   (c) goals   (d) needs

3. A teacher can develop social values among students by *[UPTET-2011-I]*
   (a) telling them about great people
   (b) developing a sense of discipline
   (c) behaving ideally
   (d) telling them good stories

4. Children's attitudes towards persons of different ethnic groups are generally based upon *[UPTET-2011-I]*
   (a) attitudes of their parents
   (b) attitudes of their peers
   (c) influence of television
   (d) attitudes of their siblings

5. Socialization is a process by which children & adults learn from: *[PTET-2011-I]*
   (a) Family   (b) School
   (c) Peers   (d) All of these

6. In the present situation, the children must possess an important factor of *[TNTET-2011-I]*
   (a) intelligence   (b) personality
   (c) moral value   (d) experience

7. Print media and electronic media must project *[TNTET-2011-I]*
   (a) acceptable negative side of life
   (b) acceptable positive side of life
   (c) positive and negative sides of life
   (d) seamy side of life

8. Peer group is formed by *[TNTET-2011-I]*
   (a) Teacher + Controlled environment
   (b) Parents + Independent environment
   (c) Society + Controlled environment
   (d) Unexpected + independent environment

9. In which of the following stages do children become active members of their peer group? *[UPTET-2011-II]*
   (a) Adolescence   (b) Adulthood
   (c) Early childhood   (d) Childhood

10. "If the people of the society has high achievement motivation, the economic growth increases and the society gets modernized". It is given in the book *[TNTET-2011-II]*
    (a) The achieving Society
    (b) Achievement of the Society
    (c) Society and Achievement
    (d) Society and its Development

11. A group which has completely negative influence is *[TNTET-2011-II]*
    (a) primary group
    (b) intermediate group
    (c) secondary group
    (d) tertiary group

12. In the context of education, socialization means *[CTET-2012-I]*
    (a) respecting elders in society
    (b) adapting and adjusting to social environment
    (c) always following social norms
    (d) creating one's own social norms

13. Teachers are advised to involve their learners in group activities because, besides facilitating learning, they also help in *[CTET-2012-II]*
    (a) Socialization   (b) Value conflicts
    (c) Aggression   (d) Anxiety

14. 'Social development means acquisition of the ability to have in accordance with social exceptions.' *[UPTET-2014-I]*
    (a) Hurlock   (b) T.P. Nunn
    (c) McDougall   (d) Ross

15. Self-centered person is *[UPTET-2014-I]*
    (a) Introvert
    (b) Extrovert
    (c) Ambivert
    (d) Socially dependent

16. Socialization is a process by which children & adults learn from: *[PTET-2014-I]*
    (a) Family   (b) School
    (c) Peers   (d) All of these

17. An example of media that transports learners to remote places by means of visualized reports is: *[PTET-2014-II]*
    (a) educational television
    (b) educational broadcasts
    (c) overhead projector
    (d) telephone

18. The first teacher of a child is　　*[TNTET-2014-I]*
    (a) Pre Primary School teacher
    (b) Primary School Teacher
    (c) Parents
    (d) Society

19. Socialization is　　　　　　*[CTET-July-2013-I]*
    (a) Rapport between teacher and taught
    (b) Process of modernization of society
    (c) Adaptation of social norms
    (d) Change in social norms

20. Features assigned due to social roles and not due to biological endowment are called
    　　　　　　　　　　[CTET-July-2013-II]
    (a) Gender role attitudes
    (b) Gender role strain
    (c) Gender-role stereotype
    (d) Gender role diagnosticity

21. Socialisation includes cultural transmission and
    　　　　　　　　　　[CTET-July-2013-II]
    (a) discourages rebellion.
    (b) development of individual personality.
    (c) fits children into labels.
    (d) provides emotional support.

22. In the progressive model of education as implemented by CBSE, socialization of children is done in such a way so as to expect them to
    　　　　　　　　　　[CTET-Feb.-2014-I]
    (a) give up time-consuming social habits and learn how to score good grades
    (b) be an active participant in the group work and learn social skills
    (c) prepare themselves to conform to the rules and regulations of society without questioning
    (d) accept what they are offered by the school irrespective of their social background

23. Fourteen-year-old Devika is attempting to develop a sense of herself as a separate, self-governing individual. She is developing *[CTET-Feb.-2014-I]*
    (a) hatred for rules
    (b) autonomy
    (c) teenage arrogance
    (d) maturity

24. What kind of errors is common between a learner who is learning his mother tongue and the learner who learns the same language as a second language?　　*[CTET-Feb.-2014-I]*
    (a) Overgeneralization
    (b) Simplification
    (c) Developmental
    (d) Hypercorrection

25. In the context of socialization, schools often have a hidden curriculum which consists of
    　　　　　　　　　　[CTET-Feb.-2014-II]
    (a) forcible learning, thinking and behaving in particular ways by imitating peers and teachers
    (b) the informal cues about social roles presented in schools through interaction and materials
    (c) negotiating and resisting socialization of students through their families
    (d) teaching and assessment of values and attitudes

26. Which of the following is a passive agency of socialization ?　　*[CTET-Sep.-2014-I]*
    (a) Health club　　　　(b) Family
    (c) Eco club　　　　　(d) Public library

27. Which of the following approaches suggests interaction of the child with the people around him and with social institutions to deal with disruptive bahaviour disorder ?
    　　　　　　　　　　[CTET-Sep.-2014-II]
    (a) Psychodynamic　(b) Ecological
    (c) Biological　　　　(d) Bahavioural

28. Making students members of a cleanliness community to motivate them for the same, reflects　　　　　*[CTET-Feb.-2015-I]*
    (a) Socio-cultural conceptions of motivation
    (b) Behaviouristic approach to motivation
    (c) Humanistic approach to motivation
    (d) Cognitive approach to motivation

29. Socialization is a process of　*[CTET-Feb.-2015-II]*
    (a) socializing with friends.
    (b) acquiring values, beliefs and expectations.
    (c) assimilation and accommodation.
    (d) learning to critique the culture of a society.

30. Family plays .... role in socialisation of the child.　　　　　　*[CTET-Feb.-2016-I]*
    (a) a not-so-important　(b) an exciting
    (c) a primary　　　　(d) a secondary

31. A teacher remarks in a co-education class to boys, "Be boys and don't behave like girls." This remark　　　　　*[CTET-Feb.-2016-I]*
    (a) reflects caste discrimination.
    (b) is a good example of dealing with boys and girls.
    (c) reflects stereotypical behaviour of discrimination between boys and girls.
    (d) highlights the biological superiority of boys over girls.

32. Which of the following are secondary agents of socialization? *[CTET-Sept.-2016-I]*
    (a) Family and neighbourhood
    (b) School and neighbourhood
    (c) School and immediate family members
    (d) Family and relatives

33. 'Gender' is a/an : *[CTET-Sept.-2016-I]*
    (a) biological entity
    (b) physiological construct
    (c) innate quality
    (d) social construct

34. A textbook of Class VIII has following illustrations: 'women as teachers and maids while men as doctors and pilots'. This type of depiction is likely to promote *[CTET-Feb.-2016-II]*
    (a) gender stereotyping.
    (b) gender empowerment.
    (c) gender role play.
    (d) gender constancy.

35. ..... is a process through which a human infant begins to acquire the necessary skill to perform as a functioning member of the society. *[CTET-Feb.-2016-II]*
    (a) Socialisation   (b) Development
    (c) Learning   (d) Maturation

36. Which of the following is true of school and socialization? *[CTET-Sept.-2016-II]*
    (a) School is the first primary agent of socialization.
    (b) School is an important agent of socialization.
    (c) School does not play any role in socialization.
    (d) School plays very little role in socialization.

37. Watching her granddaughter arguing with her father for going on a school trip, the grandmother says, "Why can't you be obedient like a good girl? Who will marry you if you behave like a boy?" This statement reflects which of the following? *[CTET-Sept.-2016-II]*
    (a) Difficulties faced by families in child-rearing
    (b) Gender constancy
    (c) Gender stereotypes about attributes of girls and boys
    (d) Improper gender identification of the girl

38. Who has classified introvert personality and extrovert personality? *[UPTET-2017-I]*
    (a) Freud   (b) Jung
    (c) Munn   (d) Allport

39. The factors affecting the social development of children are *[UPTET-2017-I]*
    (a) economic elements
    (b) social-environmental elements
    (c) physical elements
    (d) hereditary elements

40. Who described different types of personality based on glands? *[UPTET-2017-I]*
    (a) Kretschmer   (b) Jung
    (c) Cannon   (d) Spranger

41. "Creativity is a mental process to express the original outcomes." This statement is given by *[UPTET-2017-I]*
    (a) Cole and Bruce (b) Drevahal
    (c) Dehan   (d) Crow and Crow

42. The following is a play that is said to be the first social activity of a child with his friends *[APTET-May.-2018-I]*
    (a) Solitary play
    (b) Parallel play
    (c) Co-operative play
    (d) Arrogant play

Answer Key

1.	(c)	6.	(c)	11.	(b)	16.	(d)	21.	**(b)**	26.	(d)	31.	(c)	36.	(b)	41.	(d)
2.	(d)	7.	(c)	12.	(b)	17.	(c)	22.	**(b)**	27.	(b)	32.	(b)	37.	(c)	42.	(b)
3.	(c)	8.	(c)	13.	(a)	18.	(c)	23.	**(b)**	28.	(a)	33.	(d)	38.	(b)		
4.	(d)	9.	(d)	14.	(a)	19.	(c)	24.	(c)	29.	(b)	34.	(a)	39.	(b)		
5.	(d)	10.	(a)	15.	(a)	20.	(c)	25.	(b)	30.	(c)	35.	(a)	40.	(c)		

19. (c) The general process of acquiring culture is referred to as socialization. During socialization, we learn the language of the culture we are born into as well as the roles we are to play in life.

20. (c) Features like attitudes, conditions or behaviors that promote stereotyping of social roles based on gender and not due to biological endowment, especially discrimination against women.

21. (b) Socialization includes cultural transmission and development of individual personality.

22. (b) Progressive education finds its roots in present experience, is more democratic in outlook. Most progressive education programmes emphasise in group work and development of social skills.

23. (b) Autonomy means, "One who gives oneself one's law". Devika is attempting to develop a sense of herself as a separate, self-governing individual. She is developing autonomy.

24. (c) The sources of second language learning errors are both interlingual and intralingual or development factors while interlingual errors are caused mainly by mother tongue interference, intralingual or developmental errors originate in the following factor: simplification, over generalization, faulty teaching, inadequate learning and false concepts hypothesized.

25. (b) Hidden curriculum is learning the rules of behaviour need to function informally organised groups. The hidden curriculum stresses such things as formalisation and standardisation, following instructions, obedience to authority figures that are not Mom and Dad, learning to control behaviour and fit into the group, pleasing (even manipulating) authority figures and working in teams.

30. (c) Family is measured to be a main foundation for a child. Family assists a child to gain knowledge of various cognitive, emotional and social aspects. It also helps a child to build up cultural ethics, characteristics, norms, etc.

31. (c) Gender bias can have a negative impact on the minds of both genders to make them believes in wrong notions about their development, significance and existence. In order to eradicate these social obstacle teachers can play a significant role to avoid such stereotyped thoughts in students by giving examples of taking genders as neutral and satisfying the needs of the children.

32. (b) School and Neighborhood comes in the later part of the childhood, first one is home and family which is the primary source.

33. (d) Gender is a social construct as it is given more importance in the society to differentiate them in respects of various aspects of life such as religion, caste and career. According to psychologists male and female should be considered at par rather than being gender –bias,

34. (a) Gender stereotyping is a thinking that one develops for a particular gender due to social inhibitions. Thus such a thought comes only relates to gender stereotyping when one thinks a particular profession for a particular gender where as it should not be there. Work should not be counted as gender biased.

38. (b) Carl Jung and the developers of the Myers–Briggs Type Indicator provide a different perspective and suggest that everyone has both an extraverted side and an introverted side, with one being more dominant than the other.

39. (b) Children's development of social skills is affected by the nature of their family and early educational experiences

42. (b) Parallel play is considered as the first play activity because in this children paly adjacent to each other without having any influence of one another's behavior. They play alone during parallel play but also interested in knowing what others are doing. This is the first activity when he completes 12 months of his birth.

Exercise 2 : Test Yourself

1. The most intense and crucial socialization takes place
   (a) Throughout the life of a person
   (b) During adolescence
   (c) During early childhood
   (d) During adulthood

2. In studies of peer status and popularity, members of which peer status group have the greatest adjustment problems?
   (a) Rejected
   (b) Controversial
   (c) Neglected
   (d) Average

3. Television viewing is related to
   (a) increased aggressive behaviour when the television content is violent
   (b) Obesity
   (c) increased pro-social behaviour when the television content includes cooperative, helpful models
   (d) All of the above

4. Researchers examining the effect of parenting style on elementary school childrens motivation have found that the highest achieving children are those whose parents use a(n) _______ style.
   (a) Authoritarian
   (b) Authoritative
   (c) Permissive
   (d) None of the above

5. Success in developing values is mainly dependent upon:
   (a) Government   (b) Society
   (c) Family   (d) Teacher

6. Empathy means
   (a) To share or experience the feelings of another person
   (b) To put yourself in the shoes of others
   (c) Understanding others' point of view
   (d) All of the above

7. Deficits in empathic capacity may make behaviour
   (a) Anti-social   (b) Obedient
   (c) Pro-social   (d) Harmless

8. The declining normative role of the family means that
   (a) Parents are clear about rules
   (b) Parents and children are too close
   (c) Parents and children are not close
   (d) Parents are not directive as they were in the past

9. The functions of socialization include cultural transmission, social integration, and
   (a) Discouraging rebellion
   (b) Force-fitting people into positions
   (c) Development of individual personality
   (d) Providing emotional support

10. Robert and Tanya are married and live with their three children.
    (a) A family of orientation
    (b) A nuclear family
    (c) An extended family
    (d) A communal family

11. One of the very important agencies of socialization is
    (a) Family
    (b) Neighborhood
    (c) Relatives
    (d) Informal groups

12. A status is
    (a) a position in the social structure
    (b) a social class
    (c) value judgment
    (d) formal pattern of relations

13. Social norms are
    (a) Descriptive   (b) Prescriptive
    (c) Evaluative   (d) Imperative

14. Values concentrate on different areas. These may be
    (a) general life values
    (b) family values
    (c) cultural & work values
    (d) all of the above

15. Which of the following is not a primary societal need necessary for the existence of any society?
    (a) Population
    (b) Specialization
    (c) Solidarity
    (d) Diversity

16. John Bowlby first became known for his contributions to object relations theory and, specifically, the significance
    (a) of early mother-infant bonds
    (b) of early parent-children bonds
    (c) of teacher-student bond
    (d) of family-community bonds

17. Children's attitudes toward persons of different ethnic groups are generally based upon
    (a) Their parent's attitudes
    (b) The attitudes of their peer
    (c) The influence of television
    (d) Their sibling' attitudes

18. Which of the following concepts is not a part of three-fold foundation of George Herbert Mead's theory of socialization?
    (a) Mind   (b) Self
    (c) Institution   (d) Society

19. The best place of social development for a 12 years old child is ....
    (a) Neighborhood   (b) Family
    (c) Playground   (d) School

20. An example of a severe emotional disturbance would be:
    (a) Crying
    (b) Not speaking
    (c) Social withdrawal
    (d) Talking back

21. The evaluation of a person by the other members of a group:
    (a) social competence
    (b) hierarchy
    (c) status
    (d) popularity

22. Social life consists of
    (a) Musics
    (b) Participation in dramas
    (c) Games
    (d) All of the above

23. How many type of social processes involved in education?
    (a) 2   (b) 3
    (c) 4   (d) 5

24. Peer Groups refers to
    (a) people of roughly the same age
    (b) friends, buddies, pals, troops
    (c) family members
    (d) All of the above

25. Socialization requires
    (a) Teachers
    (b) Rewards
    (c) Punishment
    (d) All of the above

Answer Key

1.	(b)	6.	(d)	11.	(a)	16.	(a)	21.	(c)
2.	(a)	7.	(a)	12.	(a)	17.	(a)	22.	(d)
3.	(d)	8.	(d)	13.	(c)	18.	(c)	23.	(c)
4.	(b)	9.	(c)	14.	(d)	19.	(c)	24.	(d)
5.	(c)	10.	(b)	15.	(b)	20.	(c)	25.	(d)

Individual Differences and Intelligence; Thought and Language

As the term implies, individual differences are qualities that are unique; just one person has them at a time. Variation in hair color, for example, is an individual difference; even though some people have nearly the same hair color, no two people are exactly the same.

Group differences are qualities shared by members of an identifiable group or community, but not shared by everyone in society. An example is gender role: for better or for worse, one portion of society (the males) is perceived differently and expected to behave a bit differently than another portion of society (the females).

Individuals with similar, but nonetheless, unique qualities sometimes group themselves together for certain purposes, and groups unusually contain a lot of individual diversity within them. If you happen to enjoy playing soccer and have some talent for it (an individual quality), for example, you may end up as a member of a soccer team or a club (a group defined by members' common desire and ability to play soccer).But though everyone on the team fits a "soccer player's profile" at some level, individual members will probably vary in level of skill and motivation. The group, by its very nature, may obscure these signs of individuality.

Individual Styles of Learning and Thinking

All of us, including our students, have preferred ways of learning. Teachers often refer to these differences as learning styles, though this term may imply that students are more consistent across situations than is really the case. One student may like to make diagrams to help remember a reading assignment, whereas another student may prefer to write a sketchy outline instead. Yet in many cases, the students could in principle reverse the strategies and still learn the material: if coaxed (or perhaps required), the diagram-maker could take notes for a change and the note-taker could draw diagrams. Both would still learn, though neither might feel as comfortable as when using the strategies that they prefer. This reality suggests that a balanced, middle-of-the-road approach may be a teacher's best response to students' learning styles. Or put another way, it is good to support students' preferred learning strategies where possible and appropriate, but neither necessary nor desirable to do so all of the time.

Some students may prefer to hear new material rather than see it; they may prefer for you to explain something orally, for example, rather than to see it demonstrated in a video. Some prefer to be the other way round. There is evidence that individuals, including students, do differ in how they habitually think. These differences are more specific than learning styles or preferences, and psychologists sometimes call them cognitive styles, meaning typical ways of perceiving and remembering information, and typical ways of solving problems and making decisions.

Another cognitive style is impulsivity as compared to reflectivity. As the names imply, an impulsive cognitive style is one in which a person reacts quickly, but as a result makes comparatively more errors. A reflective style is the opposite: the person reacts more slowly and therefore makes fewer errors. As you might expect, the reflective style wou   etter suited to many academic demands of school. Research has found that this is indeed the case for academic skills that clearly benefit from reflection, such as mathematical problem solving or certain reading tasks. Some classroom or school-related skills, however, may actually develop better if a student is relatively impulsive.

Language Differences in the Classroom

Linguistic diversity is one of the elements that contribute to student diversity. Your class will have language diversity, and you will have to realize that you need to be sensitive to this linguistic diversity and adjust accordingly.

Classroom Language and Literacy Learning

Sociolinguists hold that differences in oral communication reflect social variables, such as gender, ethnicity, social class, and age. When children enter school, their mode of oral communication has been influenced by these factors; they also already work within a communication system, which consists of language structure (sound structure, inflection, syntax), content (meaning), and use (purposes of communication, appropriate forms of communication). Knowledge about meaning, language functions (pragmatics), discourse genres, and more complex syntax continue to develop during schooling and into adulthood.

Vygotsky's notion of scaffolds has played a critical role in the development of theory and research on language and literacy learning. A scaffold, of course, is an external structure that braces another structure being built. Used as a metaphor in pedagogical theory, a scaffold is an interactional mechanism for learning and development. Through dialogue and associated nonverbal interaction, teachers provide graduated assistance to novice learners as they attain ever higher levels of conceptual and communicative competence. With scaffolding, learners can experiment with new concepts and strategies in ways that would not otherwise be possible. An effective scaffold provides "support at the edge of a child's competence" defining children's zones of proximal development or their potential for new learning. "Proximal development" refers to the assumption that skills the child can display with assistance are partially developed, but cannot be employed yet without support. The wider the zone, the more capable are children to perform task; the zone is activated through dynamic connections to scaffolding..

Dialect Differences and Bilingualism

In the classroom, quite a bit happens through language. Communication is at the heart of teaching. There are two kinds of language differences- Dialect differences and bilingualism.

Dialects

A dialect is a language variation spoken by a particular ethnic, social or regional group and is an element of a group's collective identity. The rules for a language define how words should be pronounced, how meaning should be expressed, and the ways the basic parts of speech should be put together to form sentences. Dialects appear to differ in their rules in these areas, but it is important to remember that these differences are not errors. Each dialect within a language is just as logical, complex and rule-governed as the standard form of the language (often called standard speech). An example of this is the use of double negative. The double negative is required by the grammatical rules. To say" I don't want anything" in Spanish, you must literally say, "I don't want nothing".

Dialects and teaching

What does all of this mean for teachers? How can they cope with linguistic diversity in the classroom? First, they can be sensitive to their own possible negative stereotypes about children who speak a different dialect. Sometimes teachers who hold negative attitudes towards such children give lower ratings to student on different tests. This can be avoided as it affects the morale of students leading to low productivity.

Bilingualism

The majority of children around the world are bilingual, meaning that they understand and use two languages. Even in the United States, which is a relatively monolingual society, more than 47 million people speak a language other than English at home. In larger communities throughout the United States, it is therefore common for a single classroom to contain students from several language backgrounds at once. In classrooms as in other social settings, bilingualism exists in different forms and degrees. At one extreme are students who speak both English and another language fluently; at the other extreme are those who speak only limited versions of both languages. In between are students who speak their home (or heritage) language much better than English, as well as others who have partially lost their heritage language in the process of learning English. Commonly, too, a student may speak a language satisfactorily, but be challenged by reading or writing it—though even this pattern has individual exceptions. Whatever the case, each bilingual student poses unique challenges to teachers.

Primary education should be bilingual. Successive stages of bilingualism are expected to build up to an integrated multilingualism. The first task of the school is to relate the home language to the school language. Thereafter, one or more languages are to be integrated, so that one can move into other languages without losing the first one. This would result in the maintenance of all languages, each complementing the other.

Mother-tongue should be the medium of instruction all through the school, but certainly in the primary school. The Working Group on the Study of Languages constituted by NCERT in 1986 recommends in its report that 'the medium of early education' should be the mother tongue of the learners.

According to UNESCO's Educational Position Paper (2003), mother-tongue instruction is essential for initial instruction and literacy and should be extended to as late a stage in education as possible. Some studies have shown that children who study through the mother-tongue medium do not suffer any disadvantage, linguistic or scholastic, when they compete with their English-medium counterparts. The mother–tongue as a medium of instruction can eliminate the linguistic and cultural gaps caused by the difference between school language and home language, i.e. the reference point might be a minor, or minority, or major language. Researchers also point out that the reason for 26 per cent of the dropouts at the level of elementary education is the 'lack of interest in education' caused partly by the lack of cultural content in educational programs; language is not only a 'component of culture' but also a 'carrier of culture'.

Cultural Differences in Language Use: The Indian Context

In a country like India, most children arrive in schools with multilingual competence and begin to drop out of the school system because, in addition to several other reasons, the language of the school fails to relate to the languages of their homes and neighborhoods. Most children leave schools with dismal levels of language proficiency in reading comprehension and writing skills, even in their own native languages.

Some reasons that are primarily responsible for these low levels of proficiency include:

- Lack of any understanding about the nature and structure of language and the processes of language teaching-learning, particularly in multilingual contexts;

- Failure on the part of educational planners to appreciate the role of language across the curriculum in contributing towards the construction of knowledge;

- Lack of attention to the fact that a variety of biases, including caste, race, and gender, get encoded in language;

- Inability to appreciate the fact that language consists of much more than just poems, essays, and stories;

- Unwillingness to accept the role of languages of the home and neighborhood in cognitive growth and failure to notice that cognitively advanced language proficiency tends to get transferred across languages.

Language, Attitudes and Motivation

The attitudes and motivation of learners often play an important role in all language learning. Similarly, the attitudes of the teacher and parental encouragement may contribute to successful language learning. Researchers working in the area of second or foreign language learning have identified several social psychological variables that influence the learning of a second language.

Some of these variables are:

(a) aptitudes	(b) intelligence;
(c) attitudes;	(d) motivation and motivational intensity;
(5) authoritarianism; and	(6) ethnocentrism

Language and Gender

The issue of gender concerns not half but the whole of humanity. Over a period of time, language has coded in its texture a large number of elements that perpetuate gender stereotypes. Several studies have addressed the issues that centre round language and gender. Detailed analysis of male–female conversation has also revealed how men use a variety of conversational strategies to assert their point of view.

The received notions of what it means to be 'masculine' or 'feminine' are constantly reconstructed in our behaviour and are, sometimes unwittingly perhaps, transmitted through our textbooks. Indeed, the damage done by the 'gender construction of knowledge' is becoming increasingly obvious. Language, including illustrations and other visual aids, plays a central role in the formation of such knowledge and we need to pay immediate attention to this aspect of language. It is extremely important that textbook writers and teachers begin to appreciate that the passive and deferential roles generally assigned to women are socio-culturally constructed and need to be destroyed as quickly as possible. The voices of women in all their glory need to find a prominent place in our textbooks and teaching strategies.

Minor, Minority and Tribal Languages

The underprivileged speakers of minor, minority, and tribal languages often suffer severe linguistic deprivation. It is important for us to realize that the major languages of this country, including English, can flourish only in the company of and not at the cost of minor languages. The ideological position that the development of one language also helps in the development of other languages leads one to expect that the development of even some of the languages could provide a marked impetus to the rest of the languages in the case of the linguistically diverse tribal areas, and spur the speech communities to consciously strive in that direction.

Needless to say, every teacher will evolve his or her own specific method depending on a variety of social, psychological, linguistic, and classroom variables. The new dispensation must empower the teacher to use his or her space in the classroom more effectively and innovatively. Some of these basic principles include:

- **Learner:** Whatever be the method used in the classroom, the learner should never be treated as an empty receptacle. She should be at the centre of the teaching-learning process. The teacher will gradually need to explore the cognitive potential and interests of the learner in order to adjust her own language-teaching methodology.

- **Attitude:** It is only when the teacher is positively inclined towards all pupils, irrespective of their caste, color, creed or gender that they will tend to become positively motivated to be involved in the teaching-learning process. Teachers' positive attitudes will also go a long way in lowering the anxiety levels of learners, which are known to obstruct the learning process.

- **Input:** the input should be rich, interesting, and challenging and should be woven around topics that encourage peer-group learning. Modern technology may help schools in a significant way in this regard. The teacher will gradually need to explore the cognitive potential and interests of the learner in order to adjust her own language-teaching methodology.

- **Multilingualism as a Resource:** As we have argued elsewhere in this paper, language-teaching methods can be suitable sites for utilizing the multiplicity of languages available in the classroom. A sensitive analysis of the multilingualism obtaining in the classroom in collaboration with children will help in creating a meta-linguistic awareness among the teachers and the taught. Translation may prove to be a very powerful tool in this context.

- **Issues of Gender and Environment:** It is necessary that modern language-teaching methods create awareness about gender and environmental issues among children. It should be possible to address these issues implicitly and effectively through careful and sensitive language-teaching methods.

- **Assessment:** Every possible effort should be made to make assessment a part of the teaching-learning process. Whenever we break the normal classroom processes for a test or examination, we manage to raise the anxiety levels of the learners, disrupting the learning process in a significant way.

Gender-role Identity

The word gender usually refers to traits and behaviours that a particular culture judges to be appropriate for men and for women. Gender-role identity is the image each individual has of himself or herself as masculine or feminine in characteristics-a part of self concept. People with "feminine" identity would rate themselves high on characteristics usually associated with females, such as "sensitive" and low on characteristics traditionally associated with males, such as "forceful". Most people see themselves in gender-typed terms, as high on either masculine or feminine characteristics. Some children and adults, however, are more androgynous-they rate themselves high on both masculine and feminine traits. They can be forceful or sensitive, depending on the situation. Recently, some psychologists have suggested that measures of androgyny actually assess instrumental (goal-directed) and expressive (social-emotional) traits, not masculine and feminine traits.

Gender bias in the Curriculum

During the elementary school years, children continue to learn about what it means to be male or female. Unfortunately schools often foster these gender biases in a number of ways. Most of the textbooks produced for the early grades still portray both males and females in stereotyped roles. One study found that there were four times more stories about male characters than about females. In addition, the females tended to be shown in the home, behaving passively and expressing fear or incompetence. Though the textbooks have improved in terms of gender bias, there still are more males in the titles and the illustrations, and the characters (especially the boys) continue to behave in stereotypic ways. Boys are more aggressive and argumentative, and girls are more expressive and affectionate. Videos, computer programs, and testing materials also often feature boys more than girls.

Sex Differences in Mental Abilities

From infancy through the preschool years, most studies find few differences between boys and girls in overall mental and motor development or in specific abilities. During the school years and beyond, psychologists find no differences in general intelligence on the standard measures-these tests have been designed and standardized to minimize sex differences. However, scores on some tests of specific abilities show sex differences. For example, from elementary through high school, girls score higher than boys on tests of reading and writing and fewer girls remediation in reading.

Gender Differences in the Classroom

Although there are many exceptions, boys and girls do differ on average in ways that parallel conventional gender stereotypes and that affect how the sexes behave at school and in class. The differences have to do with physical behaviours, styles of social interaction, academic motivations, behaviours, and choices. They have a variety of sources—primarily parents, peers, and the media. Teachers are certainly not the primary cause of gender role differences, but sometimes teachers influence them by their responses to and choices made on behalf of students.

There has been quite a bit research on teacher's treatment on male and female students. Some female teachers interact more with boys than with girls. This is true from preschool to college. Teachers ask more questions of males, give males more feedback (praise, criticism, correction), and give more specific and valuable comments to boys. As girls move through grades, they have less and less to say.

The imbalances of teacher attention given to boys and girls are particularly dramatic in math and science classes. In one study, boys were questioned in science class 80% more often than girls. Teachers wait longer for boys to answer and give more detailed feedback to boys. Boys also dominate the use of equipment in science labs, often dismantling the apparatus before the girls in the class have a chance to perform the experiments.

Academic and Cognitive Differences in Gender

On average, girls are more motivated than boys to perform well in school, at least during elementary school. As youngsters move into high school, they tend to choose courses or subjects conventionally associated with their gender—math and science for boys, in particular, and literature and the arts for girls. By the end of high school, this difference in course selection makes a measurable difference in boys' and girls' academic performance in these subjects. But again, consider my caution about stereotyping: there are individuals of both sexes whose behaviours and choices run counter to the group trends. Differences within each gender group generally are far larger than any differences between the groups. A good example is the "difference" in cognitive ability of boys and girls. Many studies have found none at all. A few others have found small differences, with boys slightly better at math and girls slightly better at reading and literature. Still other studies have found the differences not only are small, but have been getting smaller in recent years compared to earlier studies.

How teachers influence gender roles? Teachers often intend to interact with both sexes equally, and frequently succeed at doing so. Research has found, though, that they do sometimes respond to boys and girls differently, perhaps without realizing it. Three kinds of differences have been noticed. The first is the overall amount of attention paid to each sex; the second is the visibility or "publicity" of conversations; and the third is the type of behaviour that prompts teachers to support or criticize students.

Attention Paid

In general, teachers interact with boys more often than with girls by a margin of 10 to 30 percent, depending on the grade level of the students and the personality of the teacher. One possible reason for the difference is related to the greater assertiveness of boys that I already noted; if boys are speaking up more frequently in discussions or at other times, then a teacher may be "forced" to pay more attention to them. Another possibility is that some teachers may feel that boys are especially prone to getting into mischief, so they may interact with them more frequently to keep them focused on the task at hand. Still another possibility is that boys, compared to girls, may interact in a wider variety of styles and situations, so there may simply be richer opportunities to interact with them. This last possibility is partially supported by another gender difference in classroom interaction, the amount of public versus private talk.

Public Talk Versus Private Talk

Teachers have a tendency to talk to boys from a greater physical distance than when they talk to girls. The difference may be both a cause and an effect of general gender expectations, expressive nurturing is expected more often of girls and women, and a businesslike task orientation is expected more often of boys and men, particularly in mixed-sex groups (Whatever the reason, the effect is to give interactions with boys more "publicity". When two people converse with each other from across the classroom, many others can overhear them; when they are at each other's elbows, though, few others can overhear.

Distributing praise and criticism

In spite of most teachers' desire to be fair to all students, it turns out that they sometimes distribute praise and criticism differently to boys and girls. The tendency is to praise boys more than girls for displaying knowledge correctly, but to criticize girls more than boys for displaying knowledge incorrectly. Another way of stating this difference is by what teachers tend to overlook: with boys, they tend to overlook wrong answers, but with girls, they tend to overlook right answers. The result (which is probably unintended) is a tendency to make boys' knowledge seem more important and boys themselves more competent. A second result is the other side of this coin: a tendency to make girls' knowledge less visible and girls themselves less competent.

The Indian Context- Position Paper National Focus Group
(On gender issues in Education, NCERT-2006)

Gender is the most pervasive form of inequality, as it operates across all classes, castes and communities. The dropout rates of girls, specially from the marginalized sections of society and the rural areas continues to be sad-9 out of every 10 girls ever enrolled in school do not complete schooling, and only 1 out of every 100 girls enrolled in Class I reaches Class XII in rural areas. Factors cited for dropout include poor teaching, non-comprehension, difficulties of coping and high costs of private tuition or education. Despite the education system's focused efforts to include girls, it continues to "push out" those who are already within. Clearly issues of curriculum and pedagogy require equal and critical attention, in addition to enrolment.

Work on gender sensitization and awareness building has acquired complacency given that it circles around issues of enrolment, the relative absence of female figures or removal of gendered stereotypes in textbooks. In order to move forward serious inquiry into curricula, content, the gendered construction of knowledge, as well as a more critical and pro-active approach to issues of gender is necessary. Gender has to be recognized as a cross-cutting issue and a critical marker of transformation; it must become an important organizing principle of the national and state curricular framework as well as every aspect of the actual curricula.

Implications for girls as students: Once girls are able to access schools, the assumption is that as girls and women have entered the public sphere, empowerment will automatically follow. Their life chances will expand and they will be in a position to take greater control of their lives. But the complexity lies in the fact that schools themselves create boundaries that curb possibilities. The content, language, images in texts, the curricula, and the perceptions of teachers and facilitators have the power to strengthen the hold of patriarchy.

Schooling has become another form of domestication. For example, school textbooks depict this gender based domestic division of labor. In the classroom too, just as dalit children are expected to perform the menial tasks, girls are often relegated the work of cleaning and sweeping, reinforcing the gendered division of labor. The aspirations of young girls are unrelated to their actual intellectual and cognitive abilities. The work of gender sensitization and awareness building has acquired complacency and is limited to the issues of enrolment of girls, and to the relative absence of female figures or proliferation of gendered stereotypes in text books. Such work is clearly inadequate and there is an urgent need now for serious inquiry into curricula, content, and the gendered construction of knowledge.

SC/ST girls' schooling, gendered labor and socialization:

Various educational incentives have undoubtedly facilitated the educational progress of scheduled castes and scheduled tribes, particularly in the last two decades. However, they continue to lag behind educationally and there is great unevenness between different state and regions. The parents of SC/ST are unable to send their children to 'free' schools because of costs other than the tuition fee and of forgone income from the children's work. However, educationally the most vulnerable are girls. Dalit girls' educational aspirations are decisively shaped by labor requirements of the domestic and public economies: In the caste/gendered segmentation of the labor market women are disproportionately found in agricultural/rural labor, traditional domestic, low skilled, low status, or caste related (sweeping – scavenging) services in rural sectors. In urban sectors, poor women are located in lowly unskilled, low status feminized service sectors in urban informal economy. Educational careers of most dalit girls are shaped by this structure. Even those who can meet the expenditure of the education of their children, spend less on the schooling of their daughters than the sons. The expenses of dowry compound the problem, and the chances of girls being educated is reduced further.

Addressing the Talented, Creative, Specially-abled learners or Gifted Children

Children and youth with outstanding talent perform or show the potential for performing at remarkably high levels of accomplishment when compared with others of their age, experience, or environment. These children and youth exhibit high capability in intellectual, creative, and/or artistic areas, possess an unusual leadership capacity, or excel in specific academic fields. They require services or activities not ordinarily provided by schools. Outstanding talents are present in children and youth from all cultural groups, across all economic strata, and in all areas of human endeavour.

Truly gifted children are not the students who simply learn quickly with little effort. The work of gifted students is original, extremely advanced for their age, and potentially of lasting importance. These children may read fluently with little instruction by age 3 or 4. They may play a musical instrument like a skillful adult, turn a visit to a grocery store into a mathematical puzzle, and become fascinated with algebra when their friends are having trouble carrying in addition.

A classic study of the characteristics of the academically and intellectually gifted was started decades ago by Lewis Terman and colleagues. This huge project is following the lives of 1,528 gifted males and females and continued until the year 2010. The subjects all have IQ scores in the top 1% of the population (140 or above on the Stanford-Binet individual test of intelligence. They were identified on the basis of these test scores and teacher recommendations.

Terman and colleagues found that these gifted children were larger, stronger and healthier than the norm. They often walked sooner and were more athletic. They were more emotionally stable than their peers and became better-adjusted adults than the average. They had lower rates of delinquency, emotional difficulty, divorce, drug problems and so on.

Recognizing Gifts and Talents

Teachers are successful only about 10% to 50% of the time in picking out the gifted children in their classes. These seven questions, taken from an early study of gifted students, are still good guides today.

- Who learns easily and rapidly?
- Who uses a lot of common sense and practical knowledge?
- Who retains easily what he or she has heard?
- Who knows about many things that the other children don't?
- Who uses a large number of words easily and accurately?
- Who recognizes relations and comprehends meanings?
- Who is alert and keenly observant and responds quickly?
- Who is persistent and highly motivated on some tasks?
- Who is creative, often has unusual ideas, or makes interesting connections?

Group achievement and intelligent tests tend to underestimate the IQs of very bright children. Group tests may be appropriate for screening, but they are not appropriate for making placement decisions. Many psychologists recommend a case study approach to identifying gifted students. This means gathering many kinds of information, test scores, grades, examples of work, projects and portfolios, letters or ratings from teachers, self-ratings, and so on. Especially for recognizing artistic talent, experts in the field can be called in to judge the merits of a child's creations. Science projects, exhibitions, performances, auditions, and interviews are all possibilities. Students with remarkable abilities in one area may have much less impressive abilities in others.

Teaching gifted children

Some educators believe that gifted students should be accelerated- moved quickly through the grades or through particular subjects. Other educators prefer enrichment-giving the students additional, more sophisticated, and more thought-provoking work, but keeping them with their age-mates in school.

Many people object to acceleration, but most careful studies indicate that truly gifted students who begin primary, elementary, high school, college, or even graduate school early do as well as, and usually better than non-gifted students who are progressing at the normal pace. Social and emotional adjustment does not appear to be impaired. Gifted students tend to prefer the company of older playmates and may be miserably bored if kept with children of their own age. Skipping grades may not be the best solution for a particular student. An alternative to skipping grades is to accelerate students in one or two particular subjects or allow concurrent enrolment in advanced placement courses, but keep them with peers for most classes.

Teaching methods for gifted students should encourage abstract thinking (formal-operational thought), creativity, reading of high-level and original texts, and independence not just the learning of greater quantities of facts. On approach that does not seem promising with gifted students is cooperative learning in mixed abilities groups. Gifted students tend to learn more when they work in groups with other high ability peers. In working with gifted and talented students, a teacher must be imaginative, flexible, tolerant and unthreatened by the capabilities of these students.

THE EDUCATION OF GIFTED CHILDREN

Identification

The identification of gifted children is a big problem for educators. It is inextricably tied to one's definition of and beliefs about the nature of giftedness and also to the programs and services that are put into place for children who have been identified as gifted. For example, if you believe strongly that the aim of identification is to find children who have the potential to become creative producers in adulthood, identification procedures might include a focus on demonstration of exceptionally creative work in school coupled with task persistence and motivation to produce unusual products at a high level. On the other hand, if your beliefs about giftedness are that it is exceptional intellectual ability regardless of actual achievement or performance, measures such as IQ scores could be used for identification, and you would aim to include children with high ability yet low school achievement. If you subscribe to an educational definition of giftedness and believe that gifted children are those for whom the typical school curriculum is inadequate, you would use measures of achievement to find students who are able to perform beyond their current school placement in the subjects typically taught in schools. If you subscribe to a multiple intelligences view of ability, you would want to establish identification procedures to find children with talent in the various domains and provide programs to help them develop that talent.

INTELLIGENCE

According to Wechsler, intelligence is the aggregate or global capacity of the individual to act purposefully, to think rationally and to deal effectively with his environment. Researchers have developed various types of models of intelligence. Some of the models of intelligence are as given below:

Unitary or Monarchy Theory

This theory has been defined by Binet. According to this theory intelligence consists of only one factor namely a fund of intellectual competence which is universal for all the activities of a person. But in our practical life we see contrary to this. A genial statistics professor may be absent minded or socially ill-adjusted. A student very good at conducting Science experiments may not be equally competent in learning languages. Hence, it is suggested that the unitary approach is too simple and a complex model is needed to explain intelligence satisfactorily.

Two-factor theory of intelligence

Charles Spearman suggested that there is one mental attribute, which he called g or general intelligence that is used to perform any mental test, but that each test also requires some specific abilities in addition to g. For example, memory for a series of numbers probably involves both g and some specific ability for immediate recall of what is heard. Spearman assumed that individuals vary in both general intelligence and specific abilities, and that together these factors determine performance on mental tasks. For example, an individual's performance in English could be partly due to the general factor and partly due to some kind of specific ability in language.

Multi-factor theory of Thorndike

Thorndike did not believe in the general factor. According to the theory intelligence is said to be constituted of multitude of separate factors or elements each being a minute element or ability. In other words, intelligence is the sum total of specific capacities. There is no generality to intelligence but rather commonality in the acts that people perform. A mental act involves a number of these minute elements operating together. If any two tasks are correlated, the degree of correlation is due to the common elements involved in the two tasks.

Thorndike distinguished 4 attributes of intelligence. They are:

- Level
- Area
- Range
- Speed

Level : refers to the difficulty of a task that can be solved. If all test items are arranged in an order of increasing difficulty, then the height that we can climb on the ladder of difficulty decides our level of intelligence.

Range : This refers to the number of tasks at any given degree of difficulty that we can solve. An individual possessing a given level of intelligence should be able to solve the whole range of task at that level.

Area : It refers to the total number of situations at each level to which the individual is able to respond. Area is the summation of all the ranges at each level of intelligence processed by an individual.

Speed : This is the rapidity with which an individual can respond to items.

Group-factor theory of Thurstone

Thurstone extended Spearman's two-factor theory into multi-factor theory. According to this theory, certain mental operations have in common a PRIMARY factor that gives them psychological and functional unity and which differentiates them from other mental operations. These mental operations then constitute a group. A second group of mental operations has its own unifying Primary factor; a third group has a third Primary factor and so on. Each of these primary factors is said to be relatively independent of others. From further analysis, Thurstone and his associates concluded that seven Primary mental abilities emerged clearly enough for identification and used in test designing. They are:

- **Space Visualization:** The ability to visualize geometric pattern
- **Perceptual speed:** Speed and accuracy of noting details
- **Numeric ability:** Speed and accuracy in simple arithmetic operations
- **Verbal comprehension:** Knowledge of meaning and relationship of words
- **Word fluency:** Ability to think and use many isolated words at a rapid rate
- **Associative memory:** Immediate recall or retrieval of material learned
- **Reasoning:** Ability to see relationship in situations described in symbols

Structure of Intellect by Guilford

Guilford and his associates proposed the theory of Structure of Intellects on their attempt of factor analysis. This theory represents cubical model. This model provides for 120 factors of intelligence.

Guilford suggests that mind is composed of 3 major dimensions namely

- Operations
- Content
- Product

Operations

- Cognition
- Memory recording
- Memory retention
- Divergent thinking
- Convergent thinking
- Evaluation

Contents

- Visual content
- Auditory content
- Symbolic content
- Semantic content
- Behavioural content

Products

- Units
- Classes
- Relations
- Systems
- Transformations
- Implications

Cognitive Theories of Intelligence

Another view that has stood the test of time is Raymond Cattell and John Horn's theory of fluid and crystallized intelligence.

Fluid intelligence

It is dependent on neurological development and is relatively free form the influences of education and culture. In other words, it is derived more from biological and genetic factors and les influenced by training and experience. This type of intelligence is put to use when facing new and strange situations requiring adaptation, comprehension, reasoning, problem-solving and identifying relationships etc. It reaches its full development by the end of an individual's adolescence.

Crystallized intelligence

On the other hand, is not functioning of one's neurological development and, is, therefore not innate like fluid intelligence. Rather, it is especially learned and is, therefore dependent on education and culture. It involves one's acquired fund of general information consisting of knowledge and skills essential for performing different tasks in one's day to day life. It can be identified through one's fund of vocabulary, general knowledge of world affairs, the knowledge of customs, traditions, and rituals, manner of behaving in society, handling of machines and tools, craftsmanship and art, computation and keeping of accounts and various other such tasks requiring knowledge, experience and practice.

Measurement of Intelligence

In 1904, Alfred Binet was confronted with the following problem by the minister of public instruction in Paris. How can students who will need special teaching and extra help be identified early in their school careers, before they fail in regular classes? Binet was also a political activist very much concerned with the rights of children. He believed that having an objective measure of learning ability could protect students from poor families who might be forced to leave school because they were the victims of discrimination and assumed to be slow learners.

Binet and his collaborator Simon wanted to measure not only school achievement, but the intellectual skill students needed to do well in school. After trying many different tests and eliminating items that did not discriminate between successful and unsuccessful students, Binet and Simon finally identified 58 tests, several for each age group from 3 to 13. The tests of Binet tests allowed the examiner to determine a mental age for a child. A child who succeeded on the items passed by most 6-year olds, for example, was considered to have a mental age of 6, whether the child was actually 4, 6, or 8 years old.

The concept of intelligence quotient, or IQ, was added after the test of Binet was brought to the US and revised at Stanford University to give us the Stanford-Binet test. An IQ score was computed by comparing the mental-age score to the person's actual chronological age. The formula was

$$\text{Intelligent Quotient} = \frac{\text{Mental Age}}{\text{Chronological Age}} \times 100$$

Group versus Individual IQ Tests

The Stanford-Binet is an individual intelligence test. It has to be administered to one student at a time by a trained psychologist and takes about two hours. Most of the questions are asked orally and do not require reading or writing. A student usually pays closer attention and is more motivated to do well when working directly with n adult.

Psychologists also have developed group tests that can be given to whole classes or schools. Compared to an individual test, a group test is much less likely to yield an accurate picture of any one person's abilities. When students take tests in a group, they may do poorly because they do not understand the instructions, because they have trouble reading, because their pencils break, or they lose their place on the answer sheet, because other students distract them, or because the answer format confuses them.

There are more sophisticated versions of the IQ tests. One is the SAT. Its name originally stood for Scholastic Aptitude Test., although with the passage of time the meaning of the acronym changes- it became the scholastic assessment test. And more recently, it has been reduced to the plain old SAT-just the initials. The SAT purports to be a similar kind of measure and if you add up a person's verbal and math score, as is often done, you can rate him or her along a single intellectual dimension.(Recently, writing and reasoning components have been added). Programs for the gifted use that kind of measure.

Along with this one-dimensional view, of how to assess people's minds, comes a corresponding view of school, which is the "uniform view". A uniform school features a core curriculum- a set of facts that everyone should know. The better students, perhaps those with higher IQs are allowed to take courses that call on critical reading, calculations and thinking skills. In the uniform school, there are regular assessments, using paper and pencil instruments, of the IQ or SAT variety. These assessments yield reliable rankings of people; the best and the brightest get into the better colleges, and perhaps they will also get better rankings in life.

The uniform school sounds fair-after all, everyone is treated in the same way. But this supposed rational was completely unfair. The uniform school picks out and is addressed to a certain kind of mind-we might call it provisionally the IQ or SAT mind.

MULTIPLE INTELLIGENCES

Howard Gardner's theory of multiple intelligences

Gardner proposes that there are eight different forms of intelligence, each of which functions independently of the others. Each person has a mix of all eight abilities—more of one and less of another, that helps to constitute that person's individual cognitive profile. Since most tasks, including most tasks in classrooms require several forms of intelligence and can be completed in more than one way, it is possible for people with various profiles of talents to succeed on a task equally well. In writing an essay, for example, a student with high interpersonal intelligence but rather average verbal intelligence might use his or her interpersonal strength to get a lot of help and advice from classmates and the teacher. A student with the opposite profile might work well alone, but without the benefit of help from others. Both students might end up with essays that are good, but good for different reasons.

Gardener grouped the MIs into 4 categories: those valued in the school; those valued in the arts; those connected to the personal; and those connected to the environment.

- **Those valued in school-** Verbal/linguistic and logical/mathematical intelligences. The verbal linguistic intelligence is crucial to language and a demonstrable capacity to utilize language for a particular aim. Writers, actors and actresses, lawyers and linguists are examples of people with strengths in this intelligence. The logical/mathematical intelligence is an ability to analyze problems carefully, to manipulate mathematical processes skillfully, and to use the scientific method rigorously. Philosophers, mathematicians, and scientists show strength in this intelligence.

- **Those valued in the arts are visual**/spatial, bodily/kinesthetic, and musical/rhythmic intelligences. The visual/spatial intelligence is an ability to conceptualize and use patterns in space. Painters, Sculptors and Architects are examples of people particularly strong in this kind of intelligence. The bodily/kinesthetic intelligence is an ability to find or to create solutions through the use of the body. Dancers, athletes and crafts workers excel in this intelligence. The musical/rhythmic intelligence is an ability to appreciate, create, or perform rhythmic or musical patterns. Musicians, composers and drummers use this intelligence well.

- **Those connected to the personal** are the inter-personal and intra-personal intelligences. The inter-personal intelligence is an ability to grasp the inner workings of others in such a way as to connect with them and work with them. Politicians, sales people and teachers demonstrate great strength in this intelligence. The intrapersonal intelligence is an ability to grasp the inner workings of one's self in such a way as to understand one's own life and operate well individually. Journal writers, religious gurus and psychologists are examples of people with strength in this intelligence.

- Only one of the MI, the one added in 1990, is contained in the grouping of those **connected to the environment**. The naturalist intelligence is an ability to distinguish varieties of plants and animals and to amass knowledge of the workings of the external world. Environmentalists, fishermen, and gardeners display strength in this intelligence.

Multiple intelligences according to Howard Gardner

Form of intelligence	Examples of activities using the intelligence
Linguistic: verbal skill; ability to use language well	• verbal persuasion • writing a term paper skillfully
Musical: ability to create and understand music	• singing, playing a musical instrument • composing a tune
Logical: Mathematical: logical skill; ability to reason, often using mathematics	• solving mathematical problems easily and accurately • developing and testing hypotheses
Spatial: ability to imagine and manipulate the arrangement of objects in the environment	• completing a difficult jigsaw puzzle • assembling a complex appliance (e.g. a bicycle)
Bodily: kinesthetic: sense of balance; coordination in use of one's body	• dancing • gymnastics
Interpersonal: ability to discern others' nonverbal feelings and thoughts	• sensing when to be tactful • sensing a "subtext" or implied message in a person's statements
Intrapersonal: sensitivity to one's own thoughts and feelings	• noticing complex of ambivalent feelings in oneself • identifying true motives for an action in oneself
Naturalist: sensitivity to subtle differences and patterns found in the natural environment	• identifying examples of species of plants or animals. noticing relationships among species and natural processes in the environment

EMOTIONAL INTELLIGENCE

Emotional intelligence can be defined as the ability to perceive control and evaluate own and other people's emotions, to discriminate between different emotions and label them appropriately and to use emotional information to guide thinking and behaviour. There are three main models of EI:

1. Ability model

2. Mixed model (usually subsumed under trait EI)

2. Trait model

In 1983, Howard Gardner introduced the idea that traditional types of intelligence, such as IQ, fail to fully explain cognitive ability. He introduced the idea of multiple intelligences which included both interpersonal intelligence (the capacity to understand the intentions , motivations and desires of other people) and intrapersonal intelligence (the capacity to understand oneself , to appreciate one's feelings , fears and motivations). The first use of the term "emotional intelligence" is usually attributed to Wayne Payne's doctoral thesis, However, the concept of emotional intelligence became widely known with the publication of Goleman's *Emotional Intelligence Why it can matter more than IQ.*

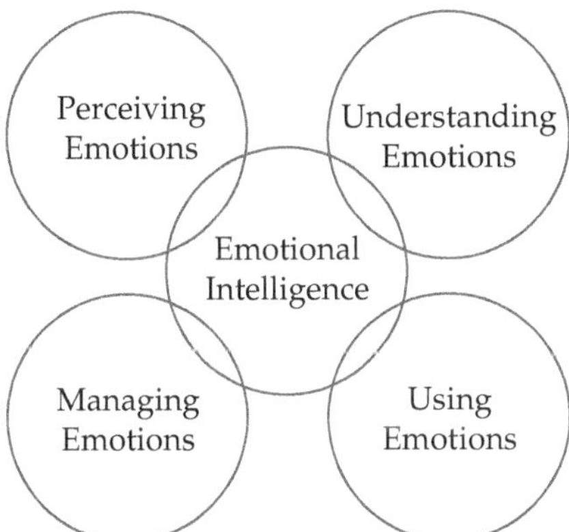

Factors of Emotional Intelligence

The Four Branches of Emotional Intelligence

Salovey and Mayer proposed a model that identified four different factors of emotional intelligence: the perception of emotion, the ability reason using emotions, the ability to understand emotion and the ability to manage emotions.

1. **Perceiving Emotions:** The first step in understanding emotions is to perceive them accurately. In many cases , this might involve understanding nonverbal signals such as body language and facial expressions.

2. **Reasoning With Emotions:** The next step involves using emotions to promote thinking and cognitive activity. Emotions help prioritize what we pay attention and react to; we respond emotionally to things that garner our attention.

3. **Understanding Emotions:** The emotions that we perceive can carry a wide variety of meanings. If someone is expressing angry emotions, the observer must interpret the cause of their anger and what it might mean. For example, if your boss is acting angry, it might mean that he is dissatisfied with your work; or it could be because he got a speeding ticket on his way to work that morning or that he's been fighting with his wife.

4. **Managing Emotions:** The ability to manage emotions effectively is a crucial part of emotional intelligence. Regulating emotions, responding appropriately and responding to the emotions of others are all important aspect of emotional management.

According to Salovey and Mayer, the four branches of their model are. "arranged from more basic psychological processes to higher , more psychologically integrated processes. For example, the lowest level branch concerns the (relatively) simple abilities of perceiving and expressing emotion. In contrast, the highest level branch concerns the conscious, reflective regulation of emotion".

LANGUAGE & THOUGHT

Language

Language is a cognition that truly makes us human. Language can be described as a " tool of thought" but we usually think of it as a tool of communication among people. Whereas other species do communicate with an innate ability to produce a limited number of meaningful vocalisations, there is no other species known to date that can express infinite ideas (sentences) with a limited set of symbols (speech sounds and words). Language is said to communicate when others understand the meaning of our sentences, and we, in turn, understand theirs.

Linguistic Competence

When we speak one of the thousands of languages of the words, we draw on our inner knowledge of the rules governing the use of language. This knowledge about language is called *linguistic competence*.

Linguistics is the study of languages as structured systems of rules, it also studies the origin of languages, the relationships among languages, how languages changes over time, and the nature of language sounds.

Language Elements

Starting with the basic sounds of speech, spoken language can be broken down into these elements:

Phones and Phonemes : Speech sounds, or phones, are made by adjusting the vocal cords and moving the tongue, lips and mouth in different precise ways. Hundreds of speech sounds can be distinguished on the basic of their frequency their intensity and their pattern of vibrations over - time. Only a limited number of all the possible phones are important to the understanding of speech, these are known as *phonemes*. English has 46 separate phonemes, a,e,i,o,u, consonant as p,m, k and d and blends of the two.

Syllables : When two or three phonemes are combined, it converts into a syllable. The syllable is the smallest unit of speech perception.

Morphemes : Morphemes are the smallest units of speech perception or language that convey meaning. These are root words that can stands alone. Morphemes can be prefixes, words, or suffixes. English has about 100,000 morphemes.

Words, Clauses and Sentences : Words are combined by the rules of grammer into clauses, and clauses are formed into sentences. A clause consists of a verb and its associated nouns, adjectives and so on. Clauses are the major units of perceived meaning in speech.

Theories of Language Development

The Learning Perspective : The Learning perspective argues that children imitate what they see and hear, and that children learn language by trying various combinations of sounds and being rewarded by their parents and others for those sounds that represent true language.

Skinner argued that adults shape the speech of children by reinforcing the babbling of infants that sound most like words.

The Nativist Perspective : The nativist perspective argues that humans are biologically programmed to gain knowledge. The main theorist associated with this perspective is *Noam Chomsky*.

Chomsky proposed that all humans have **language acquisition device** (LAD). The LAD contains knowledge of grammatical and syntactic rules common to all languages. The LAD also allows children to understand the rules of whatever language they are listening to. Chomsky also developed the concepts of transformational grammar, surface structure, and deep structure.

Transformational grammar is grammar that transforms a sentence. *Surface structures* are words that are actually written *Deep structure* is the underlying message or meaning of a sentence.

Interactionist Theory : Interactionists argue that language development is both biological and social. Interactionists argue that language learning is influenced by the desire of children to communicate with others. These theories focus mainly on the caregiver's attitudes and attentiveness to their children in order to promote productive language habits.

The Interactionists argue that "children are born with a powerful brain that matures slowly and predisposes them to acquire new understandings that they are motivated to share with others". The main theorist associated with interactionist theory is Lev Vygotsky. Interactionists focus on Vygotsky's model of collaborative learning. Collaborative learning is the idea that conversations with order people can help children both cognitively and linguistically.

Basic Components of Language

Phonological development : Phonology involves the rules about the structure and sequence of speech sound. It stands form shortly after birth to around one year. At around two months, the baby will engage in cooing, which mostly consists of vowel sounds. At around four months cooing turns into babbling which is the repetitive consonant-vowel combinations. Once the child enters the 8-12 month range the child engages in canonical babbling i.e. dada as well as variegated babbling. From 12-24 months, babies can recognise the correct pronunciation of familiar words. Babies will also use phonological strategies to simplify word pronunciation. Within the first year, two word utterances and two syllable words emerge. This period is often called the holophrastic stage of development, because one word conveys as much meaning as an entire phrase. For instance, the simple word "milk" can imply that the child is requesting milk.

Semantic development : Semantics consists of vocabulary and how concepts are expressed through words. From birth to one year, comprehension (the language we understand) develops before production (the language we use). There is about a 5 month lag in between the two. Babies have an innate preference to listen to their mother's voice. Babies can recognise familiar words and use preverbal gestures. Within the first 12-18 months semantic roles are expressed in one word speech including agent, object, location, possession, nonexistence and denial. Words are understood outside of routine games but the child still needs contextual support for lexical comprehension.

Grammatical development

Grammar involves two parts.

- The first **syntax** is the rules in which words are arranged into sentences
- The sentence, is the use of grammatical markers.

From 1-2 years, children start using telegraphic speech, which are two word combinations, for example 'wet diaper'. Brown (1973) observed that 75% of children's two-word utterances could be summarised in the existence of 11 semantic relations:

- Attributive: 'Big house'
- Agent-action: 'Daddy hit'
- Action-object: 'Hit ball'
- Agent-object: 'Daddy ball'

- Nominative: 'That ball'
- Demonstrative: 'There ball'
- Recurrence: 'More ball'
- Non-existence: 'All-gone ball'

Pragmatics development : Pragmatics involves the rules for appropriate and effective communication. Pragmatics involves three skills:

- using language for greeting, demanding etc.

- changing language for talking differently depending on who it is you are talking to;

- following rules such as turn taking, staying on topic.

Language Disorders

Mutism : Mutism refers to total absence of speech. There could be complete or partial mutism depending on the absence or decreased speech output. There could be children with hearing impairment.

Aphasia : Aphasia in children is the problems in understanding and using spoken language without any hearing loss, mental retardation, any other physical or emotional impairment in the use of language as a result of brain injury in the foetal period. These children have problems in understanding what is said to them and talking inspite of having normal sensory skills as hearing, vision, normal intelligence and good emotional adjustment.

Articulation Problems : Children learn to utter/articulate/pronounnce vowels like a/, i/, u/, o/, e, etc. first by 2-3 years and then acquire the consonants like p/t/k/ etc later. The normal production of speech sounds viz. vowels and consonants with the appropriate movements of tongue, lips, jaw and other oral structure is articulation.

Approx. age	Sound mastered
$2\frac{1}{2}$ years	b p m
$3\frac{1}{2}$ years	d t n g k n ng yj
$4\frac{1}{2}$ years	f l
$5\frac{1}{2}$ years	v s h
$6\frac{1}{2}$ years	s z r h

Omission Errors refer to omitting or deleting a particular sound in a word as in fi for fish.

Substitution Errors refer to substituting one sound for another as in tan for san (son).

Distoration Errors is where the sound is uttered nearer to the target sound but is not exactly the target sound for example fiyth for fish.

Addition Errors is where a new sound is added to sounds of a word as iskool for skuul (School).

Stuttering : It refers to the involuntary repetition, prolongation pauses or hesitation which the child struggles to end. Child has no conscious control over these blocks and hence they may be called involuntary.

Cluttering is a speech disorder characterised by an extremely rapid rate of speaking often with articulation errors.

THINKING

The mind is the idea while thinking processes of the brain involved in processing information such as when we form concepts, engage in problem solving, to reason and make decisions. Some limit the definition of thinking is as follows :

1. Thinking is the activity of human reason as a process of strengthening the relationship between stimulus and response :

2. Thinking is a reasonable working various views with the knowledge that has been stored in the mind long before the emergence of new knowledge.

3. Thinking can be interpreted to remember something, and questioned whether there is a relationship between what is intended.

4. Thinking is exploring substantive psychic awareness of human nature.

5. Thinking is processing information mentally or cognitively by rearranging the information from the environment and the symbols are stored in the memory of his past.

6. Thinking is a symbolic representation of some event train of ideas in a precise and careful that began with the problem.

7. Thinking is mental representations newly formed through the transformation of information by interaction attributes such as the assessment of mental abstraction logic, imagination and problem solving.

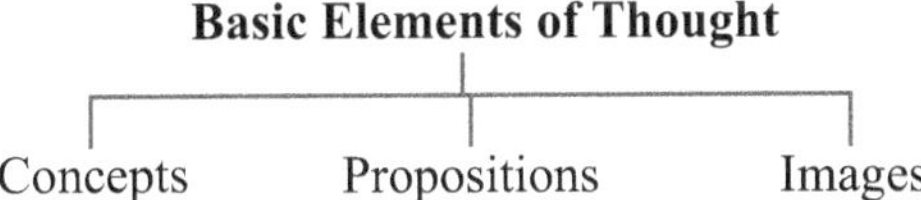

Concepts : Concepts are mental categories for objects, events, experiences, or ideas that are similar to one another in one or more respects. Concepts are closely related to **schemas**. Schemas are cognitive frameworks that represent our knowledge of and assumptions. Artificial concepts are ones that can be clearly defined by a set of rules or properties. Thus a tomato is a fruit because it possesses the properties established by botanists for this category.

In contrast, natural concepts are ones that have no fixed and readily specified set of defining features. They are fuzzy around the edges. For example, consider the following questions :

Is a pickle a vegetable ?

Is chess a sport ?

As you can readily see, these all relate to common concepts; sport, vegetable. But what specific attributes are necessary for inclusion in each concept.

Natural concepts are often based on prototypes. Prototypes are the best or cleasest examples of various objects or stimuli in the physical world.

Propositions : Propositions are sentences that relate one concept to another and can stand as separate assertions. For example, consider the following propositions.

Politicians are often self-serving. Concepts play a key role in politicians and self-serving.

Images : Images are mental pictures of the world. Mental images serve important purposes in thinking. People report using them for understanding verbal instructions, by converting the words into mental pictures of actions, for increasing motivation, by imagining successful performance, and for enhancing their own moods, by visualising positive events or scenes.

LANGUAGE AND THOUGHT

Do we think what we say or say what we think?

What is the precise relationship between language and thought? There are two possibilities :

1. Language Shapes Thought

One possibility, known as the linguistic relativity hypothesis, suggests that language actually shapes or determines thought (Whorf, 1956). According to this view, people who speak different languages may actually perceive the world in different ways because their thinking is determined by the words available to them. For example, Eskimos, who have many different words to describe snow, may actually perceive this aspect of the physical world differently from English speaking people who have only one word.

2. Thought Shapes Language

Other possibility, known as the linguistic relativity approach (Miura & Okamoto, 1989) suggests that thought shapes language. This position suggests that language merely reflects the way we think.

Exercise 1 : Previous Year Questions of CTET & STET

1. Four distinct stages of children's intellectual development are identified by *[CTET-2011-I]*
   (a) Kohlberg (b) Erikson
   (c) Skinner (d) Piaget

2. Which of the following is not a sign of an intelligent young child?
   (a) One who has the ability to cram long essays very quickly
   (b) One who has the ability to communicate fluently and appropriately
   (c) One who carries on thinking in an abstract manner
   (d) One who can adjust oneself in a new environment

3. Training in advance of normal maturation is generally *[RTET-2011-I]*
   (a) highly beneficial with respect to performance of the common skills
   (b) harmful from an overall point of view
   (c) beneficial from a long range point of view
   (d) beneficial or harmful depending on the method used in training.

4. Which of the following is not a characteristic of mental retardation ? *[RTET-2011-I]*
   (a) I.Q. between 25 to 70
   (b) Learning in a slow pace and unable to do the activities of daily routine
   (c) Poor adaptation with the environment
   (d) Poor interpersonal relations.

5. You find a student to be intelligent. You will *[UPTET-2011-I]*
   (a) remain pleased with him
   (b) not give him additional homework
   (c) motivate him so that he can make more progress
   (d) inform his parents about the fact that he is intelligent

6. Gardner formulated a list of seven Intelligencies, which among the following is not one of them: *[PTET-2011-I]*
   (a) Spatial Intelligence
   (b) Emotional Intelligence
   (c) Interpersonal Intelligence
   (d) Linguistic Intelligence

7. Which of the following is the true statement in reference to intelligence: *[PTET-2011-I]*
   (a) Intelligence is the ability to adjust
   (b) Intelligence is the ability to learn
   (c) Intelligence is the ability of Abstract Reasoning
   (d) All of these

8. Special education is related to *[PTET-2011-I]*
   (a) Educational for talented students
   (b) Educational programmes for disabled
   (c) Training programmes for Teachers
   (d) Training programme for retarded

9. Images, concepts, symbols & signs, language, muscle activities and brain functions are involved in: *[PTET-2011-II]*
   (a) adaptation
   (b) motor development
   (c) problem solving
   (d) thinking process

10. Adjusting in all stages and making happiness and usefulness to self and others is *[TNTET-2011-I]*
    (a) based on environment
    (b) based on mental health
    (c) based on attitude
    (d) based on economy

11. Individual learners differ from each other in *[CTET-2011-II]*
    (a) principles of growth and development
    (b) rate of development
    (c) sequence of development
    (d) general capacity for development

12. Every learner is unique means that *[CTET-2011-II]*
    (a) No two learners are alike in their abilities, interests and talents
    (b) Learners do not have any common qualities, nor do they share common goals
    (c) A common curriculum for all learners is not possible
    (d) It is impossible to develop the potential of learners in a heterogeneous class

13. A teacher wants the gifted children of her class to achieve their potential. Which of the following should she not do to achieve her objective? *[CTET-2011-II]*
    (a) Teach them to enjoy non-academic activities
    (b) Teach them to manage stress
    (c) Segregate them from their peers for special attention
    (d) Challenge them to enhance their creativity

14. Ability of knowing the meaning of problem, weaknesses and gaps related to environment is a characteristic of   *[RTET-2011-II]*
    (a) Gifted children
    (b) Average children
    (c) Creative children
    (d) None of them

15. Which of the following statements best shows the mental health of a person?   *[RTET-2011-II]*
    (a) Full expression, harmonization & goal direction
    (b) Lack of mental disorders
    (c) Free of personality disorders
    (d) All of these

16. In personality as well as intelligence heredity plays   *[RTET-2011-II]*
    (a) a nominal role
    (b) a great role
    (c) unpredictable role
    (d) fascinating role

17. Which of the following is the storehouse of our unfulfilled desires?   *[RTET-2011-II]*
    (a) Id
    (b) Ego
    (c) Superego
    (d) Id & Ego

18. Which of the following is not considered as a sign of 'being gifted'?   *[UPTET-2011-II]*
    (a) Creativity in ideas
    (b) Fighting with others
    (c) Novelty in expression
    (d) Curiosity

19. Schizophrenia is   *[TNTET-2011-II]*
    (a) psychoneuroses
    (b) personality behaviour disorder
    (c) psycroses
    (d) psychosomatic disorder

20. Individual attention is important in the teaching - learning process because   *[CTET-2012-I]*
    (a) teacher training programmes prescribe it
    (b) it offers better opportunities to teachers to discipline each learner
    (c) children develop at different rates and learn differently
    (d) learners always learn better in groups

21. A teacher makes use of a variety of tasks to cater to the different learning styles of her learners. She is influenced by   *[CTET-2012-I]*
    (a) Gardner's multiple intelligence theory
    (b) Vygotsky's socio-cultural theory
    (c) Piaget's cognitive development theory
    (d) Kohlberg's moral development theory

22. A school gives preference to girls while preparing students for a state level solo-song competition. This reflects   *[CTET-2012-I]*
    (a) pragmatic approach
    (b) progressive thinking
    (c) gender bias
    (d) global trends

23. Gifted students will realize their potential when   *[CTET-2012-II]*
    (a) they learn with other students
    (b) they are segregated from other students
    (c) they attend private coaching classes
    (d) they are tested frequently

24. 'Thinking is a mental activity in its cognitive aspect.'
    This statement is given by   *[UPTET-2014-I]*
    (a) Dewey
    (b) Guilford
    (c) Cruze
    (d) Ross

25. On the basis of Child Psychology, which statement is appropriate ?   *[UPTET-2014-I]*
    (a) All the children are homogeneous.
    (b) Some children are homogeneous.
    (c) Some children are unique.
    (d) Every child is unique.

26. Characteristics of good memory are   *[UPTET-2014-I]*
    (a) Rapid recall
    (b) Rapid recognition
    (c) Good retention
    (d) All of these

27. The concept of mental age is introduced by   *[UPTET-2014-I]*
    (a) Thorndike
    (b) Guilford
    (c) Spearman
    (d) Binet-Simon

28. Binet-Simson tests measure   *[UPTET-2014-I]*
    (a) General Intelligence
    (b) Specific Intelligence
    (c) Attitude
    (d) Aptitude

29. The children whose intelligence quotient (I.Q.) is above 140 will be categorized in category of   *[UPTET-2014-II]*
    (a) Moron
    (b) Dull
    (c) Average
    (d) Genius

30. "Creativity is a mental process to express the original outcomes." Who stated the above statement ?   *[UPTET-2014-II]*
    (a) Crow and Crow
    (b) James Drever
    (c) Ross
    (d) Skinner

31. What is the meaning of individual differences ?
    [UPTET-2014-II]
    (a) Differences in the physique of two individuals
    (b) Any two individual are not equal and similar in respect of physique, mental ability and emotional status.
    (c) Any two individuals are equal and similar in respect of physique and mental ability
    (d) None of these

32. The following are the marks obtained by seven students :
    40, 38, 36, 50, 51, 54, 23   *[UPTET-2014-II]*
    Median of the above will be
    (a) 36   (b) 50
    (c) 40   (d) 23

33. Interest has a relationship with
    [UPTET-2014-II]
    (a) Ability   (b) Attention
    (c) Both above   (d) None of these

34. "Thinking is mental activity in its cognitive aspect."
    Whose definition of thinking is this one ?
    [UPTET-2014-II]
    (a) Warren   (b) Ross
    (c) Valentine   (d) Skinner

35. Determinants of individual differences in human beings relate to: *[PTET-2014-I]*
    (a) Differences in Environment
    (b) Differences in Heredity
    (c) Interaction between Heredity & Environment
    (d) Both Heredity & Environment interacting separately

36. Gardner formulated a list of seven Intelligencies, Which among the following is not one of them:
    [PTET-2014-I]
    (a) Spatial Intelligence
    (b) Emotional Intelligence
    (c) Interpersonal Intelligence
    (d) Linguistic Intelligence

37. Which of the following is the true statement in reference to intelligence: *[PTET-2014-I]*
    (a) Intelligence is the ability to adjust
    (b) Intelligence is the ability to learn
    (c) Intelligence is the ability of Abstract Reasoning
    (d) All of these

38. Which of the following does not belong to the categories of Coping strategies that women commonly engaged in:
    [PTET-2014-I]
    (a) Acceptance   (b) Resistance
    (c) Revolution   (d) Adaptation

39. What should be the role of teacher in meeting the individual differences:
    [PTET-2014-I]
    (a) Try to know the abilities, interest & aptitude of individuals
    (b) Try to adjust the curriculum as per the needs of individuals
    (c) Both (a) & (b)   (d) None of these

40. If a child has mental age of 5 years & chronological age of 4 years than what will be the the the IQ of child: *[PTET-2014-I]*
    (a) 125   (b) 80
    (c) 120   (d) 100

41. A few students in your class are exceptionally bright, you will teach them:
    [PTET-2014-I]
    (a) Along with the class
    (b) Along with higher classes
    (c) By using Enriched programmes
    (d) Only when they want

42. Creative writing should be an activity planned for :
    [PTET-2014-I]
    (a) Only those children reading on grade level
    (b) Only those children spell & write cohesive sentences
    (c) Only those children who want to write for newspaper
    (d) All children

43. Which of the following are the External Factors affecting the interest of students in classroom :
    [PTET-2014-I]
    (a) Emotions & Sentiments
    (b) Culture & Training
    (c) Attitudes of students
    (d) Goals & motives

44. The thinking process involved in producing an idea or concept that is new, original and useful is termed as: *[PTET-2014-II]*
    (a) creativity   (b) innovation
    (c) intelligence   (d) synectics

45. Which one of theories of intelligence advocates the presence of general intelligence 'g' and specific intelligence 's'?
    [PTET-2014-II]
    (a) Anarchic theory
    (b) Guilford's theory of intellect
    (c) Spearman's two factor theory
    (d) Vernon's hierarchical theory

46. Ramesh and Ankit have the same IQ of 120. Ramesh is two year younger than Ankit. If Ankit is 12 years old, than the mental age of Ramesh is: *[PTET-2014-II]*
(a) 9 years   (b) 10 years
(c) 12 years   (d) 14 years

47. The gifted child: *[PTET-2014-II]*
(a) learns rapidly and easily
(b) retains what he/she has heard or read without much rote drill
(c) reasons things out
(d) attends to stimuli for a shorter period

48. The reading technique that would be employed to locate terms and references in an index or thesaurus is: *[PTET-2014-II]*
(a) key-reading   (b) re-reading
(c) scanning   (d) skimming

49. The two factor theory of intelligence was proposed by *[TNTET-2014-I]*
(a) Spearman   (b) Wechsler
(c) Piaget   (d) Binet

50. Intelligent Quotient is *[TNTET-2014-I]*
(a) $IQ = \dfrac{\text{Mental age (MA)}}{\text{Chronological age (CA)}} \times 100$

(b) $IQ = \dfrac{\text{Chronological age (CA)}}{\text{Mental age (MA)}}$

(c) $IQ = \dfrac{\text{Chronological age (CA)}}{\text{Mental age (MA)}} \times 100$

(d) $IQ = \dfrac{\text{Developmental age (DA)}}{\text{Chronological age (CA)}} \times 100$

51. "Child should be treated as child" - was said by *[TNTET-2014-I]*
(a) Roussoue   (b) Wechsler
(c) Binet   (d) Gagne

52. Average Intelligence Quotient is *[TNTET-2014-I]*
(a) 90–109   (b) 70–79
(c) 110–119   (d) 140–169

53. Logical thinking is *[TNTET-2014-I]*
(a) Convergent thinking
(b) Divergent thinking
(c) Creative thinking
(d) Exploring

54. Find the odd pair out *[TNTET-2014-II]*
(a) IQ test – Albert benae (b) Verbal test-vexler
(c) $I.Q. - \dfrac{C.A.}{M.A.} \times 100$
(a) (a) & (b) are correct
(b) (a) & (c) are correct
(c) (c) & (a) are correct
(d) (b) alone is correct

55. Name the test deviced by Thorndike in multiple theory of Intelligence *[TNTET-2014-II]*
(a) CVAD   (b) CAVD
(c) CDAV   (d) CDVA

56. The IQ correlation (r) of monozygotic twins, brought up in the same environment is *[TNTET-2014-II]*
(a) r = 0.087   (b) r = 0.0870
(c) r = 0.87   (d) r = 8.7

57. Intelligence attains its maximum level at the age of *[TNTET-2014-II]*
(a) 10 – 11   (b) 19 – 20
(c) 40 – 41   (d) 15 – 16

58. State the total number of creativity tests (Verbal + Non verbal) in Minnesota test of thinking *[TNTET-2014-II]*
(a) 10   (b) 14
(c) 12   (d) 19

59. The Chronological age of one child is 8, Mental age is 7 and another child is with (C).(A). 7 & M.(A). 8, find out their I.Q. Level. *[TNTET-2014-II]*
(a) 87.5 & 114.5   (b) 85.7 & 141.5
(c) 8.75 & 11.45   (d) 875 & 114

60. The following three aspects of intelligence are dealt by Sternberg's triarchic theory **except** *[CTET-July-2013-I]*
(a) componential   (b) social
(c) experiential   (d) contextual

61. Howard Gardner's theory of multiple intelligences emphasizes *[CTET-July-2013-I]*
(a) general intelligence
(b) common abilities required in school
(c) the unique abilities of each individual
(d) conditioning skills in students

62. The sounds th, ph, ch are *[CTET-July-2013-I]*
(a) Morphemes   (b) Graphemes
(c) Lexemese   (d) Phonemes

63. In order to avoid gender stereotyping in class, a teacher should *[CTET-July-2013-I]*
(a) try to put both boys and girls in non-traditional roles.
(b) appreciate students' good work by saying 'good girl' or 'good boy'.
(c) discourage girl from taking part in wrestling.
(d) encourage boys to take risk and be bold.

64. Schools should cater to Individual differences to *[CTET-July-2013-I]*
(a) narrow the gap between individual students.
(b) even out abilities and performance of students.
(c) understand why students are able or unable to learn.
(d) make individual students feel exclusive.

65. What kind of support can a school provide to address the individual differences in students ?
[CTET-July-2013-I]
(a) Follow a child-centered curriculum and provide multiple learning opportunities to students
(b) Apply every possible measure to remove the individual differences in students
(c) Refer slow learners to special schools
(d) Follow same level of curriculum for all students

66. "Readiness for learning" refers to
[CTET-July-2013-I]
(a) general ability level of students
(b) present cognitive level of students in the learning continuum
(c) satisfying nature of the act of learning
(d) Thorndike's Law of Readiness

67. Gifted students   *[CTET-July-2013-I]*
(a) Need support not ordinarily provided by the school
(b) Can manage their studies without a teacher
(c) Can be good models for other students
(d) Cannot be learning disabled

68. Giftedness is due to   *[CTET-July-2013-I]*
(a) Genetic makeup
(b) Environmental motivation
(c) Combination of (l) and (b)
(d) Psychosocial factors

69. Which of the following is appropriate for environment conducive to thinking and learning in children ?   *[CTET-July-2013-I]*
(a) Passive listening for long periods of time
(b) Home assignments given frequently
(c) Individual tasks done by the learners
(d) allowing students to take some decisions about what to learn and how to learn

70. Seema is desperate to score A+ grade in an examination. As she enters the examination hall and the examination begins, she becomes extremely nervous. Her feet go cold, her heart starts pounding and she is unable to answer properly. The primary reason for this is that
[CTET-July-2013-I]
(a) she may not be very confident about her preparation
(b) she may be thinking excessively about the result of this examination
(c) invigilator teacher on duty may be her class teacher and she is of very strict nature
(d) she may not be able to deal with sudden emotional outburst

71. Which one of the following is a critique of theory of multiple intelligences ?   *[CTET-July-2013-II]*
(a) Multiple intelligence are only the 'talents' present in intelligence as a whole.
(b) Multiple intdligence provides students to discover their propensities.
(c) It overemphasises practical intelligence.
(d) It cannot be supported by empirical evidence at all.

72. In a culturally and linguistically diverse classroom, before deciding whether a student comes under special education category, a teacher should

[CTET-July-2013-II]
(a) Not involve parents as parents have their own work
(b) Evaluate student on her/his mother language to establish disability
(c) Use specialised psychologists
(d) Segregate the child to neutralise environmental factor.

73. Gifted students are   *[CTET-July-2013-II]*
(a) Convergent thinkers
(b) Divergent thinkers
(c) Extrovert
(d) Very hard working

74. The shaded area represent students in a normal distribution who fall

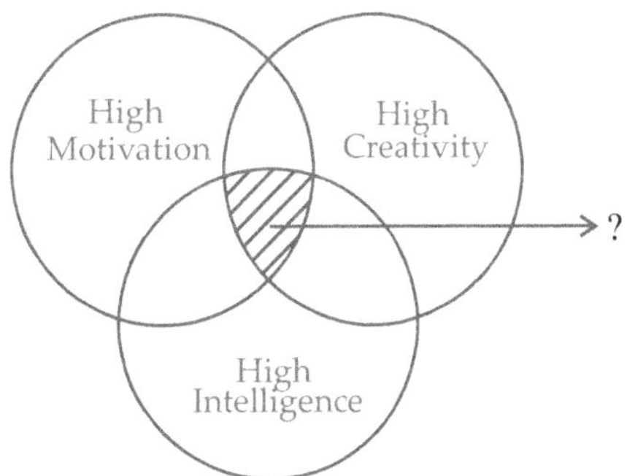

[CTET-July-2013-II]
(a) At s = 0   (b) Between 2 -3
(c) After 3   (d) Between -2

75. Intelligence theory incorporates the mental processes involved in intelligence (i.e. meta-components) and the varied forms that intelligence can take (i.e. creative intelligence)
[CTET-July-2013-II]
(a) Spearman's 'g' factor
(b) Sternberg's triarchic theory of intelligence
(c) Savant theory of intelligence
(d) Thurstone's primary mental abilities

76. Following are the critical views about the 'Theory of Multiple Intelligences', *except.*
[CTET-Feb.-2014-I]
(a) it is not research-based
(b) different intelligences demand different methods for different students
(c) gifted students usually excel in a single domain
(d) it lacks of empirical support

77. 'Theory of Multiple Intelligences' cannot be legitimized as it   *[CTET-Feb.-2014-I]*
(a) it is not possible to measure different intelligences as there are no specific tests
(b) does not place equal importance on all seven intelligences
(c) is based only on sound empirical studies done by Abraham Maslow throughout his life
(d) is not compatible with general intelligence 'g', which is most important.

78. The individual differences of students in a classroom are   *[CTET-Feb.-2014-I]*
(a) disadvantageous as teachers need to control a diverse classroom
(b) detrimental as they lead to student-student conflicts
(c) inexpedient as they reduce the speed of the curriculum transaction to the level of the slowest student
(d) advantageous as they lead teacher to explore a wider pool of cognitive structures

79. Which of the following is true about gifted learners?   *[CTET-Feb.-2014-I]*
(a) They make everyone else smarter and are essential for collaborative learning
(b) They always lead others and assume extra responsibility in the classroom
(c) They may achieve lower grades due to their heightened sensitivity
(d) Their importance is primarily due to their brainpower

80. An eleven-year-old child's score on Stanford-Binet Intelligence Scale is 130. By assuming m = 100 and s = 15 in a normal probability curve, calculate the percentage of 11-year-old children this child has scored better than.   *[CTET-Feb.-2014-II]*
(a) 98%   (b) 88%
(c) 78%   (d) 80%

81. Which of the following observations supports Howard Gardner's theory of multiple intelligences?   *[CTET-Feb.-2014-II]*
(a) Damage to one part of the brain affects only a particular ability sparing others
(b) Intelligence is an interaction of analytical, creative and practical intelligences

(c) Different intelligences are hierarchical in nature
(d) Teachers should follow one specific theory of educational innovation at the time of designing instruction

82. Shuttering problems in students can be dealt by applying which of the following methods?   *[CTET-Feb.-2014-II]*
(a) Dictated speech
(b) Prolonged speech
(c) Pragmatic speech
(d) Protracted speech

83. Which one of the following is an appropriate assignment for a gifted student?   *[CTET-Feb.-2014-II]*
(a) Many more exercises of the same type in comparison to other students
(b) Asking him/her to tutor the peers to channelize the energy and keep him/her busy
(c) Create a prototype of a new Science book based on different themes
(d) Letting him/her finish the textbook on his/her own before the entire class

84. The following skills are involved in emotional intelligence, except   *[CTET-Feb.-2014-II]*
(a) awareness of emotions
(b) management of emotions
(c) criticism of emotions
(d) amicable relation with class fellows

85. Which one of the following is a form of Sternberg's Triarchic Theory of Intelligence ?
[CTET-Sep.-2014-I]
(a) Practical Intelligence
(b) Experimental Intelligence
(c) Resourceful Intelligence
(d) Mathematical Intelligence

86. Who developed the first intelligence test ?
[CTET-Sep.-2014-I]
(a) David Wechsler
(b) Alfred Binet
(c) Charles Edward Spearman
(d) Robert Sternberg

87. Gifted students may be asked to spend more time on questions dealing with   *[CTET-Sep.-2014-I]*
(a) remembering   (b) understanding
(c) creating   (d) analyzing

88. Which of the following skills is associated with emotional intelligence ?   *[CTET-Sep.-2014-I]*
(a) Memorising
(b) Motor processing
(c) Envisaging
(d) Empathising

89. In context of 'theory of multiple intelligences', which one of the following intelligences is required for an airforce pilot ? *[CTET-Sep.-2014-II]*
(a) Interpersonal (b) Linguistic
(c) Kinesthetic (d) Intrapersonal

90. The factor 'g' in the Spearman definition of intelligence stands for *[CTET-Sep.-2014-II]*
(a) genetic intelligence
(b) generative intelligence
(c) general intelligence
(d) global intelligence

91. Renzulli is known for his _________ definition of giftedness. *[CTET-Sep.-2014-II]*
(a) four-tiered (b) four-level
(c) three-circle (d) three-sided

92. For gifted students, *[CTET-Sep.-2014-II]*
(a) it is safe to consider aptitude as a skill
(b) there is no need to monitor progress
(c) the teacher should adapt as the student changes
(d) the teacher should initiate and lead problem solving

93. Emotional intelligence may be associated with which of theory of Multiple Intelligence ? *[CTET-Sep.-2014-II]*
(a) Intrapersonal and interpersonal intelligences
(b) Naturalist intelligence
(c) Visual-spatial intelligence
(d) Existential intelligence

94. Out-of-the-box' thinking is related to *[CTET-Feb.-2015-I]*
(a) Consistent Thinking
(b) Memory-based Thinking
(c) Divergent Thinking
(d) Convergent Thinking

95. Aarjav says that language development is influenced by one's innate predisposition while Sonali feels that it is becaue of the environment. This discussion between Aarjav and Sonali is about *[CTET-Feb.-2015-I]*
(a) Critical and Sensitive feeling
(b) Stability and Instability argument
(c) Continuous and Discontinuous learning
(d) Nature and Nurture debate

96. A teacher, labelled the head of a committee, as 'chairperson' instead of 'chairman'. It indicates that the teacher *[CTET-Feb.-2015-I]*
(a) follows a more acceptable term
(b) has a good command of language
(c) is using a gender-free language
(d) has gender bias

97. We all differ in terms of our intelligence, motivation, interest, etc. This principle refers to *[CTET-Feb.-2015-I]*
(a) Individual difference
(b) Theories of Intelligence
(c) Heredity
(d) Environment

98. Which of these does not imply practical intelligence in the Triarchic theory ? *[CTET-Feb.-2015-I]*
(a) Reshaping the environment
(b) Thinking practically about oneself only
(c) Choosing an environment in which you can succeed
(d) Adapting to the environment

99. According to Gardner's theory of multiple intelligence, the factor that would contribute most for being a 'self-aware' individual would be *[CTET-Feb.-2015-II]*
(a) Intrapersonal (b) Musical
(c) Spiritual (d) Linguistic

100. A lot of debate surrounds whether girls and boys have specific sets of abilities due to their genetic materials. Which one of the following are you most likely to agree with in this context ? *[CTET-Feb.-2015-II]*
(a) Boys cannot be caring since they are born that way.
(b) Girls are socialized to be caring while boys are discouraged to show emotions such as crying.
(c) After puberty boys and girls cannot play with each other since their interests are complete opposites.
(d) All girls have inherent talent for arts while boys are genetically programmed to be better at aggressive sports.

101. Children are most creative when they participate in an activity *[CTET-Feb.-2016-I]*
(a) to escape their teacher's scolding.
(b) under stress to do well in front of others.
(c) out of interest.
(d) for rewards.

102. Mistakes and errors made by students *[CTET-Feb.-2016-I]*
(a) are a wonderful opportunity to label children as 'weak' or 'outstanding'.
(b) are indicative of the failure of the teacher and the students.
(c) should be seen as opportunities to understand their thinking.
(d) should be severely dealt with.

103. Why do individuals differ from one another?
[CTET-Feb.-2016-I]
(a) Because of the impact of the environment
(b) Due to the inborn characteristics
(c) Due to the interplay between heredity and environment
(d) Because each individual has received a different gene set from his/her'parents.

104. A child says, "Clothes dry faster in the Sun." She is showing an understanding of
[CTET-Feb.-2016-I]
(a) symbolic thought.
(b) egocentric thinking.
(c) cause and effect.
(d) reversible thinking.

105. Intelligence is   *[CTET-Feb.-2016-I]*
(a) a set of capabilities.
(b) a singular and generic concept.
(c) the ability to imitate others.
(d) a specific ability.

106. Which one of the following illustrates a person with linguistic intelligence?*[CTET-Feb.-2016-II]*
(a) Sensitivity to the meaning and order of words and the varied uses of language
(b) The ability to handle long chains of reasoning.
(c) Sensitivity to pitch, melody and tone.
(d) The ability to notice and make distinctions among others.

107. Language ...... thought processes.
[CTET-Feb.-2016-II]
(a) does not influence the
(b) cannot determine the
(c) totally governs our
(d) has an influence on our

108. There are vast differences among the students. Of these, a teacher needs to be sensitive to
[CTET-Feb.-2016-II]
I. differences based on cognitive capabilities and learning levels.
II. differences based on diversity of language, caste, gender, religion, community.
Select the correct answer using the code given below.
(a) Only I
(b) Neither I nor II
(c) Only II
(d) Both I and II

109. To cater to individual differences in his classroom, a teacher should :
[CTET-Sept.-2016-I]
(a) have uniform and standard ways of teaching and assessment
(b) segregate and label children based on their marks
(c) engage in a dialogue with students and value their perspectives
(d) impose strict rules upon his students

110. Which of the following is a characteristic of a gifted learner?   *[CTET-Sept.-2016-I]*
(a) He gets aggressive and frustrated.
(b) He can feel understimulated and bored if the class activities are not challenging enough.
(c) He is highly temperamental.
(d) He engages in ritualistic behaviour like hand flapping, rocking, etc.

111. A child sees a crow flying past the window and says, "A bird." What does this suggest about the child's thinking?
A. The child has previously stored memories.
B. The child has developed the concept of a 'bird'.
C. The child has developed some tools of language to communicate her experience.
[CTET-Sept.-2016-I]
(a) A and B
(b) B and C
(c) A, B and C
(d) Only B

112. Howard Gardner's theory of Multiple Intelligence (MI) suggests that :
[CTET-Sept.-2016-I]
(a) every child should be taught every subject in eight different ways in order to develop all of the intelligences
(b) intelligence is solely determined by IQ tests
(c) teachers should use MI as a framework for devising alternative ways to teach the subject matter
(d) ability is destiny and does not change over a period of time

113. A teacher can address diversity in her class by :
[CTET-Sept.-2016-II]
A. accepting and valuing differences
B. using socio-cultural background of children as a pedagogic resource
C. accommodating different learning styles
D. giving standard instruction and setting uniform benchmarks for performance
Select the **correct** answer using the code given below.
(a) A, B and C
(b) A, B, C and D
(c) A, B and D
(d) B, C and D

114. Gifted children are best catered to by educational programmes that :   *[CTET-Sept.-2016-II]*
(a) control their aggressive behaviour
(b) make use of gifts and rewards to motivate them to perform according to minimum standards of learning
(c) emphasize mastery of knowledge by recall
(d) stimulate their thinking and give them opportunities to engage in divergent thinking

115. Two students read the same passage yet construct entirely different interpretations of its meaning. Which of the following is true about them? *[CTET-Sept.-2016-II]*

    (a) It is not possible because learning is not meaning-making.

    (b) It is not possible and the students need to re-read the passage.

    (c) It is possible because the teacher has not explained the passage.

    (d) It is possible because different factors affect learning of individuals in varied ways.

116. Knowing the naive conceptions that students bring to the classroom : *[CTET-Sept.-2016-II]*

    (a) hampers the teacher's planning and teaching

    (b) pulls down the teacher's morale since it increases his work

    (c) does not serve any purpose of the teacher

    (d) helps the teacher to plan teaching more meaningfully

117. Match the following in the light of Howard Gardner's theory of Multiple Intelligence : *[CTET-Sept.-2016-II]*

Type of Intelligence		End State
(d)	Musical	(i) Therapist
(a)	Linguistic	(ii) Poet
(b)	Interpersonal	(iii) Athlete
(c)	Spatial	(iv) Violinist
		(v) Sculptor

	A	B	C	D
(a)	(iv)	(ii)	(v)	(iii)
(b)	(v)	(ii)	(vi)	(i)
(c)	(ii)	(iv)	(i)	(v)
(d)	(iv)	(ii)	(i)	(v)

118. The formula for calculating IQ is *[UPTET-2017-I]*

    (a) Mental age × Chronological age

    (b) $\dfrac{\text{Chronological age}}{\text{Mental age}}$

    (c) $\dfrac{\text{Mental age}}{\text{Chronological age}} \times 100$

    (d) Chronological age + Mental age

119. Fluid mosaic model of intelligence was proposed by *[UPTET-2017-I]*

    (a) Cattell   (b) Thorndike

    (c) Vernon   (d) Skinner

120. Brainstorming model of teaching is used to improve which of the following? *[UPTET-2017-I]*

    (a) Understanding   (b) Application

    (c) Creativity   (d) Problem solving

121. Goleman is associated with which of the following? *[UPTET-2017-I]*

    (a) Social intelligence

    (b) Emotional intelligence

    (c) Spiritual intelligence

    (d) General intelligence

122. The lowest level of cognitive achievement is *[UPTET-2017-I]*

    (a) knowledge   (b) understanding

    (c) application   (d) analysis

123. "Attention is the concentration of consciousness upon one object rather than upon another." This statements is given by *[UPTET-2017-I]*

    (a) Dumville   (b) Ross

    (c) Munn   (d) McDougall

124. Which test is propounded by Dr. S. Jalota in Hindi for the children of 12 to 16 years? *[UPTET-2017-I]*

    (a) Non-verbal intelligence test

    (b) General mental ability test

    (c) Army alpha test

    (d) Picture drawing test

125. Who propounded the two-factor theory of intelligence? *[UPTET-2017-I]*

    (a) Thorndike   (b) Spearman

    (c) Vernon   (d) Stern

126. Intellectual resource among the following *[APTET-May.-2018-I]*

    (a) Scientists   (b) Water falls

    (c) Farm fields   (d) Zoo

127. According to this psychologist intelligent people may have intelligent ancestors *[APTET-May.-2018-II]*

    (a) Galton   (b) Watson

    (c) Boring   (d) Woodworth

128. The defence mechanism in which a student who failed in the examination threw away his books *[APTET-May.-2018-II]*

    (a) Rationalization

    (b) Reaction formation

    (c) Displacement

    (d) Regression

129. The understanding of a person about himself and the qualities possessed by him is called *[APTET-May.-2018-II]*

    (a) Self Skill   (b) Self Respect

    (c) Self Concept   (d) Self Attitude

Answer Key

1. (d)	16. (a)	31. (b)	46. (c)	61. (c)	76. (c)	91. (c)	106. (a)	121. (b)
2. (a)	17. (a)	32. (c)	47. (c)	62. (d)	77. (a)	92. (c)	107. (d)	122. (a)
3. (d)	18. (b)	33. (b)	48. (d)	63. (a)	78. (d)	93. (a)	108. (d)	123. (a)
4. (d)	19. (d)	34. (b)	49. (a)	64. (c)	79. (c)	94. (c)	109. (c)	124. (b)
5. (c)	20. (c)	35. (c)	50. (a)	65. (a)	80. (a)	95. (d)	110. (b)	125. (b)
6. (b)	21. (a)	36. (b)	51. (b)	66. (b)	81. (a)	96. (c)	111. (a)	126. (a)
7. (d)	22. (c)	37. (d)	52. (a)	67. (a)	82. (b)	97. (a)	112. (c)	127. (c)
8. (b)	23. (a)	38. (c)	53. (d)	68. (c)	83 (d)	98. (b)	113. (a)	128. (d)
9. (d)	24. (d)	39. (c)	54. (a)	69. (d)	84. (c)	99. (a)	114. (d)	129. (c)
10. (b)	25. (d)	40. (a)	55. (b)	70. (d)	85. (a)	100. (b)	115. (d)	
11. (b)	26. (d)	41. (c)	56. (c)	71. (a)	86. (b)	101. (c)	116. (d)	
12. (a)	27. (d)	42. (d)	57. (d)	72 (b)	87. (c)	102. (c)	117. (d)	
13. (c)	28. (a)	43. (b)	58. (a)	73. (b)	88. (d)	103. (c)	118. (c)	
14. (c)	29. (d)	44. (a)	59. (a)	74. (c)	89. (c)	104. (c)	119. (a)	
15. (a)	30. (a)	45. (c)	60. (b)	75. (b)	90. (c)	105. (c)	120. (c)	

60. (b) Sternberg's three types of intelligence, called the Triarchic Theory, are:
- **Analytical, or componential, intelligence:** This type of intelligence allows a person to process information effectively and think abstractly. Most tests measure this type of intelligence.
- **Creative, or experiential, intelligence:** This type of intelligence allows a person to come up with new ideas. People high in creative intelligence can find connections between concepts that seem different and distinct.
- **Practical, or contextual, intelligence:** This type of intelligence allows a person to find practical solutions to real problems. People with this type of intelligence are often considered "street smart".

61. (c) Howard Gardner's theory of multiple intelligences emphasizes the unique abilities of each individual. Gardner's focus on human potential lies in the fact that people have a unique blend of capabilities and skills (intelligences).

62. (d) A phoneme is a basic unit of a language's phonology, which is combined with other phonemes to form meaningful units such as words or morphemes. Hence, The sounds **th, ph, ch** are phonemes.

63. (a) In order to avoid gender stereotyping in class, a teacher should try to put both boys and girls in non-traditional roles because quality, retention and achievement are essential elements of an education strategy designed to ensure that boys and girls maximize their full potential. As the Gender Equality in Education Framework indicates, that boys and girls receive the maximum benefit from their education.

64. (c) The aim of education is to enable each student to attain all-round development. To achieve this, students should be provided with suitable assistance and guidance in accordance with their abilities and learning needs. In view of these, catering for individual differences is intended neither to narrow the gap between individuals nor to even out their abilities and performance. It should aim for understanding why students are able or unable to learn well and finding appropriate ways to help them learn better.

65. (a) To address the needs of students, teachers should provide them with a variety of learning opportunities for effective learning, such as using diversified resources rather than focusing only on textbooks, and making use of a spectrum of intelligences and multi-

sensory experiences to tap the different potential of students. Schools can adopt different modes of assessment to find out the strengths and weaknesses of students before deciding on the appropriate curriculum, and learning and teaching strategies for them.

66. (b) Readiness implies a degree of concentration and eagerness. Individuals learn best when they are physically, mentally and emotionally ready to learn, and do not learn well if they see no reason for learning.

67. (a) Gifted students need support that is not provided by the schools to enhance their natural skills.

68. (c) Gifted children, sometimes referred to as children with intellectual giftedness are children with a significantly above average intellectual ability. This above average giftedness can be generic or acquired.

69. (d) Allowing students to take some decisions about what to learn and how to learn is appropriate for environment conducive to thinking and learning in children.

70. (d) The primary reason for Seema that she may not be able to deal with sudden emotional outburst.

71. (a) Gardner's theory has come under criticism from both psychologists and educators. These critics argue that Gardner's definition of intelligence is too broad, and that his eight different "intelligences" simply represent talents, personality traits and abilities. Gardner's theory also suffers from a lack of supporting empirical research.

72. (b) In a culturally and linguistically diverse classroom, before deciding whether a student comes under special education category, a teacher should evaluate student on her/his mother language to establish disability.

73. (b) Gifted children creative problem solving likely stems from their divergent thinking and ability to view things differently.

75. (b) Sternberg's Triarchic Theory is an important effort to synthesize the various theories of intelligence.

    Metacomponents: Control, monitor and evaluate cognitive processing. Used to analyze problems and pick a strategy for solving them. They decide what to do and the performance components actually do it.

    Creative Intelligence: This involves insights, synthesis and the ability to react to novel situations and stimuli. Thus he considers the experiential aspect of intelligence and reflects how an individual connects the internal world to external reality.

76. (c) The theory of multiple intelligences proposed by Howard psychologist Howard Gardner. He proposed eight intelligences. His theory has come under criticism from both psychologists and educators. Gifted students usually excel in a single domain is a view of Gardner's theory, got a criticism.

77. (a) Gardner's theory of Multiple Intelligences has eight different 'intelligences' simply represent talents, personality traits and abilities. There is a lack of specific tests to measure these intelligences.

78. (d) All individuals differ from one another not only in height, weight, colour, appearance, speed of reaction but also in behaviour. The individual differences of students in a classroom are advantageous as they lead teacher to explore a wider pool of cognitive structures and create better academic results.

79. (c) Gifted learners are those who are not only academically talented but also in all the other fields show remarkable performance. Gifted learners demonstrate high level of sensitivity, sometimes they achieve lower grades due to high sensuality.

80. (a) IQ = 130

    Assuming $\mu = 100$

    $= 13$

Normal curve and the Stanford Binet 1 Q scores

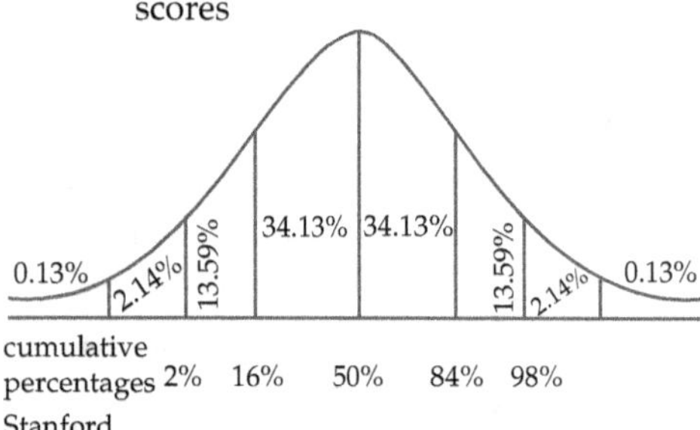

81. (a) Howard Gardner has defined Bodily-kinesthetic intelligence. According to this theory, intelligence is a potential specific connection between specific stimuli and responses. This theory supports the belief that mental and physical activity are related. So damage to one part of the brain affects only related particular ability sparing others.

82. (b) Stuttering is defined as any disturbance in the flow and time patterning of speech. The Prolonged speech is the most effective approach for fluency shaping treatment.

83. (d) Intellectually gifted children are those who have scored very high on standardised lists and usually excel in school. They are frequently very high skilled verbally and have outstanding memories and literacy ability. So, to create a prototype of a new science book will be an appropriate assignment for a gifted student.

84. (c)

Hence, criticism of emotions is not the part of EQ.

101. (c) A learner's interest is directly linked with his/her level of motivation. On the other hand, motivation assists a child to be more imaginative. Hence, children become creative when they participate in an activity of their interest.

102. (c) **"The trial and error" is a theory of learning** which was given by Thorndike, which says that individuals learn various things by their inaccuracy. Hence, inaccuracies and errors made by learners must be seen as a chance to recognize their philosophy by a teacher.

103. (c) The interaction between heredity and environment are significant parts that distinguish between individuals. Heredity involves biological aspect within an individual, and environment is associated with the external or social factors of a person.

104. (c) Children at the stage of sensorimotor, according to Piaget's cognitive development theory, start recognizing cause and effect relationships i.e. the action and the subsequent reaction that follows.

105. (c) Intelligence means an ability to attain knowledge and skills and apply them at various occasions to solve he problems by a child. Vygotsky defined intelligence as an ability to acquire learning through instructions.

106. (a) Linguistic intelligence is considered when a child acquires reading, writing, understanding of the language aspects in the best way which comes with effective learning of a language.

107. (d) Language has an influence on our thought process is the right definition of language as one expresses ones thoughts though words and expressions in the language they are proficient in.

108. (d) A teacher needs to evaluate all the aspects about the children before implementing any method to teach effectively to the students. Teacher should understand connectivity, religion, caste and community they belong to. It becomes easy for a teacher to mould her methodology accordingly.

109. (c) Assessment is done only once in a year to analyze the overall progress of a child.

118. (c) The concept of IQ was invented in the year 1904 by Alfred Binet. The equation used to calculate a person's IQ score is Mental Age / Chronological Age x 100.

120. (c) Brainstorming is a group creativity technique by which efforts are made to find a conclusion for a specific problem by gathering a list of ideas spontaneously contributed by its members.

121. (b) Emotional intelligence (EI), also known as Emotional quotient (EQ) and Emotional Intelligence Quotient (EIQ),[1] is the capability of individuals to recognize their own emotions and those of others, discern between different feelings and label them appropriately, use emotional information to guide thinking and behavior, and manage and/or adjust emotions to adapt to environments or achieve one's goal(s)

122.(a) There are six major categories of cognitive an processes, starting from the simplest to the most complex

o Knowledge

o Comprehension

o Application

o Analysis

o Synthesis

o Evaluation

124. (b) General mental ability (GMA) is a term used to describe the level at which an individual learns, understands instructions, and solves problems. Tests of general mental ability include scales that measure specific constructs such as verbal, mechanical, numerical, social, and spatial ability.

125. (b) Charles Spearman developed his two-factor theory of intelligence using factor analysis. His research not only led him to develop the concept of the g factorof general intelligence, but also the s factor of specific intellectual abilities.

126. (a) Scientists are the intellectual resources amongst the options rest are natural resources.

Exercise 2 : Test Yourself

1. Multilingual character of Indian society should be seen as
   - (a) Hindrance in teaching-learning process
   - (b) A resource for enrichment of school life
   - (c) A challenge to teacher's capacity to motivate students to learn
   - (d) A factor that makes school life a complex experience for the learners

2. The differences among individuals that distinguish them from one another and make each one a unique individual are denoted by the term ....
   - (a) Individual difference
   - (b) Heredity
   - (c) Environment
   - (d) Personality

3. An important feature of creative thinking is:
   - (a) Divergent thinking
   - (b) Convergent thinking
   - (c) Operational thinking
   - (d) Autistic thinking

4. Ramola who does not talk much at home, talks a lot at school. It shows that
   - (a) the school provides opport-unities to children to talk a lot
   - (b) teachers demand that children should talk a lot at school
   - (c) she does not like her home at all
   - (d) her thoughts get acknowledged at school

5. Which of the following is not an example of closed stratification system?
   - (a) slavery system
   - (b) Caste system
   - (c) Class system
   - (d) All of above are closed stratifica-tion systems

6. You have been told to accommodate two mentally retarded children in your class. You will
   - (a) Refuse to accept them as your students
   - (b) Tell the Principal to accommo-date them in another class that is exclusively meant for mentally retarded children
   - (c) Learn techniques to teach such students and accept them as a part of your class
   - (d) None of these

7. Intelligence testing is useful for knowing
   - (a) Individual difference
   - (b) Mental retardation
   - (c) Educational backwardness
   - (d) All of these

8. Non-verbal test of intelligence is suitable for
   - (a) Deaf and dumb
   - (b) Illiterates
   - (c) Backward children
   - (d) All of these

9. Conventional tests of intelligence measure—
   - (a) Divergent thinking
   - (b) Convergent thinking
   - (c) Both (A) and (B)
   - (d) Neither (A) nor (B)

10. Who is the father of "Theory of Multiple Intelligence"?
    - (a) Gardner
    - (b) Vygotsky
    - (c) Bruner
    - (d) Piaget

11. ...... is the ratio of mental age to the chronological age multiplied by 100.
    - (a) Emotional quotient
    - (b) Intelligence quotient
    - (c) Both
    - (d) None of these

12. Name the psychologist responsible for developing the tri-part theory of intelligence.
    - (a) Daniel Goleman
    - (b) Howard Gardner
    - (c) Robert Sternberg
    - (d) Sigmund Freud

13. Gender-role identity is the image each individual has of himself or herself as
    - (a) masculine or feminine
    - (b) positive or negative
    - (c) goal-directed or social-emotional
    - (d) cultural or stereotypical

14. The work of gifted students is
    - (a) Original
    - (b) extremely advanced for their age
    - (c) potentially of lasting importance
    - (d) All of the above

15. Teaching methods for gifted students should encourage
    (a) abstract thinking
    (b) convergent thinking
    (c) creativity
    (d) both abstract and creative thinking

16. Spearman's two-factor theory was extended into multi-factor theory by
    (a) Thorndike   (b) Thurstone
    (c) Pavlov   (d) Skinner

17. Guilford and his associates proposed
    (a) the theory of Structure of Intellects
    (b) the theory of abstract thinking
    (c) the theory of associative memory
    (d) the theory of space visualization

18. One of the primary mental abilities of the Group factor theory was
    (a) Space visualization
    (b) Divergent thinking
    (c) General Knowledge
    (d) Mechanical ability

19. Fluid intelligence depends on
    (a) Neurological development
    (b) Physical development
    (c) Social development
    (d) Aesthetic development

20. The concept of intelligence quotient, or IQ, was added after the test of ------- was brought to the US and revised at Stanford University
    (a) Binet   (b) Coleman
    (c) Collins   (d) Kohlberg

21. Journal writers, religious gurus and psychologists are examples of people with strength in which intelligence.
    (a) Inter-personal
    (b) Intrapersonal
    (c) Linguistic
    (d) Naturalist

22. Which of the following is Guilford's theory of Intelligence?
    (a) Two dimensional theory
    (b) Three dimensional theory
    (c) Multi dimensional theory
    (d) Hierachical theory

23. Individual differences have been discussed in Plato's
    (a) Republic   (b) The mind
    (c) State   (d) None of these

24. Which is Thorndike's theory about the nature of intelligence?
    (a) Uni-factor theory
    (b) Group factor theory
    (c) Multifactor theory
    (d) Two factor theory

25. The Stanford - Binet intelligence scale
    (a) was specifically designed to test adult intelligence
    (b) provides separate score for performance
    (c) is completely culturally fair, in the children of different cultures do just as well as children in this culture
    (d) assumes that intellectual ability in childhood improves as age increases.

26. Spearman's theory of intelligence explained intelligence in term of general intelligence and ________ abilities.
    (a) reasoning   (b) particular
    (c) specific   (d) regular

27. A child in school is called a problem child when
    (a) He is able to solve the problems of other children
    (b) He suggests useful approaches to teachers when they are explaining any problem
    (c) He behaves such that it becomes a problem for the teacher to understand him
    (d) He is very resourceful in suggesting good problems for the class to workout

28. Match List I with List II and select the correct answer using the codes given below the lists.

List I (1Q)		List II (Descriptions)	
A.	25-39	1	Profoundly mentally retarded
B.	40-54	2	Severely mentally retarded
C.	70-84	3	Moderately mentally retarded
D.	110-119	4	Border line
		5	Average
		6	Bright normal
		7	Superior

    (a) A-1; B-2; C-3; D-5
    (b) A-1; B-3; C-5; D-7
    (c) A-2; B-3; C-4; D-6
    (d) A-2; B-4; C-5; D-7

29. In the present intelligence classification system, the former category of Moron would now be included with in –
    (a) Profoundly retarded
    (b) Educable
    (c) Severely retarded
    (d) Mildly retarded

30. What are some characteristics of gifted children?
    (a) The enjoy puzzles, handwriting & other closed-ended, skill-based materials
    (b) They prefer to work in groups & tend to have well developed social skills
    (c) They are energized by predictable routine & structural curriculum
    (d) They demonstrate advanced language ability & very sophisticated vocabulary

31. Which of the following sentences are true in the context of Gifted child,
    1. They readily see cause-effect relationships
    2. They often display a questioning attitude and seek information for its own sake as much as for its usefulness
    3. They often display intellectual playfulness and like to fantasize and imagine
    4. They are not sensitive to beauty but are attracted to aesthetic values
    (a) only 2 and 3
    (b) only 1, 2 and 3
    (c) only 2, 3 and 4
    (d) all of the above

32. Which one of the following is not among the major Interventions for promoting education among backward minorities?
    1. Area Intensive Programme for Educational Backward Minorities
    2. Modernization of Madarsas and Maktabs
    3. Community Polytechnics
    4. Coaching Classes for Competitive Examinations
    (a) only 2 and 3
    (b) only 1, 2 and 3
    (c) only 3 and 4
    (d) all of the above

33. Which of the following intelligence 'gives one the ability to manipulate and create mental images in order to solve problems and is not limited to visual domains?'
    (a) Spatial Intelligence
    (b) Linguistic Intelligence
    (c) Musical Intelligence
    (d) Bodily-Kinesthetic Intelligence

34. The intelligence is based upon Heredity. This Principle is proposed by –
    (a) Yerks
    (b) Skinner
    (c) Binet
    (d) Spearman

35. Verbal Intelligence tests are the better option for –
    (a) Literate persons
    (b) Illiterate persons
    (c) Small children
    (d) Special children

36. For testing the intelligence of literate persons in group, you can use –
    (a) Verbal individual intelligence test
    (b) Verbal group intelligence test
    (c) Non-verbal individual intelligence test
    (d) Non-verbal group intelligence test

37. The Form Board Test of Intelligence was developed by –
    (a) Seguin and Goddard
    (b) Merrill-Palmer
    (c) Binet-Simon
    (d) Wechsler-Bellevue

38. Which theory of intelligence has taken birth through Factor - Analysis ?
    (a) Bi-factor theory
    (b) Multi-action theory
    (c) Three-dimensional theory
    (d) Sampling theory

39. What should be the role of teacher in meeting the individual differences:
    (a) Try to know the abilities, interest & aptitude of individuals
    (b) Try to adjust the curriculum as per the need of individuals
    (c) Both (a) and (b)
    (d) None of these

40. If a child has mental age of 5 years & chronological age of 4 years than what will be the IQ of child:
    (a) 125
    (b) 80
    (c) 120
    (d) 100

41. Which one of theories of intelligence advocates the presence of general intelligence 'g' and specific intelligence 's'?
    (a) Anarchic theory
    (b) Guilford's theory of intellect
    (c) Spearman's two factor theory
    (d) Vernon's hierarchical theory

42. Ramesh and Ankit have the same IQ of 120. Ramesh is two years younger than Ankit. If Ankit is 12 years old, then the mental age of Ramesh is:
    (a) 9 years
    (b) 10 years
    (c) 12 years
    (d) 14 years

43. Guilford has given the term 'convergent thinking' as equivalent to
    (a) Intelligence
    (b) Creativity
    (c) Intelligence and creativity
    (d) none of these

44. Learners display individual differences. So a teacher should
    (a) enforce strict discipline
    (b) increase number of tests
    (c) insist on uniform pace of learning
    (d) pro vide a variety of learning experiences

45. Seema learns every lesson very quickly but Leena takes longer to learn them. It denotes the developmental principle of   (a) inter-relationships
    (b) continuity
    (c) general to specific
    (d) individual differences

46. For the development of imagination
    (a) Sense organs should be trained
    (b) Story should be narrated
    (c) Attention should be paid on the development of creative tendencies
    (d) All the above activities should be carried out

47. Intelligence is transmitted in future generations. The function of ________ is to create conducive situations for the development of this innate ability.
    (a) the locality
    (b) the season
    (c) the environment
    (d) the climate

48. The measure representing the total frequency distribution is called ________ .
    (a) measure of reliable variation
    (b) measure of central tendency
    (c) measure of representative correlation
    (d) measure of representative cumulative percentage

49. Images, concepts, symbols & signs, language, muscle activities and brain functions are involved in:
    (a) adaptation
    (b) motor development
    (c) problem solving
    (d) thinking process

50. Which one of the following is an example for complex concept
    (a) Square
    (b) Rectangle
    (c) Small Blue Coloured cube
    (d) Circle

51. Non verbal test is related to ________
    (a) Creativity   (b) Intelligence
    (c) Individuality   (d) Personality

52. Gender discrimination in a classroom
    (a) does not affect the performance of the students
    (b) may lead to diminished effort or performance of the students
    (c) may lead to enhanced effort or performance of the male students
    (d) is done more by the male teachers than their female counterparts

53. Girl students
    (a) learn questions on Mathematics well but face difficulty only when they are asked to reason them out
    (b) are good in Mathematics as boys of their age
    (c) perform less competently in spatial concepts than boys of their age
    (d) possess more linguistic and musical abilities

54. Fluency, elaboration, originality and flexibility are the factors associated with
    (a) giftedness   (b) talent
    (c) divergent thinking   (d) acceleration

55. Which one of the following may be criteria of gender parity in a society ?
    (a) Comparison of number of male and female teachers in school
    (b) Equal number of distinctions achieved by boys and girls in Class 12
    (c) Comparison of number of boys and girls who survive up to Class 12
    (d) Whether the girl students are allowed to participate in competitions organised outside the school

56. The knowledge of Individual Differences helps teachers in
    (a) understanding the futility of working hard with backward students as they can never be at par with the class
    (b) accepting and attributing the failure of the students to their individual differences
    (c) making their presentation style uniform to benefit all students equally
    (d) assessing the individual needs of all students and teaching them accordingly

57. Given below are some statements about boys and girls. According to you, which one of these is true ?
   (a) Boys should help in activities outside the home.
   (b) Boys should help in household chores.
   (c) All boys should be taught Science and girls, Home Science.
   (d) Girls should help in household chores.

58. Giftedness from teacher's point of view is a combination of
   (a) High Ability - High Creativity - High Commitment
   (b) High Motivation - High Commitment - High Talent
   (c) High Ability - High Talent - High Commitment
   (d) High Talent - High Creativity - High Memory

59. A teacher in a multi-cultural classroom would ensure that the assessment considers the following :
   (a) Socio-cultural context of her students
   (b) Reliability and validity of her assessment tool
   (c) Expectations of the school administration by complying with the minimum levels of learning
   (d) Standardization of the assessment tool

60. Which one of the following would be the most effective way to identify a creative child by the teacher ?
   (a) Detailed observation of the child especially when she solves problems
   (b) Observing how the child interacts with peers in team tasks
   (c) Administering standardized intelligence tests
   (d) Giving objective type tests

Answer Key

1.	(b)	**11.**	(b)	**21.**	(b)	**31.**	(b)	**41.**	(c)	**51.**	(b)
2.	(a)	**12.**	(c)	**22.**	(b)	**32.**	(d)	**42.**	(c)	**52.**	(b)
3.	(a)	**13.**	(a)	**23.**	(a)	**33.**	(a)	**43.**	(b)	**53.**	(b)
4.	(d)	**14.**	(d)	**24.**	(c)	**34.**	(a)	**44.**	(d)	**54.**	(a)
5.	(c)	**15.**	(d)	**25.**	(d)	**35.**	(a)	**45.**	(d)	**55.**	(c)
6.	(c)	**16.**	(b)	**26.**	(c)	**36.**	(b)	**46.**	(d)	**56.**	(d)
7.	(d)	**17.**	(a)	**27.**	(b)	**37.**	(c)	**47.**	(c)	**57.**	(b)
8.	(d)	**18.**	(a)	**28.**	(a)	**38.**	(c)	**48.**	(b)	**58.**	(a)
9.	(b)	**19.**	(a)	**29.**	(d)	**39.**	(c)	**49.**	(d)	**59.**	(a)
10.	(a)	**20.**	(a)	**30.**	(b)	**40.**	(a)	**50.**	(c)	**60.**	(a)

Progressive Education

Progressive education is a movement pertaining to pedagogy that began in the late nineteenth century and has persisted in various forms till date. The term "progressive" was engaged to distinguish this education from the traditional curriculum of the 19th century, which was rooted in classical preparation for the university and strongly differentiated by socio-economic level. By contrast, progressive education finds its roots in present experience. Most progressive education programs have these qualities in common:

* Learning by doing – hands-on projects and experiential learning
* Integrated curriculum
* Problem-solving and critical thinking
* Collaborative Group work and development of social skills
* Understanding and action as opposed to rote learning
* Projects on social responsibility and democracy
* Integration of community service and service learning projects into the daily curriculum
* De-emphasis on textbooks
* Life-long learning and social skills
* Assessment by evaluation of child's projects and productions

PROGRESSIVE EDUCATION

John Dewey remembered as the "father of Progressive education," was the most eloquent and influential figure in educational Progressivism.

Dewey's vision for the school was inextricably tied to his larger vision of the good society wherein each classroom represented a microcosm of the human relationships that constituted the larger community. Dewey believed that the school, as a "little democracy," could create a "more lovely society." Dewey's emphasis on the importance of democratic relationships in the classroom setting necessarily shifted the focus of educational theory from the institution of the school to the needs of the students. This dramatic change in American pedagogy, however, was not alone the work of John Dewey.

Second, Dewey and his fellow educational Progressives drew from the work of the German philosopher Friedrich Froebel and Swiss educator Johann Pestalozzi. Froebel and Pestalozzi were among the first to coherently opine that the process of education should be concerned with educating the "whole child," wherein learning shifted from the subject matter and eventually rested upon the needs and interests of the child. Taking care of both the pupil's head and heart, they believed, was the real work of schooling. Froebel drew upon the garden metaphor of cultivating young children toward maturity, and he provided the European foundations for the late-nineteenth-century kindergarten movement in the United States. Similarly, Pestalozzi popularized the pedagogical method of object teaching, wherein a teacher began with an object related to the child's world in order to initiate the child into the world of education.

Finally, Dewey drew inspiration from the ideas of philosopher and psychologist William James. Dewey's interpretation of James's philosophical pragmatism, which was similar to the ideas underpinning Pestalozzi's object teaching, joined thinking and doing as two seamlessly connected halves of the learning process. By focusing on the relationship between thinking and doing, Dewey believed his educational philosophy could equip each child with the problem-solving skills required to overcome obstacles between a given and desired set of circumstances.

A very important feature of progressive education is student-centered learning

Theorists like John Dewey, Jean Piaget, and Lev Vygotsky whose collective work focused on how students learn are primarily responsible for the move to student-centered learning.

Student-centered learning also called child-centered learning focuses more on the needs of the students, his abilities, interests, and learning styles with the teacher as a facilitator. This classroom teaching method acknowledges student's voice as central to the learning experience for every learner. Teacher-centered learning has the teacher at its centre in an active role and students in a passive, receptive role. Student-centered learning requires students to be active participants in their own learning.

To that end, the inclusion of educational practices such as Bloom's Taxonomy and Gardner's Theory of Multiple intelligences can be helpful to a student-centered classroom because it promotes various modes of diverse learning styles. Student-centered learning should be integrated into the curriculum because it

- Strengthens student motivation
- Promotes peer communication
- Reduces disruptive behaviour
- Builds student-teacher relationships
- Promotes discovery/active learning
- Builds responsibility for one's own learning

JOHN DEWEY ON CHILD-CENTERED EDUCATION

John Dewey's contribution to education has been identified with child-centered schooling. Through such works as The School and Society, The Child and the Curriculum, and Democracy and Education, Dewey articulated a unique, indeed revolutionary, reformulation of educational theory and practice. The problem that Dewey wanted to solve was rote teaching and learning, and his solution was to adapt instruction to students' interests and to use interest-centered activities as the engine of education.

The problems that Dewey worried most about did not arise in schools and reached far beyond education.

Before the Industrial Revolution

- Education was rooted in meaningful work, in what Dewey termed "occupations".

- According to Dewey, the educative forces of the domestic spinning and weaving, the saw mill, the gristmill, the cooper shop, and the blacksmith forge, were continuously operative." As a result, learning was "a matter of immediate and personal concern".

- The clothing worn was for the most part made in the house: the members of the household were usually familiar also with the shearing of the sheep, the carding and spinning of the wool, and the plying of the loom. Not only this, but practically every member of the household had his own share in the work".

- Work experience was the curriculum for children growing up on farms and agricultural villages.

After the Industrial Revolution

- There was increase increasing economic and political inequality that resulted from concentrations of wealth and poverty increased exponentially.

- Learning grew isolated from work, because industrialism moved labor out of family and village settings and relocated it in factories.

- Learning was sent to school and there it became artificial. That was the central problem of education in an industrial age: According to Dewey, "schools have been so set apart, so isolated from the ordinary conditions and motives of life" that they are "the one place in the world where it is most difficult to get experience" This was a direct result of the great transformations associated with industrialism.

- The growing social division of labor and the rise of markets eroded self-sufficient rural economies and eliminated children's opportunities to learn from experience.

- Learning became passive. It focused on the "mere absorption of facts."

- Schools dealt with as large numbers of children as possible. Classrooms everywhere looked alike, with their "rows of ugly desks placed in geometrical order almost all of the same size."

- The language used in schools was unnatural and artificial and stifled students' ability to speak and write well.

  These evils of schooling were not the result of poor pedagogy but of the industrial division of labor, capitalist competition, and the school system that grew up as a result.

Dewey's views of a school-My Pedagogic Creed

- School must represent present life – life as real and vital to the child as that which he carries on in the home, in the neighborhood, or on the playground.

- The school, as an institution, should simplify existing social life; should reduce it, as it were, to an embryonic form. Existing life is so complex that the child cannot be brought into contact with it without either confusion or distraction; he is either overwhelmed by the multiplicity of activities which are going on, so that he loses his own power of orderly reaction, or he is so stimulated by these various activities that his powers are prematurely called into play and he becomes either unduly specialized or else disintegrated.

- As such simplified social life, the school life should grow gradually out of the home life; that it should take up and continue the activities with which the child is already familiar in the home.

- School life should exhibit these activities to the child, and reproduce them in such ways that the child will gradually learn the meaning of them, and be capable of playing his own part in relation to them.

- Education fails because it neglects this fundamental principle of the school as a form of community life. It conceives the school as a place where certain information is to be given, where certain lessons are to be learned, or where certain habits are to be formed".

- Education is the process of living and is not meant to be the preparation of future living so school must represent the present life. As such, parts of the student's home life (such as moral and ethical education) should take part in the schooling process. The teacher is a part of this not as an authoritative figure but as a member of the community who is there to assist the student.

Dewey on the subject-matter

- The social life of the child is the basis of concentration, or correlation, in all his training or growth. The social life gives the unconscious unity and the background of all his efforts and of all his attainments. The subject-matter of the school curriculum should mark a gradual differentiation out of the primitive unconscious unity of social life.

- We violate the child's nature and render difficult the best ethical results, by introducing the child too abruptly to a number of special studies, of reading, writing, geography, etc., out of relation to this social life. Therefore, that the true center of correlation on the school subjects is not science, nor literature, nor history, nor geography, but the child's own social activities.

- That education cannot be unified in the study of science, or so called nature study, because apart from human activity, nature itself is not a unity; nature in itself is a number of diverse objects in space and time, and to attempt to make it the center of work by itself, is to introduce a principle of radiation rather than one of concentration.

- Literature is the reflex expression and interpretation of social experience; that hence it must follow upon and not precede such experience. It, therefore, cannot be made the basis, although it may be made the summary of unification.

- Once more that history is of educative value in so far as it presents phases of social life and growth. It must be controlled by reference to social life. When taken simply as history it is thrown into the distant past and becomes dead and inert. Taken as the record of man's social life and progress it becomes full of meaning.

- The primary basis of education is in the child's powers at work along the same general constructive lines as those which have brought civilization into being. The only way to make the child conscious of his social heritage is to enable him to perform those fundamental types of activity which make civilization what it is.

- The study of science is educational in so far as it brings out the materials and processes which make social life what it is. One of the greatest difficulties in the present teaching of science is that the material is presented in purely objective form, or is treated as a new peculiar kind of experience which the child can add to that which he has already had. In reality, science is of value because it gives the ability to interpret and control the experience already had. It should be introduced, not as so much new subject-matter, but as showing the factors already involved in previous experience and as furnishing tools by which that experience can be more easily and effectively regulated.

- At present we lose much of the value of literature and language studies because of our elimination of social element. Language is almost always treated in the books of pedagogy simply as the expression of thought. It is true that language is a logical instrument, but it is fundamentally and primarily a social instrument. Language is the device for communication; it is the tool through which one individual comes to share the ideas and feelings of others. When treated simply as a way of getting individual information, or as a means of showing off what one has learned, it loses its social motive and end.

- According to Dewey, the curriculum in the schools should reflect that of society. The center of the school curriculum should reflect the development of humans in society. The study of the core subjects (language, science, history) should be coupled with the study of cooking, sewing and manual training. Furthermore, he feels that "progress is not in the succession of studies but in the development of new attitudes towards, and new interests in, experience".

Dewey on the nature of method

- The question of method is ultimately reducible to the question of the order of development of the child's powers and interests. The law for presenting and treating material is the law implicit within the child's own nature. Because this is so the following statements are of supreme importance as determining the spirit in which education is carried on:

  (a) The active side precedes the passive in the development of the child nature;

  (b) Expression comes before conscious impression;

  (c) The muscular development precedes the sensory;

  (d) Movements come before conscious sensations;

  (e) Consciousness is essentially motor or impulsive;

  (f) Conscious states tend to project themselves in action.

  (g) Neglect of this principle is the cause of a large part of the waste of time and strength in school work.

  (h) The child is thrown into a passive, receptive, or absorbing attitude.

  (i) The conditions are such that he is not permitted to follow the law of his nature; the result is friction and waste.

- Ideas (intellectual and rational processes) also result from action and devolve for the sake of the better control of action. What we term reason is primarily the law of orderly or effective action. To attempt to develop the reasoning powers, the powers of judgment, without reference to the selection and arrangement of means in action, is the fundamental fallacy in our present methods of dealing with this matter. As a result we present the child with arbitrary symbols. Symbols are a necessity in mental development, but they have their place as tools for economizing effort; presented by themselves they are a mass of meaningless and arbitrary ideas imposed from without.

- Much of the time and attention now given to the preparation and presentation of lessons might be more wisely and profitably expended in training the child's power of imagery and in seeing to it that he was continually forming definite, vivid, and growing images of the various subjects with which he comes in contact in his experience.

- Only through the continual and sympathetic observation of childhood's interests can the adult enter into the child's life and see what it is ready for, and upon what material it could work most readily and fruitfully. I believe that these interests are neither to be humored nor repressed. To repress interest is to substitute the adult for the child, and so to weaken intellectual curiosity and alertness, to suppress initiative, and to deaden interest. To humor the interests is to substitute the transient for the permanent. The interest is always the sign of some power below; the important thing is to discover this power. To humor the interest is to fail to penetrate below the surface and its sure result is to substitute caprice and whim for genuine interest.

- For Dewey, child-centered education will help students to retrace steps that men and women had taken to solve the crucial problems of humanity-in this case turning raw materials into clothing and mastering the agricultural practices, fabrication processes, and the technologies and science that underlay such problem solving. This work gives the point of departure from which the child can trace and follow the progress of mankind in history, getting an insight also into the materials used and the mechanical principles involved". Such a curriculum would radically resituate students' school work in several different ways.

- Dewey also firmly believed that his curriculum would solve the chronic problems of students' weak motivation, diffuse interest and boredom with school. For if school work was centered in solving practical problems that were crucial to humanity, the work would be intellectually compelling and psychologically engaging.

- Method is focused on the child's powers and interests. If the child is thrown into a passive role as a student, absorbing information, the result is a waste of the child's education. Information presented to the student will be transformed into new forms, images and symbols by the student so that they fit with their development and interests. The development of this is natural and to repress this process and attempting to "substitute the adult for the child" would weaken the intellectual curiosity of the child.

Besides Dewey, other great philosophers and educationalists like Rousseau, Froebel, Pestalozzi and Montessori too have given emphasis on the student-centred education at different times.

ROUSSEAU ON CHILD-CENTERED EDUCATION

Rousseau's principal contribution to education was the 1762 novel Emile, which influenced many later educational pioneers.

The theory that Rousseau primarily attacked in his philosophy of education was that of child depravity. The theory stated that children are born with a tendency to evil, and are naturally, therefore, inclined to misbehave. The only way to combat this is to instill authoritarian teachers that rule their classroom with an iron fist. Rousseau was certainly not the first to attack this theory, but he was one of the greatest champions of anti-child depravity. A child, he believed, must be free from "society's imprisoning institutions" and free to explore the environment and learn from direct experience of the content being taught. The encyclopedia of Informal Education breaks down his suggestions for teaching in bullet form:

- The instructor has to keep control of what the child is learning. Things that are beyond the developmental capacity of students shouldn't be taught to them. (This principle is important to Rousseau)

- Children are naturally good, they are innocent and pure.

- Children develop in stages.

- In order to teach a child, you have to consider what stage that child is in terms of his development.

- Keep in mind that individuals vary in stages: not every kid is going to be completely mature in each stage.

- Kids are going to want to move around. If this is encouraged, the physical activity will lead to mental activity.

- The student should be aware they are being socialized for public citizenship, but they should place equal importance on their personal education.

- People should develop ideas for themselves, and reason through tasks to the end, drawing their own conclusions. This as opposed to simply taking the word of the authoritarian teacher.

- The environment the child is in is a factor in how much he learns.

Friedrich Froebel on Child-centered education

Froebel's philosophy of education was based on Idealism. He believed that every human being had a spiritual essence and that every person had spiritual worth and dignity. Like Idealists, he also believed that every child had within him all he was to be at birth, and that the proper educational environment was to encourage the child to grow and develop in an optimal manner. This was the basis of the Kindergarten – a place for little ones to grow and blossom and be what they were destined to be.

One of the important contributions made by Froebel was to see play as a means by which children externalized their inner nature – and a way of imitating and trying out various adult roles. He was of the view that mothers and KG teachers needed to be fully educated about the child's development stages.

The kindergarten designed by him had a lot of gifts and occupations. A gift was given to a child to play with such as a ball or a cube which enabled the child to understand the concepts of shape, dimension, size, and their relationships. The occupations were items such as paints and clay which the children could use to make what they desired. Through the occupations, children externalized the concepts existing within their minds. Froebel thought that the whole aim of education was to prepare the human being for his immediate life. Froebel states that in nature we allow plants and animals space and time to grow because their internal laws suggest they will develop properly only in this manner. He wanted to apply the same rule to the education of children. Froebel's works included his theory of education, his idea of what good education is, his ideas on the stages in the development of the child, his development of the play-way method and the process of education-dealing with the subjects to be taught and how teaching can be made effective.

The Pedagogy of Froebel

According to Froebel, the teacher was to clear all obstacles to the self-development or "self-activity" of the child, as well as correct deviations from right and best. A teacher should not intervene and impose compulsory education, but when a child, particularly a child of kindergarten age is restless, impatient, tearful, the teacher must look for the underlying reasons and try to do away with the hindrance to the child's creative development. Froebel thought children were instructed in things they did not need. The lessons should appeal to the pupil's interests. It is clear that, in Froebel's view, the school is to concern itself not primarily with the transmission of knowledge but with the development of character and the provision of the right motivation to learn.

He emphasized the importance of games for the holistic development of a child. Froebel was particularly interested in the development of toys for children for stimulating learning. The toys he was interested in were balls, dice, globes, cylinders, shapes of wood, strips of paper, beads and buttons. The objective was aim was to enable children to distinguish between form, color, separation and association, grouping, matching, and so on When, through the teacher's guidance, the gifts are properly experienced, they connect the natural inner unity of the child to the unity of all things For example, the sphere gives the child a sense of unlimited continuity, the cylinder a sense of both continuity and limitation. Even the practice of sitting in a circle symbolizes the way in which each individual, while a unity in himself, is a living part of a larger unity.

The Montessori Method

Maria Montessori was a physician, an educator and a humanitarian known for her philosophy of education. Dr. Maria Montessori believed that no human being is educated by another person. He must do it himself or it will never be done. A truly educated individual continues learning long after the hours and years he spends in the classroom because he is motivated from within by a natural curiosity and love for knowledge. Dr. Montessori felt, therefore, that the goal of early childhood education should not be to fill the child with facts from a pre-selected course of studies, but rather to cultivate his own natural desire to learn.

In the Montessori classroom, this objective is approached in two ways: first, by allowing each child to experience the excitement of learning by his own choice rather than by being forced; and second, by helping him to perfect all his natural tools for learning, so that his ability will be at a maximum in future learning situations. The Montessori materials have this dual long-range purpose in addition to their immediate purpose of giving specific information to the child.

How do children learn?

Montessori frequently compared the young mind to a sponge. The mind literally absorbs information from the environment. The process is particularly evident in the way in which a two year-old learns his native language, without any formal instruction and without the conscious and tiresomely long effort which an adult makes to master a foreign language. Acquiring information in this way is a natural and delightful activity for the young child who employs all his senses to investigate his interesting surroundings.

She was of the opinion that a young child can learn to read, write and calculate in the same natural way that he learns to walk and talk. In a Montessori classroom, the equipment invites him to do this at his own periods of interest and readiness. Dr. Montessori always emphasized that "the hand is the chief teacher of the child". In order to learn there must be concentration, and the best way a child can concentrate is by fixing his attention on some task he is performing with his hands. All the equipment in a Montessori classroom invites the child to use his hands for learning.

The importance of the early years

According to Maria, "the most important period of life is the period from birth to the age of six. For that is the time when not only man's intelligence which is his biggest implement but also his psychic power is being formed. Parents should understand that a Montessori school is a unique learning place designed to take advantage of the child's sensitive years between three and six, when he can absorb information from an enriched environment. A child who acquires the basic skills of reading and arithmetic in this natural way has the advantage of beginning his education without drudgery, or boredom. By pursuing his individual interests in a Montessori classroom, he gains an early motivation for learning, which is the key to his becoming a truly educated person.

According to Montessori, children should be given considerable freedom. But this did not mean that they did what they felt like. She insisted that children ought to conduct themselves properly and treat others with respect. "The first idea that the child must acquire," she wrote, "is that of the difference between good and evil; and the task of the educator lies in seeing that the child does not confound good with immobility, and evil with activity, as often happens in the case of old-time discipline. And all this because our aim is to discipline for activity, for work, for good; not for immobility, not for passivity, not for obedience.... A room in which all the children move about usefully, intelligently, and voluntarily, without committing any rough or rude act, would seem to me a classroom very well disciplined indeed."

Montessori disliked conventional classrooms, where "children are tied, each to his place." She sought, instead, to teach children by supplying concrete materials and organizing situations suitable to learning with these materials. She discovered that certain simple materials aroused in young children an interest and attention not previously thought possible. These materials included beads arranged in graduated-number units for pre-mathematics instruction; small slabs of wood designed to train the eye in left-to-right reading movements; and graduated series of cylinders for small-muscle training. The age group between three and six years old would work spontaneously with these materials. Towards the end, they would not seem tired, but fresh and composed. Troublesome children became settled through such voluntary work. The materials used were designed specifically to encourage individual rather than cooperative effort. Group activity occurred in connection with shared housekeeping chores.

Exercise 1 : Previous Year Questions of CTET & STET

1. The Right to Education Act, 2009 specifies that if the number of children admitted for first class to fifth class is above two hundred then the pupil-teacher ratio required is *[RTET-2011-I]*
   (a) thirty
   (b) forty
   (c) forty-five
   (d) fifty

2. Which of the following statements is not true about teaching? *[RTET-2011-I]*
   (a) Teaching is modifiable
   (b) Teaching is formal and informal
   (c) Teaching is a science as well as art
   (d) Teaching is instruction.

3. The National Curriculum Framework, 2005 under the heading 'quality dimention' gives more importance to *[RTET-2011-I]*
   (a) Physical resources
   (b) Qualified and Motivated teachers
   (c) Experiences designed for the child in terms of knowledge
   (d) Experiences designed for the child and curriculum reform

4. The National Curriculum Framework, 2005 suggests which of the following examination reforms ? *[RTET-2011-I]*
   (a) Class X examination optional
   (b) State level exams to be conducted at different stages of school education
   (c) Competitive entrance examinations optional
   (d) All of these

5. At lower classes, play-way method of teaching is based on *[UPTET-2011-I]*
   (a) theory of physical education programmes
   (b) principles of methods of teaching
   (c) psychological principles of development and growth
   (d) sociological principles of teaching

6. To maintain interest among students in class, a teacher should *[UPTET-2011-I]*
   (a) use the blackboard
   (b) discuss
   (c) tell stories
   (d) ask questions

7. Family is a means of *[UPTET-2011-I]*
   (a) informal education
   (b) formal education
   (c) non-formal education
   (d) distance education

8. Blackboard can be included in which group / category of teaching aid? *[UPTET-2011-I]*
   (a) Audio aid
   (b) Visual aid
   (c) Audio-visual aid
   (d) None of these

9. Which of the following is related with teaching skill? *[UPTET-2011-I]*
   (a) Blackboard writing
   (b) Solving questions
   (c) Asking questions
   (d) All of these

10. In order to nurture creativity, a teacher should take help of which of the following methods? *[RTET-2011-II]*
    (a) Brainstorming
    (b) Lecture method
    (c) Audio-visual aids
    (d) All of these.

11. Right to Education Act, 2009 specifies the minimum number of working hours per week for the teacher as *[RTET-2011-II]*

(a) forty hours

(b) forty-five hours

(c) fifty hours

(d) fifty-five hours

12. Right to Education Act, 2009 states that a teacher shall perform which of the following duties?   *[RTET-2011-II]*

(a) Maintain regularity and punctuality in attending school

(b) Conduct & complete the curriculum

(c) Complete entire curriculum in a specified time

(d) All of these

13. National Curriculum Framework, 2005 suggests some activities to promote peace education. Which one of the following is enlisted in the curriculum framework?   *[RTET-2011-II]*

(a) Organise programmes to promote an attitude of respect and responsibility towards women

(b) Teach moral education

(c) Teach peace education as a separate subject

(d) Integrate peace education in the curriculum.

14. National Curriculum Framework, 2005 talks of major shifts from   *[RTET-2011-II]*

(a) knowledge as given and fixed as it evolves and is created

(b) educational focus to disciplinary focus

(c) learner centric to teacher centric

(d) none of these

15. The success of integrated education depends on   *[UPTET-2011-II]*

(a) the support of community

(b) excellence of textbooks

(c) quality of teaching-learning material

(d) attitudinal change in teachers

16. The aim of education should be   *[UPTET-2011-II]*

(a) to develop vocational skills in the students

(b) to develop social awareness in the students

(c) to prepare the students for examination

(d) to prepare the students for practical life

17. An example of media that transports learners to remote places by means of visualized reports is: *[PTET-2011-II]*

(a) educational television

(b) educational broadcasts

(c) overhead projector

(d) telephone

18. For introducing a topic in classroom, what activity should a teacher do first?   *[PTET-2011-II]*

(a) explain the rationale

(b) inform the objectives

(c) tell topic orally

(d) write topic on chalkboard

19. What is your opinion in the reforms of present education system? This question induces   *[TNTET-2011-II]*

(a) Convergent thinking

(b) Divergent thinking

(c) Logical thinking

(d) Negative thinking

20. An educationist who had the Eidetic imagery is   *[TNTET-2011-II]*

(a) Gandhiji

(b) Aurobindo

(c) Dr. Radhakrishnan

(d) Tagore

21. Which of the following is a feature of progressive education?   *[CTET-2012-I]*

(a) Emphasis on scoring good marks in examinations

(b) Frequent tests and examinations

    (c) Flexible time-table and seating arrangement

    (d) Instruction based solely on prescribed text-books

22. Frobel's most important contribution to education was his development of the: *[PTET-2014-I]*

(a) Vocational School

(b) Kindergarten

(c) Public School

(d) Latin School

23. Which of the following is NOT the benefit of integrating student-centred learning into the curriculum? *[PTET-2014-II]*

(a) strengthens student motivation

(b) promotes peer communication

(c) builds student-teacher relationships

(d) hinders discovery/active learning

24. When delivering an effective lecture in classroom, a teacher: *[PTET-2014-II]*

(a) establishes an eye contact

(b) employs meaningful gestures

(c) stands stationary at lecture stand

(d) varies pitch and tone

25. Communication with students means: *[PTET-2014-II]*

(a) asking them to do a task

(b) exchange of ideas

(c) giving them directions

(d) informing them of your idea

26. The first stage in the learning of a skill is: *[PTET-2014-II]*

(a) precision   (b) manipulation

(c) coordination   (d) imitation

27. For introducing a topic in classroom, what activity should a teacher do first? *[PTET-2014-II]*

(a) explain the rationale

(b) inform the objectives

(c) tell topic orally

(d) write topic on chalkboard

28. Self study habit can be developed in children by: *[PTET-2014-II]*

(a) citing examples of great people

(b) giving lecture on self study

(c) giving your own example

(d) making new literature available

29. In context of progressive education, which of the following statements is true according to John Dewey? *[CTET-Feb.-2014-I]*

(a) There should not be place for democracy in a classroom

(b) Students should be able to solve social problems themselves

(c) Curiosity does not belong to the inherent nature of students rather it is to be cultivated

(d) Students should be observed and not heard in the classroom

30. Multiple pedagogical techniques, assorted learning material, multiple assessment techniques and varying the complexity and nature of the content are associated with which of the following? *[CTET-Feb.-2014-I]*

(a) Universal design for learning

(b) Remedial teaching

(c) Differentiated instruction

(d) Reciprocal teaching

31. A teacher is trying to counsel a child who is not performing well after an accident. Which one of the following is most appropriate about counseling in schools? *[CTET-Feb.-2014-I]*

(a) It is about the palliative measures for making people comfortable

(b) It builds self-confidence of people by letting them explore their own thoughts

(c) It is about giving the best possible advice to students about their future career options

(d) It can be done only by the professional experts

32. Which of the following would encourage the least a student who wants to become a highly creative theater artist? *[CTET-Feb.-2014-I]*

(a) Try to win the State level competition that will ensure you scholarship

(b) Develop empathetic, amicable and supportive relationships with your peer theater artists

(c) Devote your time to those theatrical skills that you find most enjoyable

(d) Read about the performances of the world's best theater artists and try to learn

33. In the context of progressive education, the term 'equal educational opportunity' implies that all students should *[CTET-Feb.-2014-II]*

(a) receive equal education irrespective of their caste, creed, colour, region and religion

(b) be allowed to prove their capability after receiving an equal education

(c) be provided an education by using the same methods and materials without any distinction

(d) be provided an education which is most appropriate to them and their future life at work

34. Progressive education is associated with which of the following statements ? *[CTET-Sep.-2014-II]*

(a) Teachers are the originators of information and authority.

(b) Knowledge is generated through direct experience and collaboration.

(c) Learning proceeds in a straight way with factual gathering and skill mastery.

(d) Examination is norm-referenced and external.

35. By placing students in the least restricted school environment, the school *[CTET-Sep.-2014-II]*

(a) equalises the educational opportunities for girls and disadvantaged groups

(b) normalises the lives of children from deprived groups who were increasing the linkage of school with the parents and communities of these children

(c) gets disadvantaged children's involvement in activities such as science fairs and quizzes

(d) sensitises other children not to bully or to put disadvantaged children down

36. A child's notebook shows errors in writing like reverse images, mirror imaging, etc. Such a child is showing signs of *[CTET-Feb.-2015-I]*

(a) Learning disadvantage

(b) Learning disability

(c) Learning difficulty

(d) Learning problem

37. Which one of the following is not correct for the progressive model of socialization of children ? *[CTET-Feb.-2015-I]*

(a) Active participation in the group work and learning social skills.

(b) Children accept what they are offered by the school irrespective of their social backgrounds.

(c) There should be a place for democracy in the classroom.

(d) Socialization is an adoption of social norms.

38. To enable students to make conceptual changes in their thinking, a teacher should *[CTET-Feb.-2016-I]*

(a) offer rewards for children who change their thinking.

(b) discourage children from thinking on their own and ask them to just listen to her and follow that.

(c) offer an explanation in a lecture mode.

(d) make clear and convincing explanations and have discussions with the students.

39. In the context of a primary school classroom, what does active engagement mean?

[CTET-Feb.-2016-I]

(a) Memorising. Recall and Reciting

(b) Imitating and Copying the teacher

(c) Enquiry, Questioning and Debate

(d) Copying answers given by the teacher

40. Most classrooms in India are multilingual and this needs to be seen as .... by the teacher. *[CTET-Feb.-2016-I]*

(a) a bother

(b) a problem

(c) a resource

(d) an obstacle

41. Child-centred pedagogy means

[CTET-Feb.-2016-I]

(a) giving moral education to the children.

(b) asking the children to follow and imitate the teacher.

(c) giving primacy to children's voices and their active participation.

(d) letting the children be totally free.

42. A teacher can help the children to process a complex situation by *[CTET-Feb.-2016-I]*

(a) encouraging competition and offering a high reward to the child who completes the task first.

(b) not offering any help at all so that children learn to help on their own.

(c) giving a lecture on it.

(d) breaking the task into smaller parts and writing down instructions.

43. Which one of the following situations is illustrative of a child-centred classroom?

[CTET-Feb.-2016-I]

(a) A class in which the teacher dictates and the students are asked to memorise the notes.

(b) A class in which the textbook is the only resource the teacher refers to.

(c) A class in which the students are sitting in groups and the teacher takes turns to go to each group.

(d) A class in which the behaviour of students is governed by the rewards and punishments the teacher would give them.

44. Progressive education entails that the classroom is *[CTET-Feb.-2016-II]*

(a) democratic and there is space given to children for understanding.

(b) in full control of the teacher, who is dictatorial.

(c) authoritarian, where the teacher dictates and the students follow meekly.

(d) free for all with the teacher absent from it.

45. Learner-centred approach means

[CTET-Feb.-2016-II]

(a) methods where learners' own initiative and efforts are involved in learning.

(b) use of methods in which teacher is the main actor.

(c) that teachers draw conclusions for the learners.

(d) traditional expository methods.

46. Research suggests that in a diverse classroom, a teacher's expectations from her students, ... their learning. *[CTET-Sept.-2016-I]*

    (a) have a significant impact on

    (b) are the sole determinant of

    (c) should not be correlated with

    (d) do not have any effect on

47. "Having a diverse classroom with children from varied social, economic and cultural backgrounds enriches the learning experiences of all students." This statement is :

[CTET-Sept.-2016-I]

    (a) incorrect, because it can confuse the children and they may feel lost

    (b) correct, because children learn many skills from their peers

    (c) correct, because it makes the classroom more hierarchical

    (d) incorrect, because it leads to unnecessary competition

48. In a progressive classroom setup, the teacher facilitates learning by- providing an environment that : *[CTET-Sept.-2016-I]*

    (a) promotes discovery

    (b) is restrictive

    (c) discourages inclusion

    (d) encourages repetition

49. 'Child-centred' pedagogy means :

[CTET-Sept.-2016-II]

    (a) the teacher leading all the learning in the classroom

    (b) the teacher dictating the children what should be done

    (c) giving primacy to children's experiences and their voices

    (d) enabling the children to follow prescribed information

Answer Key

1.	(b)	**8.**	(b)	**15.**	(c)	**22.**	(b)	**29.**	(b)	**36.**	(b)	**43.**	(d)
2.	(d)	**9.**	(d)	**16.**	(d)	**23.**	(d)	**30.**	(c)	**37.**	(b)	**44.**	(a)
3.	(d)	**10.**	(a)	**17.**	(a)	**24.**	(a)	**31.**	(b)	**38.**	(d)	**45.**	(a)
4.	(a)	**11.**	(b)	**18.**	(a)	**25.**	(b)	**32.**	(a)	**39.**	(c)	**46.**	(a)
5.	(c)	**12.**	(d)	**19.**	(b)	**26.**	(d)	**33.**	(d)	**40.**	(c)	**47.**	(b)
6.	(d)	**13.**	(a)	**20.**	(c)	**27.**	(d)	**34.**	(b)	**41.**	(c)	**48.**	(a)
7.	(a)	**14.**	(a)	**21.**	(c)	**28.**	(d)	**35.**	(d)	**42.**	(d)	**49.**	(c)

29. (b) John Dewey remembered as the "Father of Progressive education," was the most eloquent and influential figure in educational progressivism, Dewey's vision for the school was inextricably tied to his larger vision of the good society wherein each classroom represented a microcosm of the human that constituted the larger community.

30. (c) Differentiated instruction aims high and sets out to challenge every students to excel by using multiple pedagogical techniques, assorted learning material, multiple assessment techniques.

32. (a) Except option (a) others will enhance more his creativity and his relationship with theater artists.

33. (d) Every child is a unique and special individual. Consequently, we have to teach individual children and be respectful of and account for their individual uniqueness of age, gender, learning style and future life.

38. (d) Conceptual change is a procedure that affects mental process like creativity, thinking, memory, problem solving actions, etc. A teacher can inspire conceptual modifications among children by giving them one to one discussion on how to deal with their problems in the most ethical way.

39. (c) According to NCF 2005. 'Active engagement deals with the enquiry, exploration, questioning, debates, application and reflection which lead to theory formation and to create ideas or positions.'

40. (c) According to NCF 2005. 'Multilingualism. which consists of the individuality of a child and a characteristic feature of the Indian linguistic landscape, it should be used as a source, classroom approach and an objective by an idealistic language teacher.'

41. (c) Child-centred pedagogy needs a teacher to plan the process of learning after understanding the psychology and interests of children.

42. (d) Dividing work into smaller parts is associated with content analysis, which is a significant part of the teaching -learning process This process helps teachers and students both to find the solution of the complex problems.

43. (d) A child centered classroom is the one where a method of teaching is planned according to the needs of children of a particular age group. In that classroom, a teacher acts as a facilitator by encouraging the students to actively participate in the learning process, manage their respective activities and direct their learning.

44. (a) Progressive education emphasizes on learning by doing which one gets if proper space is given to a child in the classroom i.e if a child is given freedom to express his views and learn accordingly with the help of a teacher irrespective of any fear.

45 (a) Learner centered approach refers to the method where the method of teaching is adopted according to the mental age of a child. It means his ability to learn and in the way he understands better.

Exercise 2 : Test Yourself

1. Who is remembered as the father of progressive education?
   (a) John Dewey
   (b) Pestalozzi
   (c) Mahatma Gandhi
   (d) Rousseau

2. Dewey's emphasis on the importance of --------------- relationships in the classroom setting necessarily shifted the focus of educational theory from the institution of the school to the needs of the students.
   (a) Liberal
   (b) Democratic
   (c) Directive
   (d) Authoritative

3. ------------------- were among the first to coherently opine that the process of education should be concerned with educating the "whole child".
   (a) Froebel and Pestalozzi
   (b) Montessori and Rousseau
   (c) Aurobindo and Tagore
   (d) Froebel and Rousseau

4. The cardinal principles of learner centered education are ....
   (a) Learning by doing
   (b) Learning by living
   (c) Both
   (d) None of these

5. Who popularized the pedagogical method of object teaching, wherein a teacher began with an object related to the child's world in order to initiate the child into the world of education?
   (a) Rousseau   (b) Pestalozzi
   (c) Dewey   (d) Vygotsky

6. Which type of learning focuses more on the needs of the students, his abilities, interests, and learning styles with the teacher as a facilitator
   (a) Subject-centered
   (b) Child-centered
   (c) Learning by rote
   (d) Play-way

7. Whose contribution was the School and Society?
   (a) Arthur Miller
   (b) John Dewey
   (c) Michael Apple
   (d) Michael Young

8. Rousseau's principal contribution to education was the 1762 novel
   (a) Emile
   (b) Agatha
   (c) Oscar
   (d) My pedagogic creed

9. The theory that Rousseau primarily attacked in his philosophy of education was that of
   (a) child depravity
   (b) child abuse
   (c) child play
   (d) child rights

10. Froebel's philosophy of education was based on
    (a) Naturalism   (b) Realism
    (c) Idealism   (d) Existentialism

11. -------- was of the view that mothers and KG teachers needed to be fully educated about the child's development stages.
    (a) Tagore
    (b) Vivekananda
    (c) Mahatma Gandhi
    (d) Froebel

12. The kindergarten designed by Froebel had a lot of
    (a) gifts and occupations
    (b) books and diaries
    (c) plants and animals
    (d) songs and dances

13. Who stated that in nature we allow plants and animals space and time to grow because their internal laws suggest they will develop properly only in this manner.
    (a) Froebel   (b) Montessori
    (c) Dewey   (d) Rousseau

14. Who said, "Education has two aspects: the teacher was to clear all obstacles to the self-development or "self-activity" of the child, but he was also to correct deviations from right and best"
    (a) Swami Vivekananda
    (b) Rabindranath Tagore
    (c) Mahatma Gandhi
    (d) Friedrich Froebel

15. "The hand is the chief teacher of the child" was stated by
    (a) Mahatma Gandhi
    (b) Friedrich Froebel
    (c) Maria Montessori
    (d) Adam Smith

16. NCF – 2005 was framed by –
    (a) NCERT   (b) SCERT
    (c) NCTE   (d) MHRD

17. Main objective of NCF 2005 is–
    - (a) construction of knowledge
    - (b) to memorize the lessons
    - (c) emphasize on calculations
    - (d) emphasize on discipline
18. Main objective of RTEA 2009 is –
    - (a) Free and compulsory education for children of 6 – 14 years
    - (b) Education for all till 5th class
    - (c) Education for all in Govt. school
    - (d) Free and compulsory education for children of 0–14 years
19. Computer-assisted instruction (CAI) is an educational technology that incorporates features consistent with principle of
    - (a) Classical conditioning
    - (b) Instrumental conditioning
    - (c) Operant conditioning
    - (d) Cognitive conditioning
20. Which organisation accords recognition to teacher training institutions ?
    - (a) NCTE
    - (b) NCERT
    - (c) AICTE
    - (d) SCERT
21. Which ministry in the central government looks after education ?
    - (a) Education ministry
    - (b) Education and cultural ministry
    - (c) Ministry of science and education
    - (d) Ministry of human resource development
22. Which institution develops national curriculum framework for school education?
    - (a) NCERT
    - (b) CBSE
    - (c) SCERT
    - (d) DIET
23. 'John Dewey', an educationist, belonged to –
    - (a) Pragmatism
    - (b) Idealism
    - (c) Proressivism
    - (d) Naturalism
24. District Institute of Education of Training (Diets), have been set up to improve the quality of
    - (a) Pre-primary education
    - (b) Elementary education
    - (c) Primary Education
    - (d) Senior secondary education.
25. The project method is based on
    - (a) The principle of selection
    - (b) The principle of learning by doing
    - (c) The principle of regulation
    - (d) The principle of inspiration
26. The basic education policy was based on this view that a child :
    - (a) Learns from the co-operation of the society.
    - (b) can achieve knowledge by reading books.
    - (c) can get education by doing any purposeful activity.
    - (d) can not learn anything without financial incentive
27. Navodaya Vidhalayas are for :
    - (a) Rural children
    - (b) Urban children
    - (c) Brilliant children of both rural and urban.
    - (d) The children who want to become soldiers.
28. Modern education system –
    - (a) Makes the students professional
    - (b) Make the students social
    - (c) Does not give practical knowledge
    - (d) Makes the students spiritual
29. Concept of Curriculum flexibility was introduced to benifit
    - (a) disabled children
    - (b) Madarsas and Maktabs
    - (c) Scheduled Castes, Scheduled Tribes and Others Backward Sections
    - (d) All of the above

Answer Key

1.	(a)	**6.**	(b)	**11.**	(d)	**16.**	(a)	**21.**	(d)	**26.**	(c)
2.	(b)	**7.**	(b)	**12.**	(a)	**17.**	(a)	**22.**	(a)	**27.**	(c)
3.	(a)	**8.**	(a)	**13.**	(a)	**18.**	(a)	**23.**	(a)	**28.**	(b)
4.	(c)	**9.**	(a)	**14.**	(d)	**19.**	(c)	**24.**	(b)	**29.**	(a)
5.	(b)	**10.**	(c)	**15.**	(c)	**20.**	(a)	**25.**	(b)		

Inclusive Education

6

Inclusive education is an approach to educating students with special educational needs. Under the inclusion model, students with special needs spend most or all of their time with non-disabled students though the implementation of these practices varies from school to school. Schools most frequently use them for selected students with mild to severe special needs.

Inclusive education differs from notions held earlier of 'integration' and 'mainstreaming', which tended to be concerned principally with disability and 'special educational needs' and implied learners changing or becoming 'ready for' or deserving of accommodation by the mainstream. By contrast, inclusion is about the child's right to participate and the school's duty to accept the child. Inclusion rejects the use of special schools or classrooms to separate students with disabilities from students without disabilities. It seeks to address the learning needs of all children, youth and adults with a specific focus on those who are vulnerable to marginalization and exclusion. It emphasizes full participation by students with disabilities and respect for their social, civil, and educational rights.

NATIONAL CURRICULUM FRAMEWORK- 2005

The Social Context of Education

Caste hierarchies, socio-economic status, gender bias, cultural diversity etc. characterize Indian society and deeply influence access to education and participation of children in school. This is evident in the sharp differences between different social and economic groups, which are reflected in school enrolment and completion rates. Thus, girls from SC and ST communities in both rural and urban areas and the disadvantaged sections of religious and other ethnic minorities are educationally most vulnerable. In urban areas and a lot of villages, the school system itself is stratified and provides children with appallingly different educational experiences. Differences in gender relations not only perpetuate domination but also create anxieties and stifle the freedom of both boys and girls to develop their capacities to their fullest.

The impact of globalization in every sphere of society has important implications for education. On the one hand, we are witnessing the increasing commercialization of education, and, on the other hand, inadequate public funding for education and the thrust towards 'alternative' schools. These factors indicate a shifting of responsibility for education from the state to the family and the community. We need to be alert about the commodification of schools and the application of market-related concepts to schools and school quality. The increasingly competitive environment into which schools are being drawn and the aspirations of parents place a tremendous burden of stress and anxiety on all children, including the very young, to the detriment of their personal growth and development, and thus hampering the inculcation of the joy of learning.

RTE-SSA REPORT (Right to Education - Sarva Shiksha Abhiyan Report)

The RTE Act has important implications for the overall approach and implementation strategies of Sarva Shiksha Abhiyan and it is necessary to harmonize the SSA vision, strategies and norms with the RTE mandate. The RTE has defined children belonging to disadvantaged group and children belonging to weaker sections as follows:

- Disadvantaged group is defined as those that belong to the Schedules caste/tribe, socially and educationally backward class or such other group having disadvantage owing to social, cultural, economical, gender, geographical, linguistic or other factor as may be specified by the appropriate government by notification.

- Weaker sections are defined as those "belonging to such parent or guardian whose annual income is lower than the minimum specified by the appropriate government by notification".

The Act calls for close collaboration between different government departments, especially Ministries/Department of Social Justice and Empowerment, Tribal Affairs, Minority Affairs, Women and Child, and Labor, as they all have important roles to play with respect to different disadvantaged groups. Bringing about a synergy in their efforts will be an important aspect of the task ahead.

Exclusion of Dalit Children

- The following are some of the documented experiences of exclusion faced by Dalit children. For the successful implementation of the RTE, these will have to be systematically addressed.

Exclusion of Dalit children by teachers:

- Separate seating arrangements in the classroom, with Dalit children made to sit separately or outside the classroom.

- Undue harshness towards Dalit children. For example, scolding children for coming late to school, in resolving fights between children, condoning name-calling by upper caste children, etc.

- Not giving time and attention to Dalit children in the classroom, such as not checking their homework or class work, not answering their queries – even rebuking them for asking questions in class.

- Exclusion of these children from public functions in the school such as non-participation in the morning assembly or other public events such as on Republic Day or Independence Day.

- Making derogatory remarks about Dalit children that is their lack of cleanliness and inability to keep up with academic work.

- Denying children the use of school facilities, including water source. Keeping water segregated even preventing Dalit children from using the school taps or containers used to store drinking water.

- Making children do menial tasks in school, including cleaning the school premises and even the toilets.

Exclusion of Dalit children by peer groups

- Calling Dalit children by derogatory caste names.

- Not including Dalit children in games and play activities in the classroom or in break time when children go out to play; Dalit children often return to their own neighborhoods to play with non-enrolled Dalit children.

- Not sitting with Dalit children in the classroom.

Exclusion of Dalit children by the system

- Incentives schemes and scholarships meant for Dalit children not being properly administered.

- Lack of acknowledgement of Dalit role models, such as Dr B.R Ambedkar, in the curriculum.

- Lack of sensitization of teachers in teacher education and trainings.

- Insufficient recruitment of Dalit teachers.

Based on the above known practices of discrimination the following recommen-dations are made for Inclusion of Dalit Children :

- Establishing norms of behaviour within the school for teachers and students.

- Timely detection of the forms of discrimination practiced in a particular context by either teachers or students. This is not an easy task as many forms of discrimination have become part of accepted behaviour and go unnoticed and unchallenged by the majority. Finding ways of listening to children's voices would be crucial to this exercise.

- Setting up a system of reporting on discriminatory practices at the school level would be a place to start. Complaint boxes that are regularly dealt with at SMC meetings is a suggested intervention.

- Timely redressal of instances of discrimination at the level of the school or local authority. Delays in taking action can lead to discouragement on the part of the parents and teachers.

- Establishing norms for classroom interactions such as seating patterns that ensure that children are not segregated on the basis of caste, community or gender.

- Extra-curricular activities, such as sports, music and drama with sensitivity towards participation of Dalit children, could help in breaking caste stereotype.

- Recognizing the agency of teachers. The teacher is a key figure in the school and can help to either perpetuate or obliterate discriminatory practices. But her role in this process has been largely neglected so far.

- Through proper training, setting norms of teacher behaviour, strict monitoring and supervision and taking exemplary action where norms of behaviour are flouted would help enhance school inclusivity.

- Special effort must be made to fill the posts reserved for SC and their placement in areas with dalit concentration.

- Encouraging formation of and recognizing, separate associations of SC teachers and expecting them to address issue relating to their service condition as well as the treatment meted out to dalit children in schools.

Exclusion of Scheduled Tribe Children:

Children belonging to tribal families face some of the exclusionary practices mentioned above for Dalit children and, additionally difficulties mentioned below:

- Derogatory references to their communities, names, and cultural practices.
- Exclusion from classroom processes and school activities.
- Lack of understanding of their diverse background. Primary focus is often on integrating into mainstream cultural and educational norms often resulting in de-valuing of tribal culture and heritage.
- Children from such backgrounds tend to feel inferior and often drop out or those that persist do so at the cost of losing their own sense of identity and cultural background.
- Stereo-typing of tribal culture in syllabi and textbooks.
- Lack of recognition of tribal system of knowledge, role models etc.,

In addition, tribal children face some problems peculiar to their situation.

- Tribal populations tend to be concentrated in remote, hilly or forested areas with dispersed populations where even physical access to schools is difficult.
- If there are schools and teachers, the teachers are unlikely to share the students' social and cultural background or to speak the students' language, leading to a sense of alienation among the children.
- However, the biggest problem faced by tribal children is that of language. Analysis of the educational indicators shows that majority of tribal children who drop out of the primary school is due to the difference in the school and home language. Teaching materials and textbooks tend to be in a language the students do not understand; content of books and syllabi ignore the students' own knowledge and experience and focus only on the dominant language and culture. Not understanding the standard school language and therefore the courses content, the children are unable to cope with their course and end up repeating grades and eventually dropping out.
- While instruction in the mother tongue is widely recognized as beneficial to language competencies in the first language, achievement in other subject areas, and second language learning, there is no explicit obligation on the states on institute mother tongue education. The "three language formula" that has been the cornerstone of the language policy in India has not been uniformly implemented across the country. In some states such as Jharkhand, Orissa and Chhattisgarh, which are linguistically diverse, the problem is compounded by the multiplicity of linguistic backgrounds represented in a single classroom.

Providing multilingual education is not a simple task. Education in the medium of a tribal language in initial years is challenged by a host of problems such as:

- the language may not have a script;
- the language may not even be generally recognized as constituting a legitimate language;
- there may be a shortage of educational materials in the language;

- there may be a lack of appropriately trained teachers;

- there may be resistance to schooling in the mother tongue by students, parents and teachers.

- If there are several mother tongues represented in one class, it compounds the problem even further

The National Curricular Framework 2005 has made a serious attempt at meeting the learning needs of persons belonging to tribal communities. We recommend that those recommendations be adopted by all state governments and UT Administrations. Some specific recommendations for inclusion of tribal children are made below:

- Teaching in the local language by recruiting teachers who can speak tribal languages.

- Development of educational material in local languages using resources available within the community.

- Establishing regional/state resource centers in tribal dominated states for providing training, academic and other technical support for development of pedagogic tools and education materials catering to multi-lingual situations.

- Training of teachers in multilingual education.

- Sensitization of teachers to tribal cultures and practices.

- Incorporation of local knowledge in the curriculum and textbooks.

- Creating spaces for cultural mingling within schools so as to recognize tribal cultures and practices and obliterate feelings of inferiority and alienation among tribal children.

- Involvement of community members in school activities to reduce social distance between the school and the community.

Children of most under-privileged groups

In our country there are hierarchies among the poor. There are groups which are not only the most deprived and exploited, but also quite neglected. These persons deserve a special priority. Appropriate governments and local authorities will have to make careful survey to identify persons of this category. At this stage, the following seem to us to deserve special treatment.

- Child labour, particularly bonded child labour and domestic workers;

- Children in ecologically deprived area where they are required to fetch fuel, water, fodder and do other household chores;

- Children in very poor slum communities and uprooted urban habitations;

- Children of families of scavengers;

- Children of itinerant or seasonal labor who have mobile and transient lifestyle like construction workers, road workers and workers on large construction sites;

- Children of landless agriculture labour;

- Nomadic communities and pastoralists;

- Forests dwellers and tribal people in remote areas and children residing in remote desert hamlets.

Exclusion of Muslim Children

There is enough evidence that educationally Muslims are an extremely disadvantaged community. There is need to draw them into educational and social mainstream through necessary measures, including that concerned State Governments be advised to notify them as disadvantaged groups under section 2(d) of the Act.

Not only is there no comprehensive policy for the education of Muslim children, there are no specific programs for increasing participation from this large and important minority group. Barring a few scholarships offered by the Minority Affairs Department, no special incentives exist for children from these backgrounds, unlike the other marginalized groups such as the SC and the ST. In fact very little documented evidence about the specific constraints and barriers faced by children from Muslim communities is available as very little research has been done in this area. From the scattered bits of evidence that does exist it can be said that in addition to the general issues of discrimination and harassment faced by children from other disadvantaged and excluded groups, children from Muslim families face some of the following constraints as well:

- Discouragement in school enrolment
- Hostile, threatening school and classroom environments
- Cultural and religious domination of the majority community
- Early withdrawal of male children to enable them to apprentice with artisans, mechanics etc. after because parents believe that other employment may not come their way
- Early withdrawal of female children to enable them to find grooms more educated than themselves
- Demand for Urdu, at least as a second language
- Lack of Muslim teachers

Madrassa Education

While discussing education of Muslim children the question of madrassas is usually at the forefront. Two points are worth keeping in mind while exploring strategies for their inclusion:

Demand for madrassa education is not as high as often assumed and in most cases is not seen as a substitute for mainstream education by Muslim families. As sense of losing their identity and feeling threatened by the dominant community has led to a demand for some religious education, but this must not be mistaken for a shift in demand away from a secular education.

Incorporating elements of religious history in the mainstream curriculum, offering Urdu as a language, and other such measures would go a long way in keeping Muslim children in mainstream schools.

Under RTE, madrassas have not been excluded from the purview of the Act implying that all norms and standards mentioned in the Act would apply to madrassas as well. The only exception relates to the norms governing SMCs, where these institutions have been allowed to follow their own norms. There is an important opportunity here to include a secular curriculum into the ambit of madrassa education over above their religious syllabi, which may continue to be taught.

Both these measures could contribute to building confidence in the minority community and lead to the reduction of marginalization of Muslim children from the education process.

Recommendations for Inclusion of Muslim Children

- Systematic research on specific constraints faced by Muslim children in different areas. Muslims are a heterogeneous community and exhibit wide differences in social and cultural practices in different states. A more thorough understanding of these issues will help formulate better interventions for inclusion of Muslim children into the education process.

- Option of teaching Urdu as a second language.

- Recruitment of more Muslim teachers, especially in Muslim dominated areas.

- Sensitization of all teachers on issues of cultural and religious diversity especially in relation to Muslims.

- Incorporation of practices, such as

- Celebration of Muslim festivals in schools;

- Creation of spaces for religious expression including prayer areas;

- Sensitive handling of Muslim children during Ramazan when they may be fasting;

- Encouraging discussion of Muslim cultural and religious practices in the school or classroom with the help of community members.

- A large part of exclusion results from social distance caused by lack of knowledge and understanding about minority communities. Finding spaces to break these information barriers would go a long way in reducing the hostilities and insecurities that exist on both sides.

Strategies for dealing with Reservation in Private Schools:

One of the strategies for dealing with marginalization of disadvantaged communities within the Act is to provide for 25% reservation in private and unaided schools. This provision has generated a lot of debate and discussion amongst educationists as well the public at large. While those in favor of private provision of education see this as a potential spoiler of quality within private schools, many proponents of the reservation see it as a sort of "prize" now available to children from disadvantaged backgrounds.

- The dominant thinking reflected in the Act is of inclusive quality education for all children in all schools, i.e. irrespective of the school a child attends.

- There is an explicit recognition of the fact that schools in general – be they owned and controlled by government or the private schools – need to be governed by basic norms of quality and the principles enshrined in the Constitution including those of equality, inclusiveness and diversity.

- Since, the cost implications of private school education prohibit children from certain backgrounds from accessing them, these schools tend to be "exclusive" and less diverse in the representation of children that study in them.

- The idea behind the 25% admission for children from disadvantaged groups and weaker sections in private schools is to seek to redress this imbalance. It is also to ensure that the guarantee of free and compulsory education in a neighborhood school does not completely exclude those children in the neighborhood who cannot "afford" to go to the neighborhood school.

- Hence the principle of universality that is inclusive, to the extent possible, of all the diversity that exists among children is the real purpose of the reservation. And it is with keeping this principle in mind that every effort must be made to ensure that its provision is adhered to in letter and spirit.

- In other words, ensuring that the 25% reservation represents a diversity of backgrounds from amongst the disadvantaged groups will be important. For instance, it should not result in only boys or only children from a particular caste group from being admitted under this provision.

- Exclusion of Muslim minority children in particular will have to be carefully monitored. Ideally the reservation should follow a pattern of proportionate representation from the disadvantaged and weaker sections of the neighborhood in question. It should reflect a healthy gender balance.

- While the Act mandates a random selection of children from those that apply to these schools, it will be important to ensure that children from diverse backgrounds, and gender, apply so that a random selection can be representative of the population. If not, efforts to follow a method of stratified random selection may need to be considered in the interest of maintaining diversity.

- In either case, ensuring that this provision is implemented will require careful and regular monitoring. Stringent Transparency Rules that make it mandatory for the private schools to disclose their lists of children taken in this category can be a start in this direction.

- Regular social audits that report on the practices inside the school and classrooms regarding the included children will also help in monitoring the continued and active participation of these children in the private schools. All interventions regarding discrimination mentioned above will have to apply to private school as well.

Coverage of children with disabilities in India within the RTE Act (RTE Act 2009)

- Children with disabilities have not been explicitly included as a category in section 2(d) of the RTE Act, which otherwise lists children belonging to disadvantaged groups. However, the same section also allows the appropriate government to specify, by notification, any other group of children who are disadvantaged as a result of any other factor. Thus, appropriate governments can issue a notification in section 2(d) of the RTE Act to include children with disabilities, within the category of 'children belonging to disadvantaged groups'.

- Section 3(2) of the Act qualifies that only a child suffering from disability as defined under clause (i) of section (2) of the PWD Act, 1996 shall have a right to pursue free and compulsory elementary education in accordance with provisions of chapter V of the said Act. The PWD Act,1996 excludes children suffering from certain disabilities such as cerebral palsy, autism and learning disabilities like dyslexia, disprassia etc. Further, chapter V of the PWD Act 1996 permits a multi option model for education of CWSN, which includes 'special schools' etc.

- Section 3(2) of the RTE Act is not in sync with section 3(1), in as much as it excludes children with certain disabilities from the ambit of the Act. This internal contradiction within the RTE Act needs to be addressed.

Approach and Coverage

- The SSA scheme covers all children in 6-14 years age group. The SSA Framework of Implementation explicitly states: "SSA will ensure that every child with special needs, irrespective of the kind, category and degree of disability, is provided education in an appropriate environment. SSA will adopt 'zero rejection' policy so that no child is left out of the education system".

- The RTE Act 2009, in section 3(1) entitles all children in the 6-14 years age group to a right to free and compulsory elementary education in a neighborhood school.

Identification of Children with Disabilities

As per the most recently published (DISE) data, the proportion of children with disabilities enrolled to total enrolment is only 0.84%. The total number of identified children with disabilities to total population of all children in the age group 6-14 at 1.48% is also very low (as per 2001 Census). SSA has provision for collection of data regarding children with disabilities through household surveys, assessment camps etc. There is an urgent need to streamline the process of identification through the above as well as DISE. This must be accompanied by training of the surveyors, enumerators and other government functionaries at different levels. A study by MHRD has revealed that 40% of all out-of-school children are children with special needs. Therefore early identification must be given due importance.

Educational Placement

An inclusive space for education of all children should be made available and appropriate strategies need to be followed. The SSA Framework provides that 'as far as possible every child with special needs should be placed in regular schools, with needed support services'. Under SSA, a wide range of options for educational services have been given, including for example, open school, non-formal and alternative schooling, distance education, special schools and home-based education. This range of options and strategies should be reviewed in the context of the RTE Act, which entitles all children to elementary education in regular schools that meet the norms and standards specified in the Schedule to the Act.

Children with disabilities need to be facilitated to acquire certain skills that will enable them to access elementary education as envisaged in the Act. For instance, they may need mobility training, training in Braille, sign language, tactile sign-language, and postural training, etc. Thus, school preparedness of children with disabilities must be ensured by providing 'special training' as envisaged under section 4 of the RTE Act. This training may be residential, non residential or even home based, as per their specific requirements.

- The existing non formal and alternate schooling (including home based education) options for children with disabilities can be recast as 'special training'. This means that

(a) All children with special needs who are not enrolled in schools or have dropped out, will first be enrolled in a neighborhood school in an age appropriate grade,

(b) Children will be entitled to 'special training' through regular teachers or teachers specifically appointed for the purpose.

- After completion of special training, children with special needs will continue regular classes in the age appropriate grade in which they have been enrolled. They will continue to receive special attention even after completion of 'special training' for their successful academic and emotional integration in the class. 'Special schools' will have to become inclusive schools (neighborhood schools). They will continue to function as resource centers for special inputs to regular and resource teachers, for teaching of children with special needs. The nature of this resource support can cover aspects like teacher training, development of appropriate syllabi and textbooks for children with special needs, development of individualized education plans and assessment methods, appropriate TLMs etc. Special schools would simultaneously need to work towards becoming inclusive neighborhood schools.

Education of the backward- Scheduled Caste and Tribes

Historically, the education of both the Scheduled Castes and Scheduled Tribes has been adversely affected by the ubiquity of unequal diffusion and provision of schooling. For several decades after independence, their habitations were not adequately provided with educational facilities due to paucity of resources and the gap between the massive scale of the required operation and the political will equally of state and society. The situation improved over the years, yet inadequate provision continues to serve as the most fundamental of educational deterrents to educational participation of SC/ST children. What is most alarming is the reversal today of earlier policy of equitable provision under the impact of structural adjustment. We will examine this issue shortly.

Existing schooling conditions for SC and ST vary from non-provision and under provision to the provision of the most inferior facilities, even at the basic primary level. Pre-primary education for them is even more minimal. Furthermore, both the spread and organization of the Indian education system reflect quite clearly the caste-class-tribe-gender stratified structure of society and its hierarchical ideology. The schooling system is organized in a pyramid-type hierarchy in terms of quality and social composition. Urban elite schools rank at the top and rural schools especially those located in SC and ST habitations rank at the bottom in terms of quality. Low caste and tribal children are disproportionately located in the worst schools. The effective result has been continued educational deprivation and exclusion. Several dimensions of unequal provision and unequal quality are:

1. Inadequate availability of schools

2. Poor implementation of school level policies of positive discrimination

3. Poor physical infrastructure of schools

4. Inadequacy of teachers and teaching

5. Poor provision of teaching learning materials

Inadequate Availability of Schools

Geographical location continues to be a significant predictor of whether a child will attend school, how far she will continue in school and in what type of school. Schooling within easy access has been relatively poor for the SC/ST children as compared to the general population. Scheduled Caste families, usually live in spatially segregated clusters or habitations in multi-caste villages. These residential patterns have important implications for physical and social access. School provision in predominantly Scheduled Caste habitations is much less as compared to general rural habitations. Upper-primary schooling is available within an even smaller number of habitations. On the whole, higher caste habitations within larger villages are better provided.

Poor Physical Infrastructure of Schools

A majority of studies suggest that physical/infrastructural facilities are totally inadequate and particularly deplorable in schools accessed by SC and ST, including the private schools. The majority of SC/ST children are in regular government schools. Buildings are dilapidated or badly in need of repair and basic furniture and teaching equipment is non-existent or of pathetic quality. There are of course state and regional variations. The poorest of physical infrastructure and basic amenities afflict schools in remote tribal areas. There is also a high incidence of very poorly and irregularly functioning schools.

There are reports from rural Punjab, Odisha, and Rajasthan's SC and Tribal dominated districts that reveal shortage of basics such as classrooms, drinking water facilities and teachers. Reports of neglect, indifference, greater teacher absenteeism from dalit and tribal dominated schools have accumulated, pointing to the grim reality that exists on the ground. Exceptions too have been noted, for example studies of Garhwal, Himachal Pradesh, Gujarat, Maharashtra and Kerala show that there are several regions in which the SC and ST have a fairly good provision for education. In certain areas in Maharashtra for e.g., Zilla Parishad schools are fairly good. Further, it is important to break the common misconception that rural schools are necessarily worse than urban. There are indications from Maharashtra that government rural schools may be in far better shape than urban municipal schools because most rural schools have a mix of higher and lower castes and classes whereas in urban areas where the choice of school is greater, the municipal schools cater almost exclusively to the poor, lower castes and tribes.

Inadequacy of Teachers and Teaching Transaction

A highly inadequate teaching force has been the most critical factor of equality of opportunity. Teacher-pupil ratios in schools frequented by SC and ST have been much higher than those in other schools meant for higher caste villagers. Multi-grade teaching often amounts to very limited teaching or no teaching at all! The problem of insufficient number of teachers has been compounded by the problem of unmotivated teachers, which is reflected in teacher absenteeism. Teachers for SC and ST children primarily belong to non-SC or non tribal backgrounds. They are highly irregular in attending since they live outside the villages. This is a common feature in schools located in remote areas. There are reports of `paper schools' which remain closed during the year and yet others for years on end especially in remote tribal areas. This is the situation particularly in remote tribal areas.

Dysfunctional and poorly organized school environments, inadequate number of teachers, the adoption of most conventional and uninteresting teaching methods together makes for a situation where the teaching transaction is poor and inadequate. Poor teacher competence is also a critical negative factor. At the same time however, poor working conditions which can de-motivate and demoralize even the most motivated of the primary school teacher need to be highlighted. Teachers are expected to work in isolation under harsh conditions. Worse still their teaching function is disrupted by the mandatory rules of performing all kinds of government work.

Curriculum, Pedagogy and Evaluation: Implications for SC and ST children

Curriculum is a mediator of dominance and hegemony, exploring ideological issues in the selection and structuring of knowledge and in pedagogic practice. The concept of curriculum is used here to designate the experiences pupils have under the guidance of the school. Most issues in this area are predicated upon the assumption that appropriate school experiences can indeed make a significant difference to learning and lives of SC/ST children. Content of curriculum and internal operations are thus key issues that need to be addressed. Also very important are related areas of pedagogic methods, assessment and evaluation.

In India, curriculum and the content of education have been central to the processes of reproduction of caste, class, cultural and patriarchal domination-subordination. In post independence educational policy, modification of content supposedly aimed at indigenization resulted in Brahmanisation as a key defining feature of the curriculum. Brahmanisation has been evident in the emphasis on

1. Pure language

2. Literature and other "knowledge" of society, history, polity, religion and culture that is produced by higher castes which reflects Brahmanical world view and experiences and Brahmanical perspectives on Indian society, history and culture, and

3. High caste, cultural and religious symbols, linguistic and social competencies, modes of life and behaviour.

Furthermore, the overarching stress has been on eulogizing mental as against manual labor. The heavily gendered nature of school curricular content was evident in that women's specialized knowledge and skills systems found no place in it or in the general curricular discourse. Rather they were used for devaluation and stereotyping of the female sex in curriculum. Curriculum is thus urban elite male-centric and bereft of the country's rich cultural diversity. There has been a corresponding devaluation of "lesser" dialects, cultures, traditions, and folklore of dalits and adivasis as also of peasantry. The second defining feature of the curriculum on the other hand, was its 'colonial' character which privileged western modernization. The ideology however was adopted in truncated, superficial ways – the emphasis being on the incorporation of knowledge of Western science and technology, viz. that of the "hard Western sciences", the English language and Western styles of life. Curricular structure and culture of the colonial model has remained unchanged.

Today, things have changed substantially and large numbers of parents are prepared to forego children's labor and send them to school. However school organization and curricula have not been sensitive as yet to fundamentally different economic situations, life aims and social circumstances of children belonging to poorer strata households or communities in the shaping of the school structure. What is problematic for ST and ST students is school norms of attendance, discipline, homework, tests and exams, and ethnocentric demands of concentration and memorization of the content of the text by `rote'. Furthermore, the curriculum itself as a tool of cultural dominance and hegemony has an alienating and intimidating impact. Teaching-learning material such as blackboards, chalk, texts and other reading material, laboratory equipment, instructional aid is always in short supply, of poor quality or simply nonexistent.

Curriculum and the Scheduled Castes and Scheduled tribes

Dominant forms of inequality and hierarchy are made invisible in the discourse on common nationhood and common and equal citizenship, which the school curriculum propagates. Professor Krishna Kumar's studies have focused attention on how the dominant groups' ideas about education and the educated get reflected in the curriculum. Following the curriculum, Indian texts uphold symbols of the traditional, male dominated feudal society and its obsolete cultural values and norms. However, that the value content of education is out of tune with the reality of the changing, dynamic India is a matter of choice – a choice consciously or unconsciously made by those selecting textbook material from the available body of literature and by those creating it. Worthwhile knowledge is that which is linked to the values and lifestyles of dominant groups!

Like the Scheduled castes, the curriculum does not acknowledge cultural rights of the Scheduled tribes too who are denied their own culture and history. School curriculum fails to take account of tribal cultures as autonomous knowledge systems with their own epistemology, transmission, innovation and power. Like the Scheduled Castes, Scheduled Tribes rarely feature in textbooks, and when they do, it is usually in positions servile to upper caste characters. The 'cultural discontinuity' between school and home draws attention to the rigidity of school organization and the emphasis on discipline and punishment in contrast with socialization practices and the lives of children, as reasons for non-attendance.

The Language Question:

Exclusion of their language has been a critical factor in the dropout rates of these children. Despite several policy documents and a constitutional provision (350A) recognizing that linguistic minorities should be educated in their mother tongue at primary level, there is practically no education in Scheduled Tribe languages. Although states in India were organized on linguistic grounds, political powerlessness of Scheduled Tribes prevented the formation of states based on tribal languages. They are confined to minority status within large states and are compelled to learn the state language in school. Primary teachers are predominantly from non-ST communities. And despite the pedagogic significance of initial instruction in the mother tongue, teachers do not bother to learn the tribal language even after several years of posting. The general picture at primary level is often one of mutual incomprehension between ST students and their non-ST teachers. Several studies have pointed to the significance of the language question at the primary levels.

HIDDEN CURRICULUM AND SC/ST CHILDREN

In the school and in classrooms, teacher-pupil interaction is central to teaching and learning processes. Teacher's social background (caste, religion, language), affect their interactions with students. Middle class higher caste teachers are very unhappy with the environments of schools for the poor and are poorly motivated to teach children of the poor, particularly of SC/ST background, who are `derogatorily' categorized as uneducable. There is an appalling body of evidence that suggests that teacher's preconceptions, bias and behaviour, subtle or overt, conscious or unconscious operate to discriminate against children of SC and ST background. Teachers are observed to have low expectations of SC and ST children and girls and a condescending attitude towards children from slums. Teachers also have stated or unstated assumptions of "deprived" and "deficient" cultural backgrounds, languages and inherent intellectual deficiencies of SC and/ ST children. They follow discriminatory pedagogic practices of labeling, classifying and teaching styles and operate on the basis of "realistic" perceptions of low caste children's limited cognitive capacities and life chances. For e.g. teachers beliefs about Mushar children in Bihar are that they are just not interested in education and that they do not have any 'tension' in life

Recommendations of the Focus Group is as follows:

Institutional Context

(a) **Provision :** We strongly reiterate the need for equitable provision in terms of quality of schooling at different levels, educational infrastructure and other facilities, qualified teachers, teaching learning materials, texts and others. It is crucial to enhance the autonomy and working conditions of teachers, and teacher self-esteem. All nonteaching work load must be taken off the teacher. The educational environment of substandard dysfunctional schools must change for any meaningful and effective curricular reform.

(b) We recommend the need to identify areas and groups which continue to suffer marked exclusion and neglect to enable a more focused implementation of positive discrimination policies. We also emphasize the need to invest greater financial and educational resources for their educational development.

(c) School Organization: There is need for flexibility in school structures and cultures. School times, calendars and holidays must keep in mind local contexts.

(d) The school system requires a more generous and efficient provision of facilities meant for SC and ST children. It is important for all concerned to engage with those struggling for rights of these communities, especially those committed to their educational advancement.

School Curriculum

(a) Curricular goals must emphasize critical thinking and critical evaluation and appreciation of Indian society and culture. Equal opportunity for intellectual growth, cognitive development, social and emotional development of underprivileged children must be sought. Curriculum must aim at promotion of creative talents, productive skills, dignity of labor, underlined by values of equality, democracy, secularism, social and gender justice.

(b) Curricular content: An approach rooted in critical theory and critical multiculturalism is essential to critique the unjust social order, to indigenize and incorporate diverse cultures and prevent loss of valuable cultural heritage. We must make a commitment to the preservation of all languages as a matter of communities' cultural rights as well as of national pride.

(c) Curriculum should lead to identification and creativity, not alienation. There is need to incorporate all creative arts, crafts and oral expression, especially those rooted in indigenous knowledge and skill systems.

(d) Curriculum must develop a critical social science and humanities; content aimed at the achievement of curricular goals. A balance between curricular subjects is essential.

(e) There is need to develop critical multicultural texts and reading material.

Pedagogy

(a) Incorporation of diverse pedagogic methods and practices towards enhancing learning and democratic classroom practice is essential.

(b) We need to develop constructive critical pedagogy and specific guidance on classroom practices with a view to eschew discrimination against children on the basis of caste, class, tribe, gender, identity/ ability etc.

(c) Improvement is required in the affective climate of school, to enable teachers and students to participate freely in knowledge construction and learning.

(d) There is need to develop pedagogic practices that aim at improving self esteem and identity of SC and ST.

(e) Non-graded instruction with judicious use of tests for evaluation of learning may be considered.

(f) Making available a wide range of texts and other reading and instructional material is absolutely essential.

Language

(a) Home languages must be made the media of instruction / communication in the early years of school education. They must be seen as integral to creating an enabling school environment for children and crucial for the process of learning. The pedagogic rationale is that moving from the known to the unknown facilitates learning. Language is a critical resource that children bring to school and aids thought, communication and understanding.

(b) Home languages in classroom process are also essential to build child's self-esteem and self confidence.

(c) Transition to regional language will be facilitated through learning of home language.

(d) Where there are more than one tribal languages used in any village, we recommend the use of the regional lingua franca or the majority language after consultation with villagers.

(e) Teacher training must include the stipulation that teachers pass an exam in a local language.

Gender inequality in education

The social barriers inhibiting parents from sending girls to school are:

- Poverty
- Household chores such as looking after home and siblings, farm work,
- Early marriage,
- Misconception that girls do not need education,
- Irrelevance of education for girls,
- More economic benefits from son's education,
- Lack of women teachers
- Lack of separate schools for girls
- Lack of supportive facilities like adequate and clean toilets in schools
- No transport facilities to travel to school and back.

All these inhibit parents from getting their girls enrolled. Girls have to stay at home once they attain puberty and must be protected till they are married. And they become part of another family, leaving the parental home. Add to this, the commonly held belief that marriage is the be-all and end-all for girls, leading to early marriage and pregnancy. So naturally the son is sent to the school, not the daughter.

Innovations that have made a difference

There is no dearth of interesting innovations in India – in both the government as well as the non-government sector. The table below captures the range of innovations that are underway across the country. What is, however, worrisome is that many of them have remained small-scale pilot efforts and have not led to systemic reforms in the mainstream.

India Case Study, 20 June 2003

Table IV: Some Key Issues and Successful Models Issue	Successful models/ innovations	NGOs	Government
Lack of access in rural/remote areas and dysfunctional schools	Running non-formal schools/alternative schools in rural/remote areas; Residential schools for tribal children and/ or children of specific communities/erstwhile child workers; Short-term bridge courses followed by admissions into residential schools.	Agragamee (Orissa) MV Foundation (AP) Cini Asha (W. Bengal) CREDA (UP) Maya (Karnataka)	Shiksha Karmi Project of Rajasthan Education Guarantee Scheme of Madhya Pradesh Sahaj Shiksha Kendras (Alternative Schools) in Rajasthan Lok Jumbish Ashram Shalas in Odisha, Andhra Pradesh Learning Guarantee Scheme in Karnataka (with Corporate partner) Balika Shikshan Shivir of Lok Jumbish

Community apathy towards girls' education	Community mobilisation — especially of women and youth; Campaign against child labour; Mother-daughter fairs/ girls' education and health fairs to kindle interest in education and provide advice/ counselling; Special Programmes with adolescent girls.	Concerned for Working Children (Karnataka) BGVS – several states of India Doosra Dashak (Rajasthan)	Lok Jumbish of Rajasthan DPEP Model Cluster Approach in Uttar Pradesh Back-to-school (Chaduvula Panduga) campaigns in Andhra Pradesh Chinnara Angala of Karnataka
Irrelevant curriculum	Developing relevant curriculum and provide training to teachers in both formal as well as alternative streams.	Nirantar (Delhi) Eklavya (MP) Digantar, Bodh, Sandhaan, (Rajasthan)	DPEP efforts in Kerala and Karnataka
Non-availability of women teachers	Mahila Shikshan Kendra (of Mahila Samakhya Programme), Mahila Shikshan Vihar of Lok Jumbish and Mahila Prashikshan Kendra of Shiksha Karmi Project have tried to provide intensive, good quality education for school dropouts and never-been-to-	Mahila Shikshan Kendras run under Mahila Samakhya Programme of GOI in Karnataka, Andhra Pradesh, Uttar Pradesh,	

The DPEP (District Primary Education Program) is a special program of the Government of India to increase enrolment of girls at the primary level and helping sustain it. One of its thrusts is the elimination of gender discrimination in the schools. In fact, there is a substantial gender focus in it. The decentralized implementation of the program provides for specific interventions for girls. Program goals include concentrated effort on reduction of gender disparities in education, as reflected in lower enrolment, retention and achievement of girls, particularly those from socially and economically disadvantaged groups. It emphasizes the role of the community in helping the school to combat sex stereotyping. It encourages local communities, particularly women to play an active role in every aspect of the program. This includes intensive capacity building for groups in the community to focus on issues relating to the education of girls and boys. Involvement of the community is also required in monitoring enrolment, retention and levels of achievement and classroom behaviour and transaction, with emphasis on girls. Moreover, the mid-day meal scheme is intended to attract children of the poorer sections to enroll in schools.

CHILDREN WITH SPECIAL NEEDS

Learning Disabilities

Learning disabilities is a generic term that refers to a heterogeneous group of disorders manifested by significant difficulties in the acquisition and use of listening, speaking, reading, writing, reasoning, or mathematical abilities. These disorders are intrinsic to the individual and are presumed to be due to central nervous system dysfunction. Even though a learning disability may occur concomitantly with other handicapping conditions (e.g., sensory impairment, mental retardation, social or emotional disturbance) or environmental influences (e.g., cultural differences, insufficient/inappropriate instruction, psychogenic factors), it is not the direct result of these conditions or influences.

Students with learning disabilities are not all alike. The most common characteristics are specific difficulties in one or more academic areas; poor coordination; problems paying attention; hyperactivity and impulsivity; problems organizing and interpreting visual and auditory information; disorders of thinking, memory, speech, and hearing; and difficulties making and keeping friends. Most students with learning disabilities have difficulties reading. These difficulties appear to be caused by problems with relating sounds to letters that make up words, making spelling hard as well.

SPECIFIC LEARNING DISABILITIES

Auditory Processing Disorder (APD)

Professionals may refer to the ability to hear well as "auditory processing skills" or "receptive language."

Also known as Central Auditory Processing Disorder, this is a condition that adversely affects how sound that travels unimpeded through the ear is processed or interpreted by the brain. Individuals with APD are not able to distinguish between sounds in words, even when the sounds are loud and clear enough to be heard. They can also find it difficult to tell where sounds are coming from, to make sense of the order of sounds, or to block out competing background noises.

Dyscalculia (Learning Disabilities in Math)

A specific learning disability that affects a person's ability to understand numbers and learn math facts. Individuals with this type of LD may also have poor comprehension of math symbols, may struggle with memorising and organizing numbers, have difficulty in operating signs and number "facts", (like $5 + 5 = 10$ or $5 \times 5 = 25$) have difficulty telling time or have trouble with counting principles (such as counting by 25 or counting by 55.)

Dysgraphia (Learning Disabilities in Writing)

A specific learning disability that affects a person's handwriting ability and fine motor skills. Problems may include illegible handwriting, inconsistent spacing, poor spatial planning on paper, poor spelling, and difficulty composing writing as well as thinking and writing at the same time.

Dyslexia (Learning Disabilities in Reading)

The most commonly known is a reading disability, sometimes called dyslexia. There is no difference in meaning between the terms dyslexia and reading disability. Dyslexia involves difficulties with phonological processing, including such abilities as knowing the relationship between letters and sounds and phonological awareness—that is, the ability to segment the speech stream into separate elements. Over the years, a consensus has emerged that one core deficit in dyslexia is a severe difficulty with phonological processing (Usually individuals with dyslexia have spelling problems, but the presence of spelling difficulties without reading difficulties does not indicate dyslexia.

Language Processing Disorder (LPD)

A specific type of Auditory Processing Disorder (APD) in which there is difficulty attaching meaning to sound groups that form words, sentences and stories. While an APD affects the interpretation of all sounds coming into the brain, a Language Processing Disorder (LPD) relates only to the processing of language. LPD can affect expressive language and/or receptive language.

Non-Verbal Learning Disabilities

A disorder which is usually characterised by a significant discrepancy between higher verbal skills and weaker motor, visual-spatial and social skills. Typically, an individual with NLD (or NVLD) has trouble interpreting nonverbal cues like facial expressions or body language, and may have poor coordination.

Visual Perceptual/Visual Motor Deficit

A disorder that affects the understanding of information that a person sees, or the ability to draw or copy. A characteristic seen in people with learning disabilities such as Dysgraphia or Non-verbal LD, it can result in missing subtle differences in shapes or printed letters, reversing letters or numbers, skipping words, misperceiving depth or distance, losing place frequently, struggles with cutting, holding pencil too tightly, or poor eye/hand coordination.

ADHD (Attention Deficit Hyperactivity Disorder)

A disorder that includes difficulty staying focused and paying attention, have problems sitting still, difficulty controlling behaviour and unable to follow instructions. Although ADHD is not considered a learning disability, research indicates that from 30 to 50 percent of children with ADHD also have a specific learning disability, and that the two conditions can interact to make learning extremely challenging.

Dyspraxia (Learning disabilities in motor skills)

A disorder that is characterised by difficulty in muscle control, which causes problems with movement and coordination, language and speech, and can affect learning. Although not a learning disability, dyspraxia often exists along with dyslexia, dyscalculia or ADHD.

Autism

Children with autism spectrun disorders may have trouble communicating, reading body language, learning basic skills, making friends and making eye contact.

Executive Functioning : An inefficiency in the cognitive management systems of the brain that affects a variety of neuropsychological processes such as planning organisation, strategising, paying attention to and remembering details, and managing time and space. Although not a learning disability, different patterns of weakness in executive functioning are almost always seen in the learning profiles of individuals who have specific learning disabilities or ADHD.

Communication Disorders

Language disorders may arise from many sources, because so many different aspects of the individual are involved in learning language. A child with a hearing impairment will not learn to speak normally. A child who hears inadequate language at home will learn inadequate language. Children who are not listened to, or whose perception of the world is distorted by emotional problems, will reflect these problems in their language development. Because speaking involves movements, any impairment of the motor functions involved with speech can cause language disorders. And because language development and thinking are so interwoven, any problems in cognitive functioning can affect ability to use language.

Speech disorders

Students who cannot produce sounds effectively for speaking are considered to have a speech disorder. Articulation problems and stuttering are the two most common problems.

Articulation disorders include substituting one sound for another (thunthine for sunshine), distorting a sound (shoup for soup), adding a sound (ideer for idea), or omitting sounds (po-y for pony).

Stuttering generally happens between the ages of 3 and 4. It is not yet clear what causes stuttering, but it can lead to embarrassment and anxiety for the sufferer. In about 50% of the cases, stuttering disappears during early adolescence.

Voicing problems, a third type of speech impairment, include speaking with an inappropriate pitch, quality or loudness or in a monotone. A student with any of these problems should be referred to a speech therapist.

Reading habits and errors

Do any of your students show these signs? They could be indications of learning disabilities.

Poor Reading Habits

- Frequently loses his or her place
- Jerks head from side to side
- Expresses insecurity by crying or refusing to read
- Prefers to read with the book held within inches from face
- Shows tension while reading; such as reading in a high-pitched voice, biting lips and fidgeting

Word Recognition Errors

- Omitting a word (e.g., "He came to the park," is read, "He came to park")
- Inserting a word (e.g., "He came to the (beautiful) park"
- Substituting a word for another (e.g. "He came to the pond")

- Reversing letters or words (e.g. was is read saw)
- Mispronouncing words(e.g., park is read pork)
- Transposing letters or words(e.g., "The dog ate fast is read "The dog fast ate")
- Not attempting to read an unknown word by breaking it into familiar units
- Slow, laborious reading, less than 20-30 words per minute

Comprehension Errors

- Recalling basic facts (e.g., cannot answer questions directly from a passage)
- Recalling sequence (e.g., cannot explain the order of events in a story)
- Recalling main theme (e.g., cannot give the main idea of a story)

Attention deficit hyperactivity disorder

Attention deficit hyperactivity disorder (or ADHD) is a problem with sustaining attention and controlling impulses. As students, almost all of us have these problems at one time or another, but a student with ADHD shows them much more frequently than usual, and often at home as well as at school. In the classroom, the student with ADHD may fidget and squirm a lot, or have trouble remaining seated, or continually get distracted and off task, or have trouble waiting for a turn, or blurt out answers and comments. The student may shift continually from one activity to another, or have trouble playing quietly, or talk excessively without listening to others. Or the student may misplace things and seem generally disorganized, or be inclined to try risky activities without enough thought to the consequences. Although the list of problem behaviours is obviously quite extensive, keep in mind that the student will not do all of these things. It is just that over time, the student with ADHD is likely to do several of them chronically or repeatedly, and in more than one setting (American Psychiatric Association, 2000). In the classroom, of course, the behaviours may annoy classmates and frustrate teachers.

Hearing loss

A child can have a hearing loss for a variety of reasons, varying from disease in early childhood, to difficulties during childbirth, to reactions to toxic drugs. In the classroom, however, the cause of the loss is virtually irrelevant because it makes little difference in how to accommodate a student's educational needs. More important than the cause of the loss is its extent. Students with only mild or moderate loss of hearing are sometimes called hearing impaired or hard of hearing; only those with nearly complete loss are called deaf. As with other sorts of disabilities, the milder the hearing loss, the more likely you are to encounter the student in a regular classroom, at least for part of the day.

Signs of hearing loss

A serious hearing loss tends to be noticed quickly and therefore often receive special help sooner. Mild or moderate hearing loss is much more common, however, and is probably overlooked or mistaken for some other sort of learning problem.

Teaching students with hearing loss

Adjustments in teaching students with hearing loss are easy to make though they do require deliberate actions or choices by the teacher and by fellow students. Interestingly, many of the strategies make good advice for teaching all students!

- Seat the student close to you: Do this while doing the talking or make the student sit close to key classmates if the students are in a work group. Keep noise levels to a minimum as such noise is especially distracting to someone with a hearing loss. Keep instructions concise and to-the-point. Ask the student occasionally if he or she is following what is being taught.

- Use visual cues liberally. Make charts and diagrams wherever appropriate to illustrate what you are saying. Look directly at the student when you are speaking to him or her to facilitate lip reading. Gesture and point to key words or objects. Provide handouts or readings to review visually the points that you make orally.

- Include the student in the community of the classroom. Recruit one or more classmates to assist in "translating" oral comments that the student may have missed.

Visual impairment

- Students with visual impairments have difficulty seeing even with corrective lenses.

- Students with visual impairments often show some of the same signs as students with simple, common nearsightedness.

- The students may rub their eyes a lot, for example, blink more than usual, or hold books very close to read them. They may complain of itchiness in their eyes, or of headaches, dizziness, or even nausea after doing a lot of close eye work.

- The difference between the students with visual impairment and those with "ordinary" nearsightedness is primarily a matter of degree: the ones with impairment show the signs more often and more obviously.

- If the impairment is serious enough or has roots in certain physical conditions or disease, they may also have additional symptoms, such as crossed eyes or swollen eyelids.

- For classroom teachers, the best strategy may be to keep track of a student whose physical signs happen in combination with learning difficulties, and for whom the combination persists for many weeks.

Teaching students with visual impairment

In general, advice for teaching students with mild or moderate visual impairment parallels the advice for teaching students with hearing loss, though with obvious differences because of the nature of the students' disabilities.

- Take advantage of the student's residual vision. If the student still has some useful vision, place him or her where he can easily see the most important parts of the classroom—whether that is you, the chalkboard, a video screen, or particular fellow students. Make sure that the classroom, or at least the student's part of it, is well lit (because good lighting makes reading easier with low vision). Make sure that handouts, books and other reading materials have good, sharp contrast (also helpful with a visual impairment).

- Use non-visual information liberally. Remember not to expect a student with visual impairment to learn information that is by nature only visual, such as the layout of the classroom, the appearance of photographs in a textbook or of story lines in a video. Explain these to the student somehow. Use hands-on materials wherever they will work, such as maps printed in three-dimensional relief or with different textures. If the student knows how to read Braille (an alphabet for the blind using patterns of small bumps on a page) allow him to do so.

- Include the student in the community of the classroom. Make sure that the student is accepted as well as possible into the social life of the class. Recruit classmates to help explain visual material when necessary.

Learn a bit of basic Braille and encourage classmates to do the same, even if none of you ever become as skilled with it as the student himself.

Exercise 1 : Previous Year Questions of CTET & STET

1. Education of children with special needs should be provided *[CTET-2011-I]*
   (a) along with other normal children
   (b) by methods developed for special children in special Schools
   (c) in special school
   (d) by special teachers in special schools

2. A student of V-grade with 'visual deficiency' should be *[CTET-2011-I]*
   (a) excused to do a lower level of work
   (b) helped with hislher routine-work by parents and friends
   (c) treated normally in the classroom and provided support through Audio CDs
   (d) given special treatment III the classroom

3. A provision for education for the children with disabilities can be done through *[RTET-2011-I]*
   (a) Inclusive education
   (b) Mainstreaming
   (c) Integration
   (d) None of these

4. 'Child belonging to weaker section' means *[RTET-2011-I]*
   (a) A child belonging to such parents whose annual income is low
   (b) A child belonging to such parents who come under the disadvantaged group
   (c) A child belonging to such parents who come under the category of below poverty line
   (d) A child belonging to such parents whose annual income is lower than the minimum limit specified by the appropriate government.

5. A student of grade 5 with visual deficiency should be *[UPTET-2011-I]*
   (a) excused to do a lower level of work
   (b) helped with his / her routine work by parents and friends
   (c) treated normally in the classroom and provided support through audio CDs
   (d) given special treatment in the classroom.

6. Why should students play games in school? *[UPTET-2011-I]*
   (a) It makes them physically strong
   (b) It makes work easier for teachers
   (c) It helps in passing time
   (d) It develops co-operation and physical balance.

7. You have been told to accommodate two mentally retarded children in your class. You will *[UPTET-2011-I]*
   (a) refuse to accept them as your students
   (b) tell the principal to accommodate them in another class exclusively for mentally retarded children
   (c) learn techniques to teach such students
   (d) none of these

8. Which article enjoins that "All minorities whether based on religion or language shall have the right to establish & administer education institutions of their choice" *[PTET-2011-I]*
   (a) Article 29 (1)   (b) Article 29 (2)
   (c) Article 30 (1)   (d) Article 30 (2)

9. "It is the duty of mankind to give the best to the children" - UNO proclaimed it on *[TNTET-2011-I]*
   (a) August 15, 1969 (b) April 20, 1969
   (c) June 16, 1959   (d) November 20, 1959

10. Expansion of RTE is *[TNTET-2011-I]*
    (a) Right of children to free and compulsory education
    (b) Right to teacher education
    (c) Right of children to education
    (d) Right towards education

11. 'Dyslexia' is associated with *[CTET-2011-I]*
    (a) Mental disorder
    (b) Mathematical disorder
    (c) Reading disorder
    (d) Behavioural disorder

12. The best way, specially at primary level, to address the learning difficulties of students is to use *[CTET-2011-I]*
    (a) a variety of teaching methods suited to the disability
    (b) expensive and, glossy support material
    (c) easy and interesting textbooks
    (d) story-telling method

13. Centrally sponsored scheme of Integrated Education for disabled children aims at providing educational opportunities to children with disabilities in *[CTET-2011-II]*
    (a) regular schools
    (b) special schools
    (c) open schools
    (d) Blind Relief Association schools

14. Which of the following is a better strategy for teaching children with special needs?
[RTET-2011-II]
  (a) Discussion in the classroom involving maximum number of students
  (b) Demonstration by teacher involving students
  (c) Cooperative learning and peer tutoring
  (d) Ability grouping for teaching

15. The objective of action research is to
[RTET-2011-II]
  (a) gain new knowledge
  (b) develop the science of behaviour in educational situations
  (c) modify the educational practices in school and classroom
  (d) all of these.

16. Girl's education should be given priority because *[UPTET-2011-II]*
  (a) girls are more intelligent than boys
  (b) girls are less in number than boys
  (c) girls were badly discriminated against in the past
  (d) only girls are capable of leading a social change

17. Inclusive Education *[CTET-2012-I]*
  (a) encourages strict admission procedures
  (b) includes indoctrination of facts
  (c) includes teachers from marginalized groups
  (d) celebrates diversity in the classroom

18. Inclusive education refers to a school education system that *[CTET-2012-II]*
  (a) emphasizes the need to promote the education of the girl child only
  (b) includes children with disability
  (c) includes children regardless of physical, intellectual, social, linguistic or other differently able conditions
  (d) encourages education of children with special needs through exclusive schools

19. It is not Speech Disorder : [UPTET-2014-I]
  (a) Lisping and Slurring
  (b) Talking in slow or fast Speed
  (c) Stammering and Stuttering
  (d) Sharp unclear speech

20. A child of class-4 is always suffers with anxiety and frustration, you will *[UPTET-2014-I]*
  (a) complain to his guardian
  (b) bring him to psychiatrist
  (c) do the role of a counsellor
  (d) leave him on his fortune

21. The main objective of the mental hygiene is ______. [UPTET-2014-II]
  (a) to protect the mental health of the child
  (b) to remove maladjustment
  (c) Both above
  (d) None of these

22. Special education is related to *[PTET-2014-I]*
  (a) Educational for talented students
  (b) Educational programmes for disabled
  (c) Training programmes for Teachers
  (d) Training programmes for retarded

23. Which article enjoins that "All minorities whether based on religion or language shall have the right to establish & administer education institutions of their choice" *[PTET-2014-I]*
  (a) Article 29(1)   (b) Article 29(2)
  (c) Article 30(1)   (d) Article 30(2)

24. If a child writes 16 as 61 & gets confused between b & d, this is case of : *[PTET-2014-I]*
  (a) Visual Impairment
  (b) Learning Disability
  (c) Mental impairment
  (d) Mental Retardation

25. Special needs education is the type of education: *[PTET-2014-II]*
  (a) given to very special people
  (b) given to persons with disabilities
  (c) provided to intelligent people
  (d) established by colonial masters

26. Children with speech impairment can be assisted by: *[PTET-2014-II]*
  (a) encouraging them to express thoughts in the classroom
  (b) helping him/her to pronounce correct sounds
  (c) helping him /her to hear his/her spoken errors
  (d) referral to specialist for complete evaluation

27. One's personality disorder is based on
[TNTET-2014-I]
  (a) Emotional shocks
  (b) Simple feelings
  (c) Emotional enjoyment
  (d) Mental health

28. In which country was the Juvenile Psychopathic Institute established in the year 1909
[TNTET-2014-II]
  (a) Australia   (b) India
  (c) Chicago   (d) Saudi Arabia

29. A teacher has some physically challenged children in her class. Which of the following would be appropriate for her to say ? *[CTET-July-2013-I]*

(a) Wheel-chaired bound children may take help of their peers in going to hall.

(b) Physically inconvenienced children may do an alternative activity in the classroom.

(c) Mohan why don't you use your crutches to go to the playground.

(d) Polio afflicted children will now present a song.

30. Learning disabilities may occur due to all of the following except *[CTET-July-2013-I]*

(a) Cerebral dysfunction

(b) Emotional disturbance

(c) Behavioural disturbance

(d) Cultural factors

31. An inclusive school. *[CTET-July-2013-I]*

(a) Is committed to· improve the learning outcomes of all students irrespective of their capabilities

(b) Differentiate between students and sets less challenging achievement targets for specially abled children

(c) Committed particularly to improve the learning outcomes of specially abled students

(d) Decides learning heeds of students according to their disability

32. Learning Disability in motor skills is called *[CTET-July-2013-I]*

(a) Dyspraxia (b) Dyscalculia

(c) Dyslexia (d) Dysphasia

33. Learning Disability [CTET-July-2013-I]

(a) is a stable state

(b) is a variable state

(c) need not impair functioning

(d) does not improve with appropriate input

34. Learning disabilities may occur due to all of the following **except** *[CTET-July-2013-II]*

(a) Teachers way of teaching

(b) Prenatal use of alcohol

(c) Mental Retardation

(d) Meningitis during infancy

35. An inclusive school reflects on all the following questions **except** : *[CTET-July.-2013-II]*

(a) Do we believe that all students can learn

(b) Do we work in teams to plan and deliver learning enabling environment

(c) Do we properly segregate special children from normal to provide better care

(d) Do we adopt strategies catering for the diverse needs of students

36. A disorder related to language comprehension is *[CTET-Feb.-2014-I]*

(a) apraxia (b) dyslexia

(c) aspeechxia (d) aphasia

37. Which of the following is the most effective way to convey students way to convey students from disadvantaged sections that you except them to participate and succeed? *[CTET-Feb.-2014-I]*

(a) Articulate your confidence in their ability to succeed

(b) Develop your own interest in the topics to be taught

(c) Compare them with other children as frequently as possible to make them realize their goal

(d) Emphasize the point that you have high expectation of them

38. Following are the examples of developmental disorder, except *[CTET-Feb.-2014-I]*

(a) autism

(b) cerebral palsy

(c) post-traumatic stress

(d) attention deficit hyperactivity disorder

39. Inclusion in schools primarily focuses on *[CTET-Feb.-2014-I]*

(a) making subtle provisions for special category children

(b) fulfilling the needs of children with disabilities only

(c) meeting the need of the disabled child at the expense of entire class

(d) including the educational needs to illiterate parents in schools

40. The cause of learned helplessness in children is their *[CTET-Feb.-2014-I]*

(a) acquired behaviour that they will not succeed

(b) callous attitude towards classroom activities

(c) non-compliance with expectations of their parents

(d) moral decision for not taking up studies seriously

41. If a student is consistently getting lower grades in school, her parents can be advised to help her by *[CTET-Feb.-2014-I]*

(a) working in close association with teachers

(b) withholding mobile phones, movies, comics and extra time for play

(c) narrating her the hardships of life for those who do not possess proper education

(d) forcing her to work harder at home

42. Teachers must believe in which of the following values in the context of dealing with disadvantaged learners? *[CTET-Feb.-2014-II]*
(a) Personal accountability for students' success
(b) High expectations of appropriate behaviour
(c) No demands of any sort on the student
(d) For immediate compliance of students, use of being shocked and angry

43. In the context of learning-disabled children, providing immediate connections, stressing collaboration and leveraging non-learning technologies such as instant messaging, intelligent search and content management are associated with which of the following designs?*[CTET-Feb.-2014-II]*
(a) Embedded learning
(b) Interventionist learning
(c) Reply to remediation
(d) Universal design for learning

44. An inclusive classroom is that where *[CTET-Feb.-2014-II]*
(a) assessments are repeated till the time every learner achieves minimum grades
(b) teachers teach from only prescribed books to lessen the burden of the students
(c) there is an active involvement of children in solving as many problems as possible
(d) teachers create diverse and meaningful learning experiences for every learner

45. Learning disabilities are *[CTET-Feb.-2014-II]*
(a) objective facts and culture has no role in determining them
(b) synonymous with dyslexia
(c) also present in children with average or above average IQ
(d) not immutable irrespective of time and nature of interventions

46. Which of the following may be the best way to deal with an inattentive child in the classroom? *[CTET-Feb.-2014-II]*
(a) Nag the child as frequently in front of the class to make her/him realize
(b) Make the child sit in the most distraction-reduced area
(c) Allow the child to stand while working so as to enable the child to focus attention
(d) Provide the child frequent breaks to refresh her/his attention

47. Which of the following is the most appropriate method to monitor the progress of children with learning disabilities? *[CTET-Sep.-2014-II]*
(a) Case-study
(b) Anecdotal records
(c) Behaviour-rating scale
(d) Structured behavioural observation

48. The best way to increase the chances of learning disabled students to lead a full and productive life, is by *[CTET-Sep.-2014-II]*
(a) focussing on weaknesses of such students
(b) maintaining a high expectation from such students
(c) teaching a variety of skills and strategies that can be applied across a range of contexts
(d) encouraging these children to define their own goals

49. Students of disadvantaged groups should be taught along with the normal students. It implies *[CTET-Feb.-2015-I]*
(a) Inclusive Education
(b) Special Education
(c) Integrated Education
(d) Exclusive Education

50. Deficiency in the ability to write, associated with impaired handwriting, is a symptom of *[CTET-Feb.-2015-I]*
(a) Dysgraphia   (b) Dyspraxia
(c) Dyscalculia   (d) Dyslexia

51. Which one of the following statements best describes 'Inclusion'? *[CTET-Feb.-2016-I]*
(a) It is the belief that children need to be segregated according to their abilities.
(b) It is the belief that some children cannot learn at all.
(c) It is the philosophy that all children have a right to get equal education in a regular school system.
(d) It is the philosophy that special children are 'a special gift of God'.

52. To cater to the children from 'disadvantaged' background, a teacher should*[CTET-Feb.-2016-I]*
(a) give them a lot of written work.
(b) try to find out more about them and involve them in class discussions.
(c) make them sit separately in the class.
(d) ignore them as they cannot interact with other students.

53. Which one of the following behaviours is an identifier of a child with learning disability? *[CTET-Feb.-2016-I]*
   - (a) Frequent mood swings
   - (b) Abusive behaviour
   - (c) Writing 'b' as 'd', 'was' as 'saw', '21' as '12'
   - (d) Low attention span and high physical activity

54. A child who can see partially *[CTET-Feb.-2016-I]*
   - (a) should be put in a 'regular' school with no special provisions.
   - (b) should not be given education, since it is not of any use to him.
   - (c) needs to be put in a separate institution.
   - (d) should be put in a 'regular' school while making special provisions.

55. A teacher has a 'hearing impaired' child in her middle school class. It is important for her to *[CTET-Feb.-2016-II]*
   - (a) make the child sit at a place from where she can see the teacher's lips and facial expressions clearly.
   - (b) ask the school counsellor to talk to the child's parents and tell them to withdraw their child from school.
   - (c) keep pointing to what the child cannot do over and over again.
   - (d) ridicule the child and make her sit separately so that she joins an institution for hearing impaired.

56. A teacher can effectively respond to the needs of the children from 'disadvantaged sections' of society by *[CTET-Feb.-2016-II]*
   - (a) ignoring their background and asking them to do chores in the school.
   - (b) adapting her pedagogy to the needs of every child in the classroom.
   - (c) making them sit separately in the classroom so that they do not mix with other children.
   - (d) telling other children to treat the children from disadvantaged background with sympathy.

57. Children with learning disability *[CTET-Feb.-2016-II]*
   - (a) are very wise and mature.
   - (b) are very active, but have a low IQ.
   - (c) cannot learn anything.
   - (d) struggle with some aspects of learning.

58. Which one of the following philosophical perspectives needs to be followed to deal with children with special needs? *[CTET-Feb.-2016-II]*
   - (a) They do not need any education at all.
   - (b) They have a right to inclusive education and study in regular schools.
   - (c) They should be segregated and put in separate educational institutions.
   - (d) They should be given only vocational training.

59. Inclusion of children with special needs : *[CTET-Sept.-2016-I]*
   - (a) is an unrealistic goal
   - (b) is detrimental to children without disabilities
   - (c) will increase the burden on schools
   - (d) requires a change in attitude, content and approach to teaching

60. A child with hearing impairment : *[CTET-Sept.-2016-I]*
   - (a) should be sent only to a school for the hearing impaired and not to a regular school
   - (b) will not benefit from academic education only and should be given vocational training instead
   - (c) can do very well in a regular school if suitable facilitation and resources are provided
   - (d) will never be able to perform on a par with classmates in a regular school

61. A teacher asks her class to cover sharp edges of furniture with cotton and use Touch and Feel' notice boards and books. The needs of which category of special learners is she attempting to cater to? *[CTET-Sept.-2016-II]*
   - (a) Socially disadvantaged learners
   - (b) Visually-impaired learners
   - (c) Hearing-impaired learners
   - (d) Learning-impaired learners

62. One of the following is a reason for mental ill health in students *[APTET-May.-2018-I]*
   - (a) Pleasant school atmosphere
   - (b) Over burdened learning programs
   - (c) Flexible examination system
   - (d) Healthy habits of students

63. Among the following 'Educable mentally retarded' are *[APTET-May.-2018-I]*
   - (a) Profound mentally retarded
   - (b) Severe mentally retarded
   - (c) Moderate mentally retarded
   - (d) Mild mentally retarded

Answer Key

1.	(a)	**10.**	(a)	**19.**	(b)	**28.**	(c)	**37.**	(a)	**46.**	(b)	**55.**	(a)
2.	(c)	**11.**	(c)	**20.**	(c)	**29.**	(c)	**38.**	(c)	**47.**	(d)	**56.**	(b)
3.	(a)	**12.**	(a)	**21.**	(c)	**30.**	(d)	**39.**	(a)	**48.**	(c)	**57.**	(d)
4.	(d)	**13.**	(a)	**22.**	(b)	**31.**	(a)	**40.**	(a)	**49.**	(a)	**58.**	(b)
5.	(c)	**14.**	(c)	**23.**	(b)	**32.**	(a)	**41.**	(a)	**50.**	(a)	**59.**	(d)
6.	(d)	**15.**	(c)	**24.**	(b)	**33.**	(b)	**42.**	(a)	**51.**	(c)	**60.**	(c)
7.	(c)	**16.**	(d)	**25.**	(b)	**34.**	(a)	**43.**	(a)	**52.**	(b)	**61.**	(b)
8.	(b)	**17.**	(d)	**26.**	(d)	**35.**	(c)	**44.**	(d)	**53.**	(c)	**62.**	(b)
9.	(d)	**18.**	(c)	**27.**	(a)	**36.**	(d)	**45.**	(c)	**54.**	(d)	**63.**	(d)

29. (c) A teacher must have encouraged the physically challenged children in her class. So, option (c) is the appropriate way to say her physically challenged children.

30. (d) Except cultural factors, all are learning disabilities.

31. (a) Inclusive schools recognize and respond to the diverse needs of their students, accommodating both different styles and rates of learning and ensuring quality education to all through appropriate curricula, organizational arrangements, teaching strategies, resource use and partnerships with their communities.

32. (a) Learning disability in motor skills is called Dyspraxia. Dyspraxia is a disorder that affects motor skill development. People with dyspraxia have trouble planning and completing fine motor tasks. This can vary from simple motor tasks such as waving goodbye to more complex tasks like brushing teeth.

33. (b) Learning disability is a variable state.

35. (c) In an inclusive school we can't separate special children from normal child to provide better care because a children with special need expressed a strong desire for inclusive schooling with special attention.

36. (d) Aphasia is a disturbance of the comprehension and expression of language caused by dysfunction in the brain. This class of language disorder ranges from having difficulty remembering words to losing the ability to speak, read or write.

37. (a) Some sections of the population are socially and educationally backward due to socio-cultural and economic reasons. This is the biggest challenge for a teacher to create a positive self-image in these groups.

38. (c) Others are developmental disorder, while post traumatic stress is a environmental disorder.

39. (a) Inclusive education is an approach to educating students with special educational needs. It makes subtle provisions for special category children.

40. (a) 'Learned Helplessness' is a condition in which a person has come to believe that he is helpless in a situation, even when this is untrue. The first person to do research on this topic was Martin 'Seligman'.

41. (a) If a student is consistently getting lower grades in school, her parents should work in close association with teachers because only teachers may give them the progress report of the student.

42. (a) Some sections of the population are socially and educationally backward due to socio-cultural and economic reasons. Girls, children from weaker section of society, SC/ST, backward minorities and disabled children are educationally disadvantaged. So teachers must believe personal accountability for student's success.

43. (a) Embedded learning opportunities (ELO) involve systematic instructions that is incorporated into the natural learning environment. Instructional procedures teacher can use to implement. ELO include curriculum modifications, naturalistic instructional procedures, prompting and fading, and feedback strategies.

44. (d) As an approach, inclusive education, seeks to seeks to address the learning needs of all children with a special focus on those who are vulnerable to marginalization and exclusion. It implies all learners, with or without disabilities being able to learn together through access to common pre-school provisions, schools and community educational setting with an appropriate network of support services.

45. (c) Children with learning disability may have average or even above average intelligence, but somehow these children show a lag in learning when provided with the same opportunities to learn as normal children. LDs are not objective facts not synonymous with dyslexia.

46. (b) To make child sit in the most distraction reduced are a will be the best way to deal with an inattentive child. Proper seating arrangement may divert the attention of a child into a proper channel.

51. (c) Inclusive education has main focus to make the child learn who is suffering from any disability and without disabilities in the same class or group. It is with an objective to impart equal knowledge, skills and information to every child and make them feel confident to combat with the society.

52. (b) If an instructor intends a disadvantaged student to do well, he/she should take account of such student In group discussions, build up trust in the student allocate him/her a responsibility and support the student to contribute in group activities.

53. (c) Dyslexia is a disorder related to reading disabilities found in a child instead of a normal intelligence. These children face difficulties in reading smoothly, spellings of words, writing words, etc.

54. (d) Visually impaired child should be put in a regular school according to the theory of inclusive education. Though they can get better support in Special schools but if they are made to sit with normal student they will feel normal and confident too.

55. (a) Hearing impaired child has the ability to read the facial expressions quickly there he or she should be seated at a place where he or she can see the facial expressions and movement of lips clearly. it will make him learn and understand easily.

56. (b) Teacher can effectively impart learning to the disadvantaged sections of the society by understanding their needs. It is an important aspect to give the best to the children who are not able to get knowledge elsewhere. By understating their needs teacher can adapt the method suitable to their learning abilities.

57. (d) Learning disability means when a child suffers the ability of understanding a normal situation or concept with great efforts and repetitions.

58. (b) Inclusive education aims at giving equal rights to all the children to sit in the same class i.e child with disabilities and abilities should be made to sit together in a class.

60. (c) If a child with special needs is sent to a special school and not allowed to sit with normal students then he will not be able to well if proper faculties and facilities are not given to him to suit the needs.

Exercise 2 : Test Yourself

1. Which of the following statements regarding attention-deficit hyperactivity disorder is true?
   (a) ADHD is primarily a behavioural disorder, with little heritability
   (b) Most cases of ADHD involve both inattention and hyperactivity
   (c) ADHD is diagnosed equally among girls and boys
   (d) The belief that ADHD children are brain-damaged has been supported by brain imaging studies

2. 'Dyslexia' is associated with
   (a) Mental disorder
   (b) Mathematical disorder
   (c) Reading disorder
   (d) Behavioural disorder

3. Which of the following statements regarding dyslexia is false?
   (a) Dyslexia is the most commonly diagnosed learning disability
   (b) Estimates of the prevalence of dyslexia range from 5 to 17.5%
   (c) Dyslexia is heritable and runs in families
   (d) Dyslexia affects boys more often than girls

4. Centrally sponsored scheme of Integrated Education for disabled children aims at providing educational opportunities to children with disabilities in
   (a) Regular schools
   (b) Special schools
   (c) Open schools
   (d) Blind Schools

5. The statement 'Men are generally more intelligent than women'
   (a) Is true
   (b) May be true
   (c) Shows gender bias
   (d) is true for different domains of intelligence

6. Education of children with special needs should be provided
   (a) along with other normal children
   (b) by methods developed for special children in special Schools
   (c) in special school
   (d) by special teachers in special schools

7. While discussing gender roles in the classroom, you would assert that
   (a) there are different professions for men and women
   (b) boys need to attend school as they are the future earning members of the family
   (c) gender stereotypes in society need to be addressed meaningfully
   (d) household work should not be seen as productive

8. What is the term used to describe any program provided for children and adolescents with disabilities instead of, or in addition to, the regular classroom?
   (a) Enrichment programs
   (b) Special education
   (c) Inclusive education
   (d) Adolescent education

9. Someone who supports full inclusion would advocate
   (a) hiring only teachers who are certified in special education.
   (b) Keeping students with disabilities in separate classes for an entire day
   (c) Mainstreaming without pull out
   (d) Use of pull-out strategies as the primary intervention

10. Research shows that individuals with mild retardation who are placed in regular classrooms
    (a) perform at the same level as the typical student
    (b) learn more than they would if placed in special classrooms
    (c) learn about the same as they would if placed in special classrooms
    (d) learn less than they would if placed in special classrooms

11. Research shows that the number of individuals who need special education services could be greatly reduced if
    (a) There were more special education teachers trained as general education teachers.
    (b) All those who need special services were identified.

    (c) Programmed instruction was used to teach all students.

    (d) Prevention and early intervention programs were widely applied.

12. Which of the following best expresses the text author's viewpoint on the use of labels to classify learners with exceptionalities?

    (a) Use labels with care: avoid dehumanizing, stigmatizing or segregating students.

    (b) Simplify the language of labeling, for instance, by referring to students as "the retarded", "the disturbed" or "the speech impaired."

    (c) Abandon the use of labels because of their potentially damaging effects.

    (d) Return to labels of the past (e.g., "problem child", "idiot", "genius") because they are more meaningful than today's labels.

13. Physical disabilities such as deafness, blindness, and orthopedic handicaps are

    (a) Decreasing at a rapid rate.

    (b) Increasing at a rapid rate.

    (c) Relatively rare.

    (d) Relatively difficult to diagnose.

14. Which of the following matching between two classification systems of mental retardation is correct?

    (a) trainable: severe

    (b) educable: moderate

    (c) custodial: mild

    (d) trainable: moderate

15. Simran is in fourth grade but is still reading at the first grade level. She has normal intelligence and is able to understand concepts and contribute to class discussions. When Simran is given a written quiz, however, she hands in a blank paper. Which of the following best describes Simran's underlying difficulty?

    (a) Simran has autism.

    (b) Simran has mental retardation.

    (c) Simran has a behavioural disorder.

    (d) Simran has a learning disability.

16. Mr. Kapoor understands that Rahul sometimes means to obey, but fails to control his behaviour. Rahul loves to play with his peers, but tends to annoy them with impulsive actions. Mr. Kapoor avoids using long time-outs at recess to discipline Rahul, because he wants Rahul to have a chance to be active. Mr. Kapoor helps Rahul by making rules extra clear, adjusting seating arrangements as needed and sending home daily report cards. Which of the following disabilities best fits Rahul's characteristics?

    (a) ADHD

    (b) Withdrawn behaviour

    (c) Hearing impairment

    (d) Autism

17. Which of the following statements concerning speech disorders is correct?

    (a) Language and speech disorders are really the same.

    (b) Most mild speech disorders improve with time.

    (c) Therapy should always be delayed until the secondary grades.

    (d) Teacher's should help students with speech disorders by calling on other students to help them finish sentences more quickly.

18. Which of the following statements are true regarding the use of computers for instructing exceptional students? (1) Computers can help individualize instruction in terms of method of delivery and level of instruction. (2) Computers can give immediate feedback and emphasize the active role of students in learning. (3) Computers can hold the attention of learners who are easily distracted. (4) Computer instruction is motivating and patient.

    (a) 1, 3, and 4 (not 2).

    (b) All four statements.

    (c) 1, 2, and 3 (not 4).

    (d) 2 and 4 (not 1 and 3).

19. Communication between the classroom teacher and special education personnel should begin

    (a) any time after the first day of class.

    (b) before students are placed in the classroom.

    (c) at the time that students are placed in the classroom.

    (d) after students are placed in the classroom.

20. Which of following is the cause of birth disorders?

    (a) Dominant & recessive transmission of genetic defects

    (b) Sex-linked inheritance of genetically-based diseases.

    (c) Chromosomal abnormalities & mutations

    (d) All of the above

21. Most of the students who have been diagnosed with a learning disability have which type of disability?
    (a) Emotional disturbances
    (b) Autism
    (c) Hearing impairments
    (d) Speech & language impairments

22. Inclusive education covers –
    (a) children with learning disability
    (b) children with hearing impairment
    (c) children with visual impairment
    (d) all of the above

23. Main aim of inclusive education is –
    (a) to organise material to be targeted
    (b) knowing the diversity of the class
    (c) to conduct the test
    (d) to prepare the result

24. In inclusive education a teacher gets appreciation who –
    (a) has strict control over his students
    (b) knows the problems of students and helps them
    (c) has a charming personality
    (d) is not friendly with the students

25. 'Operation Black Board' is a symbolic name of the movement to –
    (a) Provide basic facilities in primary schools
    (b) Provide facility of blackboards
    (c) Provide training to teachers to use blackboard properly
    (d) Provide education to every child

26. Which of the following is not the Goal of Inclusive Education
    1. Recognizing Education for All children as a fundamental right
    2. To ensure that no child is denied admission in mainstream education multiple choice questions
    3. To provide for home based learning for persons with severe, multiple and intellectual disability
    4. To emphasize job-training and job - oriented vocational training
    5. To facilitate access of girls with disabilities and disabled students from rural and remote areas to government hostels
    (a) 1 only   (b) 1 and 5 only
    (c) 5 only   (d) none

27. Vygotsky proposed that Child Development is:
    (a) Due to genetic components of a culture
    (b) A product of social interaction
    (c) A product of formal education
    (d) A product of assimilation & accommodation

28. Which one of the following cues does NOT indicate visual problems in the children?
    (a) difficulty in following direction
    (b) frowning
    (c) stumbling
    (d) unable to estimate distance

29. Slow learners whose educational attainment falls below their natural abilities are labeled as:
    (a) backward
    (b) gifted
    (c) juvenile delinquent
    (d) mentally retarded

30. Difficulty in recalling sequence of letters in words and frequent loss of visual memory is associated with
    (a) Dyslexia   (b) Dyscalculia
    (c) Dysgraphia   (d) Dyspraxia

31. 'Education-of-all-in-schools-for-all' could be a tagline for which of the following ?
    (a) Cohesive education
    (b) Inclusive education
    (c) Cooperative education
    (d) Exclusive education

32. Reducing the time allotted to complete an assignment to make it coincide with time of attention and increasing this time in a phased manner will be best suited to deal with which of the following disorders ?
    (a) Disruptive behaviour disorder
    (b) Dysphasia
    (c) Sensory integration disorder
    (d) Attention deficit hyperactivity disorder

33. Research has pointed out that several levels of discrimination exist in the schools. Which of these is not an example of discrimination at upper primary level ?
    (a) Teachers have low expectations of children from lower socio-economic strata.
    (b) Many teachers use only lecture method to teach.
    (c) Dalit children are made to sit separately during mid-day meals.
    (d) Girls are not encouraged to take up maths and science.

34. The rationale behind inclusive education is that
- (a) the benchmarks for performance of each child should be uniform and standardized.
- (b) society is heterogeneous and schools need to be inclusive to cater to heterogeneous society.
- (c) we need to take pity on special children and provide them access to facilities.
- (d) it is not cost-effective to provide for separate schools for special children.

35. A teacher can effectively respond to the needs of children from 'disadvantaged sections' of society by
- (a) sensitizing the disadvantaged children to the norms and strictures of schools so that they can comply with those.
- (b) telling the 'other children' to co-operate with the 'disadvantaged children' and help them learn the ways of the school.
- (c) reflecting on the school system and herself about various ways in which biases and stereotypes surface.
- (d) ensuring that the children do not get a chance to interact with each other to minimize the chances of their being bullied.

36. Which of these is a characteristic of a child with learning disability ?
- (a) Difficulty in reading fluently and reversing words
- (b) An IQ below 50
- (c) Bullying other children and engaging in aggressive acts
- (d) Doing the same motor action repeatedly

Answer Key

1.	(b)	**6.**	(a)	**11.**	(d)	**16.**	(a)	**21.**	(d)	**26.**	(d)	**31.**	(b)	**36.**	(a)
2.	(c)	**7.**	(c)	**12.**	(a)	**17.**	(b)	**22.**	(d)	**27.**	(b)	**32.**	(d)		
3.	(d)	**8.**	(b)	**13.**	(c)	**18.**	(b)	**23.**	(b)	**28.**	(c)	**33.**	(b)		
4.	(a)	**9.**	(c)	**14.**	(d)	**19.**	(b)	**24.**	(b)	**29.**	(d)	**34.**	(b)		
5.	(c)	**10.**	(b)	**15.**	(d)	**20.**	(d)	**25.**	(a)	**30.**	(a)	**35.**	(c)		

Learning, Motivation and Emotion

How do children learn?

Plato: "Children are born with knowledge that simply awaits activation".

John Locke: was of the view that the main objective of education is self-control. Children will learn properly and with interest only when the find the instruction enjoyable. Adults should use positive reinforcement such as praise rather than punishment to enable a child to learn.

Jean Jacques Rousseau: Development occurs according in a series of stages. Children should not be compelled to learn things they may not be ready for. They will learn when they are curious and it is our responsibility as adults to let the learning unfold naturally. He wrote books about a hypothetical child, Emile, where he allowed nature to raise the child so that the child is unencumbered by the pressures of the civilized society. The only way to interfere is to present lessons that were suited to the child's age and with minimal guidance and never correct Emile's mistakes.

Friedrich Froebel: saw young children as individuals who need a certain degree of freedom but also need to participate in and give society something good in return. He opened experimental preschools in Germany that he called "kindergartens" illustrating his idea that the child will grow well if properly nurtured and cared for. Froebel is best known for his emphasis on guided play as a method for learning.

John Dewey: Dewey's ideas are much like Froebel's in terms of child-centered education based on children's interests and that they learn best through play and real life experiences. School life should grow out of home life and experience. Teachers should know their children well and accordingly plan and document a purposeful curriculum. The major tenet for Dewey was problem solving that is learning through doing'.

Erik Erikson: His theory comprised of eight stages where each stage (birth to old age) has a particular issue to be resolved or accomplished before moving satisfactorily to the next stage. The stages are:

- Trust versus mistrust
- Autonomy versus Shame and doubt
- Initiative versus Guilt
- Industry versus Inferiority
- Identity versus Identity confusion
- Intimacy versus Isolation
- Generativity versus Stagnation
- Ego integration versus Despair

Jean Piaget: Swiss psychologist Jean Piaget showed that intelligence is the result of a natural sequence of stages and it develops as a result of the changing interaction of a child and its environment. He devised a model describing how humans go about making sense of their ' by gathering and organizing information.

Stages of development all children go through:

- Sensori-motor
- Preoperational
- Concrete operations
- Formal operations

Cognitive development is much more than the addition of new facts and ideas to an existing store of information. According to Piaget, our thinking processes change radically, though slowly from birth to maturity because we constantly strive to make sense of the world. Piaget identifies four factors namely biological maturation, activity, social experiences, and equilibration that interact to influence thinking.

Lev Vygotsky: is of the view that social learning is inseparable from cognitive learning; they work together & build on each other. Much learning takes place in play.

Children learn cultural norms both from each other and from their parents. Vygotsky studied how speech, memory aids, writing and symbols transform the child's mind. His theory of the zone of proximal development is the distance between the most difficult task a child can do alone and the most difficult task a child can do with help. The child on the verge of learning a new concept can benefit from the interaction with a teacher or another child or his parents; this help is now referred to as scaffolding. Teachers need to plan activities carefully to challenge the children's next level. Talking is important to clarify ideas so teacher's need to encourage conversations and provide opportunities for collaborative work. Private talk is also important to thinking.

Howard Gardner:

He maintains that people have not just one but at least seven or eight separate kinds of intelligence:

- linguistic -bodily/kinesthetic
- logical/mathematical -interpersonal (social understanding)
- musical - intrapersonal (self understanding)
- spatial - naturalistic

Every normal person has all of these but may be high in some, and low in others and these intelligences develop at different rates.

Why children fail to achieve success in school performance?

Fear and failure: Some schools promote an atmosphere of fear and insecurity. This could be the fear of failure, humiliation, disapproval etc. that most severely affects a student's ability to grow intellectually. Extrinsic motivation such as rewards and grades and stars reinforce children's fear of failing in exams and receiving disapproval from people around them. Instead of learning the actual content of the lessons, students learn how to avoid embarrassment. This atmosphere of fear not only kills a child's love of learning and suppresses his curiosity, but also makes him afraid of taking risks which may be necessary for real learning to happen.

Boredom: Boredom serves as another big hindrance, stifling both the child's inborn motivation to learn and his love of learning. Before joining school, children feel free to explore and discover those things that interest them. But once the child becomes part of our modern school system, both the institutions and the parents unknowingly sabotage their child's education. Schools demand that children perform dull, repetitive tasks which do not give an outlet to their wide range of capabilities.

- Developing strategies for students to apply what they learn in the classroom to real-life experiences will prove effective in understanding and integrating knowledge. The case method is an instructional strategy that engages students in active discussion about varied real life issues. This approach works well in cooperative or collaborative learning or role-playing to stimulate critical thinking on different perspectives.

- There are a variety of ways to use effective discussion. A successful class discussion involves planning on the part of the teacher and preparation on the part of the students.

- Cooperative learning is a strategy that encourages small groups of students to work together for the achievement of a common goal.

Schools focus on extrinsic rewards: These compel children to crave for petty rewards, recognition and praises rather than cultivate their intrinsic love of learning. Holt advocates that children be encouraged to learn by following their natural curiosities and interests, without fear and guilt. Extrinsic rewards take the child's attention away from intrinsic ones. The child may never understand the real reasons for doing something and may never appreciate the inherent rewards that a task will provide. For example, a child who reads a book in order to receive a sticker from the teacher may miss the point that reading has its own charm and enjoyment.

Lack of positive reinforcement: This is yet another practice prevalent in some schools. Positive reinforcement is used sparingly by some teachers. But the correct use of positive reinforcement in the classroom will work wonders in managing behaviour in classrooms. Skinner advocated for immediate praise, feedback, and/or reward when seeking to change a troublesome child or encourage correct behaviour in the classroom.

- Use verbal positive reinforcement loudly and openly.

- When praising a student or group of students, praise them loudly. You want the other students to hear and then ape the behaviour of the good students.

- Be immediate with your positive reinforcement.

- Catch the good behaviour immediately when it happens. A positive reinforcement which gets delayed is of no use. Sometimes it even confuses those students who have a short memory.

- Catch the good, not the bad. You have to deal with behaviour issues when they arise, but try to look for good behaviour as well. For every negative you have to address, find some positives to praise.

Strategies: Current teaching strategies increase the fear of humiliation in children, and do more to harm young people than they do to meet their needs. Such fear drives students to adopt various defense mechanisms - mumbling, acting like they don't understand, acting overly enthusiastic so they won't be called upon, etc to evade the demands placed upon them by adults or to avoid being humiliated in front of their peers.

Learning as Behaviour Change

Behavioural psychology, also known as behaviourism is a theory of learning based upon the idea that all behaviours are acquired through different methods of conditioning. Learning from a behavioural perspective involves examining the relationship between what animals or humans do and what the environment does. When there is a change in one's behaviour in relation to environmental stimuli, behaviourists refer to such learning in terms of a conditioning process.

There are two types of conditioning based on different learning principles.

Classical Conditioning

Based on the work of Ivan Pavlov, the basis for this model lies in the range of relatively permanent and unlearned reflexes that nearly all members of a species possess. Examples include our automatic reactions to hot surfaces, food smells and a whole range of stimuli that may cause fear, anxiety, flight, or a sense of well-being. These automatic reflexes are composed of two elements: an unconditional stimulus and an unconditional response.

Again, no learning is required for these responses to take place. Where the learning, or conditioning, comes in is when another neutral stimulus is introduced in just the right way when these automatic reflexes are occurring. The classic experiments from Pavlov's laboratory involved his work with the digestive process in dogs. As the story goes, Pavlov noticed that not only would dogs salivate in the presence of food (this is the unconditional stimulus-unconditional response reflex), they also would initiate the salivary secretions even before the food arrived. This curious phenomenon set Pavlov on a course of experiments in which he discovered that various neutral stimuli, such as the sound of the attendant carrying the food or the sight of the food bowl, were enough to induce the dogs to salivate. This learning process simply required that the neutral stimuli occur in some close relationship with the food itself. Essentially then, the events just prior to actual feeding became conditional stimuli causing the conditional response of salivary secretions.

Consider, for example, a child who responds happily whenever meeting a new person who is warm and friendly, but who also responds cautiously or at least neutrally in any new situation. Suppose further that the "new, friendly person" in question is you, his teacher. Initially the child's response to you is like an unconditioned stimulus: you smile (the unconditioned stimulus) and in response he perks up, breathes easier, and smiles (the unconditioned response). This exchange is not the whole story, however, but merely the setting for an important bit of behaviour change: suppose you smile at him while standing in your classroom, a "new situation" and therefore one to which he normally responds cautiously. Now respondent learning can occur. The initially neutral stimulus (your classroom) becomes associated repeatedly with the original unconditioned stimulus (your smile) and the child's unconditioned response (his smile). Eventually, if all goes well, the classroom becomes a conditioned stimulus in its own right: it can elicit the child's smiles and other "happy behaviours" even without your immediate presence or stimulus.

Classical conditioning occurs when a conditioned stimulus is paired with an unconditioned stimulus. Stimulus is a physical event capable of affecting behaviour. Usually, the conditioned stimulus (CS) is a neutral stimulus (e.g., the sound of a tuning fork), the unconditioned stimulus (US) is biologically potent (e.g., the taste of food) and the unconditioned response (UR) to the unconditioned stimulus is an unlearned reflex response (e.g., salivation). After pairing is repeated the organism exhibits a conditioned response (CR) to the conditioned stimulus when the conditioned stimulus is presented alone. The conditioned response is usually similar to the unconditioned response, but unlike the unconditioned response, it must be acquired through experience and is relatively impermanent.

A chart of events in classical conditioning

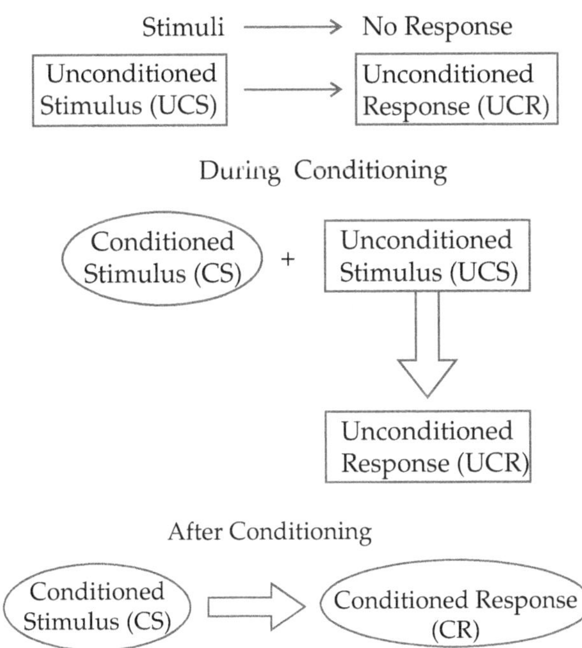

During his research on the physiology of digestion in dogs, Pavlov developed a procedure that enabled him to study the digestive processes of animals over long periods of time. He redirected the animal's digestive fluids outside the body, where they could be measured. Pavlov noticed that the dogs in the experiment began to salivate in the presence of the technician who normally fed them, rather than simply salivating in the presence of food. Pavlov called the dogs' anticipatory salivation, *psychic secretion*.

Phenomena Observed in Classical Conditioning

Acquisition : In classical conditioning acquisition is a gradual process in which a conditioned stimulus gradually acquires the capacity to elicit a conditioned response as a result of repeated pairing with an unconditioned stimulus.

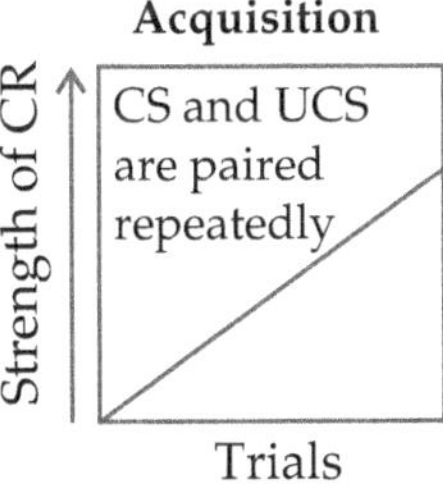

The speed of conditioning depends on a number of factors, such as the nature and strength of both the CS and the US, previous experience and the one's motivational state. Acquisition may occur with a single pairing of the CS and US, but usually, there is a gradual increase in the conditioned response to the CS. This slows down the process as it nears completion.

Extinction : In the extinction procedure, the conditioned stimulus (CS) gradually loses the ability to elicit CR when it is no longer followed by the unconditioned stimulus (US). When this is done the CR frequency eventually returns to pre-training levels.

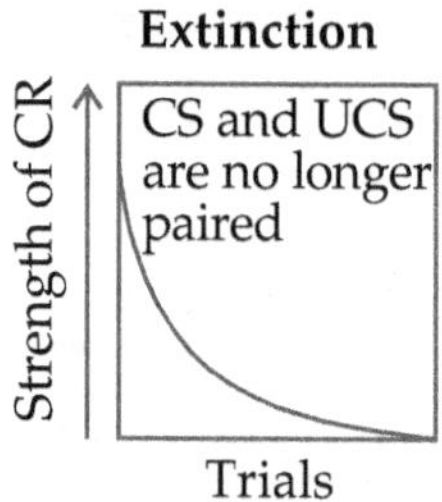

Reacquisition or Reconditioning : If the CS is again paired with the US, a CR is again acquired, but this second acquisition usually happens much faster than the first one.

Spontaneous Recovery : Spontaneous recovery is defined as the reappearance of the conditioned response after a time interval. That is, if the CS is tested at a later time (for example an hour or day) after conditioning it will again elicit a CR. This renewed CR is usually much weaker than the CR observed prior to extinction.

Stimulus Generalization : Stimulus generalization is said to occur if, after particular CS has come to elicit a CR, another similar stimulus will elicit the same CR. Usually the more similar are the CS and the test stimulus the stronger is the CR to the test stimulus. The more the test stimulus differs from the CS, the more the conditioned response will differ from that previously observed.

Stimulus Discrimination : *Stimulus discrimination* is a process in which one stimulus ("CS1") elicits one CR and another stimulus ("CS2") elicits either another CR or no CR at all. This can be brought about by, for example, pairing CS1 with an effective US and presenting CS2 with no US.

Learning process is affected by temporal arrangement of the CS-UCS pairings. Temporal means time-related: the extent to which a conditioned stimulus preceds or follows the presentations of an unconditioned stimulus.

Forward Conditioning : Learning is fastest in forward conditioning. During forward conditioning, the onset of the CS preceds the onset of the US in order to signal the US will follow. Two common forms of forward conditioning are delay and trace conditioning.

- **Delay Conditioning:** In delay conditioning the CS is presented and is overlapped by the presentation of the US.

- **Trace Conditioning :** During trace conditioning the CS and US do not overlap. Instead, the CS begins and ends before the US is presented. The stimulus-free period is called the *trace interval*. It may also be called the conditioning interval. For example : If you sound a buzzer for 5 seconds and then, a second later, puff air into a person's eye, the person will blink. After several pairings of the buzzer and puff the person will blink at the sound of the buzzer alone.

  The difference between trace conditioning and delay conditioning is that in the delayed procedure the CS and US overlap.

  Simultaneous Conditioning : During simultaneous conditioning, the CS and US are presented and terminated at the same time. *For example*: If you ring a bell and blow a puff of air into a person's eye at the same moment, you have accomplished to coincide the CS and US.

  Second-order and Higher-order Conditioning : This form of conditioning follows a two-step procedure. First a neutral stimulus ("CS1") comes to signal a US through forward conditioning. Then a second neutral stimulus ("CS2") is paired with the first (CS1) and comes to yield its own conditioned response. For example : a bell might be paired with food until the bell elicits salivation. If a light is then paired with the bell, then the light may come to elicit salivation as well. The bell is the CS1 and the food is the US. The light becomes the CS2 once it is paired with the CS1.

Backward Conditioning : Backward conditioning occurs when a CS immediately follows a US. Unlike the usual conditioning procedure, in which the CS precedes the US, the conditioned response given to the CS tends to be inhibitory. For example, a puff of air directed at a person's eye could be followed by the sound of a buzzer.

Temporal Conditioning : In temporal conditioning a US is presented at regular intervals, for instance every 10 minutes. Conditioning is said to have occurred when the CR tends to occur shortly before each US. This suggests that animals have a biological clock that can serve as a CS.

Little Albert Experiment (Phobias)

Ivan Pavlov showed that classical conditioning applied to animals. Did it also apply to humans? In a famous experiment Watson and Rayner (1920) showed that it did.

Little Albert was a 9-month-old infant who was tested on his reactions to various stimuli. He was shown a white rat. Albert showed no fear to the rat. He smiled and attempted to play with it. However what did startle him and cause him to be afraid was if a hammer was struck against a steel bar behind his head. The sudden loud noise would cause little Albert to burst into tears.

Classical Conditioning in the Classroom : If a student associates negative emotional experiences with school then this can obviously have bad results, such as creating a school phobia.

For example, if a student is bullied at school they may learn to associate school with fear. It could also explain why some students show a particular dislike of certain subjects that continue throughout their academic career. This could happen if a student is humiliated or punished in class by a teacher.

In one procedure termed flooding a student suffering from a specific fear may be forced to confront the fear-eliciting stimulus without an avenue of escape. Cases in which fearful thoughts are too painful to deal with directly are treated by systematic desensitization. It is a progressive technique designed to replace anxiety with a relaxation response.

Operant Conditioning

The better known and broadly applied behavioural model is connected with the pioneering work of E. L. Thorndike and B. F. Skinner. This approach to learning is based on the simple proposition that behaviour is a function of its consequences.

The earliest expression of this principle is Thorndike's Law of Effect, which observes that when any response is followed by a satisfactory state of affairs, it tends to be repeated. Similarly, when a behaviour is followed by an unsatisfactory or annoying result, it tends to reduce in frequency and strength.

Building on the Law of Effect, Skinner and others created an elaborate set of ideas that explained how to increase behaviours of interest, how to teach totally new behaviours, how to maintain learned behaviour, and how to reduce unwanted behaviour. All of these explanations rested on understanding the relationship between three elements of the puzzle: the behaviour of interest, the antecedent conditions in which the behaviour of interest was occurring, and the consequences following behaviour. The relationships among the three elements are sometimes referred to as the contingencies of reinforcement.

Building on the central idea that behaviour is a function of its consequences, the next step is to examine four types of possible consequences and their effects. Two of these, positive reinforcement and negative reinforcement, tend to strengthen or increase behaviours because they result in a positive state of affairs for the subject.

Punishment can be used to suppress behaviour, but the most effective long-term solution to reduce unwanted behaviour is simply to deny reinforcement. This procedure is referred to as extinction. The most effective combination of these tools would be to use positive reinforcement to strengthen desired aspects of a subject's behaviour, while simultaneously using extinction to reduce less desired or competing behaviours. An important point to note is that punishment can be effective in the short run, but it is never a desirable long-term solution because of the negative side effects that can result, such as hostility and fear.

People respond predictably to particular stimulus situations (e.g., traffic signals, classrooms, restaurants) because they have been systematically reinforced for appropriate behaviour in those settings. Following such selective reinforcement, the stimulus situation itself comes to control behaviour, as when a red light shows at a traffic intersection or people politely stand in line at a ticket counter. Learning is also a matter of acquiring completely new behaviours that are not presently in existence.

Language-delayed children, for example, may be unable to make certain sounds that need to be part of their speech repertoire. If the children could correctly produce the sounds even occasionally, the strategy would be to simply reinforce the correct behaviour. However, if the sounds are never produced, the strategy is to use a shaping procedure in which the closest approximations are reinforced. Over time, with skilled use of reinforcement, the approximations become closer and closer to the target. This is the same strategy used in animal training, where the object is to teach behaviours the animal is capable of but are not part of their natural repertoire. Again, the strategy is to selectively reinforce closer and closer approximations until the target is reached. Finally, one important issue in behavioural learning is the maintenance of behaviour at desired strength and frequency levels. This is where reinforcement schedules come into play. This is a complex area in itself, but the main idea is that constant reinforcement never produces the strongest and most extinction-resistant behaviour. Rather, once a behaviour is learned and can reliably occur in a particular stimulus environment, the reinforcement schedule needs to be adjusted so that reinforcement occurs only intermittently.

The Nature of Operant Conditioning

Antecedents as well as the following consequences: reinforcement and punishment are the core tools of operant conditioning. "Antecedent stimuli" occurs before a behavior happens. "Reinforcement" and "punishment" refer to their effect on the desired behaviour.

1.   Reinforcement increases the probability of a behaviour being expressed or repeated.

2.   "Punishment decreases the probability of a behaviour being expressed or repeated.

      Positive" and "negative" refer to the presence or absence of the stimulus.

1.   Positive is the addition or presence of a stimulus.

2.   Negative is the removal or absence of a stimulus (often adverse).

1.   **Positive Reinforcement** (reinforcement): Occurs when a behaviour (response) is followed by a stimulus that is appetitive or rewarding, increasing the frequency of that behavior. In the Skinner box experiment, a stimulus such as food or a sugar solution can be delivered when the rat engages in a target behaviour, such as pressing a lever. This procedure is usually called simply reinforcement. Preferred activities can also be used to reinforce behaviour, a principle referred to as the Premack Principle.

2.   **Negative Reinforcement** (escape): Occurs when a behaviour (response) is followed by the termination of an aversive stimulus, thereby increasing that behaviour's frequency. In the Skinner box experiment, negative reinforcement can be a loud noise continuously sounding inside the rat's cage until it engages in the target behaviour, such as pressing a lever, upon which the loud noise is removed.

3.   **Positive Punishment** (Punishment): is also called "Punishment by contingent stimulation. It occurs when a behaviour (response) is followed by a stimulus, such as introducing a shock or loud noise, resulting in a decrease in that behaviour. Positive punishment is sometimes a confusing term, as it denotes the "addition" of a stimulus or increase in the intensity of a stimulus that is aversive (such as spanking or an electric shock). This procedure is usually called simply punishment.

4.   **Negative Punishment** (penalty): is also called "Punishment by contingent withdrawal. It occurs when a behaviour (response) is followed by the removal of a stimulus, such as taking away a child's toy following an undesired behaviour, resulting in a decrease in that behaviour.

5.   **Extinction** The procedure of not reinforcing a particular response is known as extinction. For example, a rat is first given food many times for lever presses. Then, in "extinction", no food is given. Typically the rat continues to press more and more slowly and eventually stops, at which time lever pressing is said to be "extinguished."

6.   **Escape and Avoidance** In escape learning, a behaviour terminates an (aversive) stimulus. For example, shielding one's eyes from sunlight terminates the (aversive) stimulation of bright light in one's eyes. In avoidance learning, the behavior precedes and prevents an (aversive) stimulus, for example putting on sun glasses before going outdoors. Because, in avoidance, the stimulation does not occur, avoidance behavior seems to have no means of reinforcement.

7.   **Schedules of Reinforcement** Schedules of reinforcement are rules that determine when and how reinforcements will be delivered. The rules specify either the time that reinforcement is to be made available, or the number of responses to be made, or both.

     - **Fixed interval schedule:** Reinforcement occurs following the first response after a fixed time/interval has elapsed after the previous reinforcement.

     - **Variable interval schedule:** Reinforcement occurs following the first response after a variable time has elapsed from the previous reinforcement.

     - **Fixed ratio schedule:** Reinforcement occurs after a fixed number of responses have been emitted since the previous reinforcement.

     - **Variable ratio schedule:** Reinforcement occurs after a variable number of responses have been emitted since the previous reinforcement.

     - **Continuous reinforcement:** Reinforcement occurs every time after each response.

- **"Discrimination"** typically occurs when a response is reinforced only in the presence of a specific stimulus. For example a pigeon might be fed for pecking at a red light and not at a green light; in consequence, it pecks at red and stops pecking at green. Many complex combinations of stimuli and other conditions have been studied; for example an organism might be reinforced on an interval schedule in the presence of one stimulus and on a ratio schedule in the presence of another.

- **"Generalization"** is the tendency to respond to stimuli that are similar to a previously trained discriminative stimulus. For example, having been trained to peck at "red" a pigeon might also peck at "pink", though usually less strongly.

- **"Context"** refers to stimuli that are continuously present in a situation, like the walls, tables, chairs, etc. in a room, or the interior of an operant conditioning chamber. Context stimuli may come to control behaviour as do discriminative stimuli, though usually more weakly. Behaviors learned in one context may be absent, or altered, in another.

Token Economy : Token economy is a system in which targeted behaviors are reinforced with tokens (secondary reinforcers) and are later exchanged for rewards (primary reinforcers). Tokens can be in the form of fake money, buttons, poker chips, stickers, etc. While rewards can range anywhere from snacks to privileges or activities Teachers also use token economy at primary school by giving young children stickers to reward good behaviour.

Programmed Learning: In programmed learning, the material to be learned is broken up into small, easy steps. Since each step is easy, the learner makes few errors and has a sense of accomplishment. Programmed learning has three characteristics:

(1)   the final complex task is broken up into small steps.

(2)   reinforcement is contingent upon the performance of each step, and

(3)   the learner makes responses at his or her own pace.

Programmed learning is thought to be an effective way of learning facts, rules and formulae.

PSI (Personalised System of Instruction) : In the *personalised system of instruction* the material in the course is divided into small units, each of which must be mastered at a high level of proficiency before the next unit is attempted. For instance, students might be required to pass an examination at the end of each unit with a core of 90 percent, if they do not, they must study the material again until they can pass at this level.

Operant conditioning and students' learning:

Consider the following examples in which the operant behaviour tends to become more frequent on repeated occasions:

- A grade 1 child raises her hand in response to the teacher's question about an author (the operant). The teacher calls on her and she makes her comment (the reinforcement).

- A twelfth-grade student, a member of the track team, runs one mile during practice (the operant). He notes the time it takes him as well as his increase in speed since joining the team (the reinforcement).

- A child who is usually very restless sits for ten minutes to do an assignment (the operant). The teacher compliments him for working hard (the reinforcement).

Social Learning Theory

The social learning theory proposed by **Albert Bandura** has become perhaps the most influential theory of learning and development. His theory added a social element, arguing that people can learn new information and behaviours by watching other people. Known as observational learning (or modeling), this type of learning can be used to explain a wide variety of behaviours.

Basic Social Learning Concepts

There are three core concepts at the heart of social learning theory:

1. The idea that people can learn through observation.
2. The idea that internal mental states are an essential part of this process.
3. The theory recognizes that just because something has been learned it does not mean that it will result in a change in behaviour.

1. **People can learn through observation**

   Observational Learning : In his famous "Bobo doll" studies, Bandura demonstrated that children learn and imitate behaviours they have observed in other people. The children in Bandura's studies observed an adult acting violently toward a Bobo doll. When the children were later allowed to play in a room with the Bobo doll, they began to imitate the aggressive actions they had previously observed.

   Bandura identified three basic models of observational learning:

   1. A live model, which involves an actual individual demonstrating or acting out a behaviour.
   2. A verbal instructional model, which involves descriptions and explanations of a behaviour.
   3. A symbolic model, which involves real or fictional characters displaying behaviours in books, films, television programs, or online media.

2. **Mental states are imperative to learning**

   Intrinsic Reinforcement : Bandura noted that external, environmental reinforcement was not the only factor to influence learning and behaviour. He described intrinsic reinforcement such as pride, satisfaction, and a sense of accomplishment. This emphasis on internal thoughts and cognitions helps link learning theories to cognitive developmental theories.

3. **Learning does not necessarily lead to a change in behaviour**

   While behaviourists believed that learning led to a permanent change in behaviour, observational learning demonstrates that people can learn new information without demonstrating new behaviours.

The Modeling Process

All observed behaviours are not learned effectively. There are four factors that involve both the model and the learner and which can play an important role in successful social learning. The following steps are involved in the observational learning and modeling process:

- **Attention :** In order to learn, you need to be paying attention. Anything that detracts your attention is going to have a negative effect on observational learning. If the model interesting or there is a novel aspect to the situation, you are far more likely to dedicate your full attention to learning.

- **Retention :** The ability to store information is also an important part of the learning process. Retention can be affected by a number of factors, but the ability to pull up information later and act on it is vital to observational learning.

- **Reproduction :** Once you have paid attention to the model and retained the information, it is time to actually perform the behaviour you observed. Further practice of the learned behaviour leads to improvement and skill advancement.

- **Motivation :** Finally, in order for observational learning to be successful, you have to be motivated to imitate the behaviour that has been modeled. Reinforcement and punishment play an important role in motivation. While experiencing these motivators is highly effective, so is observing others experience some type of reinforcement. For example, if you see another student rewarded with extra credit for being to class on time, you might start to show up a few minutes early each day.

Learning is a function of the interaction of personal and environmental factors.

Personal factors

Personal factors are the intra individual factors like motivation, interests, abilities etc which predispose an individual towards learning.

Environmental factors on the other hand, are those contextual factors which highlight the role of the environment in learning, such as the socio-emotional, societal and cultural factors. Although the two factors represent different categories, they operate in a common system. The environmental factors provide the context within which the personal factors operate. The learner and the learning process can only be completely understood with reference to the interaction of both environmental and personal factors.

Intelligence

One of the key factors influencing our ability to learn effectively is intelligence. There are wide variations across individuals and cultures as to what actually constitutes intelligence.

Aptitude

- It must have been a matter of wonder that a lot of times individuals having the same level of intelligence do not necessarily show the same output when put to the same task or activity. Further, you must have heard frustrated people saying, "No matter what I do, I can't get my sums right", or "I just can't learn a foreign language", or "The cake I bake, never rises", or "I simply can't memorize the poem."

- It is evident that no one finds all tasks easy to master and learn. While there may be some people good at languages or math, others simply can't handle these although they are as bright as their counterparts. Similarly, some persons can learn to dance or play a musical instrument with ease, while others struggle to get their dance steps and movement skills right or keep to the tunes and notes. This is because individuals vary greatly in their aptitudes or their specific capacities to do a task well or to profit from specific types of training.

- The knowledge about different types of aptitudes helps us to economize our efforts and maximize learning. For example, by choosing personnel who can demonstrate an aptitude for a specific job, an employer is likely to benefit from sending them for advanced training program. Likewise, teachers encourage students having an aptitude for scholastic ability to strive towards excellence and high achievement by providing them additional learning opportunities.

Goals

- A goal is an outcome or attainment that an individual sets and strive to accomplish. Goals motivate people to act in order to reduce the discrepancy between 'what they are' and 'what they want to be'. They can be understood with reference to the vision of the future that each individual constructs for himself. Goals have been understood and classified in various ways. They can be short-term, long-term or personal or societal in nature and tangible or abstract. Let us now examine each one of these.

- Short term goals are those which one can achieve in the near future. They involve less time as, the required time can be specified and it does not seem inordinate and endless. For a graduate clearing the B.A or Journalism entrance examinations is an example of a short term goal. For an overweight adolescent, losing weight by going on a regulatory diet and exercise schedule is an example of a short term goal.

- Long term goals are those which are distant and oriented towards the future. For example, a child's wish to be a doctor or a teacher, are low term goals. For the rural girl, being able to pursue education and a suitable career at the end of it, are long term goals.

- Immediate goals are those which can be fulfilled quickly. Resorting to crash dieting to lose weight within a week is an example of an immediate goal. Studying for an exam only to pass it is another example of an immediate goal.

- Personal goals deal with the needs and motives of the individual and are self-rewarding. For example, wanting to be a good dancer, a good human being, maintaining good health, etc., are all illustrations of personal goals since they enable an individual to feel good about him herself. Societal goals are those which are concerned with changes in society, such as wanting better gender equality, sensitivity towards the poor, developing a more broad-minded attitude towards social reforms among the rural folk, etc.

- Tangible goals are those which are clearly definable and achievable like wanting to be a doctor, or getting a distinction in the Board examinations. Abstract goals are those which deal with qualitative changes that are difficult to specify and measure quantitatively. For example, wanting to be a good human being, or a contented person are abstract goals, since 'good' and 'contented' are difficult to define or measure precisely.

- Goals play a significant role in learning since they give strength and direction to it. When we learn only to meet the immediate goal of passing the examination, our leaning is usually temporary and ineffective and we forget it soon after the goal is accomplished. For effective learning to take place, we should be able to relate it to all that we learn. This will enable us to achieve our life goals.

- When learning is guided or motivated by long term goals, it helps us to reach newer heights and contributes productively and positively to our life. Thus, the types of goals that we set, influence the amount of motivation to achieve them. Further the nature of our goal setting activity has been found to be directly proportionate to improvement in our leaning and performance. This is because the goals help to direct our attention to the task at hand, they mobilize our effort, they increase our persistence at the task and they also help us to adopt new strategies when old ones fail to help us.

Interest

- You often hear teachers complaining to parents at the Parent Teacher Meetings that their children can do very well in studies provided parents take interest in them. You may have also heard students saying "Math kills", "Hindi is so boring"; "I just can't do physics - its subject matter doesn't interest me" or "why should I go for the cricket match when I am not interested in cricket!"

- Interest is one of the most important factors which mediates learning and which motivates to act. Without interest, as is evident from the examples cited above, there can be no learning.

- Interests are actually deep rooted constructs and are determined by the need structure of an individual. An individual with strong social needs such as belongingness, affiliation and recognition will direct all his her energies into activities which enable him her to fulfill these needs such as meeting people, going to dubs, associations, parties, meetings etc. In theoretical terms, an interest may be defined as a learnt or acquired motive stemming from some inherent needs of the individual which drive him her to act in a way that will sustain or satisfy his inner need structure.

- Individuals differ greatly in their patterns of interests because their need structures vary. For some persons, social and emotional needs become the guiding forces, for others, aesthetic or higher cognitive needs may be the preponderant factors. Age variations are also visible.

- Young children have a need for activity, play, adventure etc. and thus they learn much better through a play way approach. This arouses their interest in studies and helps to sustain their involvement in work.

- For adolescents and older learners, the needs for affiliation and group belongingness are very high and thus they always show an interest in recreational m u p activities like parties, picnics, social outings etc.

- Interests are thus determined by both age related and human needs factors. They influence not only what one will learn best, but also serve to explain why learning sometimes flags or becomes inadequate. Interests are usually classified on the basis of the nature of activity involved, for example, spiritual interests, recreational interests, scholarly or academic interests, social interests etc.

Readiness to learn and maturation

- As the term suggests, there is an optimal or most appropriate time for each individual to learn a specific skill or concept with ease and efficiency. This appropriate time comes when ones physical, neural and intellectual aspects of development have advanced enough to enable one to perceive the problem and solve it with relative ease and comfort.

- For instance, seven month old child cannot walk since it lacks the physical maturation or level of development required to promote walking. Similarly, it is impossible for a five year old to comment on democracy or socialism as he or she is not 'ready' or cognitively adept at understanding these concepts.

- Maturation can be best interpreted as relatively permanent change in an individual - be it cognitive, emotional or physical, that occurs as a result of biological ageing, regardless of personal experience. Maturation is preprogrammed and occurs regardless of the interactions a child has with the environment.

- Most expert teachers in schools know that no matter how hard they work or how good they are, they cannot force a student to think or do what he she is not biologically ready to do. Thus, cognitive 'coming of age', or maturation is another specific aspect of 'readiness to learn'. It implies that a child should have the requisite level of cognitive skills necessary for solving a problem or accomplishing a task set before her.

- It is also important for you to understand that there are large individual differences in maturation. Some children for instance walk at nine months, while others, at two years. Some children speak a language quite competently at three years, while others may be as late as five years. Puberty comes to some girls at eleven while to others at fourteen. Maturation has to be thus understood as a natural process of unfolding of the development stages, resulting in functionally preparing an individual to acquire mastery over his her environment.

- It must have become clear to you that any attempt to teach things before an adequate level of readiness is acquired by the child is futile. This also serves to explain why non-performance on the part of learners or their inability to grasp a concept, can be attributed to lack of adequate maturation and readiness to learn.

- Since maturation determines the readiness for learning, it is critical for curriculum planners and teachers to take note of this. It enables them to decide what to teach, how to teach, when to teach and correspondingly be guide on what to expect from their learners. You will now be able to appreciate why very young children should not be encouraged to write. Similarly, if teenagers are undergoing mood swings, it is because of their developmental pattern - they are not pretending moods or deliberately misbehaving.

Locus of control

- Locus of control can be best understood as the degree and location of what we believe the causes that determine the events in our life.

- Many psychologists are of the view that parenting styles, socio-cultural values and the individual's own motivational structure, beliefs, perceptions and learning style determine his/her locus of control. The locus of control may be either external or internal.

- You must have noticed how young children have to be coaxed by external forces (parents, teachers others) to learn, study, do their home work etc. However, as they grow older, there is a shift to a sense of responsibility flowing from within them. They, then, themselves plan and study, do their homework and resist help, unless required for academic support. This may be seen as a shift in the locus of control or centre of operation from external to internal forces. Individuals with an internal locus of control are usually high on achievement motivation and are mastery oriented in their learning.

- In contrast, individual's who perceive the locus of control of their learning to be external such as success being experienced because of luck factors, or failure happening because of low ability, suffer from what is called learned helplessness. They never engage in learning tasks on their own, seldom take initiative and always wait for guidance from an adult or peer.

Learning styles

- Individuals show preference for different learning conditions. These are called learning styles, or learning preferences. The learning style theories recognize that individuals learn in different ways and that each individual has a unique style of learning.

- You must have noticed that some students learn well in the morning while some others prefer to study at night. Some students like to sit in quiet places, while some others like to have music accompanying their learning.

- Many students report optimal learning while sitting on the dining table and also eating snacks along with their studies. Students who live in joint families actually develop styles of learning which are set in public spaces.

- Learning styles can thus range from straightforward preferences for physical surroundings to more fundamental differences that may be rooted in culture or personality.

- Individual differences in personality also affect the way different students approach the same learning task. One such personality difference in learning style is the depth to which persons process the information they learn.

- Some persons take a 'deep processing approach', seeking the underlying concepts and meanings of what they are attempting to learn. Others take a surface - processing approach, focusing on memorization rather than analysis and understanding.

- It is generally observed that persons who adopt a surface approach are motivated by getting good marks and other external rewards, whereas those who take a deep approach enjoy learning for the sake of learning and are less concerned with external evaluations.

Socio-cultural or environmental factors influencing learning

- The socio-cultural environment, within which a child grows, has a significant impact on learning. In fact, all learning occurs with special reference to the cultural context of an individual. The social constructivist view of psychology holds that all learning is culturally oriented and guided. For our own understanding we can subdivide socio-cultural factors into: a) family, b) neighborhood and community; and, c) class, caste, religion and ethnicity.

- Family is the first and most fundamental influence in the socialization process of an individual. It is in the family that he or she undergoes conscious, subconscious and, subliminal learning. It is within the family that the individual learns behaviour patterns ' for survival, social skills, attitudes, interpersonal skills, social norms, the do's and do not's of his/her culture and community, acquires a sense of right and wrong, a value orientation etc. Thus we can say that the family is the site of all learning.

- The neighborhood and community in which one lives also have a potent impact on what one learns and acquires. Many attitudes, habits, beliefs, perceptions, stereotypes and social roles and responsibilities are shaped directly or indirectly by our experiences with the persons in our neighborhood. These persons include our peers and age-mates and all the elders wound us.

- Through conditioning, social learning, direct instruction and modeling we learn a number of things from them. ' In our country, caste, class and religion also play a predominant role in shaping our identity, self concept, attitudes, value orientation, goals and achievement patterns.

- For example, the socio-economic status of the group to which we belong can be directly linked with the degree of stimulation or enrichment available to us in our learning environment. It has been seen that an adequately enriching and stimulating environment provides the learner with more learning opportunities, and greater control over the environment than an impoverished or needy environment.

- Learning is also seen to vary across religious and ethnic groups, owing to the distinction in their beliefs, values, attitudes and practices. For instance in many Islamic countries, women lead a very sheltered and restricted life and are taught to be submissive and obedient.

- In the Pan Indian culture, children are encouraged to develop a sense of autonomy, independence and control over their own lives. In many orthodox Hindu communities, the social learning of girls is fraught with biases and injunctions which are justified in the name of religious beliefs. The kind of experiences learners are exposed to differ across regions and geographic locations.

Physical Environment of School:

- In general, the school environments present an educative atmosphere. The modern school site, building and equipments are adequate, safe, sanitary comfortable and attractive. It is only in the best environmental setting that the most effective learning takes place.

- The teacher can suggest about lighting arrangements in the class, as due to defective lighting and ventilation arrangements the crowded classrooms lead to overheated conditions which reduce working capacity and encourage the spread of respiratory infections. Further, it will amount to restlessness, inattention and unsatisfactory work. It is a well know fact that individuals work much better in a room with an attractive atmosphere.

- Although a teacher cannot completely recondition a dull and dilapidated room yet a better planning and efforts can work wonders to improve its condition. Actually it all depends upon the upkeep of the room. Careless disorder in the room, waste papers on the floor, and the untidy state of storage space, book shelves, teacher's table and pupil's desks definitely give a shabby look to a room.

- Thus, the rooms should be attractively decorated. Neatness, cleanliness, orderliness and suitable decoration in a room will induce pupils to take a pride in their room and should largely eliminate scribbling on the wall and desks. This all will prove to be a boosting environment for learning.

Transform of Learning

Transfer of training or learning refers to the effect that knowledge or abilities acquired in one area have on problem solving or knowledge acquisition in other areas.

Holding (1991) says that "transfer of training occurs whenever the effects of prior learning influence the performance of a later activity. The degree to which trainees successfully apply in their jobs the skills gained in training situations , is considered "positive transfer of training" (Baldwin & Ford, 1980). There are three types of transfer of training:

- **Positive Transfer :** When prior learning or training facilitates acquiring a new skill or reaching the solution to a new problem. In this situation the individual performs better than he would have without the prior training.
- **Negative Transfer :** When prior learning or training hinders acquiring a new skill or reaching the solution to a new problem . In this situation the individual performs worse than that he would have had he not been exposed to the prior training .
- **Zero Transfer :** In this situation, past experience or training neither enhances nor hinders acquiring a new skill or reaching the solution of a new problem.

MOTIVATION

Motivation is usually defined as an internal state that arouses, directs and maintains behaviour. Psychologists studying motivation focus on five basic factors

- The choices people make about their behaviour: Why do some students, for example, focus on their study and others watch television?
- Time taken to do a task: How long does it take to get started? Why do some students start their homework right away, while others procrastinate?
- Level of involvement: What is the intensity or level of involvement in the chosen activity? Once the book bag is opened, is the student absorbed and focused or just going through the motions?
- Extent of persistence: What causes a person to persist or to give up? Will a student read the entire Shakespeare assignment or just a few pages?
- State of mind while engagement: What is the individual thinking and feeling while engaged in the activity? Is the student enjoying Shakespeare, feeling competent, or worrying about an upcoming test.

In a sense, motivation is an index of the eagerness of an individual to learn. Adequate motivation not only sets in motion the activities which results in learning, but also sustains and directs these. It is thus an indispensable factor in promoting learning, as it energizes and accelerates the process and evokes a very positive response from the learner. You would have observed that some students learn the same task or subject matter more efficiently than others, because they find it more rewarding and interesting. There can thus be a great deal of variation in 'what motivates', 'how much it motivates' and what the impact on the learner is. These variations may be attributed to differences in levels and types of motivation. For instance for some individuals, their needs determine what their motivation will be. For some others, the incentives available to accomplish a task become the most important consideration. For some others, the joy of engaging in a particular activity generates a motivational drive.

Intrinsic and Extrinsic Motivation

Intrinsic motivation : Intrinsic motivation is the natural tendency to seek out and conquer challenges as we pursue personal interests and exercise capabilities. When we are intrinsically motivated, we do not need incentives or punishments, because the activity itself is rewarding. For example, I study Biology outside school simply because I love the activity; no one makes me do it.

Extrinsic motivation : In contrast, when we do something in order to earn a grade, avoid punishment, please the teacher, or for some other reason that has very little to do with the task itself, we experience extrinsic motivation. We are not really interested in the activity for its own sake; we care only about what it will gain us. For example, I am working for the grade. I have no interest in the subject.

Behavioural approaches to motivation

According to the behavioural view, an understanding of student motivation begins with a careful analysis of the incentives and rewards present in the classroom. A reward is an attractive object or event supplied as a consequence of a particular behaviour. For example, a student is rewarded with bonus points when drawn an excellent diagram. An incentive is an object or event that encourages or discourages behaviour.

If we are consistently rcinforces for certain behaviours, we may develop habits or tendencies to act in certain ways. For example, if a student is repeatedly rewarded with affection, money, praise, or privileges for doing well in cricket but receives little recognition for studying, the student will probably work longer and harder on perfecting his batting rather than understanding geometry. Providing grades, stars, stickers and other reinforcements for learning-or demerits for misbehaviour-is an attempt to motivate students by extrinsic means of incentives, rewards and punishments.

Humanistic approaches to motivation

Humanistic interpretations of motivation emphasize intrinsic sources of motivation such as a person's need for self-actualization, the inborn actualizing tendency or the need for "self-determination". From the humanistic perspective, to motivate means to encourage people's inner resources- their sense of competence, self-esteem, autonomy, and self-actualization. Maslow's theory is a very influential humanistic explanation of motivation.

Maslow's Hierarchy

Abraham Maslow suggested that humans have a hierarchy of needs ranging from lower-level needs for survival and safety to higher-level needs for intellectual achievement and finally self-actualization. Self-actualization means self fulfillment, the realization of personal potential. Each of the lower needs must be met before the next higher need can be addressed.

Maslow called the four lower level needs-for survival, then safety, followed by belonging, and then self-esteem-deficiency needs. When these needs are satisfied, the motivation for fulfilling them decreases. He labeled the three higher level needs- intellectual achievement, then aesthetic appreciation, and finally self-actualization-being needs. When they are met, a person's motivation does not cease; instead it increases to seek further fulfillment. Unlike the deficiency needs, the being needs can never be completely filled. For example, the more successful you are in your efforts to develop as a teacher, the harder you are likely to strive for even greater improvement.

Cognitive approaches to motivation

Cognitive theorists believe that behaviour is determined by our thinking, not simply by whether we have been rewarded or punished for the behaviour in the past. These theorists emphasize intrinsic motivation.

Attribution theory

This cognitive explanation of motivation begins with the assumption that we try to make sense of our own behaviour and the behaviour of others by searching for explanations and causes. To understand our own successes and failures, particularly unexpected ones, we all ask "Why?" Students ask themselves, "Why did I flunk midterm?" or Why did I do so well this time?" They may attribute their successes and failures to ability, effort, mood, knowledge, luck, help, interest, clarity of instructions, the interference of others, unfair policies, and so on. To understand the success and failures of others, we also make attributions-that the others are smart or lucky or work hard.

Bernard Weiner is one of the main educational psychologists responsible for relating attribution theory to school learning. According to Weiner, most of the attributed causes for successes or failures can be characterized in terms of three dimensions:

1. Locus (location of the cause internal or external to the person)
2. Stability(whether the cause stays the same or can change) and,
3. Controllability (whether the person can control the cause)

Every cause for success or failure can be categorized on these three dimensions. For example, luck is external(locus), unstable(stability), and uncontrollable (controllability)

Attributions in the classroom

When usually successful students fail, they often make internal controllable attributions. They misunderstood the directions, lacked the necessary knowledge, or simply did not study hard enough, for example. As a consequence, they usually focus on strategies for succeeding next time. This response often leads to achievement, pride and a greater feeling of control.

Motivation to Learn in School

Teachers are concerned about developing a particular kind of motivation in their students-the motivation to learn. Student motivation to learn is defined as "a student tendency to find academic activities meaningful and worthwhile and to try to derive the intended academic benefits from them. Motivation to learn can be construed as both a general trait and a situation specific trait. Motivation to learn involves more than wanting or intending to learn. It includes the quality of the student's mental efforts. For example, reading the text 10 times may indicate persistence, but motivation to learn implies more thoughtful, active, study strategies, such as summarizing, elaborating the basic ideas, outlining in your own words, drawing graphs of the key relationships, and so on.

It would be wonderful if all our students came to us filled with the motivation to learn, but they don't. And even if they did, work in school might still seem boring or unimportant to some students. As teachers, we have three major goals. The first is to get students productively involved with the work of the class; in other words, to create a state of motivation to learn. The second and longer term goal is to develop in our students the trait of being motivated to learn so they will be able "to educate themselves throughout their lifetime". And finally, we want our students to be cognitively engaged-to think deeply about what they study. In other words, we want them to be thoughtful.

THE TARGET MODEL FOR SUPPORTING STUDENT MOTIVATION TO LEARN

Teachers make decisions in many areas that can influence motivation to learn. The TARGET acronym highlights task, autonomy, recognition, grouping, evaluation and time.

Target area	Focus	Objectives	Examples of possible strategies
TASK	• How learning tasks are structured- what the student is asked to do	• Enhance intrinsic attractiveness of learning tasks. • Make learning meaningful	• Encourage instruction that relates to students' background and experience • Avoid payment (monetary and other) for attendance, grades or achievement • Foster goal setting and self-regulation
AUTONOMY/ RESPONSIBILITY	• Student participation in learning/ school decisions	• Provide optimal freedom for students to make choices and take responsibility	• Give alternatives in making assignments • Ask for student comments on school life-and take them seriously • Encourage students to take initiatives and evaluate their own learning • Establish leadership opportunities for all students
RECOGNITION	• The nature and use of recognition and reward in the school setting	• Provide opportunities for all students to be recognized for learning • Recognize progress in goal attainment • Recognize challenge seeking and innovation	• Foster "personal best" awards • Reduce emphasis on "honor rolls" • Recognize and publicize a wide range of school-related activities of students

GROUPING	• The organization of school learning and experiences	• Build an environment of acceptance and appreciation of all students • Broaden the range of social interaction, particularly of at-risk students • Enhance social skills development	• Provide opportunities for cooperative learning, problem solving, and decision making • Encourage multiple group membership to increase range of peer interaction • Eliminate ability-grouped classes
EVALUATION	• The nature and use of evaluation and assessment procedures	• Grading and reporting processes • Practices associated with use of standardized tests • Definition of goals and standards	• Reduce emphasis on social comparisons of achievement • Give students opportunities to improve their performance • Establish grading/ reporting practices that portray student progress in learning
			• Encourage student participation in the evaluation process
TIME	• The scheduling of the school day	• Provide opportunities for extended and significant student involvement in learning tasks • Allow the learning task and student needs to dictate scheduling	• Allow students to progress at their own rate whenever possible • Encourage flexibility in the scheduling of learning experiences • Give teachers greater control over time usage through, for example, block scheduling

EMOTION AND COGNITION

Emotions are complex. The main stream definition of emotion refers to a feeling state involving thoughts,physical and physiological reactions that influence our behaviour. The physiology of emotion is closely linked to arousal of the nervous system with various states and strengths of arousal relating, apparently, to particular emotions. Emotion is also linked to behavioral tendency. Extroverted people are more likely to be social and express their emotions, while introverted people are more likely to be more socially withdrawn and conceal their emotions. Emotion is often the driving force behind motivation, positive or negative. An alternative definition of emotion is a "positive or negative experience that is associated with a particular pattern of physiological activity".

Emotions involve different components, such as subjective experience, cognitive processes, expressive behaviour, psychophysiological changes, and instrumental behaviour. At one time, academics attempted to identify the emotion with one of the components: William James with a subjective experience, behaviorists with instrumental behavior, psychophysiologists with physiological changes, and so on. More recently, emotion is said to consist of all the components.

Emotion can be differentiated from a number of similar constructs within the field of affective neuroscience:

- **Feelings** are best understood as a subjective representation of emotions, private to the individual experiencing them.

- **Moods** are diffuse affective states that generally last for much longer durations than emotions and are also usually less intense than emotions. Moods often lack a contextual stimulus.

- **Affect** is an encompassing term, used to describe the topics of emotion, feelings, and moods together, even though it is commonly used interchangeably with emotion.

In addition, relationships exist between emotions, such as having positive or negative influences, with direct opposites existing. These concepts are described in contrasting and categorisation of emotions. Graham differentiates emotions as functional or dysfunctional and argues all functional emotions have benefits.

Components of Emotion

In Scherer's components processing model of emotion, five crucial elements of emotion are said to exist. From the component processing perspective, emotion experience is said to require that all of these processes become coordinated and synchronized for a short period of time, driven by appraisal processes.

- **Cognitive appraisal:** provides an evaluation of events and objects
- **Bodily symptoms:** the physiological component of emotional experience
- **Action tendencies:** A motivational component for the preparation and direction of motor responses.
- **Expression:** Facial and vocal expression almost always accompanies an emotional state to communicate reaction and intention of actions
- **Feelings :** the subjective experience of emotional state once it has occurred

Theories of Emotion

James-Lange Theory : In his theory, James proposed that the perception of what he called an "exciting fact" directly led to a physiological response, known as "emotion." To account for different types of emotional experiences, James proposed that stimuli trigger activity in the autonomic nervous system, which in turn produces an emotional experience in the brain.

An example of this theory in action would be as follows: An emotion-evoking stimulus (snake) triggers a pattern of physiological response (increased heart rate, faster breathing, etc.), which is interpreted as a particular emotion (fear). This theory is supported by experiments in which by manipulating the bodily state induces a desired emotional state. Some people may believe that emotions give rise to emotion-specific actions: e.g. "I'm crying because I'm sad," or "I ran away because I was scared."

$$\text{EVENT} \to \text{AROUSAL} \to \text{INTERPRETATION} \to \text{EMOTION}$$

Additional support for the James-Lange theory of emotion is provided by studies of the facial feedback hypothesis. This hypothesis suggests that changes in our facial expression sometime produce shifts in our emotional experience rather than merely mirroring them.

Cannon-Bard Theory : Walter Bradford Cannon agreed that physiological responses played a crucial role in emotions, but did not believe that physiological responses alone could explain subjective emotional experiences.

He suggested that physiological responses were too slow and often imperceptible and this could not account for the relatively rapid and intense subjective awareness of emotion. He also believed that the richness, variety, and temporal course of emotional experiences could not stem from physiological reactions, that reflected fairly undifferentiated fight or flight responses. An example of this theory in action is as follows: An emotion-evoking event (snake) triggers simultaneously both a physiological response and a conscious experience of an emotion.

$$\text{EVENT} \begin{array}{l} \longrightarrow \text{AROUSAL} \\ \longrightarrow \text{EMOTION} \end{array}$$

Schachter-Singer's Two-factor Theory : He suggested that physiological responses contributed to emotional experience by facilitating a focused cognitive appraisal of a given physiologically arousing event and that this appraisal was what defined the subjective emotional experience. Emotions were thus a result of two- stage process: general physiological arousal, and experience of emotion. For example, the physiological arousal, heart pounding, in a response to an evoking stimulus, the sight of snake in the kitchen. The brain then quickly scans the area, to explain the pounding, and notices the snake. Consequently, the brain interprets the pounding heart as being the result of fearing the snake

$$\text{EVENT} \to \text{AROUSAL} \to \text{REASONING} \to \text{EMOTION}$$

Cognitive Theories : With the two-factor theory now incorporating cognition, several theories began to argue that cognitive activity in the form of judgments, evaluations, or thoughts were entirely that necessary for an emotion to occur. One of the main proponents of this view was Richard Lazarus who stated emotions must have some cognitive intentionality. The cognitive activity involved in the interpretation of an emotional context may be conscious or unconscious and may or may not take the form of conceptual processing.

Lazarus' theory is very influential; emotion is a disturbance that occurs in the following order:

1. **Cognitive appraisal :** The individual perceives the event cognitively, which cues the emotion.

2. **Physiological changes :** The cognitive reaction starts biological changes such as increased heart rate or pituitary adrenal response.

3. **Action :** The individual feels the emotion after cognition and chooses how to react.

For example: Henry sees a snake.

1. Henry cognitively assesses the snake in her presence. Cognition allows her to understand it as a danger.

2. Her brain activates Adrenaline gland which pumps Adrenaline through her blood stream resulting in increased heartbeat.

3. Henry screams and runs away.

Lazarus stressed that the quality and intensity of emotions are controlled through cognitive processes.

$$\text{EVENT} \rightarrow \text{THOUGHT} \begin{array}{l} \rightarrow \text{EMOTION} \\ \rightarrow \text{AROUSAL} \end{array}$$

George Mandler provided an extensive theoretical and empirical discussion of emotion as influenced by cognition consciousness, and the autonomic nervous system.

A prominent philosophical exponent Robert C. Solomon claimed that emotions are cognitive activity in the form of judgments. He has demonstrated a more nuanced view which responds to what he has called the 'standard objection' to cognitivism, the idea that a judgement that something is fearsome can occur with or without emotion, so judgement cannot be identified with emotion. The theory proposed by Nico Frijda where appraisal leads to action tendencies is another example.

Perceptual Theory : Argues this theory that bodily responses are central to emotions, yet it emphasises the meaningfulness of emotions or the idea that emotions are about something, as is recognised by cognitive theories. The novel claim of this theory is that conceptually-based cognition is unnecessary for such meaning. Rather the bodily changes themselves perceive the meaningful content of the emotion because of being causally triggered by certain situations.

Affective Events Theory : Developed by Howard M. Weiss and Russell Cropanzano 1996 this is a communication-based theory that looks at the causes, structures, and consequences of emotional experience (especially in work contexts). This theory discovers that emotions are influenced and caused by events which in turn influence attitudes and behaviors. This theoretical frame also emphasises time in that human beings experience what they call emotion episodes— a "series of emotional states extended over time and organised around an underlying theme." This theory has been utilized by numerous researchers to better understand emotion from a communicative lens, and was reviewed further by Howard M. Weiss and Daniel J. Beal.

Emotion and Cognition

Our thoughts seem to exert strong effects on our emotions. This relationship works in the other directions as well. Being in a happy mood often causes us to think happy thoughts, while feeling sad lends to bring negative memories and images to mind. In short, there appear to be important links between the way we feel and the way we think.

How Affect Influences Cognition:

Affect, our current mood strongly influence our perception of ambiguous stimuli. In general, we perceive and evaluate these stimuli more favorably when we are in good mood than when we are in a negative one. Positive and negative moods exert a strong influence on memory. According to Forgas information consistent with our current mood is easier to remember than information inconsistent with it. According to Isen & Daubman, persons experiencing positive effect are seen to include a wider range of information within various memory categories than do persons in a neutral or negative mood. Our current mood often influences the process of decision making. Persons experiencing positive effect are indeed more likely to make risky decisions the potential losses involved are small or very unlikely to occur. Persons in a good mood are sometimes more creative than those in negative mood. They are more successful in performing tasks involving creative problem-solving.

Exercise 1 : Previous Year Questions of CTET & STET

1. At lower classes, play-way method of teaching is based on *[CTET-2011-I]*
   (a) theory of physical education programmes
   (b) principles of methods of teaching
   (c) psychological principles of development and growth
   (d) sociological principles of teaching

2. "A young child responds to a new situation on the basis of the response made by him/her in a similar situation as in the past." This is related to *[CTET-2011-I]*
   (a) 'Law of Analogy' of learning
   (b) 'Law of Effect' of learning
   (c) 'Law of Attitude' of learning process
   (d) 'Law of Readiness' of learning

3. Motivation, in the process of learning *[CTET-2011-I]*
   (a) sharpens the memory of learners
   (b) differentiates new. learning from old learning
   (c) makes learners think unidirectionally
   (d) creates interest for learning among young learners

4. Learning can be enriched if *[CTET-2011-I]*
   (a) situations from the real world are brought into the class in which students interact with each other and the teacher facilitates
   (b) more and more teaching aids are used in the class
   (c) teachers use different types of lectures and explanation
   (d) due attention is paid to periodic tests in the class

5. The 'insight theory of learning' is promoted by *[CTET-2011-I]*
   (a) 'Gestalt' theorists
   (b) Pavlov
   (c) Jean Piaget
   (d) Vygotsky

6. Parents should play a ___1___ role in the learning process of young children. *[CTET-2011-I]*
   (a) negative   (b) proactive
   (c) sympathetic   (d) neutral

7. _________ is considered a sign of motivated teaching. *[CTET-2011-I]*
   (a) Maximum attendance in the class
   (b) Remedial work given by the teacher
   (c) Questioning by students
   (d) Pin drop silence in the class

8. Which of the following statements is not appropriate to motivation as a process? *[RTET-2011-I]*
   (a) It causes a person to move towards a goal
   (b) It satisfies the person's biological needs
   (c) It helps in achieving a psychological ambition
   (d) It keeps away from an unpleasant situation

9. Five years old Raju is watching a storm from his window. A huge bolt of lightning is followed by a tremendous thunderclap and Raju jumps at the noise. This happens several more times. There is a brief lull and another lightning bolt. Raju jumps in response to bolt. Jumping of Raju is an example of learning theory of *[RTET-2011-I]*
   (a) Classical conditioning
   (b) Operant conditioning
   (c) Trial and Error
   (d) None of these

10. Which of the following statements regarding achievement motive is true ? *[RTET-2011-I]*
    (a) Achievement motive is necessary for survival
    (b) If the satisfaction of personal potentialities is emphasized, the achievement motive may be classified as a growth motive
    (c) If the stress is on competition among people, the achievement motive can be considered a social motive
    (d) All of these

11. .... in considered a sign of motivated teaching. *[UPET-2011-I]*
    (a) Maximum attendance in class
    (b) Remedial work given by the teacher
    (c) Questioning by students
    (d) Pin drop silence in the class.

12. As a teacher what techniques you would follow to motivate students of your class: *[PTET-2011-I]*
    1. By setting induction
    2. Use of blackboard
    3. By illustration
    4. By active participation of students
    (a) 1, 2 & 3   (b) 1 & 4
    (c) 2 & 4   (d) All of these

13. What are the factors related to learner that effects the learning: *[PTET-2011-I]*
    (a) Physical & Mental health of the learner
    (b) Level of aspiration & achievement motivation
    (c) Readiness & Willpower
    (d) All of these

14. Who was the pioneer of Classical conditioning: *[PTET-2011-I]*
    (a) Skinner   (b) Pavlov
    (c) Watson   (d) Thorndike

15. Second stage of Maslow's Hierarchial need is   *[TNTET-2011-II]*
    (a) love and belonging needs
    (b) safety needs
    (c) esteem needs
    (d) physiological needs

16. Rate of learning =   *[TNTET-2011-I]*
    (a) $\dfrac{\text{Amount of learning proficiency achievement}}{\text{Time taken to achieve the amount learning}}$
    (b) $\dfrac{\text{Amount of content learnt}}{\text{Time taken to achieve the amount learning}}$
    (c) $\dfrac{\text{Amount of learning proficiency achieved}}{\text{Amount of the content}}$
    (d) $\dfrac{\text{Amount of content learnt}}{\text{Amount of the curriculum}}$

17. McDougall says that the emotional expressions of human being occur in which of the following sequence?   *[TNTET-2011-I]*
    (a) Action → Affection → Cognition
    (b) Cognition → Environment → Conation
    (c) Cognitation → Affection → Conation
    (d) Emotion → Affection → Cognition

18. By employing domesticated and trained pigeon, bringing down the wild pigeons sitting on temple towers is   *[TNTET-2011-I]*
    (a) Trial and error learning
    (b) Observation learning
    (c) Operant conditioning
    (d) Classical conditioning

19. Which of the following statements cannot be considered as a feature of 'learning'?   *[CTET-2011-II]*
    (a) Learning is a process that mediates behaviour
    (b) Learning is something that occurs as a result of certain experiences
    (c) Study of behaviour is learning
    (d) Unlearning is also a part of learning

20. Which of the following statements is true about 'learning' ?   *[CTET-2011-II]*
    (a) Errors made by children indicate that no learning has taken place.
    (b) Learning is effective in an environment that is emotionally positive and satisfying for the learners.
    (c) Learning is not affected by emotional factors at any stage of learning.
    (d) Learning is fundamentally a mental activity.

21. Which of the following is not a characteristic feature of intrinsically motivated children?   *[CTET-2011-II]*
    (a) They always succeed
    (b) They enjoy doing their work
    (c) They display a high level of energy while working
    (d) They like challenging tasks

22. A college girl developed the habit of dropping the coat on the floor. Mother asked the girl to get out of the room and hang up the coat on the peg. The girl enters house, keeps coat on, approaches closet, hang up the coat on the peg. It is an example of   *[RTET-2011-II]*
    (a) Chain learning
    (b) Stimulus Response learning
    (c) Concept learning
    (d) all of these.

23. Extrinsic motivation may include   *[RTET-2011-II]*
    I.   Praise & Blame
    II. Rivalry
    III. Rewards & Punishment
    IV. Knowledge of results.
    Of these :
    (a) I and III   (b) I, II and III
    (c) Only II   (d) all of these

24. Teacher behaviour ought to be   *[UPTET-2011-II]*
    (a) administrative   (b) instructive
    (c) Idealistic   (d) directive

25. A teacher can motivate students by   *[UPTET-2011-II]*
    (a) giving prizes
    (b) giving proper guidance
    (c) giving examples
    (d) delivering speeches in class

26. Which of the following is NOT the benefit of integrating student-centred learning into the curriculum?   *[PTET-2011-II]*

    (a) strengthens student motivation

    (b) promotes peer communication

    (c) builds student-teacher relationships

    (d) hinders discovery/active learning

27. Which of the following is NOT an element of learning event?   *[PTET-2011-II]*

    (a) learner

    (b) internal conditions

    (c) stimulus

    (d) teacher

28. The first stage in the learning of a skill is: *[PTET-2011-II]*

    (a) precision   (b) manipulation

    (c) coordination   (d) imitation

29. Motivation begins with needs exists in all of us. The need, that the student would tend to fulfill first pertains to: *[PTET-2011-II]*

    (a) esteem

    (b) physiological

    (c) social

    (d) self actualization

30. Which one of the following theories view that behaviour could be shaped through successive approximation and reinforcement of responses more nearly approaching desired behaviour?   *[PTET-2011-II]*

    (a) classical conditioning

    (b) instrumental conditioning

    (c) operant conditioning

    (d) social learning

31. Learning is best defined as   *[TNTET-2011-II]*

    (a) any change in behaviour

    (b) a relatively permanent change in behaviour due to past experience

    (c) a permanent change in behaviour due to physical development

    (d) any change in behaviour caused by punishment

32. Which of the following is a domain of learning?   *[CTET-2012-I]*

    (a) Affective   (b) Spiritual

    (c) Professional   (d) Experiential

33. A student works hard to clear an entrance test for admission into a medical college. The student is said to be motivated   *[CTET-2012-II]*

    (a) experientially   (b) intrinsically

    (c) extrinsically   (d) individually

34. According to theories of motivation, a teacher can enhance learning by   *[CTET-2012-II]*

    (a) setting uniform standards of expectations

    (b) not having any expectations from students

    (c) setting extremely high expectations

    (d) setting realistic expectations from students

35. Motives are classified as   *[UPTET-2014-I]*

    (a) Natural and Artificial

    (b) Less important and More important

    (c) Inborn and Acquired

    (d) Motives and Incentives

36. In a process of learning. 'Transfer of learning' can be   *[UPTET-2014-I]*

    (a) Positive   (b) Negative

    (c) Zero   (d) All of these

37. Which of the following school is based on learning by insight ?   *[UPTET-2014-I]*

    (a) Psycho analytical theory

    (b) Behaviourism

    (c) Connectionism

    (d) Gestalt theory

38. Which psychologist used non-sense syllables as a material of learning ?   *[UPTET-2014-I]*

    (a) William James   (b) Skinner

    (c) Ebbinghaus   (d) Bartlet

39. The laws of learning are given by *[UPTET-2014-I]*

    (a) Pavlov   (b) Skinner

    (c) Thorndike   (d) Kohler

40. Learning is   *[UPTET-2014-I]*

    (a) a change in behaviour

    (b) the result of experience or practice

    (c) relativley permanent change in behaviour

    (d) All of the above

41. The most appropriate meaning of learning is   *[UPTET-2014-I]*

    (a) acquisition of skills

    (b) inculcation of knowledge

    (c) modification of behaviour

    (d) personal adjustment

42. The Principle of 'trial and error' is propounded by   *[UPTET-2014-II]*

    (a) Thorndike   (b) McDougall

    (c) Kohler   (d) Pavlov

43. What should not be used in order to eliminate 'plateaus of learning' ?   *[UPTET-2014-II]*

    (a) The learner should be motivated and encouraged.

   (b) The good methodology of learning should be adapted

   (c) He should be punished

   (d) The causes of it should be studied

44. Application of knowledge skill or subject learned, in other situations is known as *[UPTET-2014-II]*

   (a) Motivation

   (b) Transfer of learning

   (c) Frustration

   (d) Worry

45. Initially the rate of learning increases and later on it decreases gradually, that curve is called *[UPTET-2014-II]*

   (a) Convex curve

   (b) Concave curve

   (c) Combination type of curve

   (d) There is no curve

46. _______ word is also often used for motivation. *[UPTET-2014-II]*

   (a) Emotion   (b) Need

   (c) Feeling   (d) Perception

47. Which of the following condition(s) is/are not the internal condition(s) of attracting attention ? *[UPTET-2014-II]*

   (a) Position of the stimulus

   (b) Need

   (c) One - above

   (d) Both the above - one and two

48. As a teacher what techniques you would follow to motivate students of your class: *[PTET-2014-I]*

   1. By setting induction

   2. Use of black board

   3. By illustration

   4. By active participation of students

   (a) 1, 2 & 3   (b) 1 & 4

   (c) 2 & 4   (d) All of these

49. What are the factors related to learner that effects the learning : *[PTET-2014-I]*

   (a) Physical & Mental health of the learner

   (b) Level of aspiration & achievement motivation

   (c) Readlness & Willpower

   (d) All of these

50. Who was the pioneer of Classical Conditioning: *[PTET-2014-I]*

   (a) Skinner   (b) Pavlov

   (c) Watson   (d) Thorndike

51. Which of the following Motives are considered as primary motives: *[PTET-2014-I]*

   (a) Physiological Motives

   (b) Psychological Motives

   (c) Social Motives

   (d) Educational Motives

52. Which of the following is NOT an element of learning event? *[PTET-2014-II]*

   (a) learner

   (b) internal conditions

   (c) stimulus

   (d) teacher

53. Which one of the following is an example of reinforcement? *[PTET-2014-II]*

   (a) No Lata, the answer is not 45

   (b) Kamla, can't you help Kirti with her answer

   (c) Oh no, as usual, you are wrong

   (d) Suniti, you have said rightly

54. The animal used for the experiment on operant conditioning by skinner is *[TNTET-2014-I]*

   (a) Monkey   (b) Rat

   (c) Dog   (d) Pigeon

55. Which one of the following pair is correct *[TNTET-2014-I]*

   (a) Kohler – Insight learning

   (b) Skinner – Law of learning

   (c) Pavlov – Operant or Emitted responses

   (d) Thorndike – Operant conditioning

56. Which one of the following is not related to learning factor *[TNTET-2014-I]*

   (a) Personal factor

   (b) Psychological factor

   (c) Social factor

   (d) None of these

57. Thondikes Law of learning insists on *[TNTET-2014-I]*

   (a) Stimulus   (b) Repetition

   (c) Prize   (d) Punishment

58. One of the Important Learning Factor is *[TNTET-2014-I]*

   (a) Retention   (b) Attitude

   (c) Attention   (d) Attraction

59. The Achievement of Learning is *[TNTET-2014-I]*

   (a) Skill   (b) Knowledge

   (c) Attitude   (d) All of these

60. Stimulus – response is due to
[TNTET-2014-II]
(a) Brain   (b) Maturity
(c) Sense organs   (d) Experience

61. Learning through insight was first shown by
[TNTET-2014-II]
(a) B.F. Skinner
(b) Mary Kavur Jones
(c) Pavlov
(d) Kohler

62. Hull's theory of learning formulae is
[TNTET-2014-II]
(a) $S^E R = DRXS^H \times K - I$
(b) $R^E S = DXSR^H \times K - I$
(c) $S^E R = XDSR^H R \times K - I$
(d) $S^E R = DXS^H R \times K - I$

63. A PT teacher wants her students to improve fielding in the game of cricket. Which one of the following strategies will best help his students achieve that goal ?   *[CTET-July-2013-I]*
(a) Tell students how important it is for them to learn to field.
(b) Explain the logic behind good fielding and rate of success.
(c) Demonstrate fielding while students observe.
(d) Give students a lot of practice in fielding.

64. Which of the following will be most appropriate to maximise learning ?   *[CTET-July-2013-II]*
(a) Teacher should identify her cognitive style as well as of her students' cognitive style.
(b) Individual difference in students should be smoothened by pairing similar students.
(c) Teacher should focus on only one learning style to bring optimum result.
(d) Students of similar cultural background should be kept in the same class to avoid difference in opinion.

65. The conclusion 'Children can learn violent behaviour depicted in movies' may be derived on the basis of the work done by which of the following psychologist ?   *[CTET-July-2013-I]*
(a) Edward L. Thorndike
(b) J.B. Watson
(c) Albert Bandura
(d) Jean Piaget

66. Students observe fashion shows and try to imitate models. This kind of imitation may be called
[CTET-July-2013-I]
(a) Primary simulation
(b) Secondary simulation
(c) Social learning
(d) Generalisation

67. A, B and C are three students studying English. 'A' finds it interesting and thinks it will be helpful for her in future. 'B' studies English as she wants to secure first rank in the class. 'C' studies it as she is primarily concerned to secure passing grades. The goals of A, B and C respectively are
[CTET-July-2013-I]
(a) Mastery, Performance, Performance Avoidance
(b) Performance, Performance Avoidance, Mastery
(c) Performance Avoidance, Mastery, Performance
(d) Mastery, Performance Avoidance, Performance

68. Even though this was clearly in violation of his safety needs, Captain Vikram Batra died fighting in the Kargil War while protecting his country. He might have   *[CTET-July-2013-I]*
(a) sought novel experience.
(b) achieved self-actualisation.
(c) ignored his belongingness needs.
(d) wanted to earn a good name to his family.

69. Mastery orientation can be encouraged by
[CTET-July-2013-I]
(a) focusing on students' individual effort.
(b) comparing students' successes with each other.
(c) assigning lot of practice material as home assignments.
(d) taking unexpected tests.

70. The stress affects performance in examinations. This fact reflects which of the following relationships?
[CTET-Feb.-2014-I]
(a) Cognition-Emotion
(b) Stress-Omission
(c) Performance-Anxiety
(d) Cognition-Competition

71. Which of the following factors supports learning in a classroom?   *[CTET-Feb.-2014-I]*
(a) Increasing the number of tests to motivate children to learn
(b) Supporting the autonomy of children by the teachers

   (c) Sticking to one particular method of instruction to maintain uniformity

   (d) Increasing the time interval of periods from 40 minutes to 50 minutes

72. Mature students   *[CTET-Feb.-2014-I]*

   (a) believe that emotion has no place in their studies

   (b) resolve easily all their conflicts with their intellect

   (c) sometimes need emotional support in their studies

   (d) do not get upset by studies in difficult situations

73. While appearing in an assessment, Devika finds her arousal as energizing, whereas Rajesh finds his arousal as discouraging. Their emotional experiences are most likely to differ with respect to   *[CTET-Feb.-2014-II]*

   (a) the duration of time

   (b) the extremity of emotion

   (c) the level of adaptation

   (d) the intensity of thought

74. The Government of India has started Midday Meal Scheme for the elementary schools. Which of the following theories of motivation supports this Scheme?   *[CTET-Feb.-2014-II]*

   (a) Behaviourist   (b) Socio-cultural

   (c) Cognitive   (d) Humanistic

75. Attaching importance to the home setting of students for understanding children's behaviour and using this information for building effective pedagogy is related to which of the following theories of learning?   *[CTET-Feb.-2014-II]*

   (a) Behaviourist

   (b) Ecological

   (c) Constructivist

   (d) Social-constructivist

76. Which one of the following is an example of learning style ?   *[CTET-Sept.-2014-I]*

   (a) Visual   (b) Accrual

   (c) Factual   (d) Tactual

77. According to the theory of social learning of Albert Bandura, which one of the following is true ?   *[CTET-Sept.-2014-I]*

   (a) Play is essential and should be given priority in school.

   (b) Modelling is a principal way for children to learn.

   (c) An unresolved crisis can harm a child.

   (d) Cognitive development is independent of social development.

78. When children learn a concept and use it, practice helps in reducing the errors committed by them. This idea was given by   *[CTET-Sept.-2014-I]*

   (a) E.L. Thorndike   (b) Jean Piaget

   (c) J.B. Watson   (d) Lev Vygotsky

79. The inner force that stimulates and compels a behavioural response and provides specific direction to that response is   *[CTET-Sept.-2014-I]*

   (a) Motive   (b) Perseverance

   (c) Emotion   (d) Commitment

80. Which one of the following may is a factor that affects learning positively ?   *[CTET-Sept.-2014-I]*

   (a) Fear of failure

   (b) Competition with peers

   (c) Meaningful association

   (d) Pressure from parents

81. Learners cannot learn unless *[CTET-Sept.-2014-II]*

   (a) they are taught according to the needs of social aims of education

   (b) they know that the material being taught will be tested in the near future

   (c) they are prepared to learn

   (d) they are asked about their learning in schools by their parents at home on a daily basis

82. Theory of social learning emphasises on which of the following factors ?   *[CTET-Sept.-2014-II]*

   (a) Nature   (b) Nurture

   (c) Adaptation   (d) Emendation

83. Which of the following is properly sequenced in the context of motivation cycle ?

    [CTET-Sept.-2014-II]

   (a) Arousal, Drive, Need, Achievement, Goal-directed behaviour, Reduction of arousal

   (b) Drive, Need, Arousal, Goal-directed behaviour, Reduction of arousal

   (c) Need, Goal-directed behaviour, Drive, Arousal, Achievement, Reduction of arousal

   (d) Need, Drive, Arousal, Goal-directed behaviour, Achievement, Reduction of arousal

84. Learning experiences should be planned in a manner so as to make learning meaningful. Which of the given learning experiences does not facilitate meaningful learning for the children?

    [CTET-Feb.-2015-I]

    (a) Repetition based on mere recall of content

    (b) Formulating questions on content

    (c) Discussion and debate on the topic

    (d) Presentation on the topic

85. Giving punishment, verbal or non-verbal, to the children results in   *[CTET-Feb.-2015-I]*

    (a) motivating them to work.

    (b) protecting the child's image.

    (c) improving their scores.

    (d) damaging their self-concept.

86. Which one of the following is an example of scaffolding?   *[CTET-Feb.-2016-I]*

    (a) Giving prompts and cues and asking questions at critical junctures

    (b) Giving motivational lectures to students

    (c) Offering explanations without encouraging questioning.

    (d) Offering both material and non-material rewards

87. Learning   *[CTET-Feb.-2016-I]*

    (a) is not affected by a learner's emotions.

    (b) has very little connection with. emotions.

    (c) is independent of a a learner's emotions.

    (d) is influenced by a learner's emotions.

88. Teachers can encourage children to think creatively by   *[CTET-Feb.-2016-II]*

    (a) asking them to think of different ways to solve a problem.

    (b) giving them multiple-choice questions.

    (c) asking them to memorise answers.

    (d) asking them recall-based questions.

89. Which one of the following is central to learning?   *[CTET-Feb.-2016-II]*

    (a) Meaning-making

    (b) Imitation

    (c) Conditioning

    (d) Rote memorisation

90. Your class has learners with different learning styles. To assess them, you would give them   *[CTET-Feb.-2016-II]*

    (a) the same set of tasks and tests.

    (b) a uniform set of instructions and subsequently label the children according to their marks in the test.

    (c) a variety of tasks and tests.

    (d) the same time to perform on the tests.

91. Which one of the following statements about motivation and learning is correct?   *[CTET-Feb.-2016-II]*

    (a) Learning is effective only when the students are motivated using external rewards.

    (b) Motivation does not have any role to play in learning.

    (c) Learning is effective only when the students have intrinsic motivation – a desire to learn from inside.

    (d) Learning is effective only when the students are extrinsically motivated – motivated by external factors.

92. Which one of the following statements about learning is correct?   *[CTET-Feb.-2016-II]*

    (a) Learning does not depend on learner's previous knowledge.

    (b) Learning is a passive receptive process.

    (c) Learning is equivalent to acquisition of skills.

    (d) Learning is facilitated by social actions.

93. Which one of the following is an important activity to enable children to learn?   *[CTET-Feb.-2016-II]*

    (a) Dialogue   (b) Reward

    (c) Lecture   (d) Instruction

94. What should a teacher tell her students to encourage them to do tasks with intrinsic motivation?   *[CTET-Sept.-2016-I]*

    (a) "Come on, finish it before she does."

    (b) "Why can't you be like him? See, he has done it perfectly."

    (c) "Complete the task fast and get a toffee."

    (d) "Try to do it, you will learn."

95. In an elementary classroom, an effective teacher should aim at the students to be motivated :   *[CTET-Sept.-2016-I]*

    (a) to learn so that they become curious and love learning for its own sake

    (b) to rate memorize so that they become good at recall

    (c) by using punitive measures so that they respect the teacher

    (d) to perform so that they get good marks in the end of the year examination

96. Which of the following is an example of effective school practice? *[CTET-Sept.-2016-I]*
   (a)   Constant comparative evaluation
   (b)   Corporal punishment
   (c)   Individualized learning
   (d)   Competitive classroom

97. Which of the following factors affect learning? *[CTET-Sept.-2016-II]*
   A.   Motivation of the learner
   B.   Maturation of the learner
   C.   Teaching strategies
   D.   Physical and emotional health of the learner
   (a)   A, B and C   (b)   A, B, C and D
   (c)   A and B   (d)   A and C

98. Meaningful learning is :   *[CTET-Sept.-2016-II]*
   (a)   active creation of knowledge structures from personal experience
   (b)   pairing and association between the stimulus and the response
   (c)   imitation of adults and more able peers
   (d)   passive receiving of the given information

99. Which of the following is not one of the primary tasks of a teacher for effective student learning? *[CTET-Sept.-2016-II]*
   (a)   Teaching students how to monitor and improve their own learning by effort
   (b)   Transmitting information to the students in a didactic manner
   (c)   Knowing the concepts that students bring to the classroom
   (d)   Requiring students to respond to higher-order questioning

100. Which of the following statements about cognition and emotions is correct? *[CTET-Sept.-2016-II]*
   (a)   Emotions affect cognition but cognition does not affect emotions.
   (b)   Cognition and emotions are intertwined and affect each other.
   (c)   Cognition and emotions are processes independent of each other.
   (d)   Cognition affects emotions but emotions do not affect cognition.

101. The period of learning, where no improvement in performance is made, is called   *[UPTET-2017-I]*
   (a)   learning curve
   (b)   plateau of learning
   (c)   memory
   (d)   attention

102. Who has propounded the law of trial and error of learning?   *[UPTET-2017-I]*
   (a)   Kohler   (b)   Pavlov
   (c)   Thorndike   (d)   Gestalt

103. Operant conditioning theory is propounded by   *[UPTET-2017-I]*
   (a)   Hull   (b)   Thorndike
   (c)   Hegarty   (d)   Skinner

104. Kohler is associated with which of the following?   *[UPTET-2017-I]*
   (a)   Theory of motivation
   (b)   Theory of development
   (c)   Theory of personality
   (d)   Theory of learning

105. Find the odd one out.   *[UPTET-2017-I]*
   (a)   Theory of learning to learn
   (b)   Theory of identical elements
   (c)   Drive reduction theory
   (d)   Theory of generalization

106. A boy who can ride a cycle is going to drive a motorbike. This is an example of *[UPTET-2017-I]*
   (a)   horizontal transfer of learning
   (b)   vertical transfer of learning
   (c)   bilateral transfer of learning
   (d)   No transfer of learning

107. Which of the following is not the cause of plateau of learning?   *[UPTET-2017-I]*
   (a)   Limit of motivation
   (b)   Non-cooperation of school
   (c)   Physiological limit
   (d)   Limit of knowledge

108. "Learning is the modificaiton of behaviour through experience and training." This statement was given by   *[UPTET-2017-I]*
   (a)   Gates and others
   (b)   Morgan and Gilliland
   (c)   Skinner
   (d)   Cronbach

109. Instincts are classified in fourteen types by   *[UPTET-2017-I]*
   (a)   Drever   (b)   McDougall
   (c)   Thorndike   (d)   Woodworth

110. Which is *not* included in primary law of learning?   *[UPTET-2017-I]*
   (a)   Law of readiness
   (b)   Law of exercise
   (c)   Law of multiple response
   (d)   Law of effect

111. Which of the following pairs is *not* true?
[UPTET-2017-I]

(a) Stimulus-response theory of learning – Thorndike

(b) Operant conditioning theory of learning – B.F. Skinner

(c) Classical theory of learning – Pavlov

(d) Holistic theory of learning – Hull

112. One of the following techniques is not mentioned by Sigmund Freud for dwelling out the repressed unconscious feelings   *[APTFT-May.-2018-I]*

(a) Free association (b) Gestaultism

(c) Dream analysis   (d) Hypnosis

113. According to instincts and its corresponding emotions the following is a right pair
[APTET-May.-2018-I]

(a) Parental urge - anger

(b) Curiosity - fear

(c) Laughter – spirit/activeness

(d) Structure - abhorrence

114. One of the following is a secondary need
[APTET-May.-2018-I]

(a) Food   (b) Recognition

(c) Sleep   (d) Water

115. Law of readiness, law of exercise, law of effect are the outcomes of the following learning theory
[APTET-May.-2018-I]

(a) Insight theory of learning

(b) Trial and error theory of learning

(c) Classical conditioning theory

(d) Operant conditioning theory

116. The type of reinforcement related to acquiring own standards without expecting anything from others   *[APTET-May.-2018-I]*

(a) Direct Reinforcement

(b) Indirect Reinforcement

(c) Self Reinforcement

(d) Negative Reinforcement

117. Even though we haven't seen the situation we are seeing now, we feel it as we have seen that before – This feeling is,

(a) Zeigarnik effect   *[APTET-May.-2018-I]*

(b) Hallo effect

(c) Deja vu

(d) Gestault effect

118. In terms of transfer of learning 'the effect of mother tongue in learning correct pronunciation of a foreign language' can be termed as,
[APTET-May.-2018-I]

(a) Positive transfer

(b) Negative transfer

(c) Bilateral transfer

(d) Zero transfer

119. The gradual disappearance of conditioned response of Salivation to bell in classical conditioning is   *[APTET-May.-2018-I]*

(a) Reinforcement

(b) Spontaneous Recovery

(c) Generalization

(d) Extinction

120. According to Bandura the first item in the process of social learning is   *[APTET-May.-2018-I]*

(a) Retention   (b) Reproduction

(c) Attention   (d) Reinforcement

121. The following is not related to Bruner's Theory of Instruction   *[APTET-May.-2018-I]*

(a) Readiness

(b) Analysis

(c) Content construction

(d) Serial order

122. In this leadership style, the leader is nominal and the members enjoy complete freedom and take final decisions by themselves.

[APTET-May.-2018-I]

(a) Democratic   (b) Autocratic

(c) Laissez faire   (d) Mixed

123. Swathi learnt to play carroms with right hand. Now she is able to play with left hand also. – The type of transfer of learning here is
[APTET-May.-2018-II]

(a) Positive Transfer

(b) Bilateral Transfer

(c) Negative Transfer

(d) Zero Transfer

124. Prasanthi prepared for Sociology examination first and then for Psychology. While taking Sociology examination she got confused due to recollection of psychological theories. This is due to
[APTET-May.-2018-II]

(a) Pro active inhibition

(b) Retro active inhibition

(c) Decay of memory traces

(d) Lack of interest in Sociology

125. The correct learning sequence in observational learning is   *[APTET-May.-2018-II]*

(a) Reinforcement → Attention → Retention → Performance

(b) Attention → Retention → Performance → Reinforcement

(c) Performance → Reinforcement → Attention → Retention

(d) Retention → Reinforcement → Attention → Performance

126. All children have done their project work because, the teacher announced a reward for those who have done their project work – The type of motivation here is *[APTET-May.-2018-II]*

(a) Achievement Motivation

(b) Extrinsic Motivation

(c) Intrinsic Motivation

(d) Individual Motivation

127. Reappearance of an extinguished conditional response unexpected after a rest period is called *[APTET-May.-2018-II]*

(a) Discrimination

(b) Extinction

(c) Insight

(d) Spontaneous Recovery

128. These play a vital role in 'learning to learn' skills *[APTET-May.-2018-II]*

(a) Intelligence, Aptitude

(b) Interest, Attitude

(c) Motivation, Self confidence

(d) Creativity, Learning

129. The learning in which learners depend on one another and also accountable to each other is *[APTET-May.-2018-II]*

(a) Inquiry based learning

(b) Co-operative learning

(c) Differentiated learning

(d) Collaborative learning

130. Characteristic feature of pupil centered learning is *[APTET-May.-2018-II]*

(a) Prominence to acquire knowledge

(b) Classroom is silent

(c) Students express their ideas freely

(d) Evaluation is done by the teacher only

Answer Key

1.	(c)	15.	(b)	29.	(d)	43.	(c)	57.	(b)	71.	(b)	85.	(d)	99.	(b)
2.	(b)	16.	(b)	30.	(c)	44.	(b)	58.	(c)	72.	(c)	86.	(a)	100.	(b)
3.	(d)	17.	(c)	31.	(b)	45.	(a)	59.	(d)	73.	(c)	87.	(d)	101.	(b)
4.	(a)	18.	(d)	32.	(a)	46.	(b)	60.	(a)	74.	(d)	88.	(a)	102.	(c)
5.	(a)	19.	(c)	33.	(b)	47.	(c)	61.	(d)	75.	(b)	89.	(a)	103.	(d)
6.	(b)	20.	(b)	34.	(d)	48.	(d)	62.	(d)	76.	(a)	90.	(c)	104.	(d)
7.	(c)	21.	(a)	35.	(c)	49.	(d)	63.	(d)	77.	(b)	91.	(c)	105.	(c)
8.	(d)	22.	(a)	36.	(d)	50.	(b)	64.	(a)	78.	(a)	92.	(d)	106.	(b)
9.	(a)	23.	(d)	37.	(d)	51.	(c)	65.	(c)	79.	(a)	93.	(a)	107.	(b)
10.	(d)	24.	(c)	38.	(c)	52.	(d)	66.	(c)	80.	(c)	94.	(d)	108.	(a)
11.	(c)	25.	(b)	39.	(c)	53.	(d)	67.	(a)	81.	(c)	95.	(a)	109.	(b)
12.	(d)	26.	(d)	40.	(d)	54.	(b)	68.	(b)	82.	(b)	96.	(c)	110.	(c)
13.	(d)	27.	(d)	41.	(c)	55.	(a)	69.	(a)	83.	(d)	97.	(b)	111.	(d)
14.	(b)	28.	(c)	42.	(a)	56.	(d)	70.	(a)	84.	(a)	98.	(a)	112.	(b)

113.	(c)	122.	(c)		
114.	(b)	123.	(c)		
115.	(b)	124.	(c)		
116.	(c)	125.	(b)		
117.	(c)	126.	(a)		
113.	(c)	127.	(b)		
114.	(b)	128.	(d)		
115.	(b)	129.	(c)		
116.	(c)	130.	(a)		
117.	(c)				
118.	(b)				
119	(d)				
120.	(c)				
121.	(b)				

64. (a) A teacher should maximize their learning to identify their cognitive style as well as of their students cognitive style.

65. (c) In social learning theory Albert Bandura states behaviour is learned from the environment through the process of observational learning. Children observe the people around them behaving in various ways.

66. (c) According to social learning theory, children are surrounded by many influential models, such as parents within the family, characters on children's TV, friends within their peer group and teachers at school. These models provide examples of masculine and feminine behavior to observe and imitate.

68. (b) Self-actualization refers to the desire for self-fulfillment, namely, to the tendency for him to become actualized in what he is potentially. This tendency might be phrased as the desire to become more and more what one is, to become everything that one is capable of becoming.

69. (a) Mastery orientation can be encouraged by focusing on students' individual efforts and also through positive parenting techniques and parental involvement in education.

70. (a) Cognition is defined as combination of processes like attention, memory, problem solving and planning. On the other hand emotions are associated with the feelings that one experiences on various different situations

Stress → Emotional State (Associated with heart)

Examination → Rational State (Associated with brain)

71. (b) Autonomy refers to the capacity to make decision independently, to manage one's life tasks without depending on others for assistance, so autonomy supports learning.

73. (c) Adaptation is a term referring to the ability to adjust to new information and experience.

74. (d) Mid day Meal Scheme started by the Government of India supports the humanistic theory of motivation. There are hierarchy of needs in Humanistic theory.

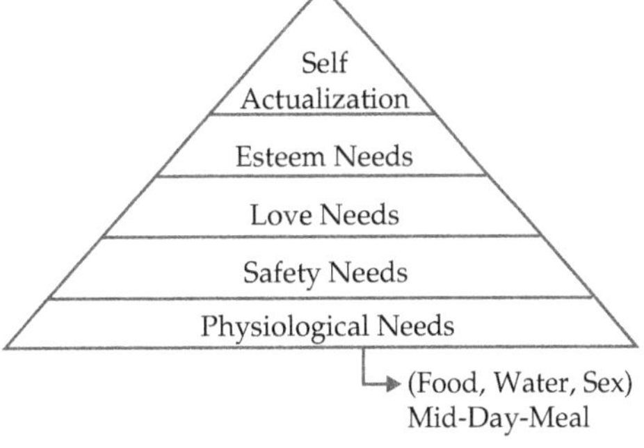

75. (b) Ecological theory of learning analyses the past life of a student and uses that information for building effective pedagogy.

86. (a) Scaffolding is a method of teaching in which a teacher provides one to one support to students to help them to solve a problem and accomplish their goals. There are various authentic tools used in scaffolding like breaking a task to smaller ones and to promote cooperative learning and to think aloud and having concrete thoughts, questioning, etc.

87. (d) it is usually observed that children are able to perform productively when they have a feeling of safety, pleasure and enthusiasm but when a child is in the state of anger, helplessness or frustration will not be able to do well either in the classroom or outside the classroom.

88. (a) There are many ways of solving a particular problem. Therefore a child should be given a problem to solve according to their abilities which will enhance their thinking power and mould it into a creative thought.

89. (a) Learning becomes easy if a child is able to decode the meaning of the concepts being taught. Language proficiency works well with the learning process that is why two languages are a must for the learner to know. One is mother tongue and the other one is for the curriculum purpose or others. Mother tongue is a medium to make a child learn the new language so that he can decode the meaning easily.

94. (d) Intrinsic motivation comes when a teacher encourages the child to do it himself and having faith in his capabilities. This encourages and motivates him to try the problems himself.

96. (c) Individualized learning is the best example of effective school learning as one gets individual marks for his or her performance.

101. (b) The **plateau effect** is a force of nature that lessens the effectiveness of once effective measures over time. An example of the plateau effect is when someone's exercise fails to be as effective as in the past, similar to the concept of diminishing returns. A

person enters into a period where there is no improvement or a decrease in performance

102. (c) The first miniature Trial and Error learning system of the method was provided by Thorndike's research on **Animal Intelligence** in 1898. This form of learning falls under S-R learning theory and also known as Connectionism.

103. (d) Skinner is regarded as the father of Operant Conditioning, but his work was based on Thorndike's (1898) law of effect. According to this principle, behavior that is followed by pleasant consequences is likely to be repeated, and behavior followed by unpleasant consequences is less likely to be repeated.

104. (d) In the 1920s, German psychologist Wolfgang **Kohler** was studying the behavior of apes. He designed some simple experiments that led to the development of one of the first cognitive theories of learning, which he called insight learning.

106. (b) **Vertical transfer**, requires that **learning** at a lower level must be transferred to a higher level of cognitive skills.

109. (b) Psychologist William **McDougall** was one of the first to write about the **instinct theory** of motivation. He suggested that **instinctive** behavior was composed of three essential elements: perception, behavior, and emotion.

110. (c) Law of Multiple Responses states that when one response does not bring satisfaction, it will initiate a new response.

112 (b) Gestaultism is a theory given by Gestalt . it is an attempt to recognize the laws behind the capacity to obtain and maintain meaningful perceptions in an actually disordered world. The essential principle of gestalt psychology is that the mind forms a worldwide thought with self-organizing propensity.

113. (c) According to instincts and its corresponding emotions the a right pair is Laughter – spirit/ activeness, because laughter shows the spirit and activeness of a listener as it is the ultimate reaction of what is delivered in front of an individual.

121. (b) Analysis is not a part of Bruner's Theory of Instruction

Exercise 2 : Test Yourself

1. Which of the following adults is helping to develop the child's intrinsic motivation?

   (a) Rahul, who praises his son for working hard on his environment project

   (b) Sharon, who gives her daughter Rs 500 for every A earned

   (c) Rohan, who takes his daughter out to dinner for winning a debate competition

   (d) Aastha, who gives her students chocolates when they are disciplined in class.

2. Which of the following statements is true about 'learning' ?

   (a) Errors made by children indicate that no learning has taken place.

   (b) Learning is effective in an environment that is emotionally positive and satisfying for the learners.

   (c) is not affected by emotional factors at any stage of learning

   (d) Learning is fundamentally a mental activity.

3. What kind of learning stems from observation of the consequences of an action?

   (a) classical conditioning

   (b) primary conditioning

   (c) operant conditioning

   (d) secondary conditioning

4. Which psychologist is famous for his pioneering work in classical conditioning?

   (a) B.F. Skinner

   (b) Sigmund Freud

   (c) John B. Watson

   (d) Ivan Pavlov

5. What is the name for the operant conditioning technique in which complicated behaviours are taught by sequential reinforcement?

   (a) instructing   (b) shaping

   (c) scaffolding   (d) modeling

6. Negative reinforcement involves:

   (a) Avoiding the aversive stimulus

   (b) Receiving the aversive stimulus

   (c) Punishment

   (d) The concept of 'negative reinforcement' does not exist, as reinforces by definition are always positive.

7. Which of the following statements is true?

   (a) In classical conditioning, the response is elicited, whereas in operant conditioning, the response is emitted

   (b) In both classical and operant conditioning, the response is elicited

   (c) In both classical and operant conditioning, the response is emitted

   (d) In classical conditioning, the response is emitted whereas in operant conditioning the response is emitted

8. Which of the following is true about learning goals?

   (a) Teachers should try to promote learning goals by making lessons interesting to students.

   (b) Instead of encouraging them, teachers should promote performance goals.

   (c) To promote learning goals, teachers should encourage students to make external attributions.

   (d) Teachers should try to promote learning goals by emphasizing the value of good grades.

9. Learners should not be encouraged to

   (a) ask as many questions as possible both inside and outside the class

   (b) actively interact with other learners in group work

   (c) participate in as many co-curricular activities as possible

   (d) memorize all the answers to questions which the teacher may ask

10. A theory that suggests that we learn from one another through observations, imitation, and modeling

    (a) Social learning

    (b) Classical conditioning

    (c) Operant conditioning

    (d) Reinforcement

11. Theory of learning which totally and only depends on 'observable behaviour' is associated with __________ theory of learning.
    (a) Cognitivist
    (b) Developmental
    (c) Behaviourist
    (d) Constructivist

12. The 'insight theory of learning' is promoted by
    (a) Piaget   (b) Vygotsky
    (c) Gestalt   (d) Pavlov

13. Aman breaks toys and dismantles them to explore their components. What would you do?
    (a) Stop Aman from playing with toys
    (b) Always keep a close watch
    (c) Encourage his curiosity and channelize his energy
    (d) Make him understand that toys should not be broken

14. Motivation is a concept that represents the energy; which moves a person to actively satisfy
    (a) Physical needs
    (b) Psychological needs
    (c) Social needs
    (d) All of the above

15. Nicole was kept awake half the night because her brother and parents were fighting. Nicole's motivation to perform school tasks will be low today, not only because she is upset about her family, but because her ______________ needs have not been met.
    (a) growth   (b) physiological
    (c) esteem   (d) higher

16. A student participates frequently and enthusiastically in class question and answer sessions. From the viewpoint of behavioural theory, one can confidently conclude that the student is motivated to
    (a) increase learning of the subject.
    (b) obtain recognition from the teacher.
    (c) demonstrate knowledge to classmates.
    (d) answer or ask questions.

17. According to research findings, which of the following types of rewards should be AVOIDED when rewarding students for performance of intrinsically interesting tasks?
    (a) feedback on progress toward developing a skill
    (b) social rewards
    (c) material rewards
    (d) praise

18. Which of the following is NOT recommended by the text author as a strategy for fostering intrinsic motivation?
    (a) student involvement in setting learning goals
    (b) employing a variety of presentation modes
    (c) games or simulations
    (d) using abstract, rather than concrete, examples

19. A teacher says to a student, "You've done well today." This type of praise may be ineffective because it is not
    (a) specific.
    (b) strong enough.
    (c) an extrinsic reward.
    (d) credible.

20. A teacher praises a student for good work, but frowns and looks displeased at the same time. By these actions, the teacher is failing to make the praise seem
    (a) credible.   (b) interesting.
    (c) contingent.   (d) specific.

21. Which of the following is not a characteristic feature of intrinsically motivated children?
    (a) They always succeed
    (b) They enjoy doing their work
    (c) They display a high level of energy while working
    (d) They like challenging tasks

22. Which of the following is not related to educational achievement?
    (a) Heredity   (b) Experiences
    (c) Practice   (d) Self learning

23. Which of the following statements cannot be considered as a feature of the process of learning?
    (a) Educational institutions are the only place where learning takes place
    (b) Learning is a comprehensive process
    (c) Learning is goal-oriented
    (d) Unlearning is also a learning process

24. Motivation, in the process of learning

    (a) sharpens the memory of learners

    (b) differentiates new learning from old learning

    (c) makes learners think objectively

    (d) creates interest for learning among young learners

25. When one learns something and makes use of what he has learned is called

    (a) Assimilation (b) Co-operation

    (c) Competition (d) Conflict

26. How do children learn concepts and attach labels to them?

    (a) From direct contact with the physical world

    (b) From social situation where language plays no part in the learning process

    (c) From social situations where language does play a definite part

    (d) All the above

27. Acquisition of information and knowledge is

    (a) Ability to learn

    (b) Ability to memories

    (c) Ability to adjust

    (d) None of the above

28. Learning is modification of ___ thoughts and experience.

    (a) emotions

    (b) behaviour

    (c) motivation

    (d) physiological drives

29. Intrinsic motivations are

    (a) Drives

    (b) Learning activity

    (c) Knowledge of progress

    (d) Praise and blame

30. Poems are the example of

    (a) Transfer of training

    (b) Serial learning

    (c) Insight learning

    (d) Cognitive learning

31. Perceptual learning does not consider –

    (a) Insight

    (b) Field conditioning

    (c) Temporal contiguity

    (d) Reinforcement

32. Knowledge of results is

    (a) promoting learning

    (b) discouraging learning

    (c) stopping learning

    (d) retarding learning

33. Motivation to be in charge, have high status & exert influence over others is

    (a) Achievement motivation

    (b) Aggressive motivation

    (c) Power motivation

    (d) intrinsic motivation

34. Which method is helpful in permanent learning?

    (a) Listening (b) Cramming

    (c) Doing (d) Reading

35. Situational approach to motivation is associated with –

    (a) S – R associationist

    (b) The Psycho-analysis

    (c) Gestalt field psychologist

    (d) Rationalists

36. Which one is not among the elements of Active learning

    (a) Materials (b) Manipulation

    (c) Language (d) Practically

37. _________ involves an interest in the learning task itself and also satisfaction being gained from task.

    (a) Intrinsic motivation

    (b) Extrinsic motivation

    (c) Expectation for success

    (d) Emotion motivation

38. Which of the following is the correct sequence in learning environment?

    (a) Interest → Attention → Memory

    (b) Memory → Attention → Interest

    (c) Attention → Interest → Memory

    (d) Memory → Interest → Attention

39. Theory of learning which totally and only depends on 'observable behaviour' is associated with ______ theory of learning.

(a) Cognitivist

(b) Developmental

(c) Behaviourist

(d) Constructivist

40. A process in which an individual learns new responses by observing the behaviour of another rather than through direct experience is known as

(a) Social learning

(b) Conditioning

(c) Experimental learning

(d) Incidental learning.

41. Which of the following is the first step in the process of conditioning ?

(a) Stimulus

(b) Frequency

(c) Generalization

(d) None of the above

42. "Memory is the direct use of what is learned." Who stated the above statement ?

(a) McDougall   (b) Woodworth

(c) Ross   (d) Drever

43. According to Gates, "______ is modification of behaviour through experience".

(a) Motivation   (b) Adjustment

(c) Learning   (d) Thinking

44. Which of the following characteristiic is not true in reference to intrinsically motivated children ?

(a) They like challenging tasks

(b) They are always successful

(c) They feel joy during the work

(d) They express high level energy in difficult tasks

45. Which one of the following theories view that behavior could be shaped through successive approximation and reinforcement of responses more nearly approaching desired behavior?

(a) classical conditioning

(b) instrumental conditioning

(c) operant conditioning

(d) social learning

46. Motivation begins with needs exists in all of us. The needs, that student would tend to fulfill first pertalns to:

(a) esteem   (b) physiological

(c) social   (d) self actualization

47. The attitude of helping others is called ______

(a) Divergent Thinking

(b) Generosity

(c) Ideals

(d) Convergent Thinking

48. The term that does not coincide with the styles of learning

(a) Oral learning

(b) Continuous learning

(c) Comparitive learning

(d) None of these

49. The principle of behaviourism is

(a) Knowledge

(b) Clarity

(c) Stimulus-response

(d) Insight

50. Robert Gagne's theory of Hierarchial learning includes ______ types of learning

(a) 5   (b) 7

(c) 8   (d) 6

51. Children in pre-primary get satisfaction from being allowed to discover. They become distressed, when they are discouraged. They do so due to their motivation to

(a) reduce their ignorance

(b) affiliate with the class

(c) create disorder in the class

(d) exercise their power

52. Extinction of a response is more difficult following

(a) partial reinforcement

(b) continuous reinforcement

(c) punishment

(d) verbal reproach

53. Which term is often used interchangeably with the term "motivation" ?

(a) Incentive   (b) Emotion

(c) Need   (d) Inspiration

54. _________ motives deal with the need to reach satisfying feeling states and to obtain personal goals.
(a) Effective
(b) Affective
(c) Preservation-oriented
(d) Safety-oriented

55. Psychosocial theory emphasises on which of the following ?
(a) Stimuli and Response
(b) Phallic and Latency stages
(c) Industry versus Inferiority stage
(d) Operant Conditioning

56. Rajesh is struggling to solve a problem of Mathematics completely. The inner force compelling him to search for a way to solve it completely, is known as
(a) Motive
(b) Personality trait
(c) Emotion
(d) Perception

57. Which of the following is a process in the social observational learning theory of Bandura ?
(a) Reflection   (b) Retention
(c) Repetition   (d) Recapitulation

58. Of the following statements, which one do you agree with ?
(a) Learning takes place in a socio-cultural context.

(b) Learning is completely governed by external stimuli.
(c) Learning cannot take place unless it is assessed externally in terms of marks.
(d) Learning has taken place only if it is evident in behaviour.

59. Which one of the following statements best describes why children should be encouraged to ask questions in the class ?
(a) Children can be made to realize that they lack intelligence by making them think of all the things they don't know about.
(b) Questions increase the curiosity of the children.
(c) Questions take learning forward by interactions and lead to conceptual clarity.
(d) Children need to practise their language skills.

60. A teacher wants to ensure that her students are motivated intrinsically. She would
(a) plan learning activities which encourage convergent thinking.
(b) specify uniform standards of achievement for all children.
(c) focus on the processes of learning of individual children rather than on the final outcome.
(d) offer tangible rewards.

Answer Key

1.	(a)	**9.**	(d)	**17.**	(c)	**25.**	(a)	**33.**	(c)	**41.**	(a)	**49.**	(c)	**57.**	(b)
2.	(b)	**10.**	(a)	**18.**	(d)	**26.**	(d)	**34.**	(c)	**42.**	(b)	**50.**	(c)	**58.**	(a)
3.	(c)	**11.**	(c)	**19.**	(a)	**27.**	(a)	**35.**	(c)	**43.**	(c)	**51.**	(a)	**59.**	(c)
4.	(d)	**12.**	(c)	**20.**	(a)	**28.**	(b)	**36.**	(d)	**44.**	(b)	**52.**	(a)	**60.**	(c)
5.	(b)	**13.**	(c)	**21.**	(a)	**29.**	(a)	**37.**	(a)	**45.**	(c)	**53.**	(c)		
6.	(a)	**14.**	(d)	**22.**	(a)	**30.**	(b)	**38.**	(a)	**46.**	(b)	**54.**	(b)		
7.	(a)	**15.**	(b)	**23.**	(a)	**31.**	(d)	**39.**	(c)	**47.**	(b)	**55.**	(c)		
8.	(a)	**16.**	(d)	**24.**	(d)	**32.**	(a)	**40.**	(a)	**48.**	(d)	**56.**	(a)		

Learning through Problem Solving and Constructivism, Memory and Forgetting

PROBLEM SOLVING

Problem solving means arriving at solution of tasks or situations that are complex or ambiguous with difficulties or obstacles of some kind. Problem solving is needed, for example, when a doctor analyzes a lung X-ray: a picture of lungs requires skill, experience, and resourcefulness to decide which obscure-looking blobs to ignore, and which to interpret as real structures. Problem solving is also needed when a store manager has to decide how to improve the sales of his product: should she price it lower or publicize it more through advertisements.

Most often, when two children take their problem to an adult to solve for them and the adult "steps in" without invitation, the adult has assumed ownership of the problem. When the adult makes an independent judgment, it usually results in a win-lose situation. One child gets what he wants, the other doesn't. However, by guiding children through a series of problem solving steps, the adult can teach students how to solve their own problems and make better decisions so it's a win-win situation.

Teachers help their students solve problems and make better decisions through a six step process.

Step 1: Define the problem or situation. Good solutions are dependent on precise identification of the problem at hand. Questions that should be asked at the start include "What is going on here?" "What problems do we have?' "What exactly do we need to do to solve?" and "is there another grave problem here?"

Step 2: Generate alternatives. Once the problem is identified and clarified, a host of feasible solutions should be generated. To think of ideas, questions such as the following are normally helpful: "What can be done differently?" What rules or procedures should be followed?" "Let's see how many ideas we can generate" and "Are there more solutions we can think of?"

Step 3: Evaluate the alternatives: Participants comment on the alternatives generated The goal is to choose a solution which has a consensus. It is appropriate to take an opinion of others on each alternative. "What do you think of this alternative or solution?" "What are its pros and cons?" "What problems does it leave unsolved?" and "if we try this idea, what can be the outcome?"

Step 4: Make the decision. After examining the alternatives, the one that seems to fit the best is selected for trial.

Step 5: Implement the solution or decision. The trial solution is put into execution with the understanding that it may or may not work as expected and that it can be altered if necessary.

Step 6: Conduct a follow-up evaluation. The results of the trial solution are analyzed and evaluated. Some useful questions include "Was this a good decision?" "Did it actually solve the problem?" "Is everyone happy with the decision" and "How effective was our decision?" If the solution or decision is judged to be satisfactory, it is retained. If not, a modified or new solution is proposed and put to the test.

Problem solving in the classroom

Problem solving happens in classrooms when teachers present tasks or challenges that are deliberately complex and for which finding a solution is not straightforward or obvious. The responses of students to such problems, as well as the strategies for assisting them, show the key features of problem solving.

Well-structured versus ill-structured problems

Problems vary in how much information they provide for solving a problem, as well as in how many rules or procedures are needed for a solution.

A well-structured problem provides much of the information needed and can in principle be solved using relatively few clearly understood rules. These are simple and well-defined. Classic examples are the word problems often taught in math lessons or classes: everything you need to know is contained within the stated problem and the solution procedures are relatively clear and precise. A well-defined problem is one that has a clear goal, a specific path to the solution and clearly visible obstacles based on the information given. For example

There are a set number of possible solutions -- and solutions are either 100% right or 100% wrong. An example of a well-structured problem is a typical mathematical (2 + 2 = ?) question. This question has a definitive "correct" answer.

Well-defined problems can be solved using a formula or algorithm; a step-by- step process that will always produce the correct result.

In contrast, an ill-structured problem has the converse qualities: the information is not necessarily within the problem, solution procedures are potentially quite numerous, and a multiple solutions are likely. Extreme examples are problems like "How can the world achieve lasting peace?" or "How can teachers insure that students learn?" Ill-defined problems are not clear-cut. There is no obvious path to the solution. These problems require investigation to define, understand and solve. Problems may have many possible answers because they are complex and ill-defined. The "best" solutions to ill-defined problems depend on the priorities underlying the situation. What is "best" today may not be "best" tomorrow. Ill-structured problems, because they are more difficult to "solve," require the development of higher order thinking skills.

An example of an ill-structured problem would be "How can we maximize water resources in our area?" In this real-life problem more than 20 solutions were proposed and local area authorities were asked to weigh the solutions.

Strategies to assist problem solving

Just as there are cognitive blockages to problem solving, there are also general strategies that help the process be successful, regardless of the specific content of a problem. One helpful strategy is problem analysis—identifying the parts of the problem and working on each part separately. Analysis is especially useful when a problem is ill-structured. Consider this problem, for example: "If the plan to improve bicycle transportation in the city." Solving this problem is easier if you identify its parts such as (1) building bicycle lanes on busy streets, (2) educating cyclists and motorists to ride safely, (3) fixing potholes on streets used by cyclists, and (4) altering traffic laws that intervene with cycling. Each separate sub-problem is more manageable than the original problem. The solution of each sub-problem contributes the solution of the whole.

Another helpful strategy is working backward from a final solution to the originally stated problem. This approach is especially helpful when a problem is well-structured but also has elements that are distracting or misleading when approached in a forward, normal direction.

A third helpful strategy is analogical thinking—using knowledge or experiences with similar features to solve the problem at hand. In planning to improve bicycle ride in the city, for example, an analogy of cars with bicycles is helpful in thinking of solutions: improving conditions for both cars and bicycles requires many of the same measures that is a better roadway and even educating drivers. Even solving simpler and more rudimentary problems enabled by understanding analogies.

CONSTRUCTIVISM

Constructivism is "the learner's contribution to meaning and learning through both individual and social activity". Constructivist perspectives are grounded in the research of Jean Piaget, Lev Vygotsky, the Gestalt psychologists, Bruner as well as the educational philosophy of John Dewey.

There is no one constructivist theory of learning. Most of the theories in cognitive science include some kind of constructivism because these theories assume that individuals construct their own cognitive structures as they interpret their experiences in particular situations. One way to organize constructivist views is to talk about two forms of constructivism: psychological and social construction. The focus is on the learner in thinking about learning (not on the subject/lesson to be taught) and no knowledge is independent of the meaning attributed to experience (constructed) by the learner, or community of learners.

Cognitive Constructivism

- Cognitive constructivism is based on the work of Swiss developmental psychologist Jean Piaget.

- Piaget proposed a sequence of cognitive stages that all humans pass through. Thinking at each stage builds on and incorporates previous stages as it becomes more organized and adaptive and less tied to concrete events.

- Piaget's special concern was with logic and the construction of universal knowledge that cannot be learned directly from the environment-knowledge such as conservation or reversibility. Such knowledge comes from reflecting on and coordinating our own cognitions or thoughts, not from mapping external reality.

- Piaget saw the social environment as an important factor in development, but did not believe that social interaction was the main mechanism for changing thinking. Some educational and developmental psychologists have referred to Piaget's kind of constructivism as "first wave constructivism" with its emphasis on individual meaning-making.

- Piaget's theory of cognitive development proposes that humans cannot be "given" information which they immediately understand and use. Instead, humans must "construct" their own knowledge. They build their knowledge through experience. Experiences enable them to create schemas- mental models in their heads. These schemas are changed, enlarged, and made more sophisticated through two complimentary processes: assimilation and accommodation.

Social Constructivism

Vygotsky believed that social interaction, cultural tools, and activity shape individual development and learning. By participating in a broad range of activities with others, learners appropriate the outcomes produced by working together; "they acquire new strategies and knowledge of the world and culture".

Putting learning in social and cultural context is "second wave" constructivism. Because his theory relies heavily on social interactions and the cultural context to explain learning, most psychologists classify Vygotsky as a social constructivist.

There is a great deal of overlap between cognitive constructivism and Vygotsky's social constructivist theory. However, Vygotsky's constructivist theory, which is often called social constructivism, has much more room for an active, involved teacher.

For Vygotsky the culture gives the child the cognitive tools needed for development. The type and quality of those tools determines, to a much greater extent than they do in Piaget's theory, the pattern and rate of development. Adults such as parents and teachers are conduits for the tools of the culture, including language.

The tools the culture provides a child include cultural history, social context, and language. Today they also include electronic forms of information access.

A constructivist teacher does not simply stand by and watch children explore and discover. Instead, the teacher may often guide students as they approach problems, may encourage them to engage in collaborative groups to work on issues and questions, and support them with encouragement and advice as they are solving problems and challenges that are rooted in real life situations. Teachers thus facilitate cognitive growth and learning as do peers and other members of the child's community.

The four important principles applied in any Vygotskian classroom.

1. Learning and development is a social and collaborative activity.
2. The Zone of Proximal Development can serve as a guide for curricular and lesson planning.
3. School learning should occur in a meaningful context and not be separated from learning and knowledge children develop in the "real world.".
4. Out-of-school experiences should be related to the child's school experience.

Complex learning environments and authentic tasks

Constructivists believe that students should not be given simplified problems and basic skills drills, but instead should encounter complex learning environments that deal with fuzzy ill-structured problems. Complex problems are not simply difficult ones; they have many parts. There are multiple, interacting elements in complex problems and multiple solutions are possible. There is no one right way of reaching a conclusion and each solution may bring a new set of problems. These complex problems should be embedded in authentic tasks and activities, the kinds of situations that students will face as they apply what they are learning to the real world. Students may need support as they work on these complex problems, with teachers helping them find resources, keeping track of their progress, breaking larger problems down into smaller ones, and so on.

Applications of Constructivist Learning

A very important teaching approach that puts the student in the center is Inquiry and Problem-based learning.

John Dewey described the basic inquiry learning format in 1910. The teacher presents a puzzling event, question, or problem. The students:

(a)   Formulate hypotheses to explain the event or solve the problem

(b)   Collect data to test the hypotheses

(c)   Draw conclusions, and

(d)   Reflect on the original problem and the thinking processes needed to solve it.

In problem based learning, students are confronted with a real problem that has meaning for them. This problem launches their inquiry as they collaborate to find solutions. In true problem-based learning, the problem is real and the students' actions matter.

Teacher's role in Problem-Based learning

Phase	Teacher behaviour
Phase 1 Orient students to the problem	Teacher goes over the objectives of the lesson, describes important logistical requirements, and motivates students to engage in self-selected problem-solving activity
Phase 2 Organize students for study	Teacher helps students define and organize study tasks related to the problem
Phase 3 Assist independent and group investigation	Teacher encourages students to gather appropriate information, conduct experiments, and search for explanations and solutions
Phase 4 Develop and present artifacts and exhibits	Teacher assists students in planning and preparing appropriate artifacts such as reports, videos, and models and helps them share their work with others
Phase 5 Analyze and evaluate the problem-solving process	Teacher helps students to reflect on their investigations and the processes they used

MEMORY

Memory is the term given to the structures and processes involved in the storage and subsequent retrieval of information.

According to Matlin, "Memory is the process of maintaining information over time." According to Sternberg" Memory is the means by which we draw on our past experiences in order to use this information in the present".

Memory is involved in processing vast amounts of information. This information takes many different forms, e.g. images, sounds or meaning.

The term memory covers three important aspects of information processing:

1. Memory Encoding

When information comes into our memory system (from sensory input), it needs to be changed into a form that the system can cope with, so that it can be stored. For example, a word which is seen (in a book) may be stored if it is changed (encoded) into a sound or a meaning (i.e. semantic processing).

There are three main ways in which information can be encoded (changed):

1.   Visual (picture)

2.   Acoustic (sound)

3.   Semantic (meaning)

The principle encoding system in long term memory (LTM) appears to be semantic coding (by meaning). However, information in LTM can also be coded both visually and acoustically.

2. Memory Storage

This concerns the nature of memory stores, i.e. where the information is stored, how long the memory lasts for (duration), how much can be stored at any time (capacity) and what kind of information is held. The way we store information affects the way we retrieve it. There has been a significant amount of research regarding the differences between Short Term Memory (STM) and Long Term Memory (LTM). Information can only be stored for a brief duration in STM (0-30 seconds), but LTM can last a lifetime.

3. Memory Retrieval

This refers the process through which information stored in memory is located. If we can't remember something, it may be because we are unable to retrieve it. When we are asked to retrieve something from memory, the differences between STM and LTM become very clear. STM is stored and retrieved sequentially. LTM is stored and retrieved by association. Organising information can help aid retrieval. You can organise information in sequences (such as alphabetically, by size or by time).

Types of Information In Memory

1.   **Semantic Memory:** Semantic memory is the sum total of each person's general, abstract knowledge about the world. Semantic memory allows us to represent and mentally operate on objects or situations that are not present to our senses.

2. **Episodic Memory:** A type of information we retain involves specific events that we have experienced personally. This is known as episodic memory. Sometimes it is called autobiographical memory. These memories allow as to travel back in time.

3. **Procedural Memory:** A memory system that retains information we cannot readily express verbally for instance, information necessary to perform skilled motor activities such as riding a bicycle.

4. **Sensory Memory:** A memory system that retains representations of sensory input for brief period of time. This memory holds fleeting representations of our sensory experiences.

5. **Short-term memory:** This type of memory is also called as temporary memory. It holds limited amounts of information for relatively short period of time. The information temporarily stored in short-term memory may last as long as thirty seconds even if the material is not being rehearsed. The existence of short-term memory is supported by the finding that words near either end of a list are remembered better than words near the middle. This effect is known as the Serial Position Curve.

6. **Long term memory:** This is also known as Permanent Memory. Here the individual learns and retains large amount of information for a very long period of time. There is an interval of time between learning and recall or reproduction. Flashbulb memories are types of long-term memories connected to dramatic events in our lives.

Other types of information in Memory:

Some of the important types of memory are as follows.

1. **Immediate memory:** Immediate memory is that which helps us to learn a thing immediately with speed and accuracy, remembering it for a short time and forgetting rapidly after use. e.g. seat number of cinema hall.

2. **Permanent memory:** Permanent memory helps us to remember a thing permanently. e.g. remembering our name.

3. **Rote memory:** Under rote memory, the things are learnt without understanding their meaning.

4. **Logical memory:** Logical memory is based on logical thinking. It takes into consideration purposeful and insightful learning.

5. **Associated memory:** The memory which helps to associate the previously learned things with so many related things and then establish multiple connections is known as associated memory.

6. **Active memory:** In active memory one has to remain active and make deliberate attempts for recollecting the past experiences.

7. **Passive memory:** Here the past experiences are recalled spontaneously without any serious attempt

Span of Memory

The amount of material that can be immediately reproduced after one repetition is called span of memory. The phenomenon of memory may be studied under four different aspects: viz the four R's.

1. Registration or Learning

2. Retention

3. Recall

4. Recognition

1. **Registration or Learning** : Before remembering, it must be registered or learnt. Learning requires time. The most efficient methods of learning or memorising that would yield the best results from the point of view of remembering effectively for a long time are as follows:

   A. *Rote Memorisation* : This is learning without understanding. Yet meaningful material is easily learnt than non-sense material. It is easier to learn poetry than prose; prose is easier to learn than disconnected words. Disconnected words are easier to learn than nonsense words. Thus logical sequence is important, along with the systematic arrangement of ideas. However, mechanical learning must be avoided as it is less effective.

   B. *Spaced V/S Mass Learning*: In spaced learning, the learner has been allowed some rest in memorisation. The subject is not required to memorise the assignment in one continuous time period. Intervals are provided. The Principle of 'work & rest' is followed. In mass learning, the subject has to memorise the assigned material at one sitting without any interval or rest, until it is mastered. Mass learning is effective when the pupils are very intelligent or are highly motivated.

   C. *Whole verses Part Learning*: When the material is read again & again from start to finish, this is whole method of learning. This method can be adopted when the material is not very lengthy and when the material is logically arranged. When material is broken down to parts or stanzas and then learnt, this is part method of learning thus slow learners and average students are benefitted. The learner is motivated each time he masters the parts.

   D. *Recitation*: The best method of learning is when the student reads the lesson few times and then reviews the lesson without the book i.e. he recites the material learnt to him. Studies have shown that self recitation is better and time saving than just reading and re-reading because permanent retention is achieved. Learner is able to detect his weakness and rectify them. Thus he knows his progress as well.

2. **Retention** : 'Retention is the inactive state of learnt activity. The learning activity leaves a mark on the brain structure. This mark is called a 'Memory Trace' which is imprinted on the Cerebral Cortex. This preservation of the memory trace in the brain is retaining of the learning activity. This can be compared to the traces or marks in the sand e.g. our footprints made on the sand. The deeper the trace, the longer the retention, while the weak traces slowly fade away.

   Memory can be improved, but the depth of the trace or retention is difficult to improve by practice, the reason being the traces that are made, depend on the genetic inheritance. Retention however can be measured in three ways:

   (a) Recall (b) Recognition & (c) Relearning.

3. **Recall** : The third aspect of memory is recall. We learn because we need to recall them at some point of time or other. So we can say that recall is the mental revival of past experiences. It is the least index of retention because we are unable to remember even though we known it. Recall depends on the mental condition and the memory trace formed.

4. **Recognition** : Recall and recognition are closely related. Recall provides the material in

memory, while recognition is the process of accepting or rejecting. Recognition is better than recall as an index of retention. Recognition starts with the object given whereas recalls find the object from the mind. Thus, when we meet a person, recognise that person's face, but may not be able to recall his name. Recognition is more a passive behaviour than an active process like recall.

Retrieval

The process of retrieval involves our ability to locate information that has previously been stored in memory. Retrieval cues are stimuli associated with information stored in memory that can aid in its retrieval.

Improving Your Memory

There are some specific aids to memory are available.

MNEMONICS : Mnemonics (pronounced "nemoniks") refers to specific memory improvement technique. Most mnemonic techniques rely on the linking as association.

The method of Loci : The word Loci means "Places". The memory pegs in this system are parts of your image of a scene. The scene can be a buildings, a hotel, kitchen, the layout of a college campus. These scenes can be visualized clearly and contains a number of discrete items in specific locations of serve as memory pegs.

Number and Letter Peg Systems: The main idea of this system is to establish a well organised set of images to which the to-be remembered items can be linked.

We have all had experiences in which we could not remember some item or piece of information. We often feel that the fact, name or item we want is somewhere "in there" but lies just beyound our reach. This is known as the *"tip-of-the tongue phenomenon"*. How does information enter long-term memory from short-term memory? The answer seems to involve a process that is rehearsal. Rather, for information to enter long-term memory, elaborative rehearsal seems to be required. It is a rehearsal in which the meaning of information is considered and the information is related to other knowledge already present in memory.

Entering Information into Long-term Memory

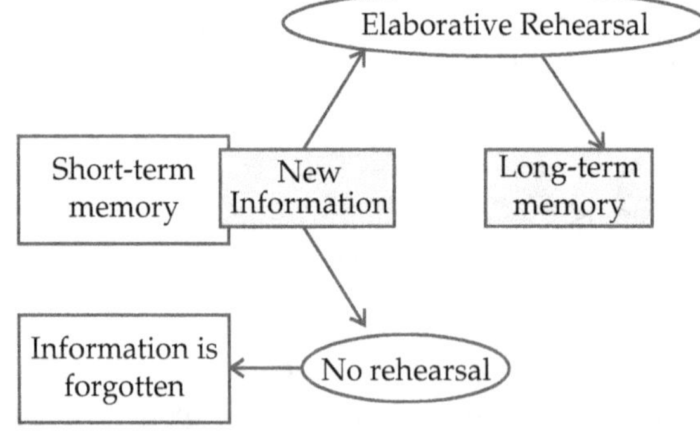

In number systems, you form an image with each number. In letter systems you can establish mnemonic pegs by forming strong, distinctive images of words that start with the sounds of the letters of the alphabet.

Stories You Tell Yourself: A made-up story is a useful mnemonic device to list of unrelated items to remember. The story starts with the first item on the list, and in order, each succeeding item is worked in. It is a form of elaborative encoding.

Chunking: This mnemonic technique is a systematic way of encoding information. Suppose you want to remember your credit-card number 1947 1601914, for example. It will help if you break the number into chunks.

In this example, the first four numbers may remind you of an important date in history (the date of the Independence of India), the next three numbers can also be "chunked" as a date, while the last four numbers form a chunk that is easy to remember by itself.

FORGETTING

According to Bhatia : "Forgetting is the failure of an individual to review in consciousness an idea or a group of ideas without the help of original stimulus."

It is not surprising that the first systematic research on memory, conducted by Ebbinghaus, was concerned with forgetting. Ebbinghaus experimented on himself and studied the rate at which he forgot nonsense syllables. The result of his investigations suggested that forgetting is rapid at first but slows down with the passage of time.

1. The Trace Decay Hypothesis

Forgetting is a process of fading of the learnt matter with passage of time. According to this view, the vivid impressions and information created in the cerebral cortex fade away as time passes. Information we acquired quite some time ago is more difficult to remember than information learned only recently. But decay is probably not the key mechanism in forgetting.

2. Forgetting As a Result of Interference

Forgetting is not a function of the passage of time and the weakening of material stored in memory. Forgetting occurs due to interference between items of information stored in memory. Interference can take two different forms.

(a) **Retroactive Interference:** Here new learned information interferes with old information present in memory.

(b) **Proactive Interference:** When previously learned information interferes with the new information. Forgetting in our daily life is more due to proactive interference; our ability to recall what we have learnt is reduced by experiences previously learnt.

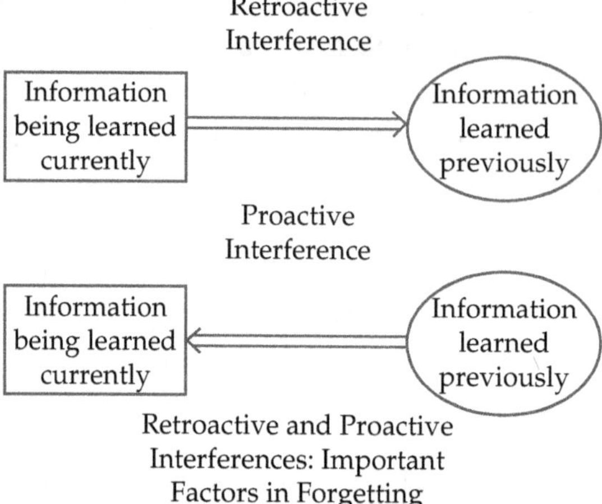

Retroactive and Proactive
Interferences: Important
Factors in Forgetting

3. Theory of Repression or Motivated Forgetting

Forgetting is a psychological process, where by will the unpleasant or conflicting experiences are repressed and pushed into the unconscious and forgotten. Thus repression is done because it may cause anxiety to remember the experiences e.g. remembering loved ones whom we will never see again, we want to forget those people who hurt us.

Exercise 1 : Previous Year Questions of CTET & STET

1. Which of the following will foster creativity among learners ? *[CTET-2011-I]*
   (a) Teaching the students the practical value of good education
   (b) Providing opportunities to question and to nurture the innate talents of every learner
   (c) Emphasizing achievement goals from the beginning of school life
   (d) Coaching students for good marks in examination

2. Which of the following is an example of positive punishment? *[RTET-2011-I]*
   (a) Redicule by friends
   (b) Loss of time with friends
   (c) Cease nagging
   (d) All of these.

3. The temporary change in behaviour due to continuous exposure to stimuli is called
   [RTET-2011-I]
   (a) Habituation
   (b) Learning
   (c) Temporary learning
   (d) Motivation

4. The teachers should not use which of the following ways to change the attitudes of students ?
   [RTET-2011-I]
   (a) Coercive persuasion
   (b) Repetition of idea or assertion
   (c) Endorsement by an admired person
   (d) Association of the message with a good feeling

5. Some people say that whenever anger draws upon children, they go to play. Until they feel better which of the defence mechanisms is represented by this behaviour ? *[RTET-2011-I]*
   (a) Projection
   (b) Displacement
   (c) Reaction formation
   (d) Sublimation

6. Which of the following is more important for keeping the good mental health of students ?
   [RTET-2011-I]
   (a) Provision for curricular activities
   (b) Freedom of expression
   (c) Variety of interests
   (d) Teacher's role and school environment.

7. A child from a disorganized home will experience the greatest difficulty with *[UPTET-2011-I]*
   (a) well-structured lessons
   (b) independent study
   (c) programmed instruction
   (d) wordbooks

8. If some students are not in a mood to study in the class, you will *[UPTET-2011-I]*
   (a) force them to study
   (b) tell those students to leave the class
   (c) warn them that they must study or else you will report the matter to the principal
   (d) tell them some interesting things related to their interest or your own subject

9. If a child writes 16 as 61 & gets confused between b & d, this is case of: *[PTET-2011-I]*
   (a) Visual Impairment
   (b) Learning Disability
   (c) Mental impairment
   (d) Mental Retardation

10. With the frequent use of brain storming method the teacher develops *[TNTET-2011-I]*
    (a) creativity   (b) intelligence
    (c) perception   (d) memory

11. Which of the following is not a sign of reading difficulty among young learners? Difficulty in *[CTET-2011-II]*
    (a) letter and word recognition
    (b) reading speed and fluency
    (c) understanding words and ideas
    (d) spelling consistency

12. Learners should not be encouraged to *[CTET-2011-II]*
    (a) ask as many questions as possible both inside and outside the class
    (b) actively interact with other learners in group work
    (c) participate in as many co-curricular activities as possible
    (d) memorize all the answers to questions which the teacher may ask

13. The personal factor(s) which affect learning is/ are *[RTET-2011-II]*
    (a) Mass media
    (b) Peer group
    (c) Teachers
    (d) Maturation and age

14. Defence mechanism helps us a lot in dealing with   *[RTET-2011-II]*
(a) violence   (b) stress
(c) fatigue   (d) strangers

15. Which of the following is not a level of teaching-learning?   *[UPTET-2011-II]*
(a) Differentiation level
(b) Memory level
(c) Reflective level
(d) Understanding level

16. The best remedy for a student's problems related with learning is   *[UPTET-2011-II]*
(a) suggestion for hard work
(b) supervised study in library
(c) suggestion for private tuition
(d) diagnostic teaching

17. In order to modify the undesirable behaviour of a student the most effective method is   *[UPTET-2011-II]*
(a) to punish the student
(b) to bring it to the notice of the parents
(c) to find out the reasons for the undesirable behaviour and provide remedies
(d) to ignore it

18. Children with speech impairment can be assisted by: *[PTET-2011-II]*
(a) encouraging them to express thoughts in the classroom
(b) helping him/her to pronounce correct sounds
(c) helping him/her to hear his/her spoken errors
(d) referral to specialist for complete evaluation

19. Communication with students means: *[PTET-2011-II]*
(a) asking them to do a task
(b) exchange of ideas
(c) giving them directions
(d) informing them of your idea

20. Self study habit can be developed in children by: *[PTET-2011-II]*
(a) citing examples of great people
(b) giving lecture on self study
(c) giving your own example
(d) making new literature available

21. Counselling which focuses on the problem of a patient is   *[TNTET-2011-II]*
(a) Directive counselling
(b) Non-directive counselling
(c) Eclectic approach in counselling
(d) Vocational counseling

22. Expansion of LAD is   *[TNTET-2011-II]*
(a) Language Abbreviation Dictionary
(b) Linguistic Appraisal Department
(c) Learner Achievement Device
(d) Language Acquisition Device

23. Which of the following is the first step in the scientific method of problem-solving?   *[CTET-2012-I]*
(a) Problem awareness
(b) Collection of relevant information
(c) Formation of hypothesis
(d) Verification of hypothesis

24. Critical pedagogy firmly believes that   *[CTET-2012-I]*
(a) what children learn out of school is irrelevant
(b) the experiences and perceptions of learners are important
(c) the teacher should always lead the classroom instruction
(d) the learners need not reason independently

25. The emphasis from teaching to learning can be shifted by   *[CTET-2012-I]*
(a) encouraging rote learning
(b) adopting frontal teaching
(c) focusing on examination results
(d) adopting child-centered pedagogy

26. In co-operative learning, older and more proficient students assist younger and lesser skilled students. This leads to   *[CTET-2012-II]*
(a) higher moral development
(b) conflict between the groups
(c) higher achievement and self-esteem
(d) intense competition

27. Term PSRN in development implies: *[PTET-2014-I]*
(a) Problem solving, reasoning & numeracy
(b) Problem solving relationship & numeracy
(c) Perceptual skill, reasoning & numeracy
(d) Perceptual skill, relationship & numbers

28. It is said that teacher should be resourceful, This means that :   *[PTET-2014-I]*
(a) He should have enough money & property so that he may not have to take up tuitions
(b) He should have contacts with high authorities so that he may not be harmed
(c) He should have adequate knowledge so that he may be able to solve the problems of students
(d) He should have good reputation among students so that authorities may not be able to take any punitive measure against him

29. An apparatus to find the span of visual attention is   *[TNTET-2014-I]*
  (a) Tachitoscope   (b) Telescope
  (c) Learning Cards   (d) Ink Blot Test

30. Long term memory is through   *[TNTET-2014-I]*
  (a) Learning by Reading
  (b) Learning by Listening
  (c) Learning by multi sensory organs
  (d) Learning by visualizing

31. The first edition of the book on 'Memory' was published by   *[TNTET-2014-I]*
  (a) Ebbinghaus   (b) John Dewey
  (c) Sigmond Freud   (d) William James

32. The best way to change the wrong doing of a child is by   *[TNTET-2014-II]*
  (a) Punishment
  (b) Teaching good moral values
  (c) by giving awards
  (d) ignoring his behaviour

33. The most potential chemical agent responsible for memory is   *[TNTET-2014-II]*
  (a) D.N.A.   (b) R.N.A.
  (c) Proteins   (d) Carbohydrates

34. The device used to measure the span of attention is   *[TNTET-2014-II]*
  (a) Kaliedascope
  (b) Mirror drawing apparatus
  (c) Tachistascope
  (d) Memory drum apparatus

35. The following are the steps in the process of problem solving except   *[CTET-July-2013-I]*
  (a) Identification of a problem
  (b) Breaking down the problem into smaller parts
  (c) Explore possible strategies
  (d) Anticipate outcomes

36. Which one of the following pair would be most appropriate choice to complete the following sentence? Children ________ faster when they are involved in the activities that seem to be ________.   *[CTET-July-2013-II]*
  (a) Forget; useful in a classroom
  (b) Recall; linked with their classwork only
  (c) Memorise; culturally neutral
  (d) Learn; useful in real life

37. Which of the following does *not* deter problem solving?   *[CTET-Feb.-2014-I]*
  (a) Insight   (b) Mental sets
  (c) Entrenchment   (d) Fixation

38. Which one of the following statements is true about ability and ability grouping?   *[CTET-Feb.-2014-II]*
  (a) Students learn better in homogeneous groups
  (b) For smooth and effective teaching, class should be homogeneous
  (c) Children are intolerant and do not accept differences
  (d) Teachers may use multilevel teaching to cater to different ability groups

39. Which one of the following represents the domain 'evaluating' in the Bloom's revised taxonomy?   *[CTET-Feb.-2014-II]*
  (a) Creating a graph or chart using the data
  (b) Judging the logical consistency of a solution
  (c) Evaluating the pertinence of the data provided
  (d) Formulating a new way for categorizing objects

40. Problem solving is more likely to succeed in schools where   *[CTET-Feb.-2014-II]*
  (a) a flexible curriculum is in place
  (b) homogeneous groups of students are present in the classes
  (c) the emphasis is only on higher order academic achievement
  (d) teacher-centric pedagogy is in effect

41. Developmental perspective of teaching demands teacher to   *[CTET-Sept.-2014-II]*
  (a) be strict disciplinarians as children experiment quite frequently
  (b) adapt instructional strategies based on the knowledge of developmental factors
  (c) treat children in different developmental stages in an equitable manner
  (d) provide learning that results in the development of only the cognitive domain

42. To explain, predict, and/or control phenomena are the goals of   *[CTET-Sept.-2014-II]*
  (a) Traditional reasoning
  (b) Inductive reasoning
  (c) Deductive reasoning
  (d) The scientific method

43. An upper primary school constructivist classroom would foresee the following role of students in their own assessment : *[CTET-Feb.-2015-I]*

(a) Denying that assessment has a role in teaching-learning.

(b) Make detailed guidelines for how marks would be correlated to students' achievement and prestige in class.

(c) Students would be the sole determinants of their own assessment.

(d) Students would plan for assessment with the teacher.

44. Expecting students to reproduce knowledge in the same way as it is received

[CTET-Feb.-2016-I]

(a) is good, since it is easy for the teacher to assess.

(b) is an effective assessment strategy.

(c) is problematic, because individuals interpret experiences and do not reproduce knowledge as it is received.

(d) is good, since we record everything as it is in our brains.

45. To enable students to think independently and become effective learners, it is important for a teacher to : *[CTET-Sept.-2016-II]*

(a) present information in an organized manner to make it easier to recall

(b) offer rewards for each success achieved by the students

(c) teach students how to monitor their own learning

(d) give information in small units or chunks

46. If a teacher wants her students to acquire problem-solving skills, the students should be engaged in activities that involve :

[CTET-Sept.-2016-II]

(a) inquiring, reasoning and decision making

(b) structured worksheets containing multiple-choice questions

(c) recall, memorization and comprehension

(d) drill and practice

47. In an inclusive classroom with diverse learners, cooperative learning and peer-tutoring

[CTET-Sept.-2016-II]

(a) should not be practised and students should be segregated based on their abilities

(b) should be used only sometimes since it promotes comparison with classmates

(c) should be actively discouraged and competition should be promoted

(d) should be actively promoted to facilitate peer-acceptance

48. Prameela got seat in a Govt. residential college. She likes to join in the college but she does not like to reside in the hostel.

The conflict is *[APTET-May.-2018-I]*

(a) Approach - Approach

(b) Approach - Avoidance

(c) Avoidance - Avoidance

(d) Double approach - Avoidance

49. In this type of memory the content is in memory for a long time *[APTET-May.-2018-I]*

(a) Rote memory

(b) Short term memory

(c) Passive memory

(d) Active memory

50. One of the following enhances memory

[APTET-May.-2018-I]

(a) Repression

(b) Disuse

(c) Interference

(d) Motivation

51. Beep sound that comes from a car when the driver doesn't wear a seat belt is called

[APTET-May.-2018-II]

(a) Negative Reinforcement

(b) Positive Reinforcement

(c) Neutral Reinforcement

(d) Unconditioned Reinforcement

52. Which of the following aspect does not contribute to memory *[APTET-May.-2018-II]*

(a) Goal behind learning

(b) Gender

(c) Interesting learning material

(d) Taking some rest after learning

53. Shaping is an important mechanism in this learning theory. *[APTET-May.-2018-II]*

(a) Classical Conditioning

(b) Operant Conditioning

(c) Insightful Learning

(d) Trial and Error Learning

54. The learners who learn through reasoning and questioning are *[APCTET-May.-2018-II]*

(a) Mastery style learners

(b) Understanding learners

(c) Self expressive learners

(d) Interpersonal learners

Answer Key

1.	(b)	**8.**	(d)	**15.**	(c)	**22.**	(d)	**29.**	(a)	**36.**	(d)	**43.**	(d)	50.	(d)
2.	(a)	**9.**	(b)	**16.**	(d)	**23**	(a)	**30.**	(c)	**37.**	(a)	**44.**	(c)	51.	(b)
3.	(a)	**10.**	(a)	**17.**	(c)	**24.**	(b)	**31.**	(a)	**38.**	(d)	**45.**	(c)	52.	(a)
4.	(a)	**11.**	(c)	**18.**	(a)	**25.**	(d)	**32.**	(b)	**39.**	(b)	**46.**	(a)	53.	(d)
5.	(b)	**12.**	(d)	**19.**	(b)	**26.**	(c)	**33.**	(b)	**40.**	(a)	**47.**	(d)	54.	(a)
6.	(d)	**13.**	(d)	**20.**	(d)	**27.**	(a)	**34.**	(c)	**41.**	(b)	**48.**	(b)		
7.	(c)	**14.**	(b)	**21.**	(a)	**28.**	(c)	**35.**	(b)	**42.**	(d)	**49.**	(d)		

35. (b) Problem solving is the mental process we follow when we have a goal but can't immediately understand how to achieve it. It's a process that depends on us - how we perceive a problem, what we know about it, and the end-state we want to reach.

Solving a problem involves a number of cognitive activities:
- ascertaining what the problem really is
- identifying the true causes of your problem and the opportunities for reaching your goal
- generating creative solutions to the problem
- evaluating and choosing the best solution, and
- implementing the best solution, then monitoring your actions and their results to ensure the problem is solved successfully

36. (d) Children learn faster when they are involved in the activities that seem to be useful in real life.

37. (a) Only 'insight' enhances problem solving, others fix the mind in a directions and deter problem solving.

38. (d) Students enter the classroom with vastly different abilities and readiness level learning. This is the reason why multi-level teaching is a necessity in any classroom. In multi-level teaching a teacher uses multi levels of teaching to meet the needs of a variety of learners.

39. (b) According to Benjamin Bloom there are six levels of cognition– Knowledge, Comprehension, Application, Analysis, Synthesis and Evaluation. Evaluation is judging or forming an opinion about the information or situation.

40. (a) Problem solving is more likely to succeed in schools where a flexible curriculum is in place so that they can explore, enjoy, learn, practise and talk about their developing understanding.

44. (c) Individuals are different in terms of their interests, intelligence, creativity and other human traits. Therefore, it can be said that expecting students to reproduce knowledge in the same way as it is given is not easy as every individual interprets situations but they do not reproduce knowledge the same way as it is received.

Exercise 2 : Test Yourself

1. Constructivism as a theory
   (a) focuses on the role of imitation
   (b) emphasizes the role of the learner in constructing his own view of the world
   (c) emphasizes on memorizing information and testing through recall
   (d) emphasizes on the dominant role of the teacher

2. The Constructivist Approach to learning means
   (a) involving the students in a variety of activities to encourage them to learn new words and structures by accommodating them with those that they have already learnt through a process of discovery
   (b) teaching rules of grammar and consolidating through rigorous practice
   (c) helping learners acquire new vocabulary by studying literature intensively
   (d) teaching new words and structures using a variety of audio-visual aids followed by practice through drill

3. Which one of the following is LEAST characteristic of the discovery learning approach?
   (a) allows students to proceed in their own way
   (b) encourages students to make intuitive guesses
   (c) makes use of deductive rather than inductive reasoning
   (d) provides specific-to-general learning strategies

4. Which of the following strategies is NOT useful when one is trying to solve a problem?
   (a) analogical thinking
   (b) functional fixedness
   (c) verbalizing
   (d) working backward

5. What is the fundamental difference between information processing and constructivist learning perspectives?
   (a) constructivists deal with accurate representations of the world; information processing theorists deal with useful associations
   (b) constructivists assume the world is "knowable" and people can understand it; information processing theorists do not
   (c) Information processing theorists are concerned with accurate representations of the world; constructivists deal primarily with useful understandings
   (d) Information processing theorists assume the world is "knowable" and people can form an understanding of it; constructivists do the same but to a lesser degree

6. Which one of the following ways of learning an applied skill is most consistent with a constructivist approach?
   (a) Have the teacher "walk" the students step-by-step through the process
   (b) Provide well-constructed worksheets with which students can practice individually
   (c) Use simplified, artificial materials in order to make the task easier for students
   (d) Use realistic materials and a group format to provide support for individuals

7. In which one of the following situations would constructivist models be LEAST applicable?
   (a) developing appreciation of science in seventh-graders
   (b) teaching basic math facts to fourth-graders
   (c) teaching English to eleventh-graders
   (d) teaching eight-graders to perform experiments in science

8. According to the _______ approach, children learn best in a teacher-centered classroom that focuses on the mastery of academic skills.
   (a) direct instruction
   (b) cognitive constructivist
   (c) social constructivist
   (d) whole learning

9. The belief that teachers should encourage collaborative learning opportunities is most characteristic of the _______ approach to student learning.
   (a) direct instruction
   (b) cognitive constructivist
   (c) social constructivist
   (d) whole learning

10. _______ theory is an example of a social constructivist approach to education.
   (a) Piaget's   (b) Vygotsky's
   (c) Watson's   (d) Elkind's

11. A criticism of the direct instruction approach is that it
    (a) does not give enough attention to the content of a discipline
    (b) is too relativistic and vague
    (c) excessively stresses critical thinking and creativity
    (d) turns children into passive learners

12. Constructivism emphasizes that individuals learn best when they:
    (a) work in collaborative groups
    (b) actively put together knowledge and understanding
    (c) learn effective strategies for retrieving information
    (d) solve real world problems

13. Scaffolding can best be described as:
    (a) Finishing a difficult task for a student
    (b) Giving enough assistance so that a student can finish a task
    (c) Decreasing the challenge of a task so that a student can successfully finish it
    (d) Grading on the curve so that a student's best effort is recognized

14. Three of the following teachers are using scaffolding to help their students learn. Which one is NOT a good example of scaffolding?
    (a) Ms Sujata gives her class some hints about how to solve an especially difficult algebra problem
    (b) Mr Kapoor teaches bowling by gently guiding each student through the correct movement a few times.
    (c) Ms Narang gives Aditya a structure to follow when he writes his first poem.
    (d) Mr Verma takes the students to the Biology lab.

15. Which of the following assignments is most consistent with the social constructivist approach to writing?
    (a) writing a book report about a novel read aloud during class
    (b) creating an outline to summarize main events studied during history class
    (c) writing a term paper about a topic studied during English class
    (d) writing an essay about a recent significant personal event

16. ______ is a social constructivist program that focuses on literacy development and biology.
    (a) Fostering a community of learners
    (b) Children teaching children
    (c) Reciprocal teaching
    (d) Schools for thought

17. Mr. Dixit is conducting a mock trial in his social studies class to teach students about the judicial branch of government. This activity exemplifies which of the following concepts?
    (a) Situated cognition
    (b) Scaffolding
    (c) Cognitive apprenticeship
    (d) Peer tutoring

18. When composing groups of students for small-group work, teachers should:
    (a) Place students with their friends
    (b) Create groups with diversity in ability, ethnicity, socio-economic status and gender
    (c) Place students of the same ability level in the same group.
    (d) Separate boys from girls.

19. Poor reading comprehension leads to academic failure in many subjects, the ways improve reading can be
    1. Read aloud to your child whenever possible
    2. Bring your child to the library weekly, and allow him or her to choose the reading
    3. Provide books on tape but he or she must not look at the words in print so that he/she can concentrate on the tape
    (a) only 1　　　　(b) only 1 and 2
    (c) only 1, 2, 3　(d) only 1 and 3

20. Instrumental conditioning is treated as problem-solving by-
    (a) Mowser　　　(b) Skinner
    (c) Kimbal　　　(d) Grant

21. Critical thinking is induced by
    (a) fore brain　　(b) right brain
    (c) left brain　　(d) hind brain

22. Experiment of memory is initially done by
    (a) Ebbinghaus　(b) Stephen
    (c) Harlow　　　(d) White

23. SQ3R method enhances
    (a) attention　　(b) aptitude
    (c) motivation　　(d) memory

24. Counselling to the counseled is
    (a) interrogation
    (b) giving advice
    (c) to understand himself thoroughly
    (d) psychoanalysis

25. Ergograph is used to explore
    (a) mental fatigue
    (b) physical fatigue
    (c) monotony
    (d) disinterest

26. The study of fluctuation of visual attention can be experimentally made with the help of a
    (a) Mason's disc
    (b) Marquis disc
    (c) Tachistoscope
    (d) Compact disc

27. Dyslexia is associated mainly with difficulties in
    (a) reading
    (b) speaking
    (c) speaking and hearing
    (d) hearing

28. Which one of the following method has a process of reasoning from general to specific ?
    (a) Inductive
    (b) Deductive
    (c) Both above
    (d) None of the above

29. The two types of memory are
    (a) STM & LTM   (b) ATM & GTM
    (c) LTM & ATM   (d) ATM & STM

30. VIBGYOR is a good example of
    (a) abbrevation   (b) Mnemonics
    (c) easy learning   (d) monics

31. Deductive reasoning involves
    (a) reasoning from general to particular
    (b) reasoning from particular to general
    (c) active construction and reconstruction of knowledge
    (d) methods including inquiry learning and heuristics

32. A student highlights the main points in a chapter, draws a visual representation and poses questions that arise in her mind at the end of the chapter. She is
    (a) trying to use method of loci.
    (b) trying to regulate her own thinking by organization of ideas.
    (c) trying to use the strategy of maintenance rehearsal.
    (d) ensuring observational learning

Answer Key

No.	Ans.	No.	Ans.	No.	Ans.	No.	Ans.	No.	Ans.	No.	Ans.
1.	(b)	7.	(b)	13.	(b)	19.	(b)	25.	(b)	31.	(a)
2.	(a)	8.	(a)	14.	(d)	20.	(a)	26.	(c)	32.	(b)
3.	(c)	9.	(c)	15.	(d)	21.	(c)	27.	(a)		
4.	(b)	10.	(b)	16.	(a)	22.	(a)	28.	(b)		
5.	(c)	11.	(d)	17.	(a)	23.	(a)	29.	(a)		
6.	(d)	12.	(b)	18.	(b)	24.	(c)	30.	(b)		

# Assessment and Evaluations

Assessment is a process of obtaining information about students' learning and making value judgments about their progress. Information about students' progress can be obtained from a variety of sources including projects, assignments, performances, observations, and tests. Students' learning is often assigned specific numbers or grades and this involves measurement.

Measurement takes into account such questions as, "How much?" and is used most commonly when the teacher scores a test or product and assigns numbers (e.g. 28 /30 on English test; 90/100 on the environmental science project).

Evaluation is the process of making judgments about the assessment information. These judgments may be about individual students (e.g. should Rahul's course grade take into account his significant improvement over the grading period?), the assessment method used (e.g. is the essay type test a useful way to obtain information about problem solving), or one's own teaching (e.g. most of the students this year did much better on the essay assignment than last year so my new teaching methods seem effective).

Assessment for learning is often formative assessment, i.e. it takes place during the course of instruction by providing information that teachers can use to revise their teaching and students can use to improve their learning. Formative assessment includes both informal assessment involving spontaneous unsystematic observations of students' behaviours (e.g. during a question and answer session or while the students are working on an assignment) and formal assessment involving pre-planned, systematic gathering of data.

Assessment of learning is summative assessment that involves assessing students in order to certify their competence and fulfill accountability mandates and is the primary focus of the next chapter on standardized tests but is also considered in this chapter. Assessment of learning is typically summative, that is, administered after the instruction is completed (e.g. a final examination in an educational psychology course). Summative assessments provide information about how well students mastered the material, whether students are ready for the next unit, and what grades should be given.

For an assessment to be high quality it needs to have good validity and reliability as well as absence from bias.

Validity

Validity of assessment means that the assessment measures what it is supposed to measure. For example, how appropriate is it to conclude that the results of a language test on grammar given to recent immigrants accurately represents their understanding of grammar? Is it alright for the teacher to conclude, based on the observation of her student, Ruhi that she has Attention Deficit Disorder because she does not follow the teachers verbal instructions? Obviously in each situation other interpretations are possible that the immigrant students have poor English skills rather than mathematics skills, or that Ruhi may be hearing impaired.

Reliability

Reliability refers to the consistency of the measurement. Suppose Mr. Kapur is teaching a unit on food chemistry in his tenth grade class and gives an assessment at the end of the unit using test items from the teachers' guide. Reliability is related to questions such as: How similar would the scores of the students be if they had taken the assessment on a Friday or Monday? Would the scores have varied if Mr. Kapur had selected different test items, or if a different teacher had graded the test? An assessment provides information about students by using a specific measure of performance at one particular time. Unless the results from the assessment are reasonably consistent over different occasions, different raters, or different tasks (in the same content domain) confidence in the results will be low and so cannot be useful in improving student learning.

STANDARDIZED TESTS

Standardized tests are created by a team—usually test experts from a commercial testing company who consult classroom teachers and university faculty—and are administered in standardized ways. Students not only respond to the same questions they also receive the same directions and have the same time limits. Explicit scoring criteria are used. Standardized tests are designed to be taken by many students within a state, province, or nation, and sometimes across nations. Teachers help administer some standardized tests and test manuals are provided that contain explicit details about the administration and scoring. For example, teachers may have to remove all the posters and charts from the classroom walls, read directions out loud to students using a script, and respond to student questions in a specific manner.

Use of standardized tests for diagnosing student's strengths and weaknesses

Standardized tests, along with interviews, classroom observations, medical examinations, and school records are used to help diagnose students' strengths and weaknesses. Often the standardized tests used for this purpose are administered individually to determine if the child has a disability. For example, if a kindergarten child is having trouble with oral communication, a standardized language development test could be administered to determine if there are difficulties with understanding the meaning of words or sentence structures, noticing sound differences in similar words, or articulating words correctly. It would also be important to determine if the child was a recent immigrant, had a hearing impairment or mental retardation. The diagnosis of learning disabilities typically involves the administration of at least two types of standardized tests—an aptitude test to assess general cognitive functioning and an achievement test to assess knowledge of specific content areas. We discuss the difference between aptitude and achievement tests later in this chapter.

Selecting students for specific programs

Standardized tests are often used to select students for specific programs. For example, the SAT (Scholastic Assessment Test) is a norm referenced tests used to help determine if high school students are admitted to selective colleges. Norm referenced standardized tests are also used, among other criteria, to determine if students are eligible for special education or gifted and talented programs. Criterion referenced tests are used to determine which students are eligible for promotion to the next grade or graduation from high school. Schools that place students in ability groups including high school college preparation, academic, or vocational programs may also use norm referenced or criterion referenced standardized tests. When standardized tests are used as an essential criteria for placement they are obviously high stakes for students.

Assisting teachers' planning

Norm referenced and criterion referenced standardized tests, among other sources of information about students, can help teachers make decisions about their instruction. For example, if a social studies teacher learns that most of the students did very well on a norm referenced reading test administered early in the school year he may adapt his instruction and use additional primary sources. A reading teacher after reviewing the poor end-of-the- year criterion referenced standardized reading test results may decide that next year she will modify the techniques she uses. A biology teacher may decide that she needs to spend more time on genetics as her students scored poorly on that section of the standardized criterion referenced science test. These are examples of assessment for learning which involves data-based decision making. It can be difficult for beginning teachers to learn to use standardized test information appropriately, understanding that test scores are important information but also remembering that there are multiple reasons for students' performance on a test.

TYPES OF STANDARDIZED TESTS

Achievement tests

K-12 achievement tests are designed to assess what students have learned in a specific content area. These tests include those specifically designed to access mastery of the academic content standards and also a general achievement test to provide normative information. Achievement tests are used as one criterion for obtaining a license in a variety of professions. Their use in teacher education is recent and there is a requirement that teacher education students take achievement tests in order to obtain a teaching license. These tests include constructed-response and multiple-choice items which tests teacher education students. The scores needed in order to pass each test vary.

Diagnostic tests

Profiling skills and abilities : Some standardized tests are designed to diagnose strengths and weaknesses in skills, typically reading or mathematics skills. For example, an elementary school child may have difficult in reading and one or more diagnostic tests would provide detailed information about three components: (1) word recognition, which includes phonological awareness (pronunciation), decoding, and spelling; (2) comprehension which includes vocabulary as well as reading and listening comprehension, and (3) fluency. Diagnostic tests are often administered individually by school psychologists, following standardized procedures. The examiner typically records not only the results on each question but also observations of the child's behaviour such as distractibility or frustration. The results from the diagnostic standardized tests are used in conjunction with classroom observations, school and medical records, as well as interviews with teachers, parents and students to produce a profile of the student's skills and abilities, and where appropriate diagnose a learning disability.

Aptitude tests

Predicting the future: Aptitude tests, like achievement tests, measure what students have learned, but rather than focusing on specific subject matter learned in school (e.g. math, science, English or social studies), the test items focus on verbal, quantitative, problem solving abilities that are learned in school or in the general culture. These tests are typically shorter than achievement tests and can be useful in predicting general school achievement. If the purpose of using a test is to predict success in a specific subject (e.g. language arts) the best prediction is past achievement in language arts and so scores on a language arts achievement test would be useful. However when the predictions are more general (e.g. success in college) aptitude tests are often used. According to the test developers, SAT Reasoning tests, used to predict success in college, assess general educational development and reasoning, analysis and problem solving as well as questions on mathematics, reading and writing. The SAT Subject Tests that focus on mastery of specific subjects like English, history, mathematics, science, and language are used by some colleges as entrance criteria and are more appropriately classified as achievement tests than aptitude tests even though they are used to predict the future.

Tests designed to assess general learning ability have traditionally been called Intelligence Tests but are now often called learning ability tests, cognitive ability tests, scholastic aptitude tests, or school ability tests. The shift in terminology reflects the extensive controversy over the meaning of the term intelligence and that its traditional use was associated with inherited capacity. The more current terms emphasize that tests measure developed ability in learning not innate capacity.

CLASSROOM ASSESSMENT

Formulating appropriate questions

When to test

- Frequent testing encourages the retention of information and appears to be more effective than a comparable amount of time spent reviewing and studying the material.

- Tests are especially effective in promoting learning if you give students a test on the material soon after they learn it, then retest on the material later.

- The use of cumulative questions on tests is a key to effective learning. Cumulative questions ask students to apply information learned in previous units to solve a new problem.

It is argued by some researchers that students will learn more if we teach them less, that is if the curriculum includes fewer topics, but explores those topics in greater depth and allows more time for review, practice, testing, and feedback.

Textbook tests

Most elementary and secondary school texts today come complete with supplemental materials such as teaching manuals, handout masters, and ready-made tests. Using these tests can save time, but is this a good teaching practice? It depends on your objectives for students, the way you taught the material, and the quality of the tests provided. If the textbook test matches your testing plan and the instruction you actually provided your students, then it may be the right test to use.

- Its important to keep these key points in mind while evaluating textbook tests
- The decision to use a textbook test must come after a teacher identifies the objectives that he or she taught and now wants to assess.
- Textbook tests are designed for the typical classroom, but since few classrooms are typical, most teachers deviate somewhat from the text in order to accommodate their pupil's needs.
- The more classroom instruction deviates from the textbook objectives and lesson plans, the less valid the textbook tests are likely to be.
- The main consideration in judging the adequacy of a textbook test is the match between its test questions and what pupils were taught in their classes:
  1. Are questions similar to the teacher's objectives and instructional emphases?
  2. Do questions require pupils to perform the behaviours they were taught?
  3. Do questions cover all or most of the important objectives taught?
  4. Is the language level and terminology appropriate for pupils?
  5. Does the number of items for each objective provide a sufficient sample of pupil performance?

Objective testing

Multiple-choice questions, matching exercises, T/F statements, and short answer or fill-in items are all types of objective testing. The word "objective" in testing means "not open to many interpretations," or "not subjective". The scoring of these types of items is relatively straightforward compared to the scoring of essay questions because the answers are more clear-cut than essay answers. These are easy to score fairly and can cover many topics.

Using multiple-choice tests

People often assume that multiple-choice items are appropriate only for asking factual questions. But multiple-choice items can test higher level objectives as well, although writing higher-level items is difficult. A multiple-choice item can assess more than recall and recognition if it requires the student to deal with new material by applying or analyzing the concept or principle being tested.

Writing Multiple-choice Questions

All test items require skillful; construction, but good multiple-choice items are a real challenge.

The stem of a multiple-choice item is the part that asks the question or poses the problem. The choices that follow are called alternatives. The wrong answers are called distracters because their purpose is to distract students who have only a partial understanding of the material.

GUIDELINES FOR OBJECTIVE-TYPE TESTS

- The stem should be clear and simple, and present only a single problem. Unessential details should be left out.

  Poor form- There are several different kinds of standard or derived scores. An IQ score is especially useful because…

  Better form An advantage of an IQ score is…

- Do not expect students to make extremely fine discrimination among answer choices

  Poor form The % of area in a normal curve falling between +1 and –1 standard deviation is about:

(a) 66%	(b) 67%
(c) 68%	(d) 69%

  Better form

  The % of area in a normal curve falling between +1 and –1 standard deviation is about:

(a) 14%	(b) 34%
(c) 68%	(d) 95%

- As much wording as possible should be included in the stem so that phrases will not have to be repeated in each alternative.

  Poor form

  A percentile score

  (a) Indicates the % of items answered correctly

  (b) Indicates the % of correct answers divided by the % of wrong answers

  (c) Indicates the % of people who scored at or above a given raw score

  (d) Indicates the % of people who scored at or below a given raw score

  Better form

  A percentile score indicates the % of

  (a) Items answered correctly

  (b) Correct answers divided by the % of wrong answers

  (c) people who scored at or above a given raw score

  (d) people who scored at or below a given raw score

- Each alternative answer should fit the grammatical form of the stem, so that no answers are obviously wrong

  Poor form

  The Stanford-Binet test yields an

(a) IQ score	(b) Reading level
(c) Vocational preference	(d) Mechanical aptitude

  Better form

  The Stanford-Binet is a test of

(a) Intelligence	(b) Reading level
(c) Vocational preference	(d) Mechanical aptitude

- You should also avoid including 2 distractors that have the same meaning. If only one answer can be right and if two answers are the same, then these two must both be wrong. This narrows down the choices considerably

Poor form

The most frequently occurring score in the distribution is called the

(a) Mode   (b) Arithmetical average

(c) Median   (d) Mean

Better form

The most frequently occurring score in the distribution is called the

(a) Mode   (b) Standard deviation

(c) Median   (d) Mean

- Avoid using the exact wording found in the textbook

  Poor students may recognize the answers without knowing what they mean

- Avoid overuse of all of the above and none of the above

Such choices may be helpful to students who are simply guessing. In addition, using all of the above may trick a quick student who sees that the first alternative is correct and does not read on to discover that the others are correct too.

ESSAY TESTING

The best way to measure some learning objectives is to require students to create answers on their own. An essay question is appropriate in these cases. The most difficult part of essay testing is judging the quality of answers, but writing good, clear questions is not particularly easy, either.

Constructing Essay Tests

Because answering takes time, true essay tests cover less material than objective tests. Thus, for efficiency, essay tests should be limited to the assessment of more complex learning outcomes.

An essay question should give students a clear and precise task and should indicate the elements to be covered in the answer. The students should know how extensive their answer should be and about how much time they should spend on each question.

Students should be given ample time for answering. If more than one essay is being completed in the same class period, you may want to suggest time limits for each. Remember, that time pressure increases anxiety and may prevent accurate assessment of some students. Do not make up for the limited amount of material an essay test can cover by including a large number of essay questions. It would be better to plan on more frequent testing than to include more than two or three essay questions in a single class period.

Advantages and Disadvantages of Different Kinds of Test Items

Type	Advantages	Disadvantages
Short answer	Can test many facts in a short time. Fairly easy to score. Excellent format for Math. Tests recall	Difficult to measure complex learning. Often ambiguous

Essay	Can test complex learning. Can assess thinking process and creativity	Difficult to score objectively. Uses a great deal of testing time.
True/False	Tests the most facts in shortest time. Easy to score. Tests recognition. Objective	Difficult to measure complex learning. Difficult to write reliable items. Subject to guessing.
Matching	Excellent for testing associations and recognition of facts. Although terse, can tests complex learning (especially concepts) Objective	Difficult to write effective items. Subject to process of elimination.
Multiple-choice	Can assess learning at all levels of complexity. Can be highly reliable, objective. Teats fairly large knowledge base in short time. Easy to score.	Difficult to write. Somewhat subject to guessing.

CONTINUOUS AND COMPREHENSIVE EVALUATIONS

- Continuous and Comprehensive evaluation refers to a system of school based assessment that covers all aspects of student's development.
- It emphasizes two fold objectives.
  - (a) Continuity in evaluation and assessment of broad based learning.
  - (b) Behavioural out come
- Comprehensive evaluation includes assessment of holistic development including cognitive, affective and psychomotor domains.
- Scholastic refers to those aspects which are related to intellect. It includes assessment of learners in curricular subjects, assignments, project work, practical and oral work, etc.
- Co-scholastic includes psychomotor skills, physical development, life skills, attitudes, values, interests, and participation in co-curricular activities.
- It also envisages improving on-going teaching-learning processes by diagnosing the learning gaps and offering corrective and enrichment input.
- In India, the Continuous and Comprehensive Evaluation has been introduced at the Secondary level in CBSE schools. Each term has two formative assessments & one summative assessment in each subject.
- Formative assessments is used by the teacher to continuously monitor student progress in a supportive environment and comprise of
  - (c) Class work
  - (d) Homework
  - (e) Oral questions
  - (f) Quizzes
  - (g) Projects
  - (h) Assignments/Tests
- Summative assessment is carried out at the end of a course of instruction and indicates and measures how much a student has learnt.

Exercise 1 : Previous Year Questions of CTET & STET

1. To make assessment a 'useful and interesting' process, one should be careful about *[CTET-2011-I]*
   (a) making comparisons between different students
   (b) labelling students as intelligent or average learners
   (c) using a variety of ways to collect information about the student's learning across the scholastic and co-scholastic boundaries
   (d) using technical language to give feedback

2. Reducing stress and enhancing success in examination necessitates *[RTET-2011-I]*
   (a) A shift towards shorter examination
   (b) Examinations to be conducted at different stages of school education
   (c) Annual and half yearly exams
   (d) Setting up of different agencies for conducting entrance exams

3. In CCE, Formative & Summative Assessment totals to: *[PTET-2011-I]*
   (a) 40% & 60% respectively
   (b) 60% & 40% respectively
   (c) 50% & 50% respectively
   (d) None of the above

4. A cricket player develops the skill of bowling, but it does not affect his skill of batting. It is known as *[RTET-2011-II]*
   (a) positive transfer of training
   (b) negative transfer of training
   (c) zero transfer of training
   (d) none of these.

5. Which one of the following is the better item of essay type of question? *[PTET-2011-II]*
   (a) Discuss Newton's laws of motion
   (b) Explain each of Newton's three laws of motion
   (c) What are Newton's laws of motion?
   (d) Write note on Newton's laws of motion

6. Army alpha test is a *[TNTET-2011-II]*
   (a) Performance test (b) Verbal test
   (c) Non-verbal test (d) Culture fair test

7. Number of verbal and picture tests in Torrance creativity test are respectively *[TNTET-2011-II]*
   (a) 5, 3   (b) 6, 2
   (c) 7, 2   (d) 7, 3

8. Aptitude test plays a significant role in *[TNTET-2011-II]*
   (a) Personal guidance
   (b) Group guidance
   (c) Educational guidance
   (d) Vocational guidance

9. Which of the following is not a projective technique *[TNTET-2011-II]*
   (a) Rorschack ink - blot test
   (b) Sentence completion test
   (c) Word association test
   (d) Interest inventing test

10. In Flander's interaction analysis ________ parts are based on teachers activity *[TNTET-2011-II]*
    (a) 1 - 8   (b) 3 - 6
    (c) 1 - 7   (d) 3 - 8

11. School-based assessment is primarily based on the principle that *[CTET-2012-I]*
    (a) students should at all costs get high grades
    (b) schools are more efficient than external bodies of examination
    (c) assessment should be very economical
    (d) teachers know their learners' capabilities better than external examiners

12. Teachers should study the errors of their students they often indicate the *[CTET-2012-II]*
    (a) need for differentiated curriculum
    (b) extent of their knowledge
    (c) remedial strategies needed
    (d) pathways for ability grouping

13. Which of the following is not the tool for Formative Assessment in scholastic domain: *[PTET-2014-I]*
    (a) Conversation Skill
    (b) Multiple Choice Questions
    (c) Projects
    (d) Oral Questions

14. Which one of the following is the better item of essay type of question? *[PTET-2014-II]*
    (a) Discuss Newton's laws of motion
    (b) Explain each of Newton's three laws of motion
    (c) What are Newton's laws of motion?
    (d) Write note on Newton's laws of motion

15. Continuous and Comprehensive Evaluation emphasizes *[CTET-July-2013-I]*
    (a) continuous testing on a comprehensive scale to ensure learning.

  (b) how learning can be observed, recorded and improved upon

  (c) fine-tuning of tests with the teaching.

  (d) redundancy of the Board examination.

16. School Based Assessment.   *[CTET-July-2013-I]*

  (a) Dilutes the accountability of Boards of Education.

  (b) Hinders achieving Universal National Standards.

  (c) Helps all students learn more through diagnosis.

  (d) Makes students and teachers nonserious and casual.

17. A teacher should   *[CTET-July-2013-I]*

  (a) treat errors committed by students as blunders and take serious note of each error

  (b) measure success as the number of times students avoid making mistakes

  (c) not correct students while they're trying to communicate ideas

  (d) focus more on lecturing and provide a foundation for knowledge

18. Rajesh is a voracious reader. Apart from studying his course books, he often goes to library and reads books on diverse topics. Rajesh does his project even in the lunch break. He does not need prompting by his teachers or parents to study for tests and seems to truly enjoy learning. He can be best described as a(n) _____ . *[CTET-July-2013-I]*

  (a) fact-centred learner

  (b) teacher motivated learner

  (c) assessment-centered learner

  (d) intrinsically motivated learner

19. All of the following promote assessment as learning except   *[CTET-July-2013-II]*

  (a) telling students to take internal feedback.

  (b) generating a safe environment for students to take chances.

  (c) tell students to reflect on the topic taught.

  (d) testing students as frequently as possible.

20. When a cook tastes a food during cooking it may be akin to   *[CTET-July-2013-II]*

  (a) Assessment of learning

  (b) Assessment for learning

  (c) Assessment as learning

  (d) Assessment and learning

21. Differentiated instruction is   *[CTET-July-2013-II]*

  (a) using a variety of groupings to meet student needs.

  (b) doing something different for every student in the class.

  (c) disorderly or undisciplined student activity.

  (d) using groups that never change.

22. CBSE prescribed group activities for students in place of activities for individual students. The idea behind doing so could be   *[CTET-July-2013-II]*

  (a) to overcome the negative emotional response to individual competition which may generalise across learning.

  (b) to make it easy for teachers to observe groups instead of individual students.

  (c) to rationalise the time available with schools most of which do not have enough time for individual activities.

  (d) to reduce the infrastructural cost of the activity.

23. If students repeatedly make errors during a lesson, a teacher should   *[CTET-July-2013-II]*

  (a) make changes in instruction, tasks, timetable or seating arrangements.

  (b) leave the lesson for the time being and come back to it after some time.

  (c) identify the erring students and talk to principal about them.

  (d) make erring students stand outside the classroom.

24. Following are some techniques to manage anxiety due to an approaching examination; **except**
  [CTET-July-2013-II]

  (a) familiarising with the pattern of question paper.

  (b) thinking too much about the result.

  (c) seeking support.

  (d) emphasising strengths.

25. Bloom's taxonomy is a hierarchical organisation of _____ .   *[CTET-July-2013-II]*

  (a) achievement goals

  (b) curricular declarations

  (c) reading skills

  (d) cognitive objectives

26. School-based assessment was introduced to
  [CTET-Feb.-2014-I]

  (a) decentralize the power of Boards of school education in the country

  (b) ensure the holistic development of all the students

  (c) motivate teachers to punctiliously record all the activities of students for better interpretation of their progress

(d) encourage schools to excel by competing with the other schools in their area

27. Which one of the following is *not* related to other options?   *[CTET-Feb.-2014-I]*
(a) Organizing question-answer sessions
(b) Taking feedback from students on a topic
(c) Conducting quiz
(d) Modeling the skills of self-assessment

28. Which one of the following questions is correctly matched with its specified domain?
[CTET-Feb.-2014-I]
(a) Could you group your: Evaluating students on the basis of their achievement in Mathematics?
(b) What was the turning: Creating points on the cricket match telecasted last night?
(c) Write down a new: Application recipe to cook chicken by using herbs.
(d) Determine which of the: Analyzing given measures would most likely lead to achieve best results.

29. A teacher is connecting a text to the previously learnt text and showing children how to summarize it. She is   *[CTET-Feb.-2014-I]*
(a) helping children to develop their own strategy to comprehend it
(b) insinuating that there is no need to go through the entire text
(c) reinforcing the importance of text from the assessment point of view
(d) encouraging children to mug it up as effectively as possible.

30. Teachers and students draw on one another's expertise while working on complex projects related to real world problems in _______ classroom.   *[CTET-Feb.-2014-II]*
(a) traditional   (b) constructivist
(c) teacher-centric   (d) social-constructivist

31. Which one of the following statements is true?
[CTET-Feb.-2014-II]
(a) The formative assessment can sometimes be summative assessment and vice versa
(b) The summative assessment implies that assessment is a continuous and integral part of learning
(c) The major objective of the formative assessment is to grade the achievement of students

(d) The formative assessment summarizes the development of learners during a time interval

32. A teacher asks his/her students to draw a concept map to reflect their comprehension of a topic. He/She is   *[CTET-Feb.-2014-II]*
(a) jogging the memory of the students
(b) conducting formative assessment
(c) testing the ability of the students to summarize the main points
(d) trying to develop rubrics to evaluate the achievement of the students

33. Many measures have been taken at institutional level to check the dropout cases in the schools run by government agencies. Which of the following is an institutional reason for children dropping out of these schools?   *[CTET-Feb.-2014-II]*
(a) There is a lack of infrastructure, such as blackboards and toilets
(b) Teachers are not having appropriate qualifications and are paid lesser salaries
(c) Teachers have not been sensitized about the need of treating children well
(d) There is no alternative curriculum for children who reject the compulsory curriculum offered

34. Which of the following should be a right way for a teacher who intends to correct errors of his/her students?   *[CTET-Feb.-2014-II]*
(a) He/She must correct every error of his/her students even if it requires late sitting in the school
(b) He/She should correct less-frequent errors more often than high-frequent and generality errors
(c) He/She should correct errors that interfere with the general meaning and understandability
(d) He/She should not correct errors if it irritates children

35. A teacher collects and reads the work of the class, then plans and adjusts the next lesson to meet student needs. He/She is doing
[CTET-Sept.-2014-I]
(a) Assessment of learning
(b) Assessment as learning
(c) Assessment for learning
(d) Assessment at learning

36. Teachers who work under School Based Assessment *[CTET-Sept.-2014-I]*
 (a) are overburdened as they need to take frequent tests in addition to Monday tests
 (b) need to assign project work in each subject to individual students
 (c) observe students minutely on a daily basis to assess their values and attitudes
 (d) feel a sense of ownership for the system

37. "How do grades differ from marks ?"
 This question belongs to which of the following classes of questions ? *[CTET-Sept.-2014-I]*
 (a) Divergent   (b) Analytic
 (c) Open-ended   (d) Problem-solving

38. Learning disabilities in Mathematics can be assessed most appropriately by which of the following tests ? *[CTET-Sept.-2014-I]*
 (a) Aptitude test   (b) Diagnostic test
 (c) Screening test   (d) Achievement test

39. Assessment for learning *[CTET-Sept.-2014-II]*
 (a) fosters motivation
 (b) is done for the purpose of segregation and ranking
 (c) emphasises the overall importance of grades
 (d) is an exclusive and a per se assessment activity

40. School Based Assessments *[CTET-Sept.-2014-II]*
 (a) focus on exam techniques rather than outcomes
 (b) offer less control to the students over what will be assessed
 (c) improve learning by providing a constructive feedback
 (d) encourage teaching to the test as they involve frequent testing

41. Students in a class are asked to assemble various artefacts of their work in a notebook, to demonstrate what they can do for their society. What kind of activity is this ?
 [CTET-Sept.-2014-II]
 (a) Essay type assessment
 (b) Anecdotal records
 (c) Problem solving assessment
 (d) Portfolio assessment

42. A Class VII student makes errors in Mathematics. As a teacher you would *[CTET-Sept.-2014-II]*
 (a) provide the student the correct answer
 (b) allow the student to use calculator
 (c) ask the student to use alternative method or redo it to find out errors on his/ her own
 (d) show the student where the errors were made and ask the student to redo it

43. Which one of the following is not a suitable formative assessment task ? *[CTET-Feb.-2015-I]*
 (a) Open-ended questions
 (b) Project
 (c) Observation
 (d) Ranking the students

44. To be an effective teacher it is important to
 [CTET-Feb.-2015-I]
 (a) emphasize dictating answers from the book.
 (b) focus on individual learning rather than group activity.
 (c) avoid disruption caused due to questioning by students.
 (d) be in touch with each and every child.

45. Teachers need to create a good classroom environment to facilitate children's learning. To create such a learning environment, which one of the given statements is not true ?
 [CTET-Feb.-2015-I]
 (a) Approval of the child's efforts
 (b) Compliance with teachers
 (c) Acceptance of the child
 (d) Positive tone of the teacher

46. Teachers, in order to help learners construct knowledge, need to focus on *[CTET-Feb.-2015-I]*
 (a) making sure the learner memorises everything
 (b) scoress marks obtained by the learner.
 (c) involving the learner for active participation.
 (d) mastering learning of concepts by the learner.

47. According to NCF 2005, errors are important because they *[CTET-Feb.-2015-I]*
 (a) are an important tool in classifying students into groups of 'passed' and 'failed'.
 (b) provide a way to the teachers to scold the children.
 (c) provide an insight into the child's thinking and help to identify solutions.
 (d) provide space for removing some children from the class.

48. The assessment of students can be used by teachers in teaching to develop insight into
 [CTET-Feb.-2015-I]

(a) identifying the students who need to be promoted to the higher class.

(b) not promoting those students who do not meet school standards.

(c) changing the teaching approach according to the learners' need.

(d) creating groups of 'bright' and 'weak' students in the class.

49. Continuous and Comprehensive Evaluation is essential for   *[CTET-Feb.-2015-I]*

(a) fine tuning of test with the teaching

(b) diluting the accountability of the Board of Education

(c) correcting less-frequent errors more than more-frequent errors

(d) understanding how learning can be observed, recorded and improved upon

50. In learning, assessment is essential for
[CTET-Feb.-2015-I]

(a) Grades and Marks

(b) Screening test

(c) Motivation

(d) Fostering of the purpose of segregation and ranking

51. How can a teacher help children become better problem solvers ?*[CTET-Feb.-2015-II]*

(a) By giving tangible rewards for solving problems

(b) By giving children a variety of problems to solve and support while solving them

(c) By encouraging children to look for answers to the problems in the textbook

(d) By providing correct solutions to all the problems they pose to students

52. In a learner-centred classroom, the teacher would
[CTET-Feb.-2015-II]

(a) use lecture method to explain key facts and then assess the learners for their attentiveness.

(b) encourage children to compete with each other for marks to facilitate learning.

(c) demonstrate what she expects her students to do and then gives them guidelines to do the same.

(d) employ such methods in which the learners are encouraged to take initiative for their own learning.

53. Which one of the following assessment practices will bring out the best in students ?
[CTET-Feb.-2015-II]

(a) When the emphasis is laid upon positive correlation between test scores and student ability

(b) When students are required to reproduce facts as tested via multiple choice questions

(c) When conceptual change and students' alternative solutions are assessed through several different methods of assessment

(d) When the marks obtained and the position secured by the student in the class are the ultimate determinants of success

54. Failure of a child to perform well in class tests leads us to believe that   *[CTET-Feb.-2015-II]*

(a) children are born with certain capabilities and deficits.

(b) assessment is objective and can be used to clearly identify failures.

(c) there is a need to reflect upon the syllabus, pedagogy and assessment processes.

(d) some children are deemed to fail irrespective of how hard the system tries.

55. There are a few children in your class who make errors. Which of these is most likely to be your analysis of the situation ?   *[CTET-Feb.-2015-II]*

(a) The children have not yet gained conceptual clarity and there is need for you to reflect on your pedagogy.

(b) The children have poor intelligence.

(c) The children are not interested in studies and want to create indiscipline.

(d) The children should not have been promoted to your class.

56. Which one of these statements do you agree with?
[CTET-Feb.-2015-II]

(a) A child's failure is primarily due to lack of parent's education and economic status.

(b) A child fails because the government is not giving enough technological resources in schools.

(c) A child's failure can be attributed directly to the genetic material he/she has acquired from his/her parents.

(d) A child's failure is a reflection on the system and its inability to respond to the child.

57. As an upper primary school mathematics teacher you believe that *[CTET-Feb.-2015-II]*
    (a) students need to possess procedural knowledge even if they don't understand conceptual basis.
    (b) students' errors provide insights into their thinking.
    (c) not all children have the ability to study mathematics in upper primary school.
    (d) boys will learn mathematics without much effort since they are 'born with it' and you need to pay more attention to girls.

58. The amount and type of scaffolding to a child would change depending on the
    [CTET-Feb.-2015-II]
    (a) child's innate abilities.
    (b) mood of the teacher.
    (c) rewards offered for the task.
    (d) level of the child's performance.

59. First step in Teaching   *[TNTET-2014-II]*
    (a) Evaluation   (b) Preparation
    (c) pursuing   (d) Planning

60. Which of the following can be evaluated using Bruce Tuckman's Teacher Feedback form
    [TNTET-2014-II]
    (a) Behaviour & Creativity
    (b) Warmth & acceptance
    (c) Dymanism & Organised   demeanor
    (d) All the above

61. Assessment   *[CTET-Feb.-2016-I]*
    (a) is a good strategy to label and categorise children.
    (b) should actively promote competitive spirit children.
    (c) should generate tension and stress to ensure learning.
    (d) is a way to improve learning.

62. Assessment by only paper-pencil tests
    [CTET-Feb.-2016-II]
    (a) limits assessment.
    (b) promotes holistic assessment.
    (c) facilitates comprehensive evaluation.
    (d) facilitates continuous evaluation.

63. Which one of the following is a good example of 'scaffolding' (learning of a problem-solving task till the student is able to do it by herself)?
    [CTET-Feb.-2016-II]
    (a) Telling her that she can do it by trying again and again
    (b) Offering a reward for solving the problem quickly
    (c) Providing a half-solved example
    (d) Telling her she cannot go home till she solves the problem

64. Which one of the following best describes a teacher's role in a middle school classroom?
    [CTET-Feb.-2016-II]
    (a) Using Powerpoint presentations to give lectures
    (b) Discouraging multiple perspectives and focusing on uni-dimensional perspective
    (c) Providing opportunities for discussions
    (d) Promoting students to compete amongst themselves for the first position

65. Assessment is purposeful if : *[CTET-Sept.-2016-I]*
    (a) it induces fear and stress among the students
    (b) it serves as a feedback for the students as well as the teachers
    (c) it is done only once at the end of the year
    (d) comparative evaluations are made to differentiate between the students' achievements

66. According to NCF, 2005, the role of a teacher has to be: *[CTET-Sept.-2016-I]*
    (a) authoritative   (b) dictatorial
    (c) permissive   (d) facilitative

67. A teacher can enhance effective learning in her elementary classroom by :   *[CTET-Sept.-2016-I]*
    (a) offering rewards for small steps in learning
    (b) drill and practice
    (c) encouraging competition amongst her students
    (d) connecting the content to the lives of the students

68. How can a teacher encourage her students to be intrinsically motivated towards learning for the sake of learning?   *[CTET-Sept.-2016-I]*

(a) By inducing anxiety and fear

(b) By giving competitive tests

(c) By supporting them in setting individual goals and their mastery

(d) By offering tangible rewards such as toffees

69. According to the National Curriculum Framework, 2005, learning is __________ and __________ in its character. *[CTET-Sept.-2016-II]*

(a) active; simple
(b) active; social
(c) passive; simple
(d) passive; social

70. Which of the following highlights assessment for learning? *[CTET-Sept.-2016-II]*

(a) The teacher assesses a student based on his/her performance in comparison to others.

(b) The teacher assesses conceptual understanding of the students besides focussing on the processes of thinking.

(c) The teacher assesses the students by comparing their responses to 'standard' responses.

(d) The teacher assesses the students based on the information given in the textbooks.

71. Which of the following statements about assessment are correct? *[CTET-Sept.-2016-II]*

A. Assessment should help students see their strengths and gaps and help the teacher fine-tune her teaching accordingly.

B. Assessment is meaningful only if comparative evaluations of students are made.

C. Assessment should assess not only memory but also understanding and application.

D. Assessment cannot be purposeful if it does not induce fear and anxiety.

(a) A and C
(b) B and C
(c) A and B
(d) B and D

72. According to the Right to Education Act, 2009, children with special needs should study : *[CTET-Sept.-2016-II]*

(a) in vocational training centres which would prepare them for life skills

(b) at home with their parents and caregivers . providing necessary support

(c) in special schools created exclusively for them

(d) in inclusive education setups with provisions to cater to their individual needs

73. An effective teacher in a classroom, where students come from diverse backgrounds, would: *[CTET-Sept.-2016-II]*

(a) create groups of students with those from the same economic background put together

(b) push students from deprived backgrounds to work hard so that they can match up with their peers

(c) focus on their cultural knowledge to address individual differences among the group

(d) ignore cultural knowledge and treat all his students in a uniform manner

74. For observing the behaviour of his students, the teacher himself involved as a player in a game played by the students, this type of observation is *[APTET-May.-2018-I]*

(a) Participatory observation
(b) General observation
(c) Non-participatory observation
(d) Macro observation

75. The present performance of an individual that shows the future achievement is *[APTET-May.-2018-I]*

(a) Interest
(b) Aptitude
(c) Attitude
(d) Performance

76. There are 151 students in a primary school. As per RTE Act -2009 the number of teachers to be placed in the school *[APTET-May.-2018-I]*

(a) 5 primary teachers + one science teacher
(b) 4 primary teachers + one language teacher
(c) 4 primary teachers + one head teacher
(d) 5 primary teachers + one head teacher

77. As per NCF-2005, the general aspect which is a physical inconvenience to children *[APTET-May.-2018-I]*

(a) Caring school staff
(b) Proximity in availability of school
(c) Well equipped Toilets
(d) Over burdened school bags

78. The type of counselling process proposed by Carl Rogers is *[APTET-May.-2018-I]*

(a) Directive counselling

(b) Non-directive counselling

(c) Eclectic counselling

(d) Dominant counselling

79. The main aim of Continuous Comprehensive Evaluation is *[APTET-May.-2018-II]*

(a) To evaluate every aspect of the student

(b) To evaluate scholastic abilities of students

(c) To evaluate the progress of a student in curricular areas

(d) To evaluate the progress of the students in co-curricular areas

80. According to RTE Act – 2009, in Primary schools if the strength of the students is above 200, the teacher pupil ratio excluding Headmaster shall not exceed *[APTET-May.-2018-II]*

(a) 1 : 30

(b) 1 : 35

(c) 1 : 50

(d) 1 : 40

81. The type of teaching model in which specially trained teacher helps differently abled students by going from one school to another.

[APTET-May.-2018-II]

(a) Alternative school model

(b) Resource model

(c) Dual teaching model

(d) Itinerant teaching model

82. Meier – Seashore Art judgment test is used to measure *[APTET-May.-2018-II]*

(a) Aesthetic Aptitudes

(b) Scholastic Aptitudes

(c) Vocational Aptitudes

(d) General Aptitudes

83. A Psychology lecturer acquainting his B.Ed. students about the employment opportunities for them after the completion of the course is called

[APTET-May.-2018-II]

(a) Educational Guidance

(b) Personal Guidance

(c) Vocational Guidance

(d) Group Guidance

84. One of the following is the limitation of observation method *[APTET-May.-2018-II]*

(a) Study of the behaviour of students directly

(b) Recording of previously decided behavioural aspects

(c) Assessing the behaviour, based on external behaviour only

(d) Study of the behaviour of animals and mental patients

85. According to Jones, Ruthstrong, help extended by others to a person to assist himself is

[APTET-May.-2018-II]

(a) Guidance

(b) Counselling

(c) Social Scaffolding

(d) Instructional Scaffolding

Answer Key

1.	(c)	11.	(d)	21.	(a)	31.	(a)	41.	(d)	51.	(b)	61	(d)	71.	(a)	81.	(c)
2.	(a)	12.	(c)	22.	(a)	32.	(b)	42.	(c)	52.	(d)	62	(a)	72.	(d)	82.	(b)
3.	(a)	13.	(b)	23.	(a)	33.	(d)	43.	(d)	53.	(c)	63	(c)	73.	(c)	83.	(c)
4.	(c)	14.	(b)	24.	(b)	34.	(c)	44.	(d)	54.	(c)	64	(c)	74.	(a)	84.	(c)
5.	(b)	15.	(b)	25.	(d)	35.	(c)	45.	(b)	55.	(a)	65	(b)	75.	(b)	85.	(b)
6.	(b)	16.	(c)	26.	(b)	36.	(d)	46.	(c)	56.	(d)	66	(d)	76.	(d)		
7.	(b)	17.	(c)	27.	(d)	37.	(b)	47.	(c)	57.	(b)	67	(d)	77.	(c)		
8.	(d)	18.	(d)	28.	(d)	38.	(b)	48.	(c)	58.	(d)	68	(c)	78.	(b)		
9.	(d)	19.	(d)	29.	(a)	39.	(a)	49.	(d)	59.	(d)	69	(b)	79.	(a)		
10.	(c)	20.	(b)	30.	(d)	40.	(c)	50.	(c)	60.	(d)	70	(b)	80.	(b)		

15. (b) In this scheme the term 'continuous' is meant to emphasize that evaluation of identified aspects of students' 'growth and development' is a continuous process rather than an event, built into the total teaching-learning process and spread over the entire span of academic session.

The second term 'comprehensive' means that the scheme attempts to cover both the Scholastic and the Co-Scholastic aspects of students' growth and development.

16. (c) School Based Assessment helps all students learn more in a pressure-free environment and reflect the standard and ability of students.

17. (c) A teacher should not correct students while they are trying to communicate ideas. The teacher should encourage students and not to intimidate them.

18. (d) Intrinsic motivation refers to motivation that comes from inside an individual rather than from any external or outside rewards. So, Rajesh can be best described as an intrinsically motivated learner.

20. (b) When a cook tastes a food during cooking, he analyzing their own progress and his success. So, it an assessment for learning.

21. (a) Differentiated instruction is an instructional theory that allows teachers to face this challenge by taking diverse student factors into account when planning and delivering instruction. Based on this theory, teachers can structure learning environments that address the variety of learning styles, interests, and abilities found within a classroom.

22. (a) CBSE prescribed group activities for students in place of activities for individual students to overcome the negative emotional response to individual competition which may generalize across learning.

23. (a) When students make repeated errors during a lesson, we make changes in how we teach (e.g., provide more examples, allow students to practice more), and provide more intensive instruction, tasks timetable or seating arrangements.

24. (b) Thinking too much about the examination result is not a right way to manage an approaching examination anxiety.

25. (d) Bloom's Taxonomy is a hierarchical representation of different types of instructional objectives. It addresses lower level thinking skills at the bottom tier then progresses to more complex thought processes when ascending to the top. While types of learning are ordered into a hierarchy and knowing, comprehending, and applying may be essential in more higher-order thinking skills.

26. (b) Assessment is a process of obtaining information about students' learning and making value judgements about their progress. These assessments ensure the holistic and all around development of all the students.

27. (d) Others are related to assessments techniques.

28. (d) According to Benjamin Bloom there are six levels of cognition: Knowledge, Comprehension. Application, Analysis, Synthesis (creation) and Evaluation. Analyzing is breaking down information into component parts.

30. (d) In social constructivist classroom, teachers and students share information about any potential real world problems and give feed back immediately. In other classrooms, teacher is the centre point and student has second place.

32. (b) Formative assessment refers to frequent interactive assessments of student progress and understanding to identify learning needs.

33. (d) Lack of differentiation in education may be an institutional reason for children dropping out of these schools. Differentiated instruction should be based upon the students readiness, interest or learning style.

34. (c) A teacher who intends to correct errors of his/her students should correct errors that interfere with the general meaning and understandability because it is basic thing to understand general words and principles.

61. (d) Assessment is a method to guage th process of learning of children by various methods. The main objective of assessment is to improve learning method by giving them timely feedback to boost their ability.

62. (a) Paper pencil test means knowing the writing ability where learning ability is judged less than the latter. It limits the overall assessment of a child. Assessment needs all types of tests which includes oral tests too where child's presence of mind is also judged.

66. (d) Teacher's role should be Facilitative as he or she should be able to deliver the needs of a learner according to his aptitude and abilities.

67. (d) A teacher can enhance effective learning in her elementary classroom by connecting the content to the lives of the students to give them first hand experience and make them recognize effectively.

74. (a) When a teacher participates in the game played by the students, teacher can observe the behavior of children and assess them better as they are in informal moods and reacts the way they think. It is called participatory contribution of a teacher where his extra efforts works well in the learning methods he is going to adapt in the classroom teaching.

75. (b) Aptitude of a child can be assessed by analyzing child's present performance and one can predict his future performance too.

78. (b) Non-directive counseling theory is given by Carl Rogers

1. The main purpose of assessment should be
   - (a) to point out the errors of the learners
   - (b) to measure the achievement of learners
   - (c) to decide if a student should be promoted to the next class
   - (d) to diagnose and remedy gaps in learning

2. Assessment
   - (a) Includes measurement but is broader
   - (b) Excludes measurement but is broader
   - (c) Is only measurement
   - (d) Is evaluation in quantitative terms

3. Which of the following is not an appropriate tool for Formative Assessment?
   - (a) Assignment
   - (b) Oral questions
   - (c) Term test
   - (d) Quiz and games

4. To make assessment a 'useful and interesting' process, one should be careful about
   - (a) making comparisons between different students
   - (b) labeling students as intelligent or average learners
   - (c) using a variety of ways' to collect information about the student's learning across the scholastic and co-scholastic boundaries
   - (d) using technical language to give feedback

5. In preparing a fifth grade class to take a standardized reading test the teacher is best advised to
   - (a) Tell the children the test is very important and they should do the best they can
   - (b) Exact key questions from a previous test and allow the pupils to answer them
   - (c) Coach the below grade level readers, as the rest of the class will do well anyway
   - (d) Give the pupils practice in answering questions similar to the type that will appear on the test

6. A test to assess the potential of students for specific abilities and skills such as music, spatial ability or logical ability is called a/an
   - (a) Proficiency test
   - (b) Aptitude test
   - (c) Attitude test
   - (d) Achievement test

7. A teacher designs a test to find out the cause of the poor grades of her learners through a/an
   - (a) Diagnostic test
   - (b) Proficiency test
   - (c) Achievement test
   - (d) Aptitude test

8. Formative Assessment is assessment
   - (a) of learning
   - (b) at learning
   - (c) in learning
   - (d) for learning

9. The term 'Comprehensive' in Continuous and Comprehensive Evaluation means
   - (a) scholastic development
   - (b) co-scholastic development
   - (c) academic skills
   - (d) scholastic and co-scholastic development

10. Diagnostic testing in Social Science will help a teacher understand
    - (a) the part of the topic the student has not memorized
    - (b) learning difficulties a student is facing in Social Science
    - (c) how revision work has helped her students
    - (d) how intelligent her students are

11. The two most important characteristics of a standardized test are ______.
    - (a) reliability and validity
    - (b) reliability and accuracy
    - (c) accuracy and equality
    - (d) practicality and validity
    - (e) validity and accuracy

12. Standardized tests are most often
    - (a) Norm-referenced
    - (b) Criterion-referenced
    - (c) Stanine tests
    - (d) Judgmental in nature

13. Evidence of validity can be related to
    - (a) Content
    - (b) Criterion
    - (c) Construct
    - (d) All of the above

14. Reliability is
    - (a) Consistency of test results
    - (b) Degree to which a test measures what is intended

(c) Hypothetical estimate of variation in scores

(d) Quality of an assessment instrument

15. Diagnostic tests are usually given individually to school students when

(a) a student's performance needs to be predicted

(b) learning problems are suspected

(c) the future potential of a student is to be revealed

(d) student's capacity to solve real life problem needs to be assessed

16. In norm referenced tests

(a) A student's performance is compared to the average performance of others

(b) Scores are compared to a pre-established standard

(c) Student's readiness for handling advanced material is assessed

(d) The mastery of very specific objectives is measured

17. What is performance test ?

(a) A power test

(b) A test which does not involve the use of language

(c) A test of mechanical ability

(d) Special ability test

18. Army Alpha and Army Beta tests are known as

(a) individual tests

(b) group tests

(c) intelligence tests

(d) personality tests

19. The evaluation of personality is best made through

(a) Inventory-test

(b) Preference-test

(c) Survey test

(d) Projective

20. Evaluation of student learning should mainly be :

(a) a continuous and comprehensive process

(b) at the end of the each term

(c) at the end of the each lesson

(d) a yearly process

21. "All those activities undertaken by teachers, and by their students in assessing themselves, which provide information to be used as feedback to modify the teaching and learning activities in which they are engaged" refers to

(a) Evaluation   (b) Assessment

(c) Examination   (d) Learning

22. In the context of the strategies used by schools with well-developed assessment systems match the following

	Strategies		Characteristics
(i)	Student Profiles	(p)	involve examining response patterns on specific standardized test items in different topic areas and generating hypotheses about the potential causes of these patterns
(ii)	Classroom Profiles	(q)	These profiles allow educators to view an assessment "snapshot" of students
(iii)	School Profile	(r)	This method, again done on a spreadsheet, allows for analyzing performance patterns and generating hypothesis within grade levels or subject areas
(iv)	Standardized Test Item Analyses	(s)	This method, typically done on a spreadsheet, allows for analyzing performance patterns and generating hypothesis

(a) (i)-p; (ii)-q; (iii)-r; (iv)-s

(b) (i)-q; (ii)-s; (iii)-p; (iv)-r

(c) (i)-r; (ii)-s; (iii)-p; (iv)-q

(d) (i)-q; (ii)-s; (iii)-r; (iv)-p

23. The purpose of evaluation is

(a) to label children as slow learner and gifted children

(b) to identify children who need remediation

(c) to diagnose learning difficulties and problem areas

(d) to provide feedback on the extent to which we have been successful in imparting education for a productive life

24. In preparing a fifth grade class to take a standardized reading test, the teacher is best advised to

(a) tell the children the test is very important and they should do the best they can

(b) mark key questions from a previous test and allow the pupils to answer them

(c) coach the below grade level readers, as the rest of the class will do well anyway

(d) give the pupils practice in answering questions similar to the type that will appear in the test

25. Today is Monday, the day before after tomorrow will be__________ .
What type of test is this?
(a) General knowledge
(b) Understanding
(c) Mathematical research
(d) Vocabulary

26. Diagnosis of the gaps in the learning of students should be followed by
(a) appropriate remedial measures
(b) intensive drill and practice.
(c) systematic revision of all lessons
(d) reporting the findings to learners and parents

27. The main purpose of assessment should be

(a) to point out the errors of the learners
(b) to measure the achievement of learners
(c) to decide if a student should be promoted to the next class
(d) to diagnose and remedy gaps in learning

28. Which of the following is not an appropriate tool for Formative Assessment?
(a) Assignment
(b) Oral questions
(c) Term test
(d) Quiz and games

29. Children's Apperception Test was designed for children between ages 3 and 10. The CAT cards substitute
(a) non-living objects for living objects
(b) animals for people
(c) females for males
(d) children for adults

30. In the National Curriculum Framework, 2005 under the heading 'Examination Reforms' which of the following reforms has been suggested?
(a) Open book exams
(b) Continuous and comprehensive evaluation
(c) Group work evaluation
(d) All of these.

31. An appropriate form of assessing students' performance in practicals is:
(a) interview   (b) observation
(c) questionnaire   (d) written test

32. Which of the following is an objective question?
(a) Open ended question
(b) True or False
(c) Essay type question
(d) Short answer question

33. A teacher uses audio-visual aids and physical activities in her teaching because they
(a) facilitate effective assessment
(b) provide a diversion to learners
(c) utilize maximum number of senses to enhance learning
(d) provide relief to the teacher

34. The major purpose of diagnostic test is that of Identifying: [PSTET-2014-I]
(a) The General area of weakness in class performance
(b) Specific nature of remedial Programme needed
(c) The causes underlying academic difficulties
(d) The specific nature of pupil difficulties

35. In CCE, Formative & Summative Assessment totals to:
(a) 40% & 60% respectively
(b) 60% & 40% respectively
(c) 50% & 50% respectively
(d) None of the above

36. An intelligent student is not doing well in studies. What is the best course of the action for the teacher:
(a) Wait till he performs better
(b) Find out reason for his under achievement
(c) Give him grace marks in the examination
(d) Ask his parents to withdraw from school

37. An appropriate form of assessing student' performance in practicals is:
(a) interview   (b) observation
(c) questionnaire   (d) written test

38. The type of evaluation which is used to monitor learning progress during instruction is called as:
(a) diagnostic evaluation
(b) formative evaluation
(c) placement evaluation
(d) summative evaluation

39. When did the UNO proclaimed "The right to learn" for children
(a) 1969 November 10
(b) 1979 December 20
(c) 1959 November 20
(d) 1949 December 10

40. Non Directive councelling was advocated by
(a) Karl Rogers   (b) Darwin
(c) Taylor   (d) Pavlov

Answer Key									
1.	(d)	**9.**	(d)	**17.**	(d)	**25.**	(b)	**33.**	(c)
2.	(a)	**10.**	(b)	**18.**	(b)	**26.**	(a)	**34.**	(b)
3.	(c)	**11.**	(b)	**19.**	(a)	**27.**	(d)	**35.**	(a)
4.	(c)	**12.**	(a)	**20.**	(a)	**28.**	(c)	**36.**	(c)
5.	(d)	**13.**	(d)	**21.**	(b)	**29.**	(b)	**37.**	(b)
6.	(b)	**14.**	(a)	**22.**	(d)	**30.**	(d)	**38.**	(b)
7.	(a)	**15.**	(b)	**23.**	(d)	**31.**	(b)	**39.**	(c)
8.	(d)	**16.**	(a)	**24.**	(d)	**32.**	(b)	**40.**	(a)

1. Which one of the following is not the aim of educational psychology and pedagogy?
   - (a) To understand the abilities, interests and potentialities of the students
   - (b) To study the developmental characteristics of the students
   - (c) To study the individual differences among the students
   - (d) To make the students free from discipline

2. Which one of the following factors does not influence the child's development?
   - (a) Heredity
   - (b) Culture
   - (c) Achievement
   - (d) Growth

3. The child can be seen in the role of active family member
   - (a) When the child becomes two years old and shares with visiting adult persons in the house
   - (b) When child becomes five years of age and accompanies the parents in the market
   - (c) When a child become 1N1½ years of age and entertains everyone at home
   - (d) When a child binds up in linguistic relationships with family members

4. In pre-primary school system, the criterion of small child's adjustment is
   - (a) he takes his own care and fulfills needs
   - (b) he remains happy with his social constraints
   - (c) tendency to play in separate groups
   - (d) development of independence among the children

5. Psychologists believe that the teacher should not use filthy words or bad language with the students in the school, because
   - (a) the children's self-concept modifies accordingly in a negative way
   - (b) the teachers' filthy language brings negative change in the children
   - (c) the children suffer from inferiority complexes and this hurts their ego-systems
   - (d) being abused in front of other children brings dishonour to them

6. The formula for Achievement Quotient (A.Q.) is
   - (a) $\dfrac{\text{Educational Age}}{\text{Mental Age}} \times 100$
   - (b) $\dfrac{\text{Mental Age}}{\text{Educational Age}} \times 100$
   - (c) $\dfrac{\text{Educational Age}}{\text{Actual Age}} \times 100$
   - (d) None of the above

7. In order to develop rapport with your pupils you should
   (a) behave with them in a democratic way
   (b) guide them
   (c) have communicative ability
   (d) all of the above

8. Teachers should not demand from their pupils something which is beyond their stage of growth. If they do so, they only cause
   (a) anger among pupils
   (b) frustration, heighten tension and nervousness in children
   (c) encouragement to students to learn more
   (d) none of the above

9. A____is one who in an standardised tests fails to attain an IQ or mental age.
   (a) Subnormal person
   (b) Very superior person
   (c) Normal person
   (d) None of the above

10. What is a criticism of identifying children based on their disabilities ?
    (a) Teachers may perceive children in terms of their disability rather than looking at the whole child
    (b) Other children may tease the child with a disability if they find out what it is
    (c) Parents will have misconceptions that their child cannot learn.
    (d) Children will blame their parents for their disabilities.

11. All of the following are approaches or theories of motivation except:
    (a) Multi-factor theory
    (b) Instinct theory
    (c) Drive theory
    (d) Need Hierarchy theory

12. Needs for security, stability & order are
    (a) safety needs
    (b) esteem needs
    (c) physiological needs
    (d) belongingness & love need

13. Operation Blackboard Program for primary schools is
    (a) Related to improve physical & material facilities
    (b) Related to admission
    (c) Related to mid-day meal
    (d) Related to blackboard

14. Nature and Nurture refer to
    (a) Internal and external environment
    (b) Temperature and character
    (c) Physical features and temperament
    (d) Heredity and Environment

15. A four year old child
    (a) does not know anything other than his play, games, his mother-father, brother-sister and things to eat and drink
    (b) Enquires about the world at every instance
    (c) make his opinion about the surrounding environment
    (d) accepts whatever people say

16. Most of the students who have been diagnosed with a learning disability have which type of disability ?
    (a) Emotional disturbances
    (b) Autism
    (c) Hearing impairments
    (d) Speech & language impairments

17. Instincts are
    (a) States of deprivation arising within the body
    (b) Patterns of behaviour assumed to be universal in a species.
    (c) The subjective feelings associated with needs.
    (d) An internal process that activates behaviour.

18. According to you, the most important component of teaching learning process is
    (a) Teacher
    (b) Class environment
    (c) Learner
    (d) Learning material

19. Aggression is very common behaviour. Psychologists think that it is a
    (a) Motive already present in all species
    (b) Motive which can't be unlearned
    (c) Motive which is biological in nature
    (d) Social motive

20. Teaching at school level implies
    (a) imparting information given in text books
    (b) asking questions and conducting examinations
    (c) preparing students to pass examination with good marks
    (d) drawing out talent of children for their all round development

21. Education equality is a
    (a) fundamental right
    (b) only a customary right
    (c) only a legal right
    (d) only a directive principle.

22. The bright normal person has an IQ of
    (a) 120-129   (b) 110-119
    (c) 130-140   (d) None of these

23. In which tests must you answer as many questions as you can in a certain amount of time
    (a) CAT   (b) TAT
    (c) Intelligence   (d) Speed

24. If we listen what we want to listen it becomes
    (a) Protective listening
    (b) Parted listening
    (c) Preferential listening
    (d) Listening partially

25. Which is not true about punishment?
    (a) It is the most common motivational drive.
    (b) It is negative and sometimes harmful.
    (c) It should never be used.
    (d) It should be used judiciously with full awareness of its dangers and limitations.

26. Which of the following categories is given free and compulsory education according to our Constitution ?
    (a) all the students
    (b) all the students upto 14 years of age
    (c) all the student and adults
    (d) all the citizens

27. Integrated leaders give equal importance to-
    (a) Task & people
    (b) Traits & behaviour
    (c) Situation & traits
    (d) None of the above

28. Habit & experience play a much larger role in the expression of sexual derive in the
    (a) Lower animal
    (b) Higher animal
    (c) Higher primates including humans
    (d) All of above

29. Women seem to have_____strong needs for power than men.
    (a) Less
    (b) More
    (c) May be more or less
    (d) Extraordinary

30. Expectancy theory is a theory of
    (a) Personality
    (b) Attitude
    (c) Motivation
    (d) Learning

Answer Key

1	(d)	6	(a)	11	(a)	16	(d)	21	(a)	26	(b)
2	(c)	7	(d)	12	(a)	17	(b)	22	(b)	27	(a)
3	(a)	8	(b)	13	(a)	18	(c)	23	(d)	28	(c)
4	(d)	9	(a)	14	(a)	19	(d)	24	(c)	29	(a)
5	(a)	10	(a)	15	(c)	20	(d)	25	(c)	30	(c)

MOCK TEST

1. The most important factor influencing human intelligence is
   - (a) heredity
   - (b) environment
   - (c) Both of the above
   - (d) None of the above

2. Sound knowledge of child development is very helpful in pedagogy. Which one of the following is not a significant statement?
   - (a) Increased awareness of developmental delays in young children has led to the creation of early intervention services
   - (b) Earlier detection of hearing deficit sometimes leads to correction of problems before serious language impairments occur.
   - (c) Schools must teach children the social and life skills that will help them to develop into healthy adolescents.
   - (d) None of the above

3. Generally the baby expresses smiling emotion when its face or cheeks are touched gently. It happens due to
   - (a) reflex actions
   - (b) emotional reactions
   - (c) display of good gestures
   - (d) conditioning

4. Social stratification can be expressed as
   - (a) the characteristics denoting socio-economic structure in the society
   - (b) the level of a family in the caste hierarchy of their community
   - (c) classification based on the demography of the population
   - (d) the difference denoting level of social respect

5. Mental hygiene includes
   - (a) physical health only
   - (b) mental health only
   - (c) physical and Mental health both
   - (d) diagnosis of Mental illness only

6. The meaning of personalized teaching is
   - (a) to teach children personally
   - (b) to give tuition individually
   - (c) to teach children as per their abilities
   - (d) None of the above

7. Teachers who are enthusiastic in the classroom teaching
   - (a) simply dramatise to hold the student's attention
   - (b) often lack proficiency in the subjects which stays hidden under their enthusiasm.
   - (c) involve their students in the teaching learning process
   - (d) All of the above

8. What will you do as a teacher if the students do not attend your class?

   (a) Keep quiet considering the present attitude of students.

   (b) Blame the students for their absence.

   (c) Think of using some interesting methods of teaching.

   (d) Know the reasons and try to remove them.

9. Which type of child has the mental age below its chronological age?

   (a) Dull child

   (b) Average child

   (c) Bright child

   (d) None of these

10. A student with epilesy will most likely display which of the following behaviours ?

    (a) Staring or convulsions

    (b) Complaining of nasal congestion & earaches

    (c) Difficulty in learning to spell

    (d) Shaking & unclear speech

11. What is the most important contribution of psychology in education ?

    (a) Proper arrangement of discipline

    (b) Change in time table

    (c) Use of co-curricular activities

    (d) Student centred education

12. Sex differences in the area of perception and personality are

    (a) Apparent before age five

    (b) Initially detectable at age seven

    (c) Indistinguishable prior to age eight

    (d) Essential mythical

13. A scheduled caste student is visiting the class only to get his scholarship. What provision will you make to attract his attention towards education?

    (a) Insulting remarks on the caste and the parents

    (b) Tell him about the importance of education in one's life

    (c) Rebuking the child

    (d) Think about the irrationality of the scheme.

14. Motives are often blocked or frustrated & the major sources of this frustration are environmental and ___ factor.

    (a) Situational

    (b) Social

    (c) Psychological

    (d) Personal

15. Computer-assisted instruction (CAI) is an educational technology that incorporates features consistent with the principle of

    (a) Classical conditioning

    (b) Instrumental conditioning

    (c) Operant conditioning

    (d) Cognitive conditioning

16. The movement from one social class to another is known as -

    (a) Migration

    (b) Immigration

    (c) Social mobility

    (d) National movement

17. The aims of lecture –cum– and demonstration strategy is

    (a) It removes the weakness of lecture strategy and enhance the quality of demonstration strategy

    (b) It combines lecture and demonstration strategy to built a new strategy

(c) It strengthens the theoretical aspect of strategies

(d) It generates a new strategy for science teaching

18. The part of the mind that is beyond awareness is called the

   (a) Unconscious

   (b) Conscious

   (c) Post conscious

   (d) Pre conscious

19. When teaching a child who is mentally retarded, a teacher should do which of the following ?

   (a) Repeat directions many times

   (b) Provide abstract examples

   (c) Set lower expectations

   (d) Give instructions only once to improve the child's focus.

20. Intrinsic motivations are

   (a) Drives

   (b) Learning activity

   (c) Knowledge of progress

   (d) Praise and blame

21. Frustration is charactersied by

   (a) Behaviour directed toward the goal of harming or injuring another living thing

   (b) The blocking of ongoing, goal directed behaviour.

   (c) Unpleasant feelings or shifts in mood.

   (d) Failling to take revenge.

22. Intelligence tests for infants

   (a) Correlate with adult tests at + 0.85 and above

   (b) Sample the same abilities tests at later ages.

(c) Provide initial information relating to aptitudes

(d) Are not accurate predictors of later IQ

23. If Adil's Intelligence quotient is 100, we know that Adil has a

   (a) perfect score on a set of age – related tests

   (b) test performance superior to 90% of other children of the same age who took the test.

   (c) mental age of typical children who have the same choronological age

   (d) mental age below those of children with the same chronological age.

24. To lead the country successfuly into the 21st century, you as a teacher will emphasize on -

   (a) energy conservation

   (b) child's right to education

   (c) mass media in education

   (d) human resource development

25. The law of experience may be taken to mean

   (a) Reward   (b) Discriminations

   (c) Generalization   (c) Repetitions

26. Which of the following statement regarding dyslexia is false?

   (a) Dyslexia is the most commonly diagnosed learning disability.

   (b) Estimates at the prevalence as dyslexia range form 5 to 175 percent.

   (c) Dyslexia is heritable and runs in families.

   (d) Dyslexia affects boys more often that girls.

27. The best educational program is one which is according to the -
    (a) ability of the child
    (b) need of the child
    (c) interest of the child
    (d) all of these along with the needs of the society

28. Which one of the following is not the defect of experimental method?
    (a) Artificial conditions of the experiment
    (b) Difficulty on the part of subject to seek help
    (c) The possibilities to gain accurate knowledge of mental state of the subject
    (d) Impossibility to control the internal state of the subject

29. There are two types of aggression, hostile aggression & _____ aggression:
    (a) Instrumental
    (b) Mild
    (c) Structural
    (d) Periodical

30. A person who has an IQ score of 60 would be considered as-
    (a) Profoundly retarted
    (b) Severely retarded
    (c) Moderately retarded
    (d) Mildly retarded

Answer Key

1	(c)	6	(c)	11	(d)	16	(c)	21	(b)	26	(d)
2	(d)	7	(c)	12	(a)	17	(a)	22	(d)	27	(d)
3	(a)	8	(d)	13	(b)	18	(a)	23	(c)	28	(c)
4	(a)	9	(a)	14	(d)	19	(a)	24	(d)	29	(a)
5	(c)	10	(a)	15	(c)	20	(a)	25	(c)	30	(d)

3 MOCK TEST

1. Verbal intelligence tests are the better option for
   (a) literate persons
   (b) illiterate persons
   (c) small children
   (d) special children

2. Generally in infancy the child's main feature is
   (a) instinctive in nature
   (b) high emotional displays
   (c) cognitive difficulties
   (d) inabilities of focusing attention

3. The cause of unreasonable emotional development of children is
   (a) rejection of the children by their parents
   (b) the excessive anxieties in parents towards their children
   (c) the over protection of children given by the parents
   (d) All the above

4. If you give the due respect to you own students, then you have in your mind that
   (a) you are exhibiting high standards of ethical relations
   (b) you are preserving your own sovereignty
   (c) you have matured attitude towards students
   (d) you feel that the students are motivated to follow this practice

5. The important characteristic of a mentally healthy person is
   (a) ability of adjustment
   (b) emotional maturity
   (c) capacity of self-estimation
   (d) All the above   .

6. Maximum participation of students is possible in teaching through
   (a) lecture method
   (b) discussion method
   (c) audio-visual aids
   (c) textbook method

7. Democracy in the class-room is best reflected through
   (a) allowing student's freedom to the observance of classroom rules and regulations.
   (b) allowing the class to decide the curricular experiences of the classroom
   (c) allowing the maximum participation of all the students in class-room activities.
   (d) None of above.

8. It is popularly said that any two students are not alike. This means

   (a) each and every student differs in their physical and mental set up.

   (b) they differ in their familiar and social status.

   (c) they are different in their mental set up.

   (d) all of the above

9. Puspendra is once again not following directions. The teacher notices that Puspendra usually has no problems following directions if he turns one ear toward her or if he asks several times to have the directions repeated. Puspendra most likely has which of these conditions?

   (a) Visual impairment

   (b) Hearing impairment

   (c) Articulation problem

   (d) Mental retardation

10. Learning is basically

    (a) Group process

    (b) Individual process

    (c) Social process

    (d) Co-operational process

11. In comparative physical growth curves, female

    (a) Develop more slowly than males.

    (b) Develop more rapidly than males.

    (c) Develop at the same rate as males.

    (d) Develop more rapidly than males during the first six years and more slowly thereafter.

12. The contribution of feedback and reinforcement is

    (a) To enhance the frequency of desired behaviour

    (b) To create obstacles in desired behaviour

    (c) They do not express any role in desired change

    (d) None of the above

13. Motive is a -

    (a) General trait

    (b) Specific trait

    (c) Desire

    (d) Particular condition of human organism.

14. What is the average correlation between the IQs of identical twins?

    (a) 90%   (b) 80%

    (c) 70%   (d) None of these

15. It is necessary for a teacher to have/do :

    (a) A lot of affinity for his country

    (b) Social service

    (c) Subject knowledge

    (d) All of the above

16. The medium at primary stage should be :

    (a) Official language

    (b) English

    (c) State language

    (d) Mother tongue

17. The advantage of using effective teaching techniques is

    (a) Enhancing students interest

    (b) Clarity of content

    (c) Understanding of the content

    (d) All the above

18. TAT stands for

   (a) Thematic Achievement Test

   (b) Thematic Apperception Test

   (c) Thematic Activity Test

   (d) None of the above

19. According to Maslow's theory the basic needs include

   (a) Physiological needs, Safety, and Security.

   (b) Safety, Love, and belonging

   (c) Physiological needs and Belonging

   (d) Security and Esteem

20. The evaluation of personality is best made through

   (a) Inventory-test

   (b) Preference-test

   (c) Survey test

   (d) Projective

21. Children with Down's syndrome typically have IQ scores in the range of

   (a) 50-70   (b) 35-49

   (c) 40-55   (d) 20-34

22. One way to select traits is to take a broad array of descriptions and simplify it by seeing which traits go together in clusters; this procedure is called

   (a) Factor Analysis

   (b) Dynamic approach

   (c) Behavioural approach

   (d) None of the above

23. Binet-Simon test was developed to

   (a) Measure IQ

   (b) Intelligence

   (c) Measure sub-normal intelligence

   (d) All

24. Which of the following interpretations would be correct about diagnostic tests?

   (a) They reveal students errors for corrective instruction.

   (b) They are meant for locating lapse in the teaching.

   (c) They help in eliminating selection of undeserving pupils.

   (d) They guide teachers selecting relevant test material.

25. A creative child is one who -

   (a) has a good academic record.

   (b) has I. Q. above normal.

   (c) has a large vocabulary.

   (d) has fluency of expression.

26. Both contraction of human eye's pupils in glaring light and salivation process on seeing food are the examples of –

   (a) Reaction behaviour

   (b) Operant behaviour

   (c) Both of the above

   (d) None of the above

27. Some children usually leave their school after one or two years of schooling. In order to complete primary education till the age of 11 and then leave the school the solution is :

(a) to give mid day meal in the school

(b) issue books free of cost

(c) not to fail any student in any class

(d) convince the parents

28. Which is a reading disability?

(a) Aphsia　　　　(b) Dyslexia

(c) Agraphia　　　(d) Apraxia

29. Learning disabled children lack -

(a) proper reasoning and thinking ability.

(b) social adjustment.

(c) motor control.

(d) hyper activity.

30. Poems are the example of

(a) Transfer of training

(b) Serial learning

(c) Insight learning

(d) Cognitive learning

Answer Key

1	(a)	6	(b)	11	(b)	16	(d)	21	(c)	26	(a)
2	(a)	7	(c)	12	(a)	17	(c)	22	(a)	27	(c)
3	(d)	8	(a)	13	(c)	18	(b)	23	(c)	28	(b)
4	(d)	9	(b)	14	(a)	19	(c)	24	(a)	29	(d)
5	(d)	10	(b)	15	(d)	20	(a)	25	(b)	30	(b)

MOCK TEST

1. The intelligence tests having language as its content are called
   - (a) Verbal tests
   - (b) Performance tests
   - (c) Projective tests
   - (d) Non-verbal tests

2. During infancy, which of the following aspect of development is not completed?
   - (a) Moral development
   - (b) Emotional development
   - (c) Social development
   - (d) Language development

3. Which one of the following is the true statement corresponding cephalocaudal principle of child's development?
   - (a) The development begins from head and moves towards legs (tail) region
   - (b) The development begins from legs region and moves towards head region
   - (c) The development from head region to legs region goes on with uniform pace
   - (d) None of the above

4. Suppose your students are not present in school on the day of a national festival; when you realise this fact, what action would you take against them as a mature teacher?
   - (a) You call the parents of those children in the school and explain them about the indiscipline done by their wards
   - (b) You will ask the students directly and make them sign an undertaking so that they will not do it again in future
   - (c) You will penalise those children and punish them
   - (d) You will call the students and ask them the reason and insist on them not to repeat the incident

5. When the parents discriminate among their children, the development of children in such an environment takes place as
   - (a) accelerated and competitive
   - (b) full of jealousy
   - (c) unbiased
   - (d) children are generally not affected

6. All of the following are the characteristic features of an effective teacher except
   - (a) emphasizing group discussion for the purpose of clarifying the objectives
   - (b) emphasis upon standard
   - (c) emphasis upon the quick control of the problematic situation
   - (d) differential treatment meted out to students of his class

7. When your friend seeks your assistance to get his ward's admission in the school, how would you extend your cooperation to him ?

   (a) You would extend all types of support as you have intimate relationship.

   (b) You would not help him.

   (c) You would put forward some lame excuse.

   (d) None of the above.

8. The primary task of a teacher is

   (a) to teach the prescribed curriculum

   (b) to stimulate and guide student's learning.

   (c) to provide diagnostic and remedial aid wherever desired.

   (d) to promote habits of conformity to adult demands and expectations.

9. Mary finds it difficult to communicate with her peers & her teacher. She easily understands what they are saying to her but when she tries to communicate her response & express her thoughts she finds it very difficult. Mary is most likely to have.

   (a) Expressive language disorder

   (b) Articulation disorder

   (c) Receptive language disorder

   (d) Voice disorder

10. When one learns something and makes use of what he has learned it is called

    (a) Assimilation   (b) Co-operation

    (c) Competition   (d) Conflict

11. Which of the following statements is true?

    (a) Individual differences between children decrease as children grow older

    (b) Most influences on development are hereditary

    (c) Most of the influences on development are environmental

    (d) Many typical changes of infancy & childhood are tied to maturation.

12. Which test attempts to predict a person's future performance, or capacity to learn

    (a) achievement test

    (b) attitude test

    (c) aptitude test

    (d) creativity test

13. Talented children can be identified through -

    (a) Intelligence

    (b) Aptitude test

    (c) Achievement test

    (d) All of the above

14. Ego is described as-

    (a) Ideal Principles

    (b) Reality Principles

    (c) Natural Principles

    (d) Pleasure Principles

15. Basic education is -

    (a) activity based

    (b) student based

    (c) handicraft based

    (d) all the three

16. Which is NOT a typical way that a visual impairment can affect a child's development?

    (a) The child may be emotionally delayed because he/she feels self-conscious about his/her in ability to see.

    (b) The child may have delayed speech & language skills & a poor ability to listen & remember.

    (c) The child may develop more slowly than typically developing children because of a lack of visual stimulation.

    (d) The child's fear of movement may affect his/her social development.

17. Teaching skills are developed by

    (a) Micro teaching

    (b) Simulation

    (c) Teaching method

    (d) All of the above

18. Navodaya Vidyalayas are for :

    (a) Rural children.

    (b) Urban children.

    (c) Brilliant children of both rural and urban back grounds.

    (d) The children who want to become soldiers.

19. Persona is the -

    (a) Basic core of human personalty

    (b) Attitude towards self

    (c) Role the individual plays in life

    (d) Self-image

20. Individuals with IQs of 90-110 are described as-

    (a) Average   (b) Dull normal

    (c) Bright normal   (d) Border line

21. A child who studies for the sake of earning a scholarship is an example of

    (a) Intrinsically motivated person

    (b) Extrinsically motivated person

    (c) Positively motivated person

    (d) None of the above

22. When a person seeks & enjoys cooperation with others he is said to have a/an

    (a) affiliation motive

    (b) dependence motive

    (c) sentimental motive

    (d) achievement motive

23. Which one of the following is most suitable for learning a skill?

    (a) Observing   (b) Listening

    (c) Reading   (d) Doing

24. The level of motivation is

    (a) High when the task is difficult

    (b) High when the task is of routine nature

    (c) Low when the task is difficult

    (d) Low when the task is interesting

25. In the face of threat, one may retreat to an earlier pattern of adaptation, possibly a childish or primitive one. It is known as.

    (a) Displacement

    (b) Regression

    (c) Sublimation

    (d) None of these

26. In order to develop a good rapport with students a teacher should -

    (a) love his students

    (b) be friendly with all

    (c) pay individual attention

    (d) communicate well

27. The Stanford - Binet intelligence scale

    (a) was specifically designed to test adult intelligence

    (b) provides separate score for performance

    (c) is completely culturally fair, in that children of different cultures do just as well as children in this culture

    (d) assumes that intellectual ability in childhood improves as age increases.

28. Which gland of the Pavlovian dogs experimentation has produced saliva?

    (a) Parotid gland

    (b) Parathyroid gland

    (c) Thyroid gland

    (d) Pituitary gland

29. In which age-group can a child differentiate between anger and affection?

    (a) In infancy

    (b) In childhood

    (c) In adolescence

    (d) In adulthood

30. The primary task of the teacher is :

    (a) To teach the prescribed curriculum.

    (b) To stimulate and guide student's learning

    (c) To ensure that all students belong to socially acceptable groups.

    (d) To promote habits of conformity to adult demands and expectations.

Answer Key

1	(a)	6	(d)	11	(c)	16	(b)	21	(b)	26	(c)
2	(a)	7	(a)	12	(c)	17	(d)	22	(a)	27	(d)
3	(a)	8	(b)	13	(d)	18	(c)	23	(a)	28	(a)
4	(d)	9	(a)	14	(b)	19	(c)	24	(a)	29	(a)
5	(b)	10	(a)	15	(d)	20	(a)	25	(b)	30	(b)